L H Russnum

Process and Method in Canadian Geography

Vegetation, Soils
and Wildlife

Process and Method
in Canadian Geography

Vegetation, Soils and Wildlife

Selected Readings
edited by
J. G. Nelson
M. J. Chambers

Methuen

Toronto   London   Sydney   Wellington

Library of Congress Card Number 79-83147

SBN 458 90260 8 (Hardbound)

SBN 458 90270 5 (Paperback)

Design by Hiller Rinaldo

Printed and Bound in Canada

73 72 71 70 69   1 2 3 4 5 6

Preface

This volume is part of a series on Canadian Geography. Companion works include *Geomorphology, Water,* and *Weather and Climate.* Volumes on other topics are being planned.

Each volume comprises a collection of recent articles gathered, for the most part, from learned journals. The series is Canadian in the sense that the papers deal with Canadian topics or have been prepared by geographers working in Canada; it is geographic in the sense that they are concerned with the landscape, and the physical and cultural processes at work on it. For purposes of general definition the landscape can be thought of as *that zone at or near the surface of the earth that is perceived, used or affected by man.* This zone obviously includes surface phenomena such as vegetation, animals, and soils. The zone changes, however, with changes in knowledge and technology, so that more and more contemporary geographers are becoming concerned about human penetration into the oceans and into space. A process can be thought of as *a change that varies in space and time.* A process can be considered as cultural when it is *totally or primarily a result of the activities of man.* Examples are: urbanization with its cities and towns; agriculture with its fields and crops. A process can be considered as physical when it is *totally or primarily a result of forces independent of man.* Examples are ocean currents and hurricanes. As the articles in these volumes will show, however, the distinction between cultural and physical processes is, in many cases, increasingly difficult to draw. Floods are influenced by cultural activities, such as lumbering, as well as by physical processes, such as thunderstorms. Climate is affected by cities as well as by the general circulation of the atmosphere.

In recent years geographers have placed increasing emphasis on the study of processes. While this is partly a result of improved instrumentation, research methods, and technique, it also reflects a general trend in geography toward a more analytical approach. In this and companion volumes, stress has therefore been placed on articles illustrating research techniques and the study of processes. An attempt, however has also been made to add to the usefulness of the volumes by including studies that are concerned with many parts of Canada in order to provide knowledge and appreciation of the Canadian landscape.

In our initial thinking about the volumes, we recognised that it would be necessary and desirable to include relevant research undertaken by biologists, geologists, and members of other landscape-oriented disciplines. Geography, as with other disciplines, interrelates with many fields of study, and a considerable amount of cross-fertilization of thought and technique occurs. Now that a number of volumes have been formulated and organized, we find that some of them contain more work by practitioners in related disciplines than we had originally anticipated. Our concern, however, is to deal with those processes, techniques, problems, and topics that we believe to be of interest and importance to geographers in the wide sense. Moreover, the broader content of some of the volumes may make them extremely useful to members of related disciplines, as well as to those many scholars and students whose work and interest carry them into the so-called interdisciplinary areas where so many important contemporary problems lie.

Aside from their possible interest and value to some members of the public, the various volumes in this series should be useful at a variety of academic levels. Many of the articles in each volume will be of interest to the beginning student. They would also seem to be suitable for more advanced undergraduate courses, for example, the first courses exclusively on biogeography, geomorphology or climatology, or for broader courses in resources or conservation. The volumes could also be valuable in certain graduate courses as they describe important recent developments in research fields. They are a guide to the state of the art—or the science—in Canada. For those wishing to investigate a topic further, all the original bibliographies have been retained. These references are considered to be of greater value to the reader than other material that might be introduced, such as comments and reviews interjected between articles by the editors. Most of the maps, diagrams, and photographs have been retained in each article.

Contents

		Page
	Preface	v
	J. G. Nelson & M. J. Chambers	
	Introduction	1
1	F. K. Hare	7
	Climate and Zonal Divisions of the Boreal Forest Formation in Eastern Canada	
2	R. T. Ogilvie	25
	The Mountain Forest and Alpine Zones of Alberta	
3	J. G. Nelson and A. R. Byrne	45
	Man as an Instrument of Landscape Change. Fires, Floods and National Parks in the Bow Valley, Alberta	
4	P. F. Maycock and B. Matthews	59
	An Arctic Forest in the Tundra of Northern Ungava, Quebec	
5	F. B. Watts	93
	The Natural Vegetation of the Southern Great Plains of Canada	
6	A. Leahey	113
	The Soils of Canada from a Pedological Viewpoint	
7	T. C. F. Tedrow and J. E. Cantlon	125
	Concepts of Soil Formation and Classification in Arctic Regions	
8	J. H. Day and H. M. Rice	139
	The Characteristics of Some Permafrost Soils in the Mackenzie Valley, N.W.T.	
9	Bentley, C. F.	155
	Soil Management and Fertility—Western Canada	
10	L. R. Webber	167
	Soil Physical Properties and Erosion Control	
11	J. H. Ellis	175
	Soil Erosion in Western Canada	

		PAGE
12	N. R. Richards Soil Erosion in Eastern Canada	185
13	C. C. Flerow On the Origin of the Mammalian Fauna of Canada	195
14	G. W. Scotter Effects of Fire on Barren-Ground Caribou and Their Forest Habitation in Northern Canada	205
15	J. G. Nelson The Effects of European Invasion on Animal Life and Certain Aspects of Landscape in the Bow Valley Area, Alberta: 1750-1885	219
16	I. M. Cowan The Fur Trade and the Fur Cycle 1825-1857	239
17	D. H. Pimlott Wolf Control in Canada	249
18	D. H. Munro Ducks and the Great Plains Wetlands	265
19	A. de Vos Insecticide Applications and Their Effects on Wildlife	279
20	D. C. Foote Remarks on Eskimo Sealing and the Harp Seal Controversy	287
21	V. Flyger The Polar Bear: A Matter for International Concern	293
22	W. A. Fuller Emerging Problems in Wildlife Management	301
23	J. S. Marsh Maintaining the Wilderness Experience in Canada's National Parks	315
24	J. R. Mackay Tundra and Taiga	327
25	I. Burton The Quality of the Environment: A Review	349
	Index	363

Contributors

Bentley, C. F.
Agricultural Advisor, External Aid Office, Ottawa.
Department of Soil Science, University of Alberta, Edmonton.

Burton, I.
Department of Geography, University of Toronto, Toronto.

Byrne, A. R.
Department of Geography, University of Wisconsin, Madison.

Cantlon, J. C.
Department of Botany and Plant Pathology, Michigan State University.

Cowan, I. M.
Dean, Faculty of Graduate Studies, University of British Columbia.

Day, J. H.
Soil Research Institute, Canada Department of Agriculture, Ottawa.

De Vos, A.
Forestry Officer, Food and Agriculture Organization of the United Nations.

Ellis, J. H.
Formerly professor of soils, University of Manitoba, Winnipeg. Now Agricultural Consultant, Manitoba Department of Mines and Natural Resources, and Department of Agriculture.

Flerow, C. C.
Paleontological Institute, Academy of Sciences of the U.S.S.R.

Flyger, V.
Department of Inland Research, National Resource Institute, University of Maryland.

Foote, D. C.
Institute of Social, Economic and Government Research, University of Alaska, College, Alaska.

Fuller, W. A.
Department of Zoology, University of Alberta, Edmonton.

Hare, F. K.
Formerly Chairman, Department of Geography, McGill University. Now President, University of British Columbia.

Leahey, A.
Formerly Pedology Research Co-ordinator, Canada Department of Agriculture, Ottawa.

Mackay, J. R.
Department of Geography, University of British Columbia.

Marsh, J. S.
Department of Geography, University of Calgary.

Matthews, B.
Department of Geography, McGill University.

Maycock, P. F.
Department of Botany, McGill University.

Munro, D. A.
Director, Canadian Wildlife Service, Ottawa.

Nelson, J. G.
Department of Geography, University of Calgary.

Ogilvie, R. T.
Department of Biology, University of Calgary.

Pimlott, D. H.
Department of Zoology, University of Toronto.

Rice, H. M.
Soil Research Institute, Canada Department of Agriculture, Ottawa.

Richards, N. R.
Dean, Ontario Agricultural College, Guelph, Ontario.

Scotter, G. W.
Canadian Wildlife Service, Edmonton, Alberta.

Tedrow, J. C. F.
Department of Soils, Rutgers University.

Watts, F. B.
Late of Department of Geography, University of Toronto.

Webber, L. R.
Department of Soil Science, Ontario Agricultural College, Guelph, Ontario.

Introduction

The articles in the present volume attempt to relate different types of vegetation, soils and wildlife to causative processes as well as to use and management problems. Considerable emphasis is placed on man's effects; the cultural influence generally being considered particularly appropriate to the professional geographer.

The articles can be grouped into roughly four divisions: vegetation; soils; wildlife; and certain articles of a more general or summary nature—on wilderness, the tundra and the taiga, and environmental quality—being included at the end. That the articles can be grouped in this way should not be taken as negating their overall unity. What happens to vegetation is generally related to soils, animals, man and other components of what is, after all, one landscape.

In the first article Kenneth Hare identifies and describes the extent and character of various divisions of the boreal forest and relates these to climate and particularly to annual evapo-transpiration. At the same time, Hare recognizes the influences of other processes, such as fire, on the boreal forest. His article clearly demonstrates the value of a fundamental geographical technique: a phenomena or process—in this case, vegetation—is mapped to establish similarities and differences in character and areal distribution and compared to a map or maps of related phenomena in an attempt to explain the character and distribution.

Although generally similar to Hare's, R. Ogilvie's paper is a more detailed description of the flora of the mountain and alpine regions of Alberta and adjacent British Columbia. Vegetation types are described and related to climatic, geomorphic and other factors, such as temperature, snow, avalanches, exposure and drainage conditions. The article by Nelson and Byrne is also concerned with vegetation in the Rocky Mountains, particularly in the Banff National Park area. The study concentrates on a man's effects on vegetation through fire, lumbering and other processes. The emphasis in the study is on historical geographic evidence and methodology.

The paper by Maycock and Matthews, *An Arctic Forest in the Tundra of Northern Ungava, Quebec,* is concerned with the vegetation which occurs under extreme climatic conditions. The study is a sophisticated one and refers to a variety of processes and research methods including tree ring and pollen analysis.

The article by F. B. Watts deals with "natural vegetation" and particularly the grasslands of the southern Great Plains of Canada. "Natural" vegetation is defined as that *fundamentally unchanged by man,* where man is thought of as the white man and not the native. The reconstruction of the natural vegetation is based largely on an analysis of historical accounts, particularly those of the early surveyors, although some reference is made to botanical field studies of vegetation. Much emphasis is placed on the linking of vegetation with climate and relatively little on the role of fire in the formation and maintenance of the grasslands and parklands.

The second section of this volume is devoted to soils. The articles can be divided into two groups. The first—by Leahey, Tedrow and Cantlon, and Day and Rice—is concerned with the definition, description and origin or genesis of soils. Climate, vegetation, slope and other influences on soil profiles and soil types are discussed, as well as areal similarities and differences in soils, problems of mapping, and difficulties in establishing consistent terminology in the face of recent advances in soil science. The article by Leahey, as amended by W. A. Ehrlich, contains a summary of the latest terminology in Canadian pedology.

The second group of articles is mainly concerned with soils from the point of view of agriculture. Bentley discusses some of the physical attributes of soils which are important to the farmer or rancher. He also describes briefly some agricultural techniques and their influence on soils. For example, he refers to some of the disadvantages of the summer fallow system as practised in western Canada. He sees a need for better rotations, including more forage crops.

The articles by Webber, Ellis and Richards are primarily concerned with soil erosion and the factors which influence it. Descriptions are given of the intensity and extent of soil erosion in western and eastern Canada. Reference is made to some of the experiments that have been conducted to determine variations in rates of soil erosion under different physical and agricultural conditions. The paper by Ellis is of additional interest because he has strong negative opinions about the utility of new government arrangements or legislation as an aid in controlling soil erosion. His opinions will not be shared by all—especially when the notion of the right of the owner to do more or less as he likes with the land is involved.

The third section contains articles on the fauna of Canada. Much of the work on the history of animals has been done by biologists or geologists who often refer to themselves as zoogeographers or paleographers. Their work can provide information and perspective that is of considerable value to anyone concerned with animals. In the first article in the section, C. C. Flerow gives a broad picture of the origin and dispersal or North American mammals and relates these mammals to the presence or absence of the Bering Strait Land Bridge and so to their ultimate area of origin, Asia.

G. W. Scotter provides us with an account of fire and its effects on the caribou. He indicates that fire destroys lichen and other forage preferred by the caribou. By the use of various field techniques, including the counting of animal pellets, he shows that caribou and moose numbers are lower in recently burned areas in northern Canada. Scotter concludes that fire has been one of the principal reasons for the decline of the caribou to present relatively low levels, with man and wolves being important reasons for the tendency for the caribou population to remain at these levels over the last several years.

Nelson's article is concerned with changes in animal life, notably the beaver and buffalo, and also in the landscapes associated with these animals, during the period c. 1750-1885, when the fur trade and other cultural and economic changes were introduced into western Canada from Europe. Little mention is made of the fur cycle as an explanation of short term fluctuations in animal populations, mainly because the effects of this process are difficult to assess, the beaver having been hunted assiduously and reduced rapidly following the appearance of the white man. Cowan's article, on the other hand, demonstrates the effects of the fur cycle on animals such as the fisher, minx, rabbit and lynx, over large parts of British Columbia during the period 1825-1857, by using historical records of fur returns recorded in the notebooks and post journals of the fur traders.

Douglas Pimlott's article on the wolf is more contemporary and discusses the validity of ideas of the wolf as a direct threat to man and cattle, and as an indirect threat through the transmission of diseases such as rabies. Pimlott also examines the effects of altitudes, legislation and government agencies on wolf populations. He raises questions about the effects of government wolf control systems, which have largely been substituted for bounty systems in Canada since the 1950's.

Munro's paper is a statement of the importance of the prairie wetlands to ducks and associated wildlife. He attempts to explain the unusually large concentrations of ducks on the prairie wetlands in terms of glacial history, the presence of moraines and associated undulating to rolling terrain, climate, and the profusion of scattered lakes in various stages of successional development. These lakes are characterized by a great variety of vegetation and animal life which can be consumed by ducks and other birds. He also discusses the destructive effects of cultivation and pothole drainage on ducks. Munro sees certain contemporary cultural and economic tendencies as being more favourable for these birds. For example, the growing demand for recreation and the apparent tendency for greater emphasis on livestock *vis-a-vis* grain production will work to reduce drainage of the wetlands. De Vos presents some evidence on the direct and indirect effects of pesticides on birds in particular. He suggests certain management methods which should be used prior to the application of pesticides.

Two articles are primarily concerned with attitudes towards animals of considerable contemporary economic and aesthetic importance—in this case the seal and the polar bear. Foote discusses the attitudes aroused during the recent controversy over the killing of harp seal by so-called inhumane methods. The strength and dispersion of these attitudes has resulted in a declining market for seals in general anad has caused economic problems for native people dependent on the hunting of seals. Foote's article clearly demonstrates how modern methods of communication, notably TV, can arouse attitudes that may work to prevent an apparent abuse, but, in the process, have other unforeseen and unwanted effects. Flyger does not believe the reasons for decline of the polar bear are clear. Certain physical changes may be involved—the retreat of pack ice, home of the seal, food of the bear—but Flyger also directs attention to the wasteful hunting methods practised by man in the name of sport and recreation. Animals are hunted down with planes, shot, skinned, beheaded and left. Flyger puts forward the very interesting suggestion that we should encourage new forms of hunting that do not lead to a kill, for example the use of syringe guns to temporarily immobilize an animal. The final article in the third section, by Fuller, is a useful summary of wildlife problems in Canada. Fuller clearly recognizes various cultural and physical processes involved in management. He refers to natural fluctuations in game populations, disease, and the persistence of certain concepts or attitudes toward game, for example the "buck law". Fuller sees the need for an "ecological conscience" as well as more and better education about wildlife and landscape.

The last three articles stand somewhat apart from the rest. Marsh's paper is concerned with the wilderness experience desired by more Canadians as population grows and urbanization proceeds. Marsh relates the wilderness experience to the national parks—the only type of Federal land in Canada specifically set aside for wilderness use. He describes the pressures being placed on the national parks by cultural processes, such as population growth, increased mobility, and automation with increased leisure time as its by-product. The pressure is basically twofold: greater demand for facilities which destroy, damage or detract from the wilderness; and the sheer wear of greater numbers of visitors. Marsh discusses a number of techniques and measures which could be used to avoid loss of wildland needed for the hiker, camper, and scientist of the future. Among these are: better federal-provincial co-operation in the creation of new wilderness areas; areal and temporal zoning; the use of alternative areas outside the national parks; restrictions in visitor use, including the probable necessity to book in advance for visits to many areas.

Mackay's article provides an integrated view of the tundra and the taiga. Of particular interest is the discussion of the effects of snow on temperatures, soils, and other aspects of landscape. The article prompts a concern for the tundra as an area particularly susceptible to disturbance and quick change, but slow to recover, and in need of careful management.

The final article, by Burton, is devoted to the recently developed idea of "quality of the environment". Burton raises certain fundamental questions—one being the problem of what a high quality environment actually is. He proceeds to analyse various approaches to environmental problems through ecology, economics, law, technology, and human behaviour and response—and is not very optimistic about any of them. Thus ecological knowledge is considered to be fundamentally weak and "unable to predict satisfactorily the changes in ecosystems which are likely to result from a specific human intervention". So far as economics is concerned, "it is not possible to reduce these problems to economic terms satisfactorily at the present time, and it may never be possible. Even if it were, a false indulging assumption is implied, namely that what is best in economic terms is necessarily best in all other ways also." So far as technology is concerned, "the Achilles heel of the technologists' approach is, of course, that the present problems of environmental quality arise precisely from the application of technological solutions to problems in the past. The new technology now being developed may in turn prove to be only palliatives that will pile up greater difficulties to be confronted at a later date."

J. G. Nelson.
M. J. Chambers.

Calgary,
January 30th, 1969.

Climate and Zonal Divisions of the Boreal Forest Formation in Eastern Canada

F. K. Hare

The boreal forest formation is the great belt of coniferous forest stretching across the subarctic latitudes of Eurasia and North America. Perhaps because of its inaccessibility and unsuitability for permanent rural settlement, the boreal forest has been little studied by geographers in North America, though Russian and Scandinavian workers have devoted much time to it. The phytogeographer and the ecologist have been concerned primarily with the southern part of the formation, which is the main home of the lumbering industries of Canada, Scandinavia, and the U.S.S.R. The greater part of the formation, beyond the limit of merchantable trees, has received scant attention.

The idea that the boreal forest consists of an endless repetition of muskeg and forest, with little difference from one place to another, is a popular delusion. In both Eurasia and eastern North America the formation resolves itself naturally into three or four zonal divisions, each with its characteristic type of cover and each standing in a definite and predictable relationship to climate. This paper is devoted to a study of these zonal divisions in Canada east of the Ontario-Manitoba boundary, and particularly in the great Labrador-Ungava peninsula, where the author himself has worked.

Reprinted from *Geographical Review,* Vol. XL (1950), pp. 615-35. Copyrighted by the American Geographical Society of New York.

Labrador-Ungava offers many advantages to the student of the zonal structure of the boreal forest. The peninsula is essentially a tilted peneplain, relatively low in latitude 58° (near the Arctic tree line) but rising southward to a general level approaching 3000 feet some 50 to 100 miles north of the St. Lawrence. Toward the river it falls in a spectacular and highly complex escarpment, the Laurentide scarp, which has yet to appear on most contour maps of North America. The southward rise of altitude has the effect of offsetting to some extent the normal southward rise of temperature. The thermally controlled zonal divisions of the boreal forest are hence widened and can be studied over much greater distances than in Russia or Finland. The same is true on a smaller scale between Hudson Bay and Lake Superior.

A further advantage springs from the fact that the entire eastern half of the Canadian boreal forest has an abundant precipitation. Control of growth by temperature, well known to be the usual climatic control of natural vegetation in high latitudes, is thus manifested in full measure. Drought effects such as those reported by Marie Sanderson in western Canada are unknown.[1]

The boreal forest formation in eastern Canada, as elsewhere, is bounded on the north by the tundra. On the south, it passes into a mixed forest formation, the Great Lakes–St. Lawrence Forest of Halliday[2] or the Lake Forest of Weaver and Clements.[3] A similar mixed forest borders the Russian boreal forest west of the Urals. As with the zonal divisions of the boreal forest itself, both the southern and northern limits are readily determinable in climatological terms.

Composition

The chief associations of the formation are dominated by white spruce (*Picea glauca*), black spruce (*P. mariana*), larch or tamarack (*Larix laricina*), and balsam fir (*Abies balsamea*). The jack pine (*Pinus banksiana*) is also an important element in the western half of the region. Tree lines of these species are given in Figure 1, but a discussion of their climatic relations is not attempted in this paper.

---

[1] Marie Sanderson, "Drought in the Canadian Northwest", *Geogr. Rev.*, Vol. XXXVIII (1948), pp. 289-99.
[2] W. E. D. Halliday, "A Forest Classification for Canada", *Dominion Forest Service Bull. 89*, Ottawa (1937).
[3] J. E. Weaver and F. E. Clements, "Plant Ecology", 2nd ed., New York and London (1938), pp. 496-500.

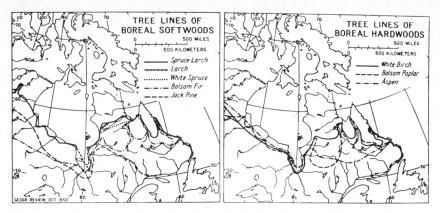

Figure 1. Tree lines of boreal softwoods. Note absence of the jackpine from much of Labrador-Ungava. The two spruces and the larch have coincident tree lines in most places.

Figure 2. Tree lines of boreal hardwoods. Note limited extent of aspen in Labrador-Ungava.

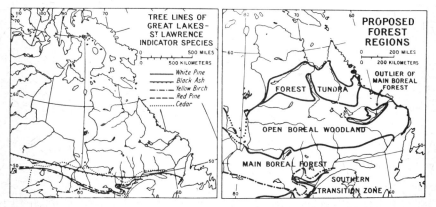

Figure 3. Tree lines of species typical of the Great Lakes-St. Lawrence mixed-forest formation. Two species, the cedar and the black ash, invade the main boreal forest.

Figure 4. Proposed zonal divisions of the boreal forest in Labrador-Ungava. The term "region" is applicable because the map was originally drawn to establish natural regions in the peninsula; "zonal division" is a better term as applied to the boreal forest as a whole. The classification closely follows that of Hustich but the terminology and the positions of boundaries are revised. "Southern transition zone" refers to the ecotone between the boreal and Great Lakes-St. Lawrence forests.

The black spruce, white spruce, and tamarack have almost identical northern tree lines, and all three range throughout the formation in North America, though the tamarack is rare in Alaska. Their relative abundance, however, varies greatly. In Labrador-Ungava, black spruce is overwhelmingly the most common. In northern and central districts it occurs either alone or in association with tamarack; in the south and southeast black spruce–balsam fir is the principal association.

Balsam fir and jack pine have northern tree lines for which no exact climatic equivalent can be found. The jack pine, for example, has made little progress into Labrador-Ungava, in spite of apparently favorable climate.

Associated with the dominant coniferous species is a small group of hardwoods having a widespread distribution in the boreal forest in both North America and Eurasia, though the actual species differ between the two land masses. The North American representatives are the white birch (*Betula papyrifera*), balsam poplar (*Populus balsamifera*), aspen (*Populus tremuloides*), and certain alders (*Alnus* spp.). None of these trees form part of the climax, but all are important elements in the successions. Their tree lines are shown in Figure 2.

Birch and aspen attain their greatest significance in areas recently burned. Huge areas of birch-aspen associes[4] extend today over the fire-devastated parts of Labrador-Ungava and northern Ontario. Beneath the pale green foliage of the hardwoods, spruce, larch, and fir seedlings grow rapidly, and in a few decades the climax coniferous association is re-established. White birch and aspen also occur as individual relict trees in the coniferous associations, though aspen does not appear in northern Labrador-Ungava.

Balsam poplar occurs widely throughout the region, though it is always local in distribution. The alders are found almost exclusively along watercourses and lake shores, forming impenetrable thickets through which landings can hardly be forced.

Along the southern margins of the formation the boreal forest is invaded by isolated individuals or groves of species proper to the Great Lakes–St. Lawrence mixed forest formation. Among the softwoods, these include the white cedar or arbor vitae (*Thuja occidentalis*), white pine (*Pinus strobus*), a dominant species of this mixed forest, and red pine (*P. resinosa*). The hardwoods include

---

4 An "associes" is the successional equivalent of "association". The birch-aspen communities of the boreal forest are short-lived, yielding place to the coniferous forest that is climax in the formation; hence the use of "associes" rather than "associations".

black ash (*Fraxinus nigra*), yellow birch (*Betula lutea*), and big tooth aspen (*Populus grandidentata*). The cedar and black ash invade the boreal forest deeply, but the others penetrate only a short distance. Tree lines of most of these species are shown in Figure 3. At the southern limit of the boreal forest, white and red pines and sugar maple become dominants.

Forest Types

The boreal forest formation is not readily divisible into associations, as is the deciduous forest. Partly because of the small number of species, partly because the region has been heavily glaciated and hence suffers from deranged drainage and highly variable soils, the forest exhibits structural types rather than fixed associations. These types differ as to the spacing of trees, the layering of the vegetation, and the nature of the ground cover. Many of them are definitely not "climax" and probably represent successional stages that must soon give way to a higher form of forest. The principles of succession in the boreal forest are, however, too vaguely understood to allow a genetic classification. Accordingly the forest types are ranked as equals in the following discussion, regardless of their status.

The classification of forest types used here is based on a study by the Finnish ecologist Hustich.[5] He has studied both the Labrador and the Scandinavian-Finnish boreal forest, and his classification for the Labrador-Ungava region can be cross-referred to both the Russian taiga and the forests of western Canada as studied by Raup.[6] Hustich's detailed subdivisions are not considered here, and new English terms are suggested for the main types. These are three in number:

1. The *close-forest* type ("Moist Series" of Hustich) is a continuous stand of closely spaced trees, in Labrador-Ungava usually a black spruce–balsam fir association. Such stands occur on well-drained land with a water-retentive soil and hence with abundant but not excessive moisture. The ground vegetation is rich in mosses, especially feather mosses, and there are some characteristic small herbs such as bunchberry (*Cornus canadensis*) and wood sorrel (*Oxalis montana*).

2. The *lichen-woodland* type ("Dry Series" of Hustich) consists of open stands of trees with a thick and beautiful floor of lichens. Black and white spruce, tamarack, and jack pine all occur in such

---

5 Ilmari Hustich, "On the Forest Geography of the Labrador-Peninsula: A Preliminary Synthesis," *Acta Geographica*, Vol. X, No. 2 (1949), pp. 36-42.
6 H. M. Raup, "Phytogeographic Studies in the Athabaska-Great Slave Lake Region, II," *Journ. Arnold Arbortum*, Vol. XXVII (1946), pp. 1-85.

woodland, though the spruces are overwhelmingly the dominants. The lichen floor consists of a layer several inches thick of the pale-gray, purple, orange, or green fruiting bodies of *Cladonia*, the genus to which the so-called "reindeer mosses" belong. The trees are from 2 to 25 yards apart. Black spruce tends to assume a beautiful "candelabrum" form in the lichen-woodlands. This type occurs only on drier sites in the south but is widespread in central and northern districts. Various subtypes of lichen-woodland probably cover more than 60 per cent of the Labrador-Ungava plateau and are wide-spread throughout the formation in North America and Eurasia. The term "woodland" is used to suggest the wide spacing of the trees.

3. The *muskeg* type ("Wet Series" of Hustich) occurs on badly drained ground and is variable in appearance. Black spruce and, to a smaller extent, tamarack are the typical trees. Both are slow-growing and slow-reproducing, appearing like gaunt sticks often largely devoid of branches or green leaves. The wet ground is cover-ed by sphagnum mosses and certain shrubs, of which Labrador tea (*Ledum groenlandicum*), leatherleaf (*Chamaedaphne calyculata*), and a heath (*Kalmia angustifolia*) are representative.

These clear-cut forest types occur throughout the formation in eastern Canada. The zonal divisions about to be discussed are de-finable in terms of the relative frequency of the forest types. This important principle has only recently emerged as the basis of divi-. sion in the boreal forest.

The Zonal Divisions

We come now to the first of the two main purposes of this article —the definition of zonal divisions within the formation. The argu-ment closely parallels that of Hustich, who laid down major forest

TABLE I – PROPOSED ZONAL DIVISIONS OF THE BOREAL FOREST
IN LABRADOR-UNGAVA

ZONAL DIVISION	HUSTICH'S TERM	DOMINANT FOREST TYPE
Forest-Tundra Ecotone	Forest-Tundra	Thin lichen-woodland in valleys; pure tundra on interfluves
Open Boreal Woodland	Taiga	Lichen-woodland
Main Boreal Forest	Southern Spruce Forests	Close-forest
Boreal–Mixed Forests Ecotone	——	Close-forest containing Great Lakes-St. Lawrence indicators

regions for Labrador-Ungava in 1949.[7] The basis of definition and the precise limits of the divisions proposed here differ significantly from his. In the next section the climatic relations of each of the divisions are reviewed.

South of the tundra four zonal divisions are proposed. These are arranged in north-south sequence in Table I.

The proposed zonal boundaries in Labrador-Ungava are shown in Figure 4. Where these differ from those of Hustich, the differences are based on an inspection of aerial photographs, on flights across the boundary zones, and in a few cases on ground traverses. The map is in any case provisional and will demand continual revision.

The dominant forest types refer to areas of well-drained soil. Throughout the formation areas of poor drainage are covered by treeless swamps and muskegs that differ little from zone to zone. The detailed character of the cover in each zone is beyond the scope of this report, but some further description is necessary.

The *forest-tundra ecotone* extends across northern Labrador-Ungava from the Hudson Bay coast to the Atlantic. Here it is truncated by the pure coastal tundra, which runs along the Atlantic shore to the Strait of Belle Isle. Along the line of the Torngat uplift, running north-south just east of the George River, the ecotone is narrow and is displaced southward by the greater altitude. The forest-tundra ecotone[8] is the zone in which associations of the tundra and boreal forest formations intermingle. The boreal forest is represented by long strings of lichen-woodland along the chief rivers, but the interfluves are covered by pure tundra entirely free of trees. Permafrost is widespread throughout the zone. The northern limit is the Arctic tree line. The southern, the line along which the lichen-woodland covers interfluves as well as valley floors, is known with some confidence from traverses by Rousseau on the George River,[9] Low on the Kaniapiskau River,[10] and Polunin at

---

[7] Hustich, *op. cit.*, pp. 47-53, Figs. 19 and 20. See also his "phytogeographical Regions of Labrador", *Arctic*, Vol. II (1949), pp. 36-42, especially Fig. 4.

[8] The term "forest tundra" is a literal translation of the Russian term *Iyesotundra* for the same belt in European Russia and Siberia. "Forest-tundra ecotone", a preferable form in English, was introduced by J. W. Marr, "Ecology of the Forest Tundra Ecotone on the East Coast of Hudson Bay", *Ecological Monographs*, Vol. XVII (1948), pp. 117-44.

[9] J. J. Rousseau, "The Vegetation and Life Zones of George River, Eastern Ungava and the Welfare of the Natives," *Arctic*, Vol. I (1948), pp. 93-96.

[10] A. P. Low, "Report on Explorations in the Labrador Peninsula . . .", *Ann. Rept. Geol. Survey of Canada*, Vol. VIII (N.S.), Ottawa (1895), Rept. L, p. 153.

Lac Bienville.[11] The present author was also able to traverse the boundary by air near the headwaters of the Whale River.

The *open boreal woodland* as a term seems preferable to Hustich's "taiga," since the latter is applied by Russian ecologists to the entire formation and is so understood by geographers everywhere. As the present term implies, this zone is dominated by enormous stretches of the lichen-woodland forest type; tall and well-developed spruce (more rarely other conifers) stand several yards apart in a sea of *Cladonia*. On the wetter ground muskeg supervenes, with stunted trees, Labrador tea, and sphagnum. Close-forest types are absent over most of the zone but become abundant on steeply sloping ground near the southern boundary. This boundary—one of the most significant economic limits on the continent, as it is the virtual northern limit of lumbering—is defined as that along which close-forest exceeds lichen-woodland in area.

The open boreal woodland presents one of the most picturesque, colorful, and extensive landscapes of the continent and is equally important in the Eurasian boreal forest. The beauty of its *Cladonia* floor, which retains the impress of footprints for years and whose pastel shades defy the color film, is still largely unknown to North Americans, since convenient routes nowhere penetrate its solitudes.

The *main boreal forest* is far better known, for it yields more than 90 per cent of the pulpwood cut of eastern Canada. Along its entire length it is penetrated by railways, logging roads, and power-generating rivers. In eastern Canada it extends from north of Lake Superior across southern Labrador-Ungava to Anticosti Island and Newfoundland. Large outliers cover inland Gaspé, the highlands of New Brunswick, and parts of Maine.

This zone is largely covered by close-forest associations of black spruce and balsam fir east of Lake St. John, white spruce and balsam fir to the west, thus approaching the traditionally accepted boreal climax. Lichen-woodlands occur only on dry soils and appear to be a late stage of the xerosere.[12] Muskeg, with black spruce and tamarack as dominants, is again common, especially on the dreary plains south and west of James Bay.

The northern limit of this zone was first defined by Halliday,[13] who consolidated traverse records from many transverse valleys crossing the boundary. Hustich accepted Halliday's line with few

---

[11] Nicholas Polunin, "Report on Botanical Explorations in Arctic America, 1946-48," *Arctic*, Vol. II (1949), pp. 45-47.
[12] The succession of covers achieved as the forest extends over dry surfaces like rocky outcrops or sand plains, which abound in this region.
[13] Halliday, *op. cit.*, see map in folder.

exceptions.[14] An accurate determination of its position on the Romaine River by H. N. Lash and N. Drummond showed, however, that Hustich's line was too far north.[15] The position given on Figure 4 incorporates their results.

An important outlier of the main boreal forest covers the lowlands around the head of Lake Melville and in the Hamilton Valley. This favored region of Labrador has much close-forest, though lichen-woodland is extensive on sand plains and gravels. It was formerly believed that the richness of this vegetation sprang from the deeper and more fertile soils developed on the Proterozoic sediments contained in the basin. It is now obvious, however, that this outlier is a climatic effect, a subject treated below. A revised version of Halliday's map[16] includes another outlier, the middle Kaniapiskau Valley, on the strongly folded Proterozoic sediments of the Labrador Trough. Here the vegetation consists of lichen-woodland and is included in the open boreal woodland of Figure 4.

The southern limit of the main boreal forest is the line along which the white pine–maple associations of the Great Lakes–St. Lawrence mixed forest formation replace the spruce-fir of the boreal forest. The position of this boundary as shown on Figure 4 is taken without change from "Native Trees of Canada."[17] The Lake St. John basin forms a conspicuous enclave of Great Lakes–St. Lawrence associations within the main boreal forest.

The ecotone between these two formations is less easy to define than the forest-tundra. On Figure 4 the northern edge of the ecotone is taken as the tree line of white and red pine. However, certain elements of the Great Lakes–St. Lawrence forest, notably the white cedar and black ash, extend well beyond this line.

Climatic Relations

Climatic correlation has been impossible in the past because of the lack of inland climatological stations. Not until 1937 was a station established in the interior of Labrador-Ungava, a region equal in area to the United States east of the Mississippi and south of latitude 40° N. Since then, however, many stations have been opened by the Canadian Department of Transport and the United States

---

14 Hustich, "On the Forest Geography of the Labrador Peninsula," *op. cit.*, Figs. 19 and 20.

15 Lash and Drummond made a traverse along Romaine River to determine ground control for the ecological interpretation of aerial photographs. The traverse, as yet unpublished, was carried out as part of a project directed by the present author. Mr. Lash has now assumed control of this project.

16 "Native Trees of Canada," *Forest Service Bull. 61*, 4th ed., Ottawa (1949). See map inside covers.

17 *Ibid.*

Air Weather Service, and a rudimentary climatological network is now in operation. In 1947 the author began preparation of a report on the climatology of the region, and extensive use has been made below of materials gathered during this investigation.

Raw climatic data have little application in ecoclimatology. Effort must be made to find means of combining and integrating the elements into indices having a more direct applicability to ecological problems. The best available system is C. W. Thornthwaite's classification of 1948,[18] and it is used here. An account of the climates of Canada as a whole according to this new classification has already been published by Sanderson.[19] A considerably denser network of stations has been used in the preparation of Figures 5 and 6, however, and these maps differ in detail from those of Sanderson.

Annual potential evapotranspiration is the function used by Thornthwaite to establish the degree of thermal efficiency possessed by a climate. It is an accumulating logarithmic function of monthly mean temperatures, regarded as expressing thermal efficiency on the basis of a presumed analogy with the control of growth rates by temperature.

Figure 5 shows annual potential evapotranspiration over eastern Canada and the boundaries of the thermal provinces suggested by Thornthwaite. The D'/C'_1 boundary runs north of Baker Lake, across the Ungava Peninsula from Portland Promontory to Payne Bay, and across the northernmost part of the Torngat massif. The C'_1/C'_2 boundary (separating cooler and warmer microthermal provinces) runs from the Hayes River near Gods Lake across James Bay to the northern tip of the Long Peninsula of Newfoundland. Thus the greater part of Labrador-Ungava falls into the cool microthermal province (C'_1). All the southern districts lie in the warm microthermal province (C'_2); mesothermal climates do not occur within the area of Figure 5, though they are found in the St. Lawrence lowlands near Montreal.

The records from Goose Bay airport show that an important outlier of warm microthermal climate occurs around the head of Lake Melville and the lower Hamilton Valley. Fragmentary records

---

[18] C. W. Thornthwaite, "An Approach Towards a Rational Classification of Climate," *Geogr. Rev.*, Vol. XXXVIII (1948), pp. 55-94. A more general treatment of the climate is given by F. Kenneth Hare, "The Climate of the Eastern Canadian Arctic and Sub-Arctic and Its Influence on Accessibility," 2 vols., Montreal, (1950). Doctoral Diss. (unpub.).

[19] Marie Sanderson, "The Climates of Canada According to the New Thornthwaite Classification", *Scientific Agric.*, Vol. XXVIII (1948), pp. 501-17.

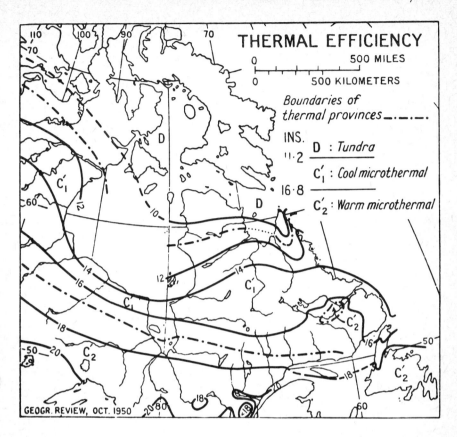

Figure 5. Thermal efficiency, expressed in terms of potential evapotranspiration (in inches), according to Thornthwaite's classification of 1948.

from North West River and the Hamilton Valley confirm that this is an extensive area, but its form can at present only be sketched in relation to the terrain (Figure 5).

The moisture index, the other main element in Thornthwaite's classification, is shown in Figure 6. Labrador-Ungava, Newfoundland, and northern Ontario have an abundant well-distributed precipitation and rank almost exclusively as humid or perhumid. The southern half of Labrador-Ungava has indices of more than 100 (A; perhumid), as does most of Newfoundland. Highest values occur along the Laurentide scarp belt, just north of the Gulf of St. Lawrence, and in southern Newfoundland. Conspicuously drier areas include the structural depressions of Lake St. John and Lake Melville, and also the Atlantic coastal strip from Nain to Cape Harrison.

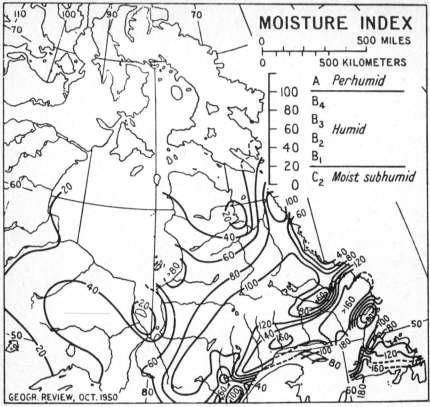

Figure 6. Moisture index, according to Thornthwaite's classification of 1948. Note high values typical of southern Labrador-Ungava, low values along western margin.

Farther north and west indices are lower but everywhere exceed 20, except in the James Bay and Ungava Bay depressions. This is in striking contrast to the condition reported for the western boreal forest by Sanderson,[20] who found indices ranging from below –20 to about +20, i.e. between arid and moist subhumid.

There is some doubt about the extent of drought in the James Bay region. The isopleth of 20 in the center is based on values computed for Fort Albany (17), Moose Factory (19), and Fort George (33). It is possible, however, that these values are too low, perhaps because of faulty exposure of the snow-measuring site. More recent observations at Moosonee, a first-order station staffed by trained professional observers, indicate a heavier winter snowfall than at near-by Moose Factory, and the index stands at 74. The point is academic, since almost the entire district is covered by muskeg in which bad drainage upsets the normal moisture cycle.

[20] Sanderson, "Drought in the Canadian Northwest, *op. cit.*

Correlations Between Climate and the Zonal Forest Divisions

It now remains only to establish the relation between the climate distributions and the zonal divisions of the forest. Such attempts were previously made by Halliday[21] and Villeneuve[22] for various parts of the region, but in both cases before data were available from the interior of Labrador-Ungava and before Thornthwaite's new system was published. Villeneuve's maps do not extend beyond the 51st parallel.

Elsewhere, a good deal of work has been done on the growth conditions of the coniferous trees composing the boreal forest climax. With few exceptions, all these investigations have suggested that midsummer temperatures control growth rates and that precipitation is largely ineffective as a control. Thus Hustich reported that the width of annual rings in Scotch pine (*Pinus sylvestris*) at Utsjoki, Lappland, was closely correlated with July mean daily temperature; vertical growth of the trees was likewise related to the July temperature of the previous year. Neither vertical nor radial growth was related to variations in summer precipitation.[23] Similar results were obtained by Erlandsson[24] and other Scandinavian workers for Scotch pine and other boreal forest conifers. Giddings stressed the dependence of the spruce on summer temperature in both Alaska[25] and the Mackenzie Valley.[26] The widely accepted view that the northern forests are governed in their growth by temperature, and that precipitation is everywhere adequate to supply the needs of the growth possible under such cool conditions, was also accepted by Thornthwaite in his earlier climatic classification.[27]

The present investigation amply confirms this view. A comparison of Figures 5 and 6 with Figure 4 shows at once that there is an obvious correlation between the zonal forest divisions and thermal efficiency (that is, potential evapotranspiration); the interdivisional

21 Halliday, *op. cit.*, pp. 40-45.
22 G. O. Villeneuve, "Climatic Conditions of the Province of Quebec and Their Relationship to the Forests", *Forest Protection Service Bull. No. 6*, Quebec (1946).
23 I. Hustich, "On the Correlation between Growth and the Recent Climatic Fluctuation", in "Glaciers and Climate . . .," *Geografisha Annaler*, Vol. XXXI, (1949), pp. 90-105.
24 S. Erlandsson, "Data 23", *Dendrochronological Studies*, Uppsala (1936).
25 J. L. Giddings, Jr., "Dendrochronology in Northern Alaska," *Univ. of Arizona Bull.*, Vol. XII, No. 4 (1941).
26 *Idem.*, "Mackenzie River Delta Chronology," *Tree-Ring Bull.*, Vol. XIII (1947), pp. 26-29.
27 C. W. Thornthwaite, "The Climates of North America According to a New Classification," *Geogr. Rev.*, Vol. XXI (1931), pp. 633-55.

boundaries tend to follow the isopleths of potential evapotranspiration. On the other hand, there is no obvious correlation between the moisture provinces and the forest divisions. No evidence whatever has been found to suggest any control of the forest structure by the moisture factor, other than the effects of poor drainage in the muskeg. Table II shows how close is the correlation between thermal efficiency and the forest divisions. With trifling exceptions, the interdivisional boundaries follow closely the isopleths of potential evapotranspiration suggested in Table II.

TABLE II—FOREST DIVISIONS AND POTENTIAL EVAPOTRANSPIRATION
IN LABRADOR-UNGAVA

DIVISION	TYPICAL VALUE OF P-E ALONG BOUNDARIES (INCHES)	DOMINANT COVER TYPE
Tundra		Tundra
	12.0–12.5	
Forest-Tundra Ecotone		Tundra and lichen-woodland intermingled
	14.0–14.5	
Open Boreal Woodland		Lichen-woodland
	16.5–17.0	
Main Boreal Forest		Close-Forest with spruce-fir associations
	18.5–19.0	
Boreal-Mixed Forest Ecotone		Close-forest with white and red pine, yellow birch, and other non-boreal invaders
	20.0	
Great-Lakes–St. Lawrence Mixed Forest		Mixed forest

The Arctic tree line, the southern limit of the tundra, nowhere reaches Thornthwaite's theoretical potential evapotranspiration value of 11.2 inches. Near the mouth of the George River, which affords a good migration route northward, a thin stand of black spruce and tamarack reaches the value of 11.5 inches, but elsewhere the tree line lies between 12 and 12.5 inches. Marr has shown, however, that white spruce is actively invading the tundra near the Great Whale River, and it may well be that there has not been time since the Wisconsin glaciation for the forest to attain its climax tree line.[28]

Near Richmond Gulf on the Hudson Bay coast and south of Hebron on the Atlantic coast, well-developed black and white spruce groves stand well north of the isotherm of 10° C. (50° F.) for the warmest month.

---

[28] Marr, *op. cit.*

The narrow strip of coastal tundra fringing the Atlantic coast of Labrador as far south as Belle Isle was formerly thought to be the reflection of the chilling effect of the Labrador Current and its pack ice. Climatological stations directly on this coastal tree line, however, show that the thermal efficiency is adequate to support-lichen-woodland (Hopedale, 15.3 inches; Cartwright, 15.3 inches; Belle Isle, 14.5 inches). Evidently temperature is not alone responsible for the lack of trees.

The open boreal woodland extends between the potential evapotranspiration values of 14.0–14.5 and 16.5–17.0 inches. Its southern limit coincides with Thornthwaite's suggested divide between warmer and cooler microthermal climates (C'_1/C'_2). In other words, the forest-tundra ecotone and open boreal woodland correspond with the cool microthermal province.

Wide variations in moisture index occur within this division, without any apparent effect on the vegetation. Since moisture is abundant everywhere, it is of interest to speculate as to the origins of the curious structure of the dominant lichen-woodland, with its widely spaced but fully developed trees and its lichen floor that requires little moisture. Farther south lichen-woodland is definitely a drought type, confined to sandy or gravelly soils.

It may well be that the widespread character of this dry type in the open boreal woodland results from physiological drought, as Schimper has called it. Where frost in the soil is still unthawed in July, the season of peak growth, the trees can derive moisture only from the topmost layers of the soil and hence are driven to assume a horizontally developed root system. Competition between neighboring trees must then mean that the space between individuals has to be greater.

The main boreal forest occupies the range of potential evapotranspiration between 16.5–17.0 and 20.0 inches. It is invaded by indicators of the Great Lakes-St. Lawrence formation as far north as the 18.5- and 19.0-inch isopleths. The southern limit, 20.0 inches, is faithfully followed from Lake Superior to Gaspé; the 20.0-inch isopleth even curves around the Lake St. John lowland, with the little enclave of mixed forest mentioned above. It is to be noted that Thornthwaite's microthermal-mesothermal boundary (C'_2/B'_1) is 22.4 inches; the main boreal forest and the Great Lakes-St. Lawrence formation thus meet in the middle of the warm microthermal province.

The small outlier of warm microthermal climate in the Lake Melville-Hamilton River region coincides reasonably well with the detached area of main boreal forest in the same districts. Though poor in species, the well-developed close-forests of this region offer one of the largest untapped reserves of pulpwood in eastern North America. The region has a thermal efficiency similar to that of the forests now being cut near Clarke City and on Anticosti Island.

The Remaining Areas

Although the delimitation of zonal divisions has not yet been undertaken beyond Labrador-Ungava, a few comments may be made concerning other parts of eastern Canada.

"Native Trees of Canada" includes a revised version of the Halliday map of Canadian vegetation. It distinguishes between a "northern transition" zone and the main boreal forest; and in Labrador-Ungava the line very nearly coincides with the boundary between the open boreal woodland and the main boreal forest. From the vicinity of James Bay west to Manitoba the boundary continues to lie between the 16.5- and 17.0-inch isopleths of potential evapotranspiration. The regions farther north in the Hudson Bay lowland are too little known to permit further correlation.

The islands of Newfoundland and Anticosti lie wholly within the range of potential evapotranspiration found in the main boreal forest, with the solitary exception of the Long Peninsula of Newfoundland. Both islands are largely covered by close-forest, with the spruces and balsam fir as the dominants. There seems no doubt that they lie within the main boreal forest division. The warmest area of Newfoundland (potential evapotranspiration 19–20 inches) lies along the railway line from St. George Bay to the Avalon Peninsula. This thermal efficiency corresponds with the boreal-mixed forest ecotone on the mainland, and it is interesting to note that many non-boreal trees occur in isolated localities (for example, white pine and red maple, *Acer rubrum*). The south coast of Newfoundland is chilled by the onshore prevailing winds crossing the offshoot of the Labrador Current that moves westward along the coast. Much of the high ground of the south is covered by treeless moss barrens. In many cases the lack of trees is an effect of altitude, but moss barrens occur also at low altitudes in regions where the thermal efficiency is ample to support high forest. Their origin has not been explained.

A preliminary glance at the Russian taiga has shown that zonal divisions comparable with those defined above for Labrador-Ungava have almost identical relationships with climate. This encourages the hope that it will ultimately be possible to extend the present review to the entire extent of the boreal forest formation. It will be of particular interest to see whether anything of the same zonal structure is revealed in the boreal forest of western Canada, where Sanderson has reported the retarding effects of drought. It may well be that the dependence of growth on thermal efficiency so strikingly confirmed in the humid east breaks down in the drier west.

2

The Mountain Forest and Alpine Zones of Alberta

R. T. Ogilvie

The Rocky Mountains of Alberta comprise a series of parallel ranges running northwest and southeast for approximately four hundred miles between 54 degrees north latitude and 49 degrees north latitude. The forest and alpine zones in the east slope of the Rocky Mountains of Alberta are bounded on the west by the Continental Divide, and bordered on the east by the foothills and plains. Grassland dominated by *Festuca scabrella* occurs in the plains and low foothills, further westward the vegetation is groveland of *Populus tremuloides*, and in the high foothills the vegetation is forest of climax *Picea glauca, P. mariana,* and successional *Pinus contorta* var. *latifolia, Populus tremuloides, P. balsamifera,* and *P. trichocarpa*. The boundaries between these vegetation regions are diffuse, they interfinger with one another and with the mountain vegetation, extending from the foothills through the Front Ranges far into the mountains along the broad, low valley bottoms.

1. Climate

Throughout the mountains the climate is highly variable. Each of the parallel series of mountain ranges has a slightly different climate. Some generalizations can be made: the prevailing winds are westerly, and the greatest amount of precipitation occurs in the western mountain ranges and decreases through the eastern ranges. Relatively speaking, there is a rain-shadow effect which increases eastwards. The Foothills and Front Ranges have a more continental boreal-like climate, with more extreme temperatures, lower precipitation, and a summer—high, winter—low distribution of precipitation. Westward to the Continental Divide there is a more maritime type of climate, with less extreme temperatures, higher precipita-

Unpublished manuscript.

tion, and a winter—high, summer—low distribution. With increasing elevation there is a similar trend from continental to maritime-type climate. Also paralleling this climatic trend is a trend in the flora and vegetation: going from east to west and from low to higher elevations there is a trend from a boreal-type of flora to a more cordilleran type of flora. These trends are illustrated by the data from two meteorological stations in Banff National Park. Banff station lies in the Front Ranges of the mountains, in a broad valley bottom at low elevation. It has a continental type of climate, with a mean annual temperature of 36°F., and a mean annual precipitation of 19 inches with most of it occurring during the summer (Figure 1). Lake Louise station is close to the Continental Divide and at a higher elevation. It shows a more maritime type of climate, with a mean annual temperature of 32°F., and a mean annual precipitation of 31 inches which occurs mostly during the winter (Figure 2).

A general climatological principle is called the lapse rate; this is the name given to the familiar phenomenon of temperature decreasing with increase in elevation. The general rate of decrease is 3°F. for every 1000 feet rise in elevation. Ecologically this is important because of the retarding effect on the growing season of plants.

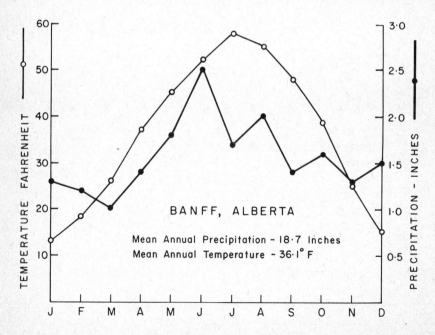

Figure 1. Temperature and precipitation trends at Banff, Alberta.

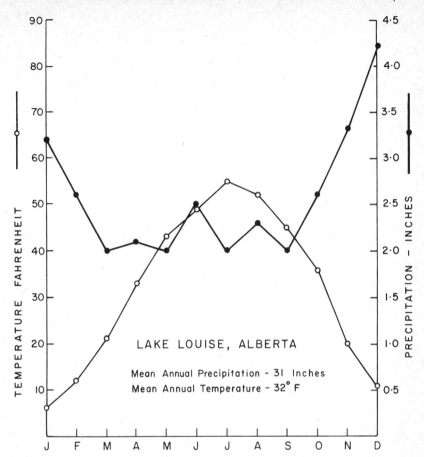

Figure 2. Temperature and precipitation trends at Lake Louise, Alberta.

As an approximate rule-of-thumb, plant development (e.g. flowering, leafing) averages four days later for every 400 feet rise in elevation. A reversal of this lapse rate occurs during what is called nocturnal temperature inversion. Instead of a continual decrease in temperature with height, there is a cold layer of air at the ground surface, a warm layer above, and then cold air above this. These temperature inversions are caused in two ways: during the night the air loses heat to the soil and becomes increasingly cooled; and cold, heavier air from higher up moves downslope and accumulates in the valley bottom below the warm air. Two examples from measurements taken in Banff can be used for illustration. One showing how temperatures can differ over a few feet in height:

Station at valley bottom, minimum night temperature = 32°F.
Station on bench 20 ft. higher, min. night temp.   = 44°F.

A second example shows the extreme temperature range that may occur during inversions:

Station at valley bottom (6600 ft. elev.) = 34°F.
Station on valley side (7450 ft. elev.) = 52°F.

Such temperature inversions occur very regularly, with a frequency of as many as 30 days in the month. The ecological importance of temperature inversions is that valley bottom communities are composed of low temperature-enduring plants; thermophilous species are prevented from occurring there. For example, the absence of forest in high valley bottoms is probably a result of low temperatures preventing the establishing of trees.

2. Topography

Mountain topography is extremely irregular; this produces a great diversity of habitats and plant communities. Direction of exposure, or aspect, is a major environmental influence: northerly and easterly exposures are cooler and moister, southerly and westerly aspects are warmer and drier. Aspect has a profound effect on vegetation pattern; one can see examples of this throughout Banff park.

3. Geology

Much of the geological strata is sedimentary: limestones, dolomites, sandstones, shales. Many of the derived soil-forming materials are calcareous, whether bedrock weathered in place, or transported glacial and alluvial materials.

4. Soils

As discussed above, many of the soils are developed from calcareous parent materials; this may be contrasted with the mountains soils of British Columbia where many of the parent materials are acidic. Some of the common types of soil profiles occurring here are:

Brunisolic—having weakly developed horizons, and occurring in the drier habitats at lower elevations.

Podzolic—having pronounced horizons and leaching, occurring in areas with greater moisture and at higher elevations.

Gleisolic—wet soils, with a high water-table.

Organic Bog Soils—saturated soils with water near the surface, and deep peat accumulation.

The Flora

1. The Historical-Geological and the Environmental Factors Determining the Flora

There are two reasons why some plants occur in Banff while other plants do not. Firstly, the environment does not permit some species to grow. In the second case, past geological events have eliminated some species from the flora. For example, a number of plants such as western hemlock, western white pine, western red cedar, and Devil's club occur in adjacent British Columbia but not in Banff. This is largely a result of events during Pleistocene glaciation when all plants were eliminated from the region and some species did not migrate back after deglaciation.

2. Floristic Elements—the distribution patterns of the different plant species

There are two general types of plant distribution patterns in the flora of Banff. Species with boreal distribution are those occurring across northern Canada. Boreal species make up about two-thirds of the Banff flora. Species with a cordilleran distribution are confined to the mountain region of western North America. About one-third of the plant species of Banff have this cordilleran type of distribution.

3. Tree Species in Banff National Park

Picea engelmannii—Engelmann spruce; cordilleran distribution.

Picea glauca—white spruce; boreal distribution. Extensive hybridization occurs between Engelmann and white spruce, in fact most of the spruce stands in Banff Park are hybrids.

Picea mariana—black spruce; boreal distribution. Restricted to a few small stands in the northern part of the park.

Abies lasiocarpa—alpine fir; cordilleran distribution.

Pinus contorta var. *latifolia*—lodgepole pine, cordilleran distribution.

Pinus albicaulis—whitebark pine; cordilleran distribution.

Pinus flexilis—limber pine; cordilleran distribution; restricted to the southern part of the park.

Pseudotsuga menziesii—Douglas fir; cordilleran distribution.

Larix lyallii—alpine larch; cordilleran distribution; restricted to the southern part of the park.

Populus tremuloides—aspen; boreal distribution.

Populus balsamifera—balsam poplar; boreal distribution.

Populus trichocarpa—western cottonwood; cordilleran distribution.

Betula papyrifera—paper birch; boreal distribution.

Ecology of Tree Species

1. Lodgepole Pine

Lodgepole pine is the first tree to colonise an area after forest fire; it is highly adapted for this. One adaptation is the feature of closed cones (serotiny), in which the cone scales are sealed shut by resin bonds. Temperatures in excess of 113°F. are required for melting the resin bonds; such temperatures are attained only in fires. The cones remain closed on trees for up to 50 years, so that immediately following a fire there is a sudden release of large quantities of seed. This condition of closed cones changes with the age of the trees. Young pine, up to 20 years, produce mostly open cones. After 20 years mostly closed cones are formed, but in the old trees a few open cones are always formed. Another adaptation is that pine has very rapid germination and seedling growth. This means that following fire this species can become rapidly established and out-compete other species. Lodgepole pine is adapted to growth in open conditions with high light intensity; it is a shade-intolerant tree which cannot establish itself inside stands. It is thus suited to the open conditions following fires. In forest succession after fires there is rapid colonisation of lodgepole pine during the first three to five years. In some cases extremely dense stands result (e.g. "dog-hair stands" with 1½ million trees per acre, and stagnating 50-year-old stands with a maximum height of 4 feet). Lodgepole pine grows rapidly for 90 to 100 years, then slows down abruptly. Spruce and alpine fir seed into the stands and form the understorey; by 200 to 250 years lodgepole pine is decadent and dying out, and spruce and fir become the dominant trees in the stand. All lodgepole pine stands are of fire origin and are successional, none are climax.

2. Spruces and Alpine Fir

Both these trees are shade tolerant; they readily reproduce under the stand. They also reproduce vegetatively by layering, especially at high elevations. Alpine fir has rapid seedling growth surpassing spruce, initially it is more abundant than spruce. In time, spruce catches up, and the final mature stand is mostly spruce with lesser amount of alpine fir. Alpine fir is a relatively short-lived species (300-350 years); the spruces are long-lived (450 up to 600 years). Spruce and alpine fir can reproduce themselves indefinitely in the stand, the stands are self-regenerating, and thus these species form the climax forest. If fire were eliminated, after several centuries most of the forest would be spruce-fir; there would be only the occasional individual example of lodgepole pine and other successional trees.

Fire History

The whole of the east slopes of the Rocky Mountains, including Banff Park, has had an extremely extensive history of fires. Climatically the region is extremely susceptible to fire, and the forest has been repeatedly burned. A few protected habitats are not burned, e.g. along streams, on north-facing slopes, and at very high elevations near timberline. But there are many areas where fires have gone right up to timberline. An approximate idea of the amount of the East Slopes Area which has been burned-over can be obtained from some figures of the Alberta Forest Service: 58% of the merchantable volume of timber in this area is lodgepole pine (merchantable is defined as trees with diameter greater than 4 inches, so this figure does not include many fire stands with smaller diameter).

The history of fires in this area can be inferred from an analysis of the ages of pine stands:

Age of Stand	*Historical Period*	*% of Stands*
50- 75 yrs.	Early Park Period: 1887-1911	30
75-110 yrs.	Prospecting and Early Railway: 1850-1886	47
110-185 yrs.	Furtrading Period: 1775-1850	15
+185 yrs.	Pre-European Period: pre-1775	8

Thus, even though fire is a natural environmental factor in this region, the amount of fires (and consequently the amount of lodgepole pine stands) has been strongly influenced by human activities. This is especially pronounced during the Prospecting and Early Railway Period of the late nineteenth century. Nowadays there is a great decrease in fires as a result of fire control measures of the National Park Warden Service and the Alberta Forest Service.

3. Aspen

Aspen is fire successional like lodgepole pine. It has the feature of reproducing vegetatively through extensive root suckers; this results in clonal stands in which all the trees are genetically identical.

4. Cottonwood Poplars

The cottonwood poplars are successional species that colonise on river deposits. These stands last for one generation, at which time the cottonwoods are replaced by spruce and alpine fir.

5. Douglas Fir

Douglas fir occurs on the driest, warmest slopes where it can out-compete other species which are more moisture-requiring. In such habitats Douglas fir forms regenerating climax stands. It forms open, widely-spaced (savanna-type) stands, which are suitable to its ecological requirements since it is a relatively shade-intolerant species and requires high light intensities for satisfactory establishment. In other habitats Douglas fir occurs sporadically as a successional species to the spruce-fir forest.

6. Alpine Larch and Whitebark Pine

These two trees are timberline species, restricted to a narrow altitudinal band at timberline.

7. Limber Pine

Limber pine is not actually typical of the mountains in Alberta; it is more typically a foothills species. It does not occur at high elevations in the mountains; its characteristic habitat is rocky ridge crests and exposed outcrops.

8. Black Spruce

As indicated above, black spruce occurs as a small stand at Saskatchewan River Crossing in Banff National Park, but is abundant along the Athabasca River Valley in Jasper National Park. It is a species of very wet, peatland habitats.

The Forest Communities

Plant species are aggregated into distinct groupings determined by historical factors, environment, and competition. The environment acts on the flora and selects out those species which are best adapted to occur in a certain habitat. Each species has its own set of optimal environmental conditions, thus for a certain environment those species which are best adapted will predominate, other species which are less adapted are less able to compete and are restricted in their abundance and vigour or are prevented from occurring there. Thus competition, along with environmental selection operates among the members of the plant community to determine the ultimate species composition and structure of the community.

A series of plant communities have been defined and described for the Rocky Mountains of Alberta. Each of these communities has a distinctive species composition and occurs in a specific habitat (Figure 3). The communities listed below have been defined by their habitat characteristics and their dominant and constant plant species.

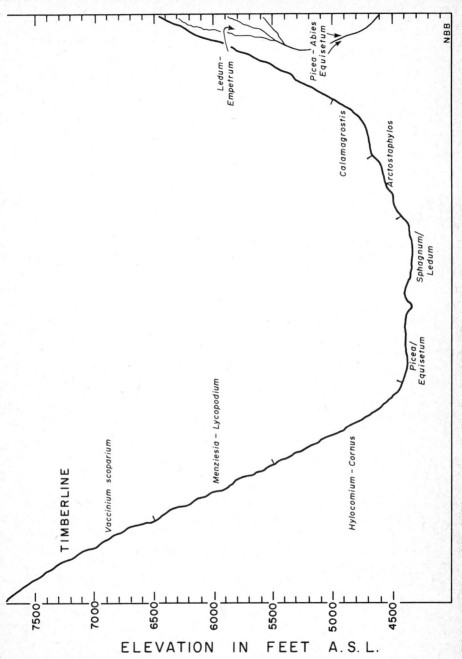

Figure 3. Picea-Abies habitat types in the Rocky Mountains of Alberta.

1. *Picea – Equisetum* Community

This is the river-flat horsetail community, occurring on alluvial flats along major rivers. The soils have a high water-table, with recurrent flooding. There is a lush cover of the herb layer, and a moderate development of the shrub and moss layers.

2. *Picea / Sphagnum – Ledum* Community

The peat moss – Labrador tea community also occurs on alluvial flats along major river valleys. The subsoil consists of fine clays which cause impeded drainage, and the water-table occurs at the surface. Deep peats accumulate to form Organic Bog Soils. There is an abundant moss layer and shrub layer, and a well-developed herb layer.

3. *Picea / Arctostaphylos* Community

The valley bottom bearberry type occurs on the dry river terraces at low elevations. The soils are coarse and stoney, droughty, and poorly developed. The shrub layer is most abundant, the herb and bryophyte layers are sparse and poorly developed. Because of the dryness of this type and its susceptibility to fires, many of the stands of this community are now dominated by lodgepole pine.

4. *Picea – Abies / Calamagrostis* Community

This is the pinegrass community, occuring at valley bottoms and on the lower south-facing slopes from 4500 to 5000 feet elevation. The soils are finer materials with a more favourable moisture status, and are weakly podzolised. There is a dense herb layer, a moderately developed low shrub layer, and a sparse bryophyte and lichen layer. This community is highly susceptible to burning and is almost completely dominated by lodgepole pine stands.

5. *Picea – Abies / Hylocomium – Cornus* Community

The feather moss type occurs on northerly slopes from 4500 to 5500 feet elevation. The shaded slopes provide favourable moisture conditions, and the soils are podzolised. There is a continuous carpet of feather mosses, a moderately developed herb layer, and a sparse cover of shrubs.

6. *Picea – Abies / Menziesia – Lycopodium* Community

This is the false azalea type occurring on the middle and upper valley slopes from 5500 to 6500 feet elevation. There is abundant moisture throughout the growing season, and the soils are strongly developed podzolic profiles. There is a dense tall shrub layer, an abundant cover of bryophytes and lichens, and a sparse herb layer.

7. *Picea – Abies / Ledum – Empetrum* Community

In small localised places on the upper valley slopes, seepage water comes close to the soil surface. In such places there is an alteration in the plant communities, with a greater abundance of Labrador tea, crowberry, and other such moist-habitat species. This seepage Labrador tea-crowberry community occurs on gleyed podzolic soils.

8. *Picea – Abies / Equisetum* Community

This is the upper streamside horsetail community. It occurs along tributary streams at higher elevations, and is a counterpart to the valley-bottom horsetail community. There is a rich herb layer, and moderately developed moss and shrub layers.

9. *Picea – Abies / Vaccinium scoparium* Community

The high elevation grouseberry type occurs from 6500 feet elevation to timberline. There is very deep snow cover, a short growing season, and the soil remains frozen late in the summer. The low shrub heath layer has high coverage, there is an abundant bryophyte and lichen layer, and a sparse herb layer.

Upper Timberline

One of the most conspicuous features in the mountains is the distinct line where forest ends and the treeless alpine region begins. Viewed from a distance, upper timberline is an abrupt vegetation change which occurs at a constant elevation throughout the area. In Banff this elevation is at approximately 7000 feet. At closer range, timberline is neither so abrupt nor is it constant in elevation. There is a gradual breaking-up of the forest into groves, tree islands, low stunted krummholz colonies, and finally dwarfed isolated trees. In Banff, this timberline pattern occurs from 6500 to 7500 feet, with straggling dwarfed trees occurring as high as 8000 feet elevation. Some generalisations on timberline can be made: timberline tends to be high on lee slopes and slopes bordering streams (but not in stream bottoms). It is low on wind-exposed slopes, on south-facing slopes, avalanche slopes, along stream bottoms, and on unstable substrata such as scree and rubble. The environmental factors controlling timberline are complex, but the major ones are: low temperature, wind desiccation, avalanching, and snow depth.

The Alpine Region

The alpine environment is cold, windy, and snowy. In Banff, the mean annual temperature from stations at 7500 feet elevation is 25°F., the highest summer temperature is approximately 75°F., the lowest winter temperature is around –30°F. The frost-free period in summer is about seven days. There is a two month period between the last heavy snowfall in spring and the first heavy snowfall in late summer, although light snowfalls occur every week during summer. Precipitation ranges between 35 and 60 inches per year, with most of it occurring as snow. One of the major factors governing alpine vegetation is the pattern of snow distribution. Ridge crests and wind-exposed slopes are blown free of snow, and the snow is accumulated to great depths on lee-slopes of ridges, in krummholz colonies, and in channels and topographic depressions. Snow depth can vary from nil to in excess of fifteen feet. The snow pattern is constant from year to year and results in a vegetation pattern closely correlated with it.

Wind in the alpine is approximately double that in the adjoining forest zone. In exposed habitats, wind speed *averages* about 20 miles per hour, and during one month amounts to around 14,000 miles.

One final feature of the alpine environment is the occurrence of soil movement. Soils saturated by snow meltwaters undergo slumping and creep, to produce terraced and lobed terrain. Frost action sorts different sized soil particles to produce stone polygons, stone stripes, and earth circles. Permafrost does not as a rule occur in alpine soils, although we have found one occurrence of it in Banff.

Alpine plants show adaptations to the rigorous environmental conditions: they are cold resistant, drought resistant, wind resistant, and certain species are resistant to deep snow cover. Low-growing cushion and mat plants are protected from the wind, and benefit from the warmer temperatures close to the ground. Many alpine plants have small, needle or scale-like leaves, and white, hairy surfaces to reduce water-loss. Alpine plants are able to grow, flower, and form seed in temperatures below freezing. One group of plants is adapted to withstand deep snow cover for long periods, and carry on rapid growth and flowering during the few weeks they are exposed in summer.

The Alpine Communities

Ten alpine plant communities have been defined in Banff Park (Figure 4).

1. *Phyllodoce – Vaccinium scoparium* Community

This is a timberline heath community occurring among tree islands and krummholz colonies, on lee-slopes with very deep snow accumulation. The soils are subject to solifluction. There is an abundance of low heath species, and a good cover of the herb and bryophyte layers.

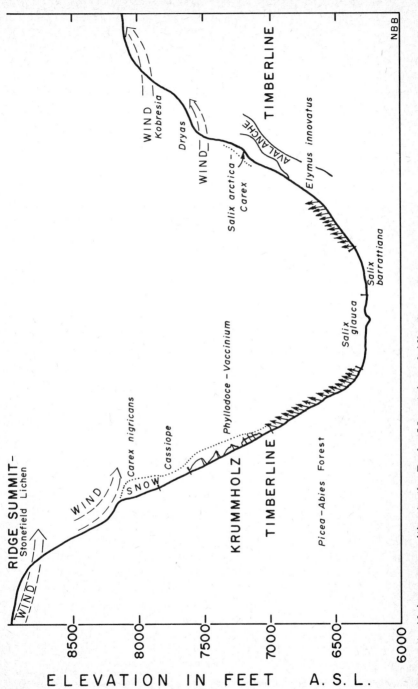

Figure 4. Alpine communities in the Rocky Mountains of Alberta.

2. *Cassiope* Community

Another heath community occurs on north-facing slopes, with deep snow cover. The soils have seepage and solifluction. There is an abundant low shrub layer, a rich bryophyte and lichen layer, and a moderately-developed herb layer.

3. *Salix glauca* Community

This is a valley-bottom tall willow community, occurring where low temperatures prohibit the establishment of trees. The soils are coarse stream deposits which have repeated flooding and a high water-table. There is a dense tall shrub layer, a moderately-developed herb layer, and a less abundant bryophyte layer.

4. *Salix barrattiana* Community

This is another tall willow community occurring in similar situations to the previous one. The soils are finer stream materials and less subject to flooding. There is a dense tall shrub layer and a well-developed herb layer.

5. *Elymus innovatus* Community

This avalanche meadow community occurs on steep south-facing slopes, on stoney, black soils. There is a moderate snow cover as a result of early snowmelt and continual avalanching. There is a lush grass and herb cover, but very few shrubs or mosses.

6. *Kobresia myosuroides* Community

This dry-sedge meadow occurs at higher elevations above the *Elymus* community, on snow-free, wind-exposed south-facing slopes and ridge-crests. The soils are shallow and stoney. There is a rich herb layer, and an abundant lichen and bryophyte layer.

7. *Salix arctica – Carex* Community

This dwarf willow-sedge meadow occurs in areas of deep snow accumulation, on soils which are moist from meltwaters. There is a rich herb layer of sedges, grasses and forbs, an abundant dwarf shrub layer, and a well-developed moss layer.

8. *Carex nigricans* Community

This is a snowpatch sedge community occurring in small channels and depressions where there is very deep snow accumulation. The soils are moist, and free of snow for only a brief period. There is an abundant herb layer of sedges, grasses and colourful forbs, with a minor occurrence of dwarf shrubs and mosses.

9. *Dryas hookeriana – Oxytropis podocarpa – Cetraria* Community
This community occurs on wind-exposed, snow-free ridges. The soils are shallow and stoney. There is an abundance of cushion and mat-plants, and a large number of lichens.

10. Stonefield Lichen Community.
This community occurs on the wind-swept summits of the highest ridges (around 9000 feet elevation) near the altitudinal limit of closed communities. The ground is snow-free, and covered with rocks and stone fragments. The vegetation is sparse, consisting mainly of lichens and mat-plants.

Appendix

Characteristic Species and Habitat Features of the Plant Communities
Picea engelmannii—Abies lasiocarpa Forest *Plant Association*

1. Picea—Abies / Vaccinium scoparium association 6400 ft. elevation to timberline. Podzolic soils. Very deep snow accumulation. Very short growing season; sub-optimal temperatures. Soil frozen late in year.
E (EI), aF, aL, wbP.
Vaccinium scoparium, Phyllodoce glanduliflora, P. empetriformis. Dicranum fuscescens, leafy liverworts, Cladonia spp. Arnica latifolia, Valeriana sitchensis, Pedicularis bracteosa, ssp. calliorthem Erigeron peregrinus.

2. Picea—Abies / Menziesia ferruginea—Lycopodium annotinum association middle and upper valley slopes, from 5,500-6,500 ft. elevation. Moisture conditions favourable throughout year. Deep snow accumulation. Soils strongly podzolised.
EI & I, aF.
Menziesia ferruginea, Rhododendron albiflorum, Vaccinium membranaceum, V. myrtillus, V. scoparium, Sorbus sitchtnsis, S. scopulina. Pleurozium schreberi, Dicranum fuscescens, D. scoparium, Hylocomium splendens Barlulophozia sp. ssp. americus, Ptilium crista-castrensis. Lycopodium annotinum, Arnica latifolia, A. cordifolia, Linnaea borealis, Cornus canadensis.

3. Picea—Abies / Hylocomium splendens—Cornus canadensis association lower valley slopes, north to east aspects, from 4,500-5,500 ft. Podzolic soils (Grey Wooded).
GI, aF. Highly productive site: rapid growth, heavy stocking, large timber volume.
Hylocomium splendens, Pleurozium schreberi, Ptilium crista-castrensis. Cornus canadensis, Linnaea borealis, Pyrola secunda,

P. virens, P. uniflora, Arnica cordifolia, Stenanthium occidentale.
Rosa acicularis, Alnus crispa var. sinuata, Lonicera involucrata.

4. Picea—Abies / Calamagrostis rubescens association lower
south-facing slopes and valley bottoms. Medium-textured soils;
Bisequa Grey Wooded Soil.
GI, aF, lP, tA. Fire-susceptible and usually dominated by successional lP. Calamagrostis rubescens, Elymus innovatus, Aster
conspicuus, A. ciliolatus, Castilleja hispida, Arnica cordifolia,
Fragaria virginiana var. glauca. Spiraea lucida, Rosa acicularis,
Vaccinium caepitosum, V. mytillus. Brachythecium spp., Dicranum rugosum, Drepanocladus uncinatus.

5. Picea / Arctostaphylos uva-ursi association valley bottom and
lower south-facing slopes, on coarse gravel and sand deposits.
Dry, weakly podzolised soils (Brunisolic).
G & GI; lP (fire successional).
Arctostaphylos uva-ursi, Juniperus horizontalis, J. communis,
Shepherdia canadensis, Potentilla fruiticosa. Elymus innovatus,
Anemone multifida, Viola adunca. Drepanocladus uncinatus,
Brachythecium spp., Tortula ruralis, Polytrichum piliferum,
Cladonia spp., Peltigera canina.

6. Picea—Abies / Equisetum association bordering rivers and
streams. Medium to fine, recently deposited alluvium; high water
table; Gleysolic Soil.
G. GI, I, aF, river successional bP.
Equisetum arvense, E. pratense, E. scirpoides, Mitella nuda,
Osmorhiza chilensis, Petasites palmatus, Carex spp., Orchis
rotundifolia. Ribes lacustre, Salix spp., Lonicera involucrata,
Rubus pubescens. Timmia austriaca, Mnium affine, Peltigera
aphthosa.

7. Picea / Sphagnum—Ledum association broad river flats; fine
clay deposits, impeded drainage, excessive water: mire (fen and
bog). Organic Bog Soils.
Sphagnum spp., Aulacomnium palustre, Tomenthypnum nitens,
Drepanocladus fluitans, D. revolvens.
Ledum groenlandicum, Betula glandulosa, Salix spp., Empetrum
nigrum Vaccinium vitis-idaea, V. oxycoccus.
Carex spp., Equisetum scirpoides, E. variegatum, E. arvense,
Juncus spp., Pedicularis groenlandicum, Habenaria dilatata,
Tofieldia glutinosa.

8. Picta—Abies/Ledun—Empetrum association (seepage association) along valley slopes in localised places where ground-water
comes close to surface and seepage occurs. Gleyed-Podzolic Soil.
Vegetation is related to communities adjoining this association,

thus seepage variants of the Vaccinium, M-L, and H-C associations. An abundance of: Ledum groenlandicum, Empetrum nigrum, Equisetum scirpoides, E. variegatum, Pedicularis bracteosa, Senecio triangularias, Trollius albiflorus.

Picea Engelmnnii—Abies lasiocarpa Province
Forest Associations of the Southern Area

1. Picea—Abies—Larix / Luzula wahlenbergii association. At high elevations, near timberline. Northerly-facing slopes. Deep snow accumulation. Well developed podzolic soils.
   aL, eS, aF.
   ssp. calliostham luzula wahlenberyii, Erigeron peregrinus, Valeriana sitchensis, Dicranum fuscescens.

2. Picea—Abies / Xerophyllum tenax association.
   At high elevations, up to timberline. Southerly-facing slopes. Soils shallow and stoney.
   aF, eS, wbP.
   Xerophyllum tenas, Viola orbiculata, Arnica latifolia, Luzula spp. Vaccinium myrtillus, V. scoparium, V. membranaceum, Sorbus sitchensis. Mnium spinulosum, Brachythecium spp. Dicranum fuscescens, Polytrichum juniperinum, Gladonia spp.

3. Picea—Abies / Menziesia ferruginea—Tiarella unifoliata association. Middle and upper slopes from 5,000-6,000 ft. Strongly developed podzolic soils.
   eS, aF.
   Menziesia ferruginea, Sorbus sitchensis, S. scopulina, Rhododendron albiflorum, Lonicera utahensis, Vaccinium scoparium, V. membranaceum Dicranum fusescens, leafy liverworts, Pleurozium schreberi, Mnium drummondii, M. spinulosum, Rhytidiopsis robusta.
   Tiarella unifoliata, Arnica Listera cordata, Pyrola secunda, P. uniflora, Clintonia uniflora, Viola orbiculata.

4. Picea—Abies / Pachistima myrsinites association. Middle valley slopes from 4,500-5,500 ft., southerly aspects. Podsolic soils. Fire susceptible.
   eS, aF, IP (fire successional).
   Pachistima myrsinites, Spiraea lucida, Mahonia repens, Rubus parviflorus, Vaccinium membranaceum.
   Arnica latifolia, Goodyera oblongifolia, Chimaphila umbellata, Aster conspicuus, Clintonia uniflora, Thalictrum occidentale, Pyrola virens, P. secunda, Hieracium albiflorum.
   Brachythecium spp., Drepanocladus uncinatus, Mnium spinulosum, Dicranum spp., Rhytidiopsis robusta, Cladonia spp.

5. Picea—Abies / Calamagrostis rubescens—Lupinus sericeus association. Valley bottom and lower slopes; dry soils, weakly podzolised and brunisolic. Fire susceptable.
   eS, aF, (lP tA fire successional).
   Calamagrostis rubescens, Lupinus sericeus, Pyrola secunda, Arnica cordifolia, Aster conspicuus, A. ciliolatus, Hieracium albiflorum, Lathyrus ochroleucus, Senecio pseudaureus, Smilacina, racemosa, Chimaphila umbellata. Spiraea lucida, Vaccinium caespitosum, V. myrtillus, Symphoricarpos albus, Amelanchier almfolia, Rosa acicularis.
   Brachythecium salebrosum, Drepanocladus uncinatus. Bryum spp. Polytrichum juniperinum, Cladonia spp.
6. Picea—Abies / Heracleum—Equisetum association. Level terrain bordering streams. High water-table, gleysolic soils with medium-textured parent material.
   eS, aF, (wC successional).
   Heracleum lanatum, Equisetum arvense, E. pratense, E. scirpoides, Actaea arguta, Angelica dawsonii, A. arguta, Osmorhiza occidentalis, O. chilensis, O. depauperata, Thalictrum occidentale, Smilacina racemosa, Streptopus amplexifolius, Galium triflorum.
   Timmia austriaca, Mnium affine, Brachythecium spp.
   Lonicera involucrata, Ribes lacustre, Lonicera utahensis, Rubus strigosus, R. parviflorus.
6a. Fern variant.
   Gymnocarpium dryopteris, Dryopteris dilatata, Athyrium filix-femina.
6b. Devil's Club variant.
   Oplopanax horridum.
   Symbols: aF=Abies lasiocarpa, aL=Larix lyallii, eS=Picea engelmannii, wS=Picea glauca, I=hybrid intermediate, EI=hybrid P. engelmannii intermediate, GI=hybrid P. glauca intermediate, lP =Pinus contorta, wbP=Pinus albicaulis, tA=Populus tremuloides, bP=Populus balsamifera, wC=Populus trichocarpa, pB=Betula papyrifera.

Alpine Plant Associations
1. Salix glauca Association—level valley bottom near streams; (below timberline—6,500'+) p.m. stratified, coarse alluvium, recurrent flooding, high water-table, Gleysolic A-C (Rendzina warp soil); moderate snow-cover 3-4'. Salix glauca, S. farriae, S. subcoerulea, Betula glandulosa; Aster foliaceous. Senecio indecorus, Deschampsia caespitosa, Equisetum scirpoides, E. pratense, E. variegatum, Delphinium glaucum; Selaginella selaginoides;

Aulacomnium palustre, Brachythecium salebrosum, Marchantia polymorpha.

2. Salix barrattiana Association—level valley bottom, at and just below timberline p.m. fine alluvium, high water-table; deep Humic Gleysolic (black muck) Warp Anmoor. moderate snow cover (4-5').

   Salix barrattiana, S. glauca, Arnica mollis, Trollius albiflorus, Senecio triangularis, Aster foliaceus, Delphinium glaucum, Deschampsia caespitosa, Epilobium alpinum' Mnium affine, Aulacomnium palustre. Hypnum spp.

3. Betula glandulosa Association—valley bottom and lower slopes around timberline, well-drained, drier soils (than previous two); Minimal podzolic (Semipodsol). Betula glandulosa, Salix glauca, Solidago multiradiata, Poa arctica, Danthonia intermedia, Erigeron peregrinus, Luzula parviflora, Festuca brachyphylla, Hypnum revolutum, Dicranum fuscescens.

4. Phyllodoce Association—at timberline among tree islands and krummholz; lee slopes with deep snow accumulation (+10 ft.); deep podzolic soils, solifluction. (Alpine Iron Humus Podzol, Alpine Sod Podzol).

   Phyllodoce glanduflora, P. empetriformis, Vaccinium scoparium, Erigeron peregrinus, Pedicularis bracteosa, Valeriana sitchensis, Arenaria capillaris, Castillega occidentalis, C. rhexifolia, Polytrichum juniperinum, Barbilophozia hatcheri, Dicranum fuscescens.

5. Cassiope Association—north-facing slopes, deep snow cover; podzolic soils with seepage, solifluction. (Alpine semipodzol).

   Cassiope tetragona, C. mertensiana, Salix arctica, Dryas hookeriana, Polygonum viviparum; Hypnum revolutum, Hylocomium splendens, Dicranum fuscescens.

6. Salix nivalis—Salix arctica Association—on north-facing avalanche slopes; deep snow cover with continual avalanching coarse colluvial regosol, (Colluvial Ranker).

   Salix nivalis, Salix arctica, Salix glauca, Astragalus alpinus, Solidago multiradiata, Poa longipila, Polygonum viviparum.

7. Elymus innovatus Association—on south-facing avalanche slopes; moderate snow-cover from snow melt and avalanching. Colluvial chernozemic soil, (Alpine Sod Braunerde). Elymus innivatus, Bromus pumpellianus, Festuca scabrella, F. saximontana, Poa spp., Hedysarum sulphurescens, Fragaria, Arctostaphylos Oxytropis spp. Campanula rotundifolia, Achillea millefolium, Tortula ruralis, Peltigera canina.

7a. Seepage Variant with high water-table: plus Heracleum, Thalictrum, Hackelia, Delphinium.

8. Kobresia myosuroides Association—higher zone above Elymus assn., on wind-exposed S-facing slopes and ridge crests; snowfree. Soils shallow, colluvial regosols (Ranker, Rendzina). Kobresia myosuroides, Carex rupestris, Agropyron latiglume, Dryas hookeriana, Selaginella rupestris, Smelowskia calycina, Potentilla ovina, Tortula, Cetraria cuc., niv., Physcia muscigena.

9. Salix arctica—Carex microptera Association—level to sloping ground; deep soils, weakly podzolized (semipodzol), solifluction, moist from snow melt-waters; deep snow.
Salix arctica, Carex microptera, C. phaeocephala, C. pyrenaica, Antennaria lanata, Poa alpina, Phleum alpinum, Polytrichum juniperinum, Dicranum fusc. Juncus drummondii, Luzula parv.

10. Carex nigricans Association—snowbeds, in small basins and channels with very deep snow accumulation (+15 ft.) soils moist from snow-melt, frozen late in year; podzolised with solifluction (Semipodzol, Pseudogley).
Carex nigricans, Antennaria lanata, Erigeron peregrinus, Ranunculus esch., Sibbaldia procumbens, Veronica alphina, Juncus drummondii, Poa alp., Phleum alp., Tortula ruralis.

11. Dryas hookeriana—Oxytropis podocarpa Association—wind-exposed, snow-free ridges and moraines; snow-free; shallow regosols (Ranker & Randzina).
Dryas hookeriana, Oxytropis podocarpa. Myositis alp., Hedysarum mack., Salix nivalis, Anemone drummondii, Arenaria rossii, Potentilla nivea, Festuca baffin, F. brachyphylla, Amemone drummondii, Saxifraga bronchialis, Cetraria islandica, C. cuc., C. niv., Thamnolia subuliformis, Encalypta, Tortula.

12. Stonefield Lichen Association—on wind-exposed summits of high ridges near altitudinal limit of closed communities (9,000 ft.); snow-free; extensive surface cover of stones shallow regosols (Rawmark), o.m. removed by wind.
Cetraria, Cladonia, Thamnolia, Cornicularia aculeata, rocklichens-Lecanora, Rhixocarpon, Umbilicaria. Oxytropis podocarpa, Silax nivalis, Smelowskia, Silene acaulis, Papaver kluanensis, Taraxacum ceratophorum.

13. Plants of talus and rock—occupying crevices and soil pockets at high elevations. Taraxacum lyratum, Crepis nana, Eriogonum androsaceum, Saussurea densa, Campanula uniflora, C. lasiocarpa, Saxifraga oppositifolia, Papaver kluanensis.

3

Fires, Floods and National Parks in the Bow Valley, Alberta

J. G. Nelson and A. R. Byrne

Little is known of the early landscape history of the Canadian National Parks, and hence of the effects of park policy and park development on hydrologic and other physical processes. Recent studies of changes in the landscape of Banff National Park, Alberta, are therefore worth discussing, for they suggest that the vegetational changes introduced under park policy have played some part in flood reduction in the Bow River valley. In addition, these studies illustrate man's short memory where his own effects on landscape are concerned.

In Banff National Park the Bow Valley cuts across massive mountain terrain, composed chiefly of folded and faulted limestones, dolomites, and quartzites. The mountains nowhere exceed 12,000 feet, though many of the peaks reach 9000-10,000 feet. Major river valleys, such as the Bow, generally lie about 4000-5000 feet below the surrounding summits. The heavy effects of glaciation are evident in the cirques and arêtes of the upper slopes and in the broad terraces and other drift deposits nearer the valley floors. As in other mountainous areas, the climate is highly variable. Although climatic

Reprinted from *Geographical Review*, Vol LVI (1966), pp. 226-38. Copyrighted by the American Geographical Society of New York.

data are relatively few,[1] the higher ranges probably receive more than fifty inches of precipitation a year, and possibly more than a hundred inches, most of which falls as snow. Lower intermontane valleys in the east probably receive less than twenty-five inches a year, much of which falls in spring and summer as rain. Of the three main vegetative divisions—coniferous forest, grassland, and tundra—forest is the most widespread. Engelmann spruce, white spruce, and alpine fir are common, as are lodgepole pine and aspen. The last two are pioneer species and generally follow fires. Large stands of lodgepole pines, usually of the same age, occur throughout the Bow Valley and provided a strong part of the motivation for the research reported in this paper.

Recent historical-geographical studies show that, contrary to general opinion, the vegetation of much of Banff National Park is neither "unspoiled" nor "natural" but, rather, owes much of its distributional pattern and successional status to the activities of the white man.[2] The significance of the pre-European population as a cause of vegetational and other landscape change is as yet difficult to assess because of a lack of relevant archeological work. Paucity of research also casts a shadow over the effects of the early white fur traders and prospectors who were increasingly active in the Banff area from 1800 to 1880. These forerunners of settlements are known to have left their mark on the land, but the degree of their influence is uncertain. The attitude of the prospectors certainly seems to have been conducive to widespread forest burning. In fact, the accusation has been made that the prospector, in general, welcomed fire, "since it laid bare the rocks in which he sought his fortune."[3]

The Role of the Railway

However, the year 1881 was undoubtedly of great significance for vegetational and other landscape change in the Banff area. In this year the decision was made to route the Canadian Pacific Railway up the Bow Valley rather than through the Yellowhead Pass farther north (Figure 1). One direct consequence of the railway was a marked increase in forest fires. Fires were started during the con-

[1] See, for example, A. H. Laycock, "Precipitation and Streamflow in the Mountain and Foothill Region of the Saskatchewan River Basin," *Prairie Provinces Water Board Rept. No. 6*, Regina (1957).
[2] A. R. Byrne, "Man and Landscape Change in the Banff National Park Area before 1911", M.A. thesis (unpub.), University of Alberta at Calgary (1964).
[3] H. N. Whitford and Roland D. Craig, "Forests of British Columbia", Commission of Conservation, Ottawa (1918), p. 126. Quoted in Byrne, *op. cit.* (see footnote 2), p. 89.

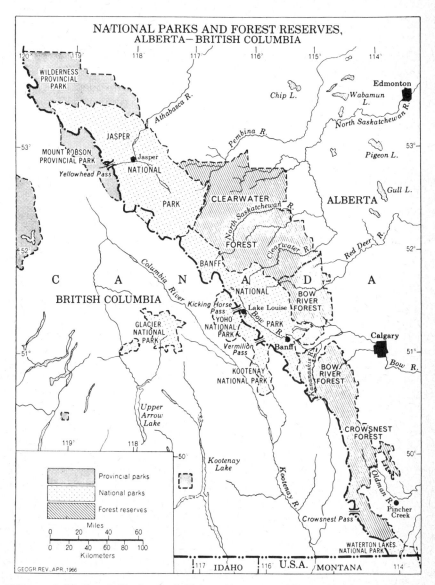

Figure 1. National Parks and Forest Reserves, Alberta-British Columbia.

struction of the track and were also caused by sparks from the engines. According to one observer, the Bow Valley from Banff to the British Columbia-Alberta summit was burned over by engineers during the survey of the Canadian Pacific main line in 1882.[4]

J. J. McArthur, the government surveyor, was moved by similar burning in the nearby Selkirk Mountains to make the following comment in his report of 1886:

"It is a matter of regret that fires incidental to railway construction have devastated much of the country in the vicinity of the railway and have spoiled much of the wonderful beauty of the environs of the mountains . . . and in most instances these fires have occurred through wanton carelessness. Apart from climatic and other considerations, the large quantities of timber in the tributary passes which have so far escaped destruction, should impress on the government the necessity of using every means in its power to suppress this species of vandalism."[5]

Cutting of the forests was likewise accelerated as a result of the coming of the railway, not only for ties but for pit props in the coal mines that were opened at Anthracite, Bankhead, and Canmore, chiefly for engine fuel. The settlers in these new towns undoubtedly also used large quantities of wood in winter. Aside from their direct effects on the forest, the lumbering activities left acres of bush and slash as a fire hazard and thus were probably a frequent indirect cause of more burning.[6]

Fires and forest destruction continued after the establishment of the Banff National Park in 1886. In June, 1889, a large fire swept down the Bow Valley from the west and threatened the park. Fortunately, it was stopped by a treeless area on the northwestern boundary, but not before it had almost completely destroyed the forest on the slopes south of the Bow from the Vermilion Lakes to and beyond Baker Creek (Figure 2). In the same year fires burned over the country drained by Forty Mile Creek, the Sawback Lakes, the head of the North Saskatchewan, Cuthead Creek, and the Cascade River. In 1891 a heavy fire three to four miles west of Banff, alleged to have

---

4 Several large fires are discussed by H. Ritchie in an incomplete manuscript entitled "Causes of Floods in Previous Years as Compared to the Last Few Years and What Effect of Reforestation on Stream Flow as Well as Burning of Forest." The manuscript appears to have been written in the period 1912-1915. A copy is on file at the Water Resources Branch, Department of Northern Affairs and National Resources, Calgary.
5 *Canada Dept. of the Interior Ann. Report for the Year 1886*, Part II, Ottawa (1887) pp. 41-42. Quoted in Byrne *op. cit.* (see footnote 2), p. 87.
6 Information in this and following paragraphs is from Byrne, *op. cit.* (see footnote 2), Chapter 6 and 7 (pp. 74-109).

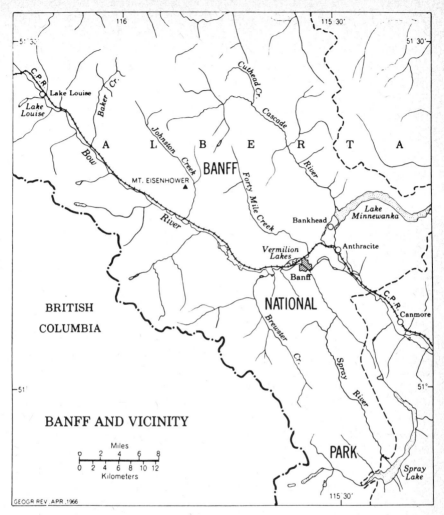

Figure 2. Banff and vicinity, Alberta.

been started by a C.P.R. locomotive, spread eastward to the Vermilion Lakes. In 1894 a large fire spread from British Columbia to the headwaters of the Spray and down the Spray Valley to the Spray Lakes, where it burned itself out on the side of the mountains. In May of 1903 a serious fire occurred on the north side of the railway track some three miles west of Banff station. In the same year another fire destroyed the forest on the north side of the Bow from the east gate of the park to Anthracite. In 1904 a fire burned the forest in the Bow Valley north of the river from the Vermilion Lakes west to Baker Creek.

As a result of such fires, much of the Bow Valley and the eastern slopes of the Rockies in southern Alberta was by 1910 characterized by young, fire-following lodgepole pine or by dead timber and deforested ground. According to government foresters who studied the area on the east side of the park from north of the Elbow River to the North Saskatchewan River in the early years of the present century, "Eighty percent of the territory surveyed has been burned over in the last fifty years and sixty percent of this, or forty-eight percent of the entire country has been burned over in the last twenty-five years."[7]

Study of old and modern photographs (Figures 3, 4, and 5) gives some idea of the difference between conditions in the late nineteenth century and the early twentieth and at present. The Banff National Park area, in the early days, was obviously a departure from the scene familiar to the visitor today. Indeed, the Banff landscape was a disappointment to early tourists, one of whom described Banff townsite in 1887 as being surrounded by "grand and majestic [mountains], but almost devoid of vegetation, except for a few trees growing apparently out of the solid rock."[8]

Effects of Vegetation Change on Flooding

Although Banff National Park encompasses the upper watershed of the Bow River, little attention has been paid to the possible influence of the vegetation changes on flooding—not surprisingly, when the changes themselves are unknown, unacknowledged, or forgotten. National Park publications and other literature stress the idea of the Banff area as an original wilderness, where the natural vegetation has been preserved unharmed for future generations. Burning is not thought of, and no consequent change in run-off or flooding is expected.

However, historical evidence indicates a link between the burned and cleared state of the Bow Valley in the nineteenth century and the severe floods of these same early days. Basically, two types of floods occur on the Bow: ice-jam floods and climatic floods. The ice-jam floods are usually local, caused by large blockages of ice, the reasons for which are still not well understood.

---

[7] P. Z. Caverhill, "Rocky Mountain Forest Reserve: Report of P. Z. Caverhill," *Canada Dept. of the Interior, Forestry Branch, Bull. No. 18* (1910), pp. 19-27. Quoted in Byrne, op. cit. (see footnote 2), p. 98.
[8] W. Henry Bameby, "The New Far West and the Old Far East", London (1889), p. 17.

Figure 3. These photographs were taken from approximately the same position, the upper one in 1885 and the lower one in 1964. The Rundle Massif provides the background. Except for the disappearance of the settlement and the innovation of the Trans-Canada Highway, the main contrast between the two pictures lies in the change in forest cover. This is seen particularly well along the top of the terrace where the earlier photograph shows a thin tree cover and evidence of recent burning, and the later photograph a relatively thick cover of coniferous trees. 1885 photograph courtesy Ernest Brown Collection, Department of Industry and Development, Edmonton, Alberta; 1964 photograph courtesy J. S. Marsh.

Figure 4. The top photograph was taken about 1912 and shows the briquetting plant at the Bankhead coal mines, with Cascade Mountain in the background. Here the mountain slope behind the buildings appears either to have been cut over extensively, or burned. However, if the picture was not taken in summer, some of the slope (for example, at center right) is probably covered with leafless aspen poplar. The lower photograph, taken in the summer of 1963, shows the foundations of the mine buildings and indicates how well the aspen poplar and coniferous trees, mainly lodgepole, have recolonized the cleared areas. (1912 photograph courtesy the Glenbow Foundation, Calgary, Alberta; 1963 photograph by A. R. Byrne.)

Figure 5. The upper view is of Castle Mountain (now Mount Eisenhower) and Silver City as they appeared about 1887, several years after the collapse of a short-lived copper-mining boom. The lower photograph was taken from approximately the same position in the summer of 1964. The most striking change, other than the obvious disappearance of the buildings, is again the increase in tree cover. The difference is particularly noticeable on the terrace but it is also clearly evident on the lower slopes of Mount Eisenhower. Today the predominant tree species is the lodgepole pine, but it is impossible to determine what trees were present in the earlier picture. (1887 photograph courtesy of the Glenbow Foundation, Calgary, Alberta; 1964 photograph courtesy J. S. Marsh.)

The extensive floods of yesterday and today are climatic in origin. An examination of relevant reports[9] suggests that these floods often occur in spring, as a result, principally, of four factors: copious precipitation in a short period, high temperatures, deep snow, and high ground-moisture levels. The greater the coincidence of these factors, the more severe the flood is likely to be. Thus if a mass of maritime tropical air brings heavy precipitation and relatively high, melt-inducing temperatures to the wet soils and deep snow of the Bow Valley in May, large floods are likely.

Two of the largest floods known on the Bow were brought about in approximately this manner, though in neither case was the coincidence of the four conditions "ideal" in the sense that the maximum flood possible was produced. A report on the 1923 floods notes:

"The precipitation of the eastern slope of the Rockies throughout the month of May, 1923 was well above normal and culminated in a storm of great severity which started about May 30th in the southwestern corner of Alberta and southeastern corner of British Columbia. This storm which was probably quite local in effect at first, widened out as it travelled northward to the Red Deer basin. It is believed that the whole of the precipitation in the south fell as warm rain melting what was left of the winter accumulation of snow on the mountains and causing unusual floods."[10]

And a similar report on the 1932 floods reads:

"Following a winter of unusually heavy snow fall on the eastern slope of the Rocky Mountains, the months of April and May were characterized by heavy precipitation which caused some improvement in runoff and a saturated condition of the surface soil after the dry summer of 1931.

"Beginning with May 31st a torrential rainstorm developed in the foothill and lower mountain areas of the Bow, Elbow and Highwood Rivers which continued till June 3rd and caused extremely high water in those streams of the storm area.

"A study of the few meteorological records available as shown earlier in this report reveals the fact that the extreme headwaters of the Bow River did not record an abnormal precipitation during

---

9 Reports on floods of 1902, 1912, 1915, 1923, 1932, etc., mimeographed by the Department of the Interior, Dominion Water Power Branch, Canada. On file at the Water Resources Branch, Department of Northern Affairs and National Resources, Calgary.
10 A. L. Ford, "Floods in the Southern Part of Alberta and Saskatchewan during 1923", (mimeographed, Department of the Interior, Dominion Water Power Branch, Calgary, 1923). Copy on file, Water Resources Branch, Department of Northern Affairs and National Resources, Calgary.

the flood and the temperatures were not extremely high. The conditions were therefore not by any means 100% ideal for the production of a maximum flood that could be easily possible on these streams."[11]

One of the greatest known floods on the Bow was the flood of 1897. Large floods are certainly known to have occurred earlier, but information on their magnitude and, in the case of the late-nineteenth-century floods, on their possible relation to the activities of the white man is difficult to obtain. For example, George M. Dawson, an eminent geologist of the early Canadian West, recorded evidence for large-scale flooding in at least part of the Bow Valley in 1884. He also expressed the belief, based on field observations, that "no such flood could have occurred for fifty or a hundred years previously."[12] However, these brief remarks of Dawson's are insufficient basis for comparing the flood whose effects he observed with better-known floods such as those of 1897 and later. Moreover, even though Dawson recognized that fires had increased during historical time, and particularly during the few years before his arrival in the Banff area, and even though he saw these fires as attributable to the carelessness of the white man,[13] he did not postulate a relationship between the fires, the destruction of vegetation resulting from them, and flooding.

The first known citation of such a link appeared in the *Calgary Herald* of June, 1897, when flood damage was heavy at Banff, at Calgary, and in the valley as a whole. In reporting on this situation the *Herald* noted:

"During recent years much of the heavy timber which covered the sides of the Mountains has been burnt off, and when the cloud burst between the Gap and Castle Mountain [Mount Eisenhower] the steep slopes of the mountains and foothills became chutes along which the floods rushed, swelling the rivers and valleys, into a wild torrent of seething, descalating [*sic*] waters."[14]

Another reference to the link between fires, vegetation change, and flooding is found in an incomplete manuscript on file in the

11 O. H. Hoover and W. T. McFarlane, "Floods in Southern Alberta during 1932" (mimeographed, Department of the Interior, Dominion Water Power Branch, Calgary, 1932), p. 60. Copy on file, Water Resources Branch, Department of Northern Affairs and National Resources, Calgary.

12 George M. Dawson, "Preliminary Report on the Physical and Geological Features of that Portion of the Rocky Mountains between Latitudes 49° and 51° 30'," *Canada Geol. Survey Ann. Rept.*, (N.S., Vol. I (1885), Montreal (1886), 6. 33B.

13. Ibid., pp. 36B-37B.

14 Calgary Herald, June 21, 1897.

records of the Water Resources Branch, Calgary.[15] In this document, which seems to date from 1912-1915, Mr. H. Ritchie, an engineer, gives us his ideas on the factors affecting floods. He notes that precipitation was unusually high at the turn of the century— an observation confirmed by study of available weather records —and postulates a link between the extensive fires of the nineteenth century and the large floods of the same period. As he puts it:

"This goes to show that the heavy floods of 1897 and thereabouts came shortly and sometimes a few years after they had big fires. It is thirty-two years after the big fire of the Bow Valley [presumably the burning during the 1882 survey by the C.P.R. engineers] and what do we see? a heavy undergrowth starting up which for several reasons offers the best condition for absorption and ground storage."[16]

Ritchie then points out some of the ways in which vegetation slows runoff and reduces floods—interference by trees, absorption by moss and similar vegetation, lower temperatures, slower melting of snow beneath forest cover. He concludes:

"These conditions are growing stronger and stronger each day and trusting to no fires for years to come which will spoil the work being accomplished by nature in the woods the time will come when a more gradual or mean flow over a longer period will be noticed in streams and not such excessive floods unless by causes which man cannot avoid."[17]

That reforestation continued is evident from a report on the 1923 floods in Alberta and Saskatchewan,[18] which occurred over a wide area, including the Bow River basin. In the discussion of their cause, particular attention is paid to heavy rains in late May and June. However, reference is also made to the forest growth:

". . . owing to the greater protection of forest growth in recent years, it can be safely assumed that on the eastern slope of the Rockies from which most of the run-off is derived, there was more rather than less vegetation than in 1915, the last year in which floods occurred in these streams."[19]

But the author of the report expresses uncertainty about the degree to which reforestation reduces runoff:

"It however is a question as to just what extent tree life actually retards run-off. It doubtless has a marked effect on the winter snow

---

[15] Ritchie, *op. cit.* (see footnote 4).
[16] *Ibid.*, p. X.
[17] *Ibid.*, p. XI.
[18] Ford, *op. cit.* (see footnote 10).
[19] *Ibid.*, p. 8.

by protecting it from the direct rays of the sun, and in turn causing the runoff from the source to occur late in the season. The result is that much of the snow must be added to the rain which melts it, causing an increased run-off, very probably during the flood period. Whether or not the residue of the winter snow which becomes run-off under such conditions exceeds the amount of precipitation absorbed by transpiration is open to question."[20]

The problem of the effect of vegetation change on runoff and flooding is still unsolved today, and for this and other reasons the quantitative importance of reforestation to flooding in the Bow must remain uncertain. To separate the effects of variation in natural factors, such as precipitation, from those of fire and man is impossible, if only because data on discharge are rare before 1908. Moreover, the flow of the Bow has been affected by dams for more than four decades. One way of assessing the possible magnitude of the effects of burning and clearing would be to study research results from other areas. For example, studies in California[21] and in the Colorado mountains[22] indicate increases of more than 50 percent in stream-flow peaks in various years after burning or clearing. However, the application of these results to Bow floods cannot be strict and is considered unwise, particularly until more is known about other influential variables—for example, forest density, maximum twenty-four-hour precipitation, and watershed physiography—in the Bow Valley.

The evidence presented here seems sufficient to permit several conclusions. In Alberta, as elsewhere, the recent history of natural phenomena is largely unknown, the memory of landscape changes short, and the effect of human intervention unappreciated. Even the so-called "preserves" of the recently and sparsely settled National Parks of western Canada seem to have been changed appreciably by man. Thus the large floods in the Bow during the late nineteenth century and the early twentieth seem to have been at least partly induced by destruction of vegetation through fire, lumbering, and other processes. Since these early days vegetation has reestablished

[20] *Ibid.*, pp. 8-9.
[21] For example, H. W. Anderson and H. K. Trobitz, "Influence of Some Watershed Variables on a Major Flood," *Journ. of Forestry*, Vol. XLVII (1949), pp. 347-356. Abstract in A. G. Underhill, "Report of a Change in Vegetation on the Runoff Chracteristics of Alberta Streams" (mimeographed, Water Resources Branch, Alberta Department of Agriculture, Calgary, n.d.), p. 37.
[22] B. C. Goodell and H. G. Willm, "How to Get More Snow Water from Forest Lands," in "Water" (edited by Alfred Stefferud), *Yearbook of Agriculture 1955*, U.S. Dept. of Agriculture (1955), pp. 228-34; reference on pp. 232-33.

itself on the slopes of the Bow Valley as a result of the protective policy of the National Parks and other conservation agencies. The reestablishment of vegetation has undoubtedly had the effect of reducing floods in the Bow, though to what degree is unknown. More historical-geographical studies are needed in preserves such as the National Parks. They will probably reveal a surprising amount of human effect on the park landscapes and, together with studies in unprotected surrounding areas, should also demonstrate just how far man can change an environment in a short time without being fully aware of it.

4

An Arctic Forest in the Tundra at Northern Ungava, Quebec

P. F. Maycock and B. Matthews

Introduction

The vegetation of arctic regions is frequently described as treeless, or as occurring beyond the limit of trees or tree growth. This emphasis on treelessness is an anomaly since it attempts to describe a phenomenon in terms of what it is not, rather than in terms of what it is. The fact that trees do not grow in the tundra should be no more surprising than that they are absent from lakes.

The lack of trees in the tundra, and the consequent lack of shade, is nevertheless one of the striking aspects of the landscape and, combined with the absence of tall shrubs, is an extremely important ecological feature. Although there are situations at the foot of cliffs or adjacent to ledges, bluffs, and large boulders that are protected from direct sunlight for short periods, there are virtually no habitats that are permanently shaded throughout the growing season. Thus the majority of tundra plants are heliophytes and develop and grow in full sunlight.

It is interesting to speculate on the effects that continuous shading of various degrees might have on tundra species that have evolved in unshaded habitats and have become adapted to abundant light, particularly the effect of the shade cast by a natural forest canopy.

An unusual opportunity to investigate the influence of shading on arctic plant species occurred during the summer of 1961 when Matthews was conducting geomorphological studies in the extreme

Reprinted from *Arctic*, Vol. 19 (1966), pp. 114-44.

northwestern section of the Ungava Peninsula in northern Quebec and discovered an extensive wooded community. This find was rather unusual because the site was some 300 miles beyond the extreme limit of trees and the community was growing under arctic tundra conditions.

The community can be considered a forest in the strict ecological meaning of the term because members of the dominant stratum are frequently of tree form with boles exceeding 12 sq. in. basal area at breast height, and sometimes attaining heights of 16 ft. A more or less continuous tree layer is formed at 12 ft. and thus the criterion of forming a solid shade-casting canopy is also satisfied. This community type occurs sporadically in several situations in this region and covers several hundred acres in at least one locality.

It was immediately realized that the occurrence of a *willow forest* so far north of the tree-line was so unusual as to merit careful study. Matthews was primarily interested in the initial development and postglacial history of the community but after consultation with Maycock it was agreed that a study of the composition and environmental features, and possibly of the historical patterns, would also assist in understanding the factors responsible for the development and persistence of the community in a region where climatic conditions would seem to prohibit it. An opportunity to investigate shading effects as well as possible floristic peculiarities was also provided.

A study of the composition and structure of the community and the surrounding vegetation was undertaken in early July 1962. Attempts were made to relate these features to environmental conditions. Matthews and assistants obtained the compositional data according to instructions from Maycock and gathered environmental information on topography, geology, climate, and geomorphology. Maycock compiled the floristic material and carried out the growth ring analysis of the trees.

Previous Reports of Arctic Thicket Communities

The first reports of unusual shrub communities in the Canadian Arctic are those of Soper (1930, 1933). These were discovered north of Lake Harbour in south Baffin Island and the most spectacular, along the Willow River, contained *Salix* that attained heights up to 12 ft.

> One of the interesting discoveries . . . a stand of willows over twelve feet in height. This came as a surprise in latitude 63°10′N, over 400 miles north of the timberline in northern Quebec. (Soper 1933)

Polunin (1948, p. 134) says the tallest specimens reported by Soper are probably all *Salix planifolia*.

Polunin also describes many occurrences in the Canadian Eastern Arctic of shrub or thicket communities that are dominated by a variety of woody species and restricted to various favourable environmental situations. A thicket of up to half a metre in height, dominated by *Salix richardsonii* is described near Pond Inlet, and a *Betula-Salix* community near Lake Harbour, Baffin Island, is related to exceptionally favourable conditions of shelter, snow cover, moisture, drainage, and southerly exposure. The same author (1948, pp. 215-16) reports a willow thicket that approaches the type and size treated in this paper in the vicinity of Wakeham Bay in northern Ungava. *Salix cordifolia* the dominant shrub there, grew to almost a metre. Unfortunately no presence list is provided for such an unusual community, but of four underherbs mentioned, three are found in the "Willow Valley" thicket.

Porsild (1955) refers frequently to localized thicket types, usually of low stature and dominated by *Salix alaxensis* and *Salix richardsonii* in the western Arctic Islands. An extensive tall thicket is also described at Orpiksoit, near Holman Post on Victoria Island, in a sheltered valley along a stream.

In the isolated reports of similar thicket communities, the site characteristics that have permitted their development — favourable exposure, deep snow cover, plentiful moisture, good drainage and shelter — are emphasized. Unfortunately the internal environments of the thickets and their influence on microclimate and on the herbs and shrubs growing within, have not been discussed. A series of presence lists from a large number of communities of this kind, with careful environmental observations, would provide very useful information on tundra species that can tolerate varying degrees of shade and provide an indication of their performance under exceptionally favourable microclimatic conditions.

Description of the Area
Topography
The "Willow Valley" forest is located in a 1500-ft. deep glaciated valley at the southeastern end of Watts Lake which is 170 ft. above sea-level and 32 miles south of Deception Bay (61°31′N., 74°5′W.). The exact location of the community and the region is shown in Figure 1.

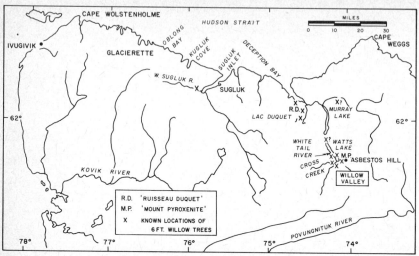

Figure 1. Location map of the area surrounding "Willow Valley", Arctic Quebec.

Surrounding the valley is a gently undulating plateau, 1,500 to 2,300 ft. above sea-level, which is dissected by deep glaciated valleys especially the south-north trending Murray Lake-Watts Lake Trough. The local topographic features are presented in Figure 2 and Figure 3.

Geology and Geomorphology

The "Willow Valley"— Asbestos Hill area lies in the Povungnituk group of metamorphosed sediments and lavas and presents a marked contrast to the area of resistant rocks of the Proterozoic granite-gneiss complex to the north. Here occur relatively easily eroded schists, lavas, and quartzites penetrated by more resistant ultrabasic dykes and isolated plugs of intrusive rocks that form the isolated monadnocks on the plateau surface, such as "Mount Pyroxenite". (Recently named features not yet accepted by the Canadian Board of Geographical Names, will be enclosed in quotation marks.) Bedrock in the immediate vicinity of "Willow Valley" is mainly chlorite and sericite schists covered with morainic material, boulder clay, lake silt, deltaic gravels and sand, and scree and solifluction materials.

The area was extensively glaciated during the Pleistocene. Evidence collected by Matthews points to a late glacial movement of ice from a minor centre in the Asbestos Hill area and its concentration as an outlet glacier in the Murray Lake-Watts Lake Trough. In postglacial times the valley was invaded by a 24-mile-long lake

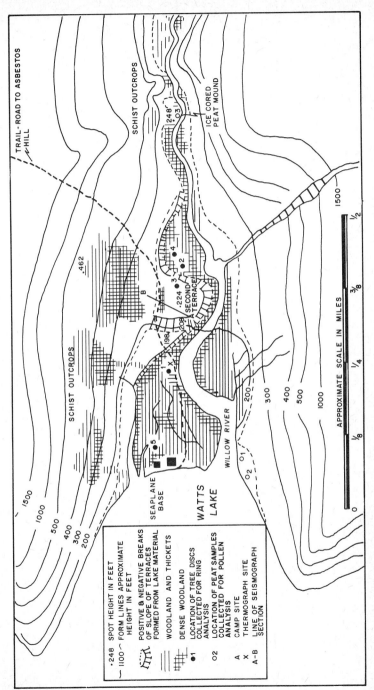

Figure 2. General environmental features of "Willow Valley".

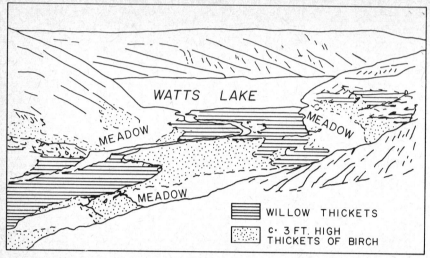

Figure 3. General topography and vegetation of "Willow Valley", looking northwest down the valley.

or possibly an arm of the sea. This event took place at least 7,000 years ago because the highest fossil marine shells (148 ft. a.s.l.) 8 miles inland from Deception Bay have been dated as 6,760 ± 140 years B.P. (the shells were collected by the junior author in 1961 and dated by the National Physical Laboratory, England). Thus the ice must have vacated the Deception Bay area by that time at the latest to allow the sea to invade. After an unknown period the land began to rise and the long lake drained gradually northwards until it eventually separated into the present Watts Lake and Murray Lake. The old raised beaches and deltas can still be traced along the sides of the trough valley and especially in the tributary valleys. On these beaches an early "Willow Valley" forest became established, probably during the hypsithermal period, as evidenced by a layer of wood in the thick peat deposits.

Soil and peat deposits

The existence of a *forest* in arctic Quebec is an unusual feature and it is therefore not surprising that the soil that has developed is quite different from normal tundra soils. It possesses some of the characteristics of a brown forest soil and is possibly an arctic equivalent. The local soil might be termed an *arctic thicket* type.

Soil profiles are shown in Figure 4, and an outstanding feature is the great depth of soil that has developed in contrast to arctic findings. It is doubtful if it could be classed as an arctic brown soil, for apart from colour differences, Tedrow and Cantlon (1958) claim this type is the arctic equivalent of the temperate podsols, and no

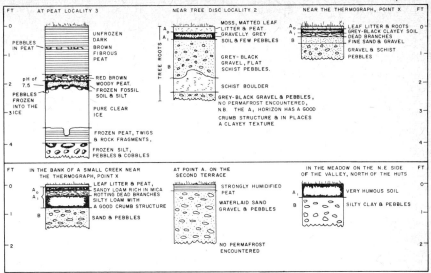

Figure 4. Peat and soil profiles of "Willow Valley". Localities and points refer to Figure 2.

signs of leaching were observed below the willows. In addition, these well-drained soils are only slightly acid whereas arctic brown soils are usually strongly acid. This was especially true near tree disc locality 2, Figure 2, where a 3-ft. pit was excavated in the mature willow forest.

This pit was located on the first terrace of the valley and the parent material was composed of poorly sorted sand, gravel pebbles and cobbles, mainly of schist. In Figure 4 the soil profile has been divided into three horizons: an A_0 (0-3 in.), an A_1 (3-6.5 in.), and a third (6.5-12 in.), termed a B horizon, as there was no evidence of illuviation. The A_1 horizon consisted of a grey gravelly loam with a medium crumb structure and a moderate amount of humus. The greyish colour appears to be the result of melanization of the soil by humus rather than the effect of gleying as there were no signs of drainage impedence. Samples of the 3 horizons were taken for laboratory analysis.

The results of the analysis of structural components are presented in Table I. The major feature of the different horizons was the high proportion of stony material which increased greatly with the depth. When the stony material was removed from the B horizon material, there was insufficient left for nutrient analysis emphasizing the almost complete lack of fine materials. The textural analysis emphasizes the extreme skeletal nature of these soils and the importance of the role of the A_0 layer and the upper A_1 layer in supporting the luxuriant growth of the willows.

TABLE I. TEXTURAL CLASSES CALCULATED ON BASIS OF PERCENTAGE WEIGHT OF TOTAL SAMPLE. "WILLOW VALLEY" FOREST SOILS

Portion	Horizon		
	A_0	A_1	B
2 mm.+	19.1	51.4	70.1
1 mm.−<2 mm.	not separated	20.6	14.2
<1 mm.	80.9	28.0	15.7

The chemical analyses presented in Table II re-emphasize the importance of the organic horizons. The A_1 layer contained significantly less organic matter than the A_0 but was richer in calcium, potassium, magnesium, and phosphate.

TABLE II. ANALYSIS OF NUTRIENT CONTENT AND REACTION, "WILLOW VALLEY" FOREST SOILS.

	A_0	A_1
Organic matter	22.9%	3.1%
pH	6.0	5.8
Exchangeable bases		
P_2O_5	5.4 mg./100 g.	6.0 mg./100 g.
Ca	62 mg./100 g.	450 mg./100 g.
K	7 mg./100 g.	44 mg./100 g.
Mg	8 mg./100 g.	27 mg./100 g.

Climate

The nearest station for which reliable climatic data are available is Cape Hopes Advance, but it lies almost 180 miles southeast of "Willow Valley" and on an exposed coast. These records are of little value for the inland thicket site where conditions are undoubtedly less severe.

At Cape Hopes Advance the mean annual temperature, based on a 22-year record, is 19.0°F. and this is 3.1° colder than Fort Chimo, 200 miles to the south. The total annual precipitation, based on the same period, is 13.74 in., and 8.14 of this falls as rain. The mean annual snowfall of 56.0 in. is high for a tundra climate. Most of the snow falls between October and May although traces have been recorded in all months. Prevailing winds are from the north-west. The average frost-free period of 27 days (13-year record) is very short for the growth of the vigorous shrubs that led to the development of this community.

Vegetation of the "Willow Valley" area

From the air the vegetation in the deep U-shaped valley is seen in sharp contrast to that on the plateau. The plateau is sparsely covered with dry open rocky tundra. Most of the surface is bare glacial rubble, felsenmeer or exposed bedrock. Lichens, mosses, grasses, and a few dwarf shrubs form the depauperate communities.

The shrub stands in the valley present a luxuriant plant cover in comparison with the bleak plateau. The willow forest forms a solid green canopy at 12 ft. and contains specimens that attain a height of almost 16 ft. Two species of willow dominate the thickets: *Salix planifolia* Pursh and *S. alaxensis* (Anderss.) Cov. The thickets can be divided into two groups, a dense valley bottom forest, growing on gravels and sands, and an equally dense forest on the southwest facing slope. The latter was growing on stabilized scree material and glacial deposits up to a height of 460 ft. above sea-level or 290 ft. above the lake.

Both situations are well drained, although this fact was obscured in early July 1962, in the valley bottom, because of flooding in the lower half of the valley when the lake suddenly rose 8 ft. due to an ice jam in the outlet river during breakup.

The tallest trees (16 ft.) in the slope thickets grow immediately below sheer schist cliffs and may benefit from the rapidly disintegrating bedrock which may produce a constant supply of nutrients. These willows are predominantly *Salix alaxensis* and have diameters at the base of 4 in. Both *S. alaxensis* and *S. planifolia* grow in the valley bottom forest and there attain trunk diameters of up to 8 in. at base. Specimens of *S. alaxensis* tended to be taller than those of *S. planifolia*.

The site requirements of the two dominant *Salix* differ somewhat. *S. planifolia* occurs in wetter areas and tends to border the many interlacing streams to the northeast of the main river channel, a feature noted also by Polunin (1940) in various parts of the eastern Arctic. On the other hand *S. alaxensis* occupies most of the less moist interfluve areas and hence covers the largest section of the valley bottom. In adjacent "Rivière à la Croix" valley, however, the better drained areas are those immediately adjacent to the fast-flowing streams and so *S. alaxensis* tends to border the water courses whereas *S. planifolia* occupies the more waterlogged areas (see Figure 5).

All trees in both the slope and valley bottom thickets showed evidence of vigorous growth of terminal shoots during 1962. By July 6, 1.5 in. of new growth had been added on both species in the valley bottom and by July 13 this had increased to 3 to 4 in.

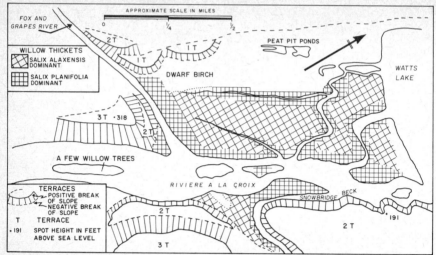

Figure 5. Map showing vegetation and topography of "Rivière à la Croix" valley forest; based on air photographs and mapping in the field.

This rapid growth was probably due to the exceptionally high temperatures of early July. Temperatures of 70°F. and higher prevailed at a time when there were only a few hours of darkness and very little cloud and hence up to 20 hours of sunshine per day.

The oldest part of the valley bottom thicket is near tree disc localities 2 and 4 (Figure 2). There the understory is relatively sparse and the trees are larger and much farther apart and attain an average height of 16 ft. Many trees have numerous stems that have developed vegetatively from the base. One tree had over 40 full-

Figure 6. A general view of the community looking southeast up "Willow Valley".

sized stems growing from a single main root stock and over half of these were growing prostrate. In general, however, the number of fallen branches was less than would be expected in an area of high winds.

The prolific production of offshoots and the presence of numerous tall branches produces a dense canopy cover. Canopy covers as high as 85 per cent and as low as 25 per cent were recorded, although sporadic openings occurred throughout. These shading effects are important in determining the composition of the shrub and herb cover of the understory.

On the drier areas, especially on the steep edge of the second terrace, the willows give way to a heath community composed of cricaceous species, dwarf birch and willows, grasses, and other herbs. The wetter area between the slope and valley bottom thickets is occupied by a type of meadow vegetation composed of lush grasses, sedges, and herbs. This meadow is crossed by two narrow belts of trees 7 ft. high, which connect the two wooded areas. Vigorously growing willow saplings are occasionally present in the meadow, suggesting that, should present conditions continue, the meadow will eventually become a thicket. A possible reason for the gap is the extreme waterlogging that takes place in July, as noted in 1962. This condition, acting as a factor to inhibit tree growth, was also observed in Alaska by Benninghoff (1952).

The drainage in the open meadow is impeded because the 5 in. layer of peaty soil is underlain by silty clay, pebbles and stabilized solifluction material, which are more susceptible to freezing than are gravels and sands. Thus the active layer is shallow compared with the gravel and sand areas and peaty soils also have a low thermal conductivity. Moreover, before stabilization of the solifluction material by the grasses and herbs, this part of the valley would probably not offer a firm enough surface on which willows could become established.

The fauna of the thickets was rich and varied. A number of species of birds were present including the arctic sparrow which, in two unusual instances had nested in the willows instead of on the ground. One of the nests was discovered 2 ft. up in the crook of a 12 ft. high tree. This height was possibly related to the depth of late spring snow. The excreta of fox and lemming were abundant and an old prospector reported that high populations had occurred previously. In some situations lemming droppings covered more than 20 per cent of the ground. This organic debris must supply necessary nutrients to the herb layer. Spiders, beetles, and slugs were also very numerous.

Thicket Communities of Extreme Northern Ungava

The "Willow Valley" forest is the most extensive known in the northern sections of the Ungava peninsula. It covers an area of several hundred acres. An extensive survey of much of the region by helicopter, coupled with reports of pilots who had passed frequently over the territory, permits the writers to present with some assurance, the distributional pattern of the thicket communities in the extreme northern section of the peninsula.

Other thickets containing 17-ft. trees exist in the "Rivière à la Croix" valley and on various deltas along Watts Lake and Murray Lake (Figure 1). Asbestos Corporation personnel have also reported the existence of one or two small thickets along the Rivière Déception valley, and Matthews noted large thickets at the south end of Lac Duquet and especially in the west tributary valley. No other trees of this size have been found elsewhere between Cape Wolstenholme and Deception Bay. A few 7-ft. willows were noticed on the southwest side of Deception Bay in the "Renard Noir" valley, on the northwest side of Lac Duquet by Ruisseau Duquet and along the "Rivière Tourbe" valley.

It is a notable fact that the tall willow forests of arctic Quebec are established only on the deep marine, lake or river gravels and sands, except in parts of "Willow Valley" where slope types also occur.

Field and Laboratory Procedures

Environmental features of the thickets were carefully studied as it was recognized that these characteristics are critical for the development and persistence of these willow communities. Topographic, geological, pedological, and geomorphologic phenomena were carefully noted. Measurements of permafrost depth were taken both in the valley and on the surrounding plateaux. Climatic data were accumulated for a site in the valley near the fringes of the thickets (Figure 2). A thermograph and modified Stevenson screen, placed just 1 ft. above the ground were used. These modifications may have resulted in the greater diurnal range of these records compared with those from Asbestos Hill, which were taken in a standard screen, but the thermograph is correct only to $\pm$ 2°F. and thus the data are considered to be sufficiently accurate to permit a comparison with those for the same period at Asbestos Hill. The weather records for Asbestos Hill mining camp (approx. 2,000 ft. a.s.l.) had been collected only for the previous three years, since 1960, and records are missing for some of the winter months.

The growth patterns and ages of the *Salix* were also investigated, using discs that had been cut from a few of the larger trees at the site.

Floristic and compositional data were collected as follows. All vascular plants in the thicket and adjacent areas and on the nearby plateaux were collected and identified. Metre-square quadrats, placed at random, were used to record the density of ground cover plants. Nine quadrats were read, 3 in the dense willow thicket, 3 in the shrubby edges and small openings within the community and 1 in the open tundra. Within the herb and shrub quadrats estimates of the coverages of lichens, mosses and bare ground were taken. Finally a 10 x 10 m. quadrat was laid out in one of the more dense sections to record the actual density of *Salix* stems. Time prevented the expansion of this latter project and unfortunately no quadrat was recorded in that part of the thicket where the largest willows were growing.

In the laboratory the quadrat data were sorted and actual densities were calculated. The information was tabulated in the order of the occurrence of species in the thicket community proper, in the thicket openings and fringes, and finally in the surrounding tundra habitats.

Results

Floristics

A flora of 67 species of vascular plants, including 69 different taxonomic entities was determined for the valley and environs. Of these plants 2 were completely new to the flora of Quebec. It is surprising that one of these, *Salix alaxensis*, was one of the major dominants of the community and is now known to be widespread in the interior of the extreme northern section of the Ungava Peninsula. The other addition to the flora of the Province was *Stellaria edwardsii*. Several other vascular plants presented notable range extensions that have already been reported (Maycock 1963). A few species of plants, particularly grasses and sedges, may have been overlooked during the survey, owing to the short period of investigation and the inexperience of the collectors.

The affinity of the flora is undoubtedly arctic. With the exception of 2 species, *Ledum groenlandicum* and *Habenaria obtusata* var. *collectanca*, all have been recorded from the Canadian Arctic Archipelago. Both of the exceptions are wide-ranging boreal and subarctic species that have recently been collected with increasing frequency in northern Ungava (Rousseau 1966). Throughout their range they are usually found growing with coniferous trees or in habitats sheltered by boreal or subarctic shrubs.

At the time the survey was initiated the authors questioned whether a large number of boreal associates would be discovered growing under the ameliorated microclimate produced by the shrubs. It was expected that boreal relicts that had survived in the shelter of the thicket from a previous forest community that could have developed during the postglacial xerothermic, might be found. The existing complement of species does not seem to support this supposition, with the exception of the two boreal-subarctic species mentioned. In this regard it is significant that Maycock made a related discovery while botanizing in 1960 on Merry Island of the Nastapoka Group that lies just 3 miles off the southeast shore of Hudson Bay, adjacent to Great Whale River. In a few small stunted groves of spruce that had developed in the tundra, *Ledum groenlandicum* formed the shrub cover and *Habenaria obtusata* was taken nearby. These were the only boreal species in the otherwise arctic flora of the island.

The other point that should be mentioned concerning the occurrence of these boreal plants is that they may possibly be recent arrivals in the community from areas farther south, and became established because of the new conditions produced by the willows. This is assuming that the willow thickets are a recent development too.

There were also a number of cryptogams in the community. Ten species of mosses, 4 lichens and 1 fungus were collected and these were the more prevalent among those associated with the other herbs and shrubs. The following list is not considered complete and is presented to draw attention to the more conspicuous or dominant cryptogams. The fungus was growing on fallen rotted wood and was quite abundant.

FUNGI: *Polyporus elegans* Bull. ex. Fr.

BRYOPHYTA: *Abietinella abietina* (Hedw.) Fl.; *Drepanocladus uncinatus* (Hedw.) Warnst.; *Distichium* sp.; *Myurella tenerrima* (Brd.) Lindb.; *Hypnum revolutum* (Mitt.) Lindb.; *Hylocomium splendens* (Hedw.) BSG.; *Rhacomitrium canescens* Brid.; *Brachythecium* sp.; *Tortula ruralis* (Hedw.) Sin.; *Ditrichum flexicaule* (Schwaegr.) Hampe.

LICHENS: *Cladonia pyxidata* (L.) Hoffm.; *Cetraria nivalis* (L.) Ach.; *Peltigera canina* (L.) Willd. var. rufescens (Weis) Mudd.; *Stereocaulon tomentosum* E. Fr.

Structural composition and shading effects

The lack of boreal elements may seem unusual, but of greater consequence is the fact that so many arctic species seem capable of withstanding the shaded environment produced by the willows. Canopy coverages estimated at levels varying from 25 to 85 per cent prevent large amounts of sunlight from reaching the ground. 37 species were found under these reduced light conditions in the forest. Several of these are wide-ranging species that also occur in boreal forest communities farther south as well as in arctic regions and would be expected to withstand these conditions. *Ledum groenlandicum, Epilobium angustifolium, Calamagrostis canadensis, Equisetum arvense, Carex scirpoidea, Betula glandulosa, Salix reticulata* and *Campanula rotundifolia* could be included in this group. On the other hand arctic species such as *Draba nivalis, Erigeron eriocephalus, Taraxacum lacerum, Arabis alpina, Pedicularis flammea, Potentilla hyparctica, Oxytropis foliolosa* and *O. terrae-novae* would not be expected in dense shade, yet they grew in these thickets. Many of the arctic species were somewhat etiolated, had longer internodes, were taller in stature, and often had certain pigments less well developed than normally; but others were flowering and fruiting, apparently uninfluenced by the effects of shade.

A second group of 44 species occurred in situations that were only partially shaded. Canopy coverages on the edges of the thickets and in the smaller openings in the thickets varied from 0 to 5 per cent. In the open tundra sites where there was no shading at all there was a total of 26 species. The intermediate habitats supported the largest assortment of plants, apparently selected from among those species that were capable of growing under all of the light conditions available (a small group of 8 species including *Oxytropis terrae-novae, Dryas integrifolia, Epilobium latifolium, Arnica alpina, Betula glandulosa, Potentilla hyparctica, Salix reticulata* and *Potentilla nivea*) and from those occurring in the open and shaded sites. The overlap in shaded and semi-shaded habitats was 18 species, whereas in semi-shaded and open it was only 3 species; both of these figures omitting those plants which were common to all three sites. *Salix cordifolia* was the only plant found in the shaded and open communities that was absent in the intermediate.

The actual densities of the plants as tallied in metre quadrats in the different sites indicates that many were capable of growing satisfactorily under the existing conditions. Some species were vigorous enough to dominate in extensive areas on the ground under the thicket canopy and in partially shaded situations. In Table III those species that occurred in at least one of the quadrats recorded in the three related communities are presented on the basis of average density per square metre. Several species occurred with comparatively high average densities in at least one of the three sites. *Poa glauca, Arnica alpina, Epilobium latifolium* and *Oxytropis terrae-novae* possessed high values in the willow thickets. *Equisetum arvense, Stellaria longipes* and *Epilobium angustifolium* occurred as predominant members of the understory both within and on the edges of the thickets, whereas *Salix reticulata* occurred with high values in all three communities but reached optimum influence in the open tundra. *Carex scirpoidea* and *Calamagrostis canadensis* were most prominent on the thicket edges and in openings. Of the species that attained optimum density values in the open tundra, *Salix cordifolia, Dryas integrifolia, Salix calcicola* and *Stellaria monantha* were most significant. The density values for the herbs support and expand the presence data and show a more refined picture of actual composition in the three sites.

TABLE III. AVERAGE DENSITY PER SQUARE METER FOR SPECIES WHICH OCCURRED IN AT LEAST ONE OF THE NINE QUADRATS RECORDED IN THE THREE COMMUNITIES OF "WILLOW VALLEY"

Species	Willow Thicket	Shrubby Edges and Openings	Tundra
Pedicularis flammea	0.2	—	—
Taraxacum lacerum	0.8	—	—
Cerastium beeringianum	1.0	—	—
Erigeron unalaschkensis	1.8	—	—
Stellaria edwardsii	3.6	—	—
Erigeron eriocephalus	5.2	—	—
Artemisia borealis	5.6	—	—
Festuca brachyphylla	6.6	—	—
Poa glauca	8.6	—	—
Epilobium latifolium	14.0	—	—
Arnica alpina	23.0	—	—
Oxytropis terrae-novae	47.0	—	—
Campanula rotundifolia	0.4	0.3	—
Betula glandulosa	0.6	0.3	—
Potentilla hyparctica	1.4	0.3	—
Potentilla nivea	3.0	0.3	—
Pyrola grandiflora	0.6	2.0	—
Oxytropis foliolosa	0.8	2.3	—
Polygonum viviparum	4.6	6.7	—
Equisetum arvense	10.4	6.7	—
Stellaria longipes	30.0	8.7	—
Epilobium angustifolium	8.0	9.0	—
Carex scirpoidea	0.6	71.7	—
Salix reticulata	11.0	25.0	65.0
Salix cordifolia	1.2	—	10.0
Dryas integrifolia	0.8	—	17.0
Calamagrostis canadensis	—	21.7	—
Rhododendron lapponicum	—	1.3	—
Carex norvegica	—	0.7	—
Campanula uniflora	—	0.3	—
Salix calcicola	—	4.7	15.0
Pedicularis lapponica	—	0.3	7.0
Stellaria monantha	—	—	19.0
Oxytropis maydelliana	—	—	5.0

The gradual trends in the series of quantitative data that are evident in Table III emphasize that although the species are predominantly of arctic distribution they respond differently to the effects of shading and the protection from exposure afforded by the thicket community. The various herbs apparently find conditions most beneficial under one of the three vegetational situations investigated. It is perhaps dangerous to place too much reliance on the trends indicated in these tables, because scant information is available particularly for the tundra sites. The moisture conditions of the three sites are probably not similar enough for critical comparison, because the tundra on the elevated terraces is undoubtedly drier than the moist valley bottom. The data are nevertheless of sufficient magnitude to illustrate that it would be fruitful to investigate these relationships on a larger scale, to determine the influence of shade and protection on the tundra species. It may be that a more thorough study of a large number of the *thicket forests* in the region may yield a larger number of boreal species and tundra types that can withstand shade.

Thicket canopy structure

The composition and structure of the canopy was studied in a single 10 x 10 m. quadrat situated in one of the less mature sections of the community. It is unfortunate that a similar quadrat was not taken in the more mature forest, but the data available do present a satisfactory picture of the structure of the canopy in a younger area of the community.

Within the quadrat there were a total of 217 *Salex* stems. These varied in size from a diameter at base of 1 in. and a height of 4 ft. up to a diameter of 5 in. and a height of 9 ft. Approximately 65 per cent were *Salix alaxensis* and the remainder were *S. planifolia*. In the more mature areas the density of stems per metre was estimated to be greatly reduced and trunk diameters were considerably larger. The largest observed was 8 in. in diameter and had attained a height of slightly greater than 16 ft.

When the density of stems is considered it is realized that a cover of this thickness greatly reduces the percentage of incident light available for plant growth at the ground surface. In spite of this, as the data indicate, many of the species that dominated in the encircling open tundra communities were successfully growing in the shaded thickets.

Age studies

Several of the tree discs were unsatisfactory for age studies because the central areas were badly decomposed. This was particularly true for the largest discs and thus it may not have been too serious that some of the largest willows could not be felled for lack of proper tools. Five discs, the largest 4.25 in. diameter at 1 ft. above the ground, were suitable for examination. Four of these, the largest, were collected in "Willow Valley" and the other was cut from an isolated 7 ft. tree in Ruisseau Duquet valley. (See Figure 1 for tree disc location sites.)

Initially it was planned that ring width measurements would be taken so that possible correlations could be ascertained between increment fluctuations and favourable or unfavourable periods of growth caused by climatic, biotic, or other influences. This proved too difficult a task because the rings were not as clearly defined as was desirable for this purpose and because the central portions of many discs were obscured by decomposition. Thus after the rings were defined and counted they were then critically examined in series and where a ring or a group of rings appeared notably smaller than those adjacent, they were so noted on a tally sheet on which the years were listed in order corresponding to the growth rings. Years of exceptionally wide increment were also so noted. Although this procedure seemed somewhat crude, it was not without value.

The oldest disc proved to be the largest. It was 59 years old, having started growth in 1904. The other discs were 50, 49, 38, and 38 years old, having apparently started to grow in 1913, 1914, 1925, and 1925 respectively (Figure 7). The disc taken from the Ruisseau Duquet locality was 50 years old and it had a diameter slightly greater than half that of the 59-year old disc from "Willow Valley". Thus the growth in diameter or increase in girth in relation to age cannot be directly compared for the different sites. Growth patterns for "Willow Valley" discs are quite variable and no direct correlation of age and diameter can be ascertained from the materials available, although it may be possible with more intensive sampling. Such information would be of limited value because the site characteristics of any stem appear to be so variable that no direct correlation would be possible. The available information indicates simply that a stem diameter of the order of 4 in. at a foot above ground level represents a growth period of 50 years. The two other discs of 3.5 in. diameter at ages of 38 years, seem to bear this out. The prominence of heartwood deterioration also suggests that a trunk diameter of 5 in. at 60 years is approaching the growth limit for the species here. It is exceptional for stems to become much larger, but in special circumstances they did grow to 8 in. The prevalence of vegetative reproduction in *Salix*, with the possibility of renewed stem growth would emphasize that the willows are probably much older than any single trunk may indicate.

Figure 7. Polished tree sections of *Solix alaxansis* from "Willow Valley". The three discs on the left, from top to bottom, were 59, 38 and 49 years old; the top disc on the right was 38 years old. The disc on the lower right was cut in Ruisseau Duquet, and was 50 years old.

The patterns of apparent ring suppression were of particular interest. Those for "Willow Valley" and Ruisseau Duquet which are 22 miles apart, correspond quite closely. Differentiated growth suppression is clearly evident for the years 1956-54, 1934-31, and 1925-24. The period 1950-54 was notably a favourable period of growth as were the years 1959-58, 1938-37, and 1920-21. The oldest discs also possessed a marked suppression period for the years between 1913 and 1910 although none of the other cores were old enough to substantiate this.

The temperature data for Cape Hopes Advance were examined for cyclic fluctuations which, if present, could be compared with the growth fluctuations of the willows in the valley. Mean monthly temperatures for May, June, July, and August were summed up and averaged from 1943 onward, the period for which data were available. The annual sums were subtracted from this average total to determine the deviations. These deviations above or below the average were compared to the growth peaks and depressions but no valid correlations were observed although the magnitude of deviation seemed significant and the values were as cyclic as the growth patterns. There are insufficient data for such a comparison but undoubtedly the major source of difficulty is that the Cape Hopes Advance records are not valid for this inland situation. The marked similarity of the growth patterns in the two separate localities prompted the attempt at correlation. The other factor to be considered is that the willows must be at their extreme climatic limit and there is little doubt that a large number of environmental factors may have a great influence on their existence and yearly growth. Thus small variations in any of these features, not just temperature, may profoundly affect growth patterns under conditions that would seem to provide the bare minimum for existence. There is however, reason to believe that more precise and more abundant ring data and climatic information might provide a clearer picture of the climatic features that are limiting and might also provide a basis for determining features of the past climate in this inland region of Ungava.

Discussion

Knowledge of the presence of this unusual *arctic forest* community in a region so effectively isolated from others where it would be normally established, calls forth speculation as to the reason for its existence. The descriptions of the community and its relationship to the environmental features of the site and to the gross features of the surrounding area that have been presented, permit more than a speculative discussion of the conditions that are directly responsible for its establishment, development, growth, and continuance. Some factors are more important than others in this respect.

Protection afforded by topography

Protection from rigorous climatic influences would seem to be a factor of survival and yet the reverse seems to be the case. The Murray Mining Corporation Field Report for 1962 emphasizes that the dominant winds during the winter are from the northwest which is the direction of alignment of "Willow Valley". This co-incidence of exposure creates a channelling effect and intensifies wind speeds at this period. If protection from prevailing winds was the factor allowing the growth of trees, then the lack of trees in many of the deep valleys in the region that appear to offer greater protection would have to be accounted for. The unfavourable influence of strong cold winds may be effectively minimized by other factors such as an enduring protective snow cover.

The influence of aspect does not seem of importance because "Willow Valley" faces northwest and not south or southwest. The slope wood on the northeast side of the valley may be favourably situated in this respect. Geiger (1957) states that southwest-facing slopes receive the greatest intensity of insolation in mid-afternoon during summer. Ground temperatures are also higher because a greater part of the solar radiation is used in the forenoon in evaporating moisture from the top few inches of the soil. Hence it is theoretically in the afternoon that sun does its greatest work on the southwest facing slopes in "Willow Valley", provided that skies remain clear and fog does not develop, as it does near the coast, especially in August when it is frequent and dense.

Inland during the afternoon the top layers of the soil will probably be comparatively dry and thus most of the absorbed heat energy may be used in raising the ground temperature. To test these ideas ground temperatures were recorded at various places and times during the afternoons of 7, 8, and 10 July, 1962, on the northeast side (facing southwest) of "Willow Valley". There was an average ground temperature of 50°F. at 2 in. while the air temperature at 5 ft. varied from 56°F. to 71°F. This compares favourably with readings taken in a permafrost-free area, for Geiger (1957) records an average annual temperature of 9.2°C. (49°F.) at 5 cm. (2 in.) in loam in Germany. Despite the small number of measurements, they would seem to indicate a great storage of heat during the summer on the northeast slope and consequently a deep active layer above the permafrost. Unfortunately no complementary measurements could be taken on the southwest slope for comparison, because throughout the period the river was in flood and could not be crossed on foot. The asymmetrical shape of the valley would nevertheless, seem to support the theory that the depth of thaw is greater on the northeast than southwest slope, as there appears to have been greater solifluction movement on the northeast side of "Willow Valley" before stabilization by vegetation. Aspect may thus be a significant local factor in the actual location of at least a section of the thicket.

Permafrost and its effects on tree growth

Another factor that may have influenced the development and spread of the tall thickets is the presence of a deep active layer over the permafrost in summer, in the gravels and sands of the raised deltas and river terraces. The existence of continuous permafrost in the Asbestos Hill area has been proven by numerous drillings for the mining corporation which showed that permafrost depth is probably greater than 930 ft. Yet when pits deeper than 3 ft. were dug in the second terrace at point A and near tree disc location 2 (Figure 2), no permafrost was encountered. The results of seismic investigations along line A-B (Figure 2) proved that if permafrost did exist in the terrace deposits, it was more than 12 ft. below the surface. In most other valleys in the locality however, permafrost was discovered at only 6 to 12 in. below the surface in early and mid July. This was notably the case near the mouth of "Rivière à la Croix" in an area lacking tree or shrub cover. In "Willow Valley" near-surface ground ice was found only in the thick peat deposits at peat locations 1, 2, and 3 (Figure 2) but at depths of 11 in., 8.5 in. and 2 ft., respectively.

To what extent the presence of a deep active layer is a direct consequence of the modifying influences exerted by the thickets and to what extent the condition existed before the invasion of trees, is debatable. Tikhomirov (1962) stresses the fact that the cultivation of trees in the southern tundra of the U.S.S.R. has produced a significant amelioration of the harsh microclimatic conditions. Conversely, Benninghoff (1952) in Alaska maintains that the colonization of an area by vegetation leads to a raising of permafrost level because of the insulating effects of the plants and debris during the short arctic summer. In "Willow Valley" it is probable that a deeper active layer must have existed prior to the development of the thickets, possibly as a result of the general climatic amelioration in the Arctic and the unusual local microclimatic conditions. This is supported by the statement that *Salix planifolia*, the tallest shrub in the Arctic, "is limited to areas where the deeper layers of soil remain unfrozen in an average winter." (Polunin 1940).

Although there is no proof, it is quite possible that a permanently unfrozen layer does exist in certain sites in "Willow Valley" owing to the insulating effects of very deep snow, a high storage of heat in summer, and the low susceptibility of the sands and gravels to freezing.

The presence of a deep active layer in summer has two important effects on the growth of the willows. It enables the trees to gain a sure roothold and so withstand the strong winds that occasionally attain speeds of 100 m.p.h. Tap roots were observed to have penetrated deeper than 3 ft. into the unfrozen gravel and pebbles and ensured a stable foundation. Also, despite the marked channelling of winds from the south, very few trees in the area were windthrown, even in the slope thicket. The other effect of a deep active layer is that it ensures a continuous supply of flowing water for tree roots throughout the summer. This has been stated as a necessary condition for the growth of *Salix planifolia* (Polunin 1940) and probably holds true for *S. alaxensis*.

Snow depth

The depth of winter and spring snowfall would seem to be the most important of the topoclimatological factors influencing the growth of the willows. Polunin (1940) emphasized that *Salix planifolia* grows to a large size only in situations where the stems and branches are in part protected by a deep drift of snow. Bliss (1962) states that generally "tundra shrubs are found only where the winter snow cover prevails". Snow cover affords valuable protection to trees and shrubs during critical low temperatures and during periods of strong, often corrosive winds. Bliss also emphasizes that, "shrub height is quite well correlated with mean winter snow depth." If this is so then it would be expected that snow accumulation would have to be extremely deep in "Willow Valley" to protect 16 ft. trees, but this is probably the case.

Unfortunately snow depth has not been measured in the valley, but in early 1962 mining camp personnel who had to trudge from Watts Lake through the snow of "Willow Valley", reported snow of considerable depth. Nevertheless, for the spring of 1961, it was recorded in the Murray Mining Corporation Report that, "the tractor train could not be used in the canyon between Watts Lake and Asbestos Hill because of rough ground and sparse snow cover." This condition was probably due to the early dispersal of snow and early break up of that year. In the same report it is mentioned that "wind sweeps across the peninsula a great deal of the time, causing the snow to pile up in large drifts in the canyons and the lee of hills."

The depth of snow in the valleys must be relatively great in the "Willow Valley" region since more than 6 ft. of snow falls annually on the plateau top, as recorded at Asbestos Hill camp. Also, the snow is of a drier type and is blown easily from the plateau tops and frozen expanse of Watts Lake by the high winds, accumulating in the 1,500 ft. depression of "Willow Valley". Heavy accumulation would occur especially on the northeast side by the slope thickets. The trees aid in this accumulation process because they trap the drifting snow, a fact of great importance in the Schefferville area of central Quebec (Matthews 1962).

Temperature influences

Weather records have been taken at Asbestos Hill mining camp (approx. 2,000 ft. a.s.l.) since 1960, although records are missing for some of the winter months. This short record indicates that temperatures on the plateau are not extreme, seldom exceeding 70°F. and rarely falling below—40°F. (McOuat *et al.* 1961). Records for 1960 and 1961 indicate a mean monthly temperature for April of 9.6°F. and for July of 48.1°F. Temperature data were collected during 1962 to compare conditions in "Willow Valley" with those of Asbestos Hill. Theoretically higher summer temperatures were expected in the valley as it is some 1,800 ft. lower than the plateau. Greater summer heat could possibly have been an important factor in the growth and establishment of the thickets.

In theory temperatures in "Willow Valley" should be approximately 5°F. higher than those at Asbestos Hill if there is a normal change of temperature of 3°F. per 1,000 ft. of altitude. When the 7 a.m. and 7.30 p.m. mean temperature differences for the sites are compared it is seen that this does not occur, there being lower temperatures in the morning (—3.5°F.) and higher temperatures (4.5°F.) in the evening in the valley. Cold air drainage into the deep valley from the plateau and valley sides at night produces a marked temperature inversion. A spectacular difference occurred on July 15 when the 7 a.m. temperature in the valley was only 37°F. while at Asbestos Hill it was 61°F., a difference of 24°F. Some of this reduction in temperature may have been due to microclimatic influences in the tree stand, such as cold air drainage from the crown canopy and the shading effect of the relatively dense foliage (40 per cent). In spite of these possible factors there is little doubt that general air temperatures were considerably lower in the valley than on the hill at 7 a.m.

If these temperature conditions prevail throughout the growing season then it would seem that the valley bottom would be an unfavourable site for the growth of trees, for nocturnal ground and air frosts would no doubt be more frequent than on the plateau. Nevertheless, as daytime temperatures are usually higher in the valley, this may possibly compensate for the low night temperatures and raise soil temperatures accordingly. This may be reflected in the deeper than usual active layer.

The temperatures for 1962 were probably above average, for air temperatures of over 83°F. were recorded in the valley only a few days after one of the worst snow storms of the year, on 4 July. In spite of the sudden transition from winter to summer the trees had already grown 1½ in. by 6 July and 3 to 4 in. by 13 July. Many herbs were also in bloom by this date, indicating the triggering effect of high temperatures, even for a relatively short period. The willows particularly *Salix alaxensis* flowered very heavily during July and the favourable high temperatures may have been beneficial for the production of abundant viable seed.

The effects of wind

Strong winds are often cited as one of the major environmental factors that are a hazard to tree growth in subarctic and arctic regions. This factor has been held responsible for the complete lack of trees where environmental factors would seem to permit their growth. Thus if trees do exist in an arctic area it would be expected that wind velocity there would be moderate. As previously stressed, however, this is not the case in "Willow Valley" where winds up to 100 m.p.h. have frequently been experienced, the deep valley having a tendency to channel the wind, especially when it blows from the south.

That the area surrounding "Willow Valley" is extremely windy can be seen in Table IV which compares the mean monthly wind speeds at Asbestos Hill and at Schefferville, in central Quebec, for the period from May to September 1961. The figures have been extracted from reports by McOuat *et al.* (1961) and Shaw (1962).

Table IV. Comparison of mean monthly wind speeds in miles per hour (May to September) at Asbestos Hill and Schefferville, Quebec.

	Asbestos Hill 1961	Schefferville 1961	AVERAGE MEAN (1955-60)
May	14.2	12.0	10.0
June	14.6	11.3	10.0
July	9.4	9.8	10.4
August	17.2	11.4	10.3
September	16.6	11.8	12.3

In July 1962 when strong winds did blow, it was noticed that in the daytime temperatures were not lowered, in fact, in many instances they were raised. It would appear that the air descending from the plateau into the valley was warmed adiabatically producing a Föhn effect. In winter the effects of the winds are limited by the heavy protecting mantle of snow. There was moreover, no sign of wind influencing the level of the tree canopy which would project above the snow in winter. The uneven nature of the individual tree tops could be clearly seen. Probably the valley bottom thickets are protected from the strong southerly winds by the steep terrace edges which slopes at approximately 40° and rise to more than 20 ft. That the wind has played little part in affecting tree shapes is further evidenced by the absence of any noticable wind gap at their base and the lack of much misshapen growth or blowdown resulting from wind.

Interrelationships of limiting factors

There is little doubt that the valley forest community barely manages to exist under the prevailing conditions although there is some evidence that even under these limiting conditions it may be extending into adjacent sections. The fact that it is subjected to the fringes of subsistence makes it difficult to select any one environmental condition as being responsible for its survival. An environmental complex is operative and it may be that many of the specific factors involved in the complex may be limiting in regard to the community. If this assumption is reasonable then in would be of great value to study the compositional and environmental characteristics of a large number of communities of this type throughout the region to gain a clearer understanding of the factors responsible. A study of initial development stages might well be important, because the establishment of vegetational cover itself may prove to be a factor of considerable significance in overcoming the fringe-like nature of environmental factors and allowing the community to extend itself to limits that seem impossible when viewed in relation to the prevailing ecological and climatological influences.

Of the environmental factors that seem influential in controlling the location, establishment and continued growth of the "Willow Valley" forest as it exists at present, several would seem to be particularly significant and their effects are undoubtedly collective in nature. The presence of a deeper than usual active layer and perhaps the existence in places of a permanently unfrozen layer between the active layer and the permafrost table in winter is of prime importance. These influences are undoubtedly dependent on high summer temperatures, the insulating effects of a deep accumulation of snow and the nature of the parent materials. The protective nature of the deep snow cover in winter cannot be overestimated either for its direct effect on the willows or for its indirect influences on climatic and environmental features. The availability of free flowing water during the growing season has a beneficial effect on the growth of the willows not only in providing a constant source of water and nutrients but perhaps also in producing moist aerated situations that are suitable for shrubs of this nature. These conditions are undoubtedly provided in close proximity to the stream channel and in the lower terrace sections that are often flooded.

Other factors that contribute to the successful continuance of the thickets are secondary in nature. These include the production of extensive amounts of viable seed, particularly in favourable summers such as 1962, and coupled with this the good conditions for seed germination that are provided by the soils and peats in adjacent areas which, on analysis, are shown to contain a relatively high amount of exchangeable bases. In the thickets the large number of seedlings, from both seed and vegetative sprouts, that occurred and which are spreading into adjacent areas without a shrub cover, are valid evidence of the importance of these factors, and also emphasize the influences exerted by the thicket community toward ameliorating harsh climatic conditions to give rise to favourable microclimatic situations.

The existence of high summer temperatures cannot be considered the dominant factor responsible for the "Willow Valley" forest, for if this were so it would be expected that thickets of willow would be more widespread in the deep sheltered valleys, especially along the coast where temperatures of over 70 F. were experienced at Deception Bay, Otter Lake, and Sugluk at the end of July and the beginning of August, 1962.

All the summer conditions are of great importance as their influences must be considered in relation to the growth period. The frost free period for the region is only 27 days. This is a 13-year mean for Cape Hopes Advance to the southeast. Favourable microclimatic situations may extend this complement slightly for "Willow Valley" but a growth period of 30 days would seem to be the maximum. As short a period as this is undoubtedly critical for the growth of large shrubs especially of the size of the willows involved, as a relatively large amount of photosynthetic material must be replaced annually before any growth can take place. To produce this material and then permit the growth of new twigs, leaves, and wood on the trunk, the tree, in a very short growing season, may lay down sufficient food to carry it through the year and provide for this growth expansion. In this light the existing climatic conditions are surely near border-line for growth phenomena of this magnitude. It is not unrealistic to imagine that several consecutive growing seasons of short duration, or during which sunlight might be greatly reduced or temperature levels be well below normal, could lead to a serious depletion of food reserves, to a marked reduction in growth, and perhaps even to rapid die-back of the thickets. Such an argument speaks against a single environmental factor as holding complete dominance, and supports the concept of a complex of limiting but perhaps compensating factors. The willows, their patterns of growth and their present vigorous appearance also indicate that such a hypothetical situation has not arisen, at least not within the past 60 or perhaps 75 years, and in the light of evidence to be presented below perhaps even for a much more extended period of time.

Conclusions
Significance of the Willow Forest
There are several important considerations in connexion with the *willow forest* of extreme Northern Ungava. The first is simply that this unusual phenomenon exists, has been discovered and described, and that others may also be available for critical investigation in the same region or elsewhere; the second is related to the extreme conditions under which the community has developed and survived, and involves an evaluation of these critical factors; the third is the significance of the forest in relation to the historical background of the region, particularly in terms of the events since Pleistocene glaciation; the last is the question of the practical value of present knowledge that might be profitably extended by a more intensive study of thickets in the region. The first two aspects have been extensively treated above and the concluding remarks are presented largely in reference to the other two considerations.

Historical significance of the community
The oldest trunks that were critically examined from the area were of the order of 60 years. Several unexamined trunks were larger and if, as is indicated from the materials available, there is a rough relationship between size and age (although this does not necessarily follow in this situation), these larger specimens may well be considerably older. Nevertheless, on the basis of the heartwood deterioration in the speciments examined it appears that an age of 75 to 100 years is maximum under the existing conditions. The presence of fallen trunks attested to this assumption. The growth habits of these willows and the evidence available from excavations that

uncovered several layers of buried wood, undoubtedly of similar origin, indicate that the existence of the willow community might well have spanned a period of time much longer than 100 years. The breakage of old stems is actually a stimulus to the further production of stems, especially in the case of the genus *Salix*.

On purely theoretical grounds it might be suggested that the willow forest is a depauperate relic of a much more extensive interglacial community that has survived the effects of the glacial advances during the Pleistocene period. From geomorphological evidence, however, this would seem impossible as there is every reason to believe that the "Watts Lake-Murray Lake Trough" was glaciated intensively during the maximum of the last glaciation, although, as Matthews (1962*a*) points out, certain upland areas, such as the Asbestos Hill region might have remained as nunataks. A more reasonable supposition is that the forest was first established during the hypsithermal interval (between 9,000 B.P. and 2,600 B.P.) having survived the climatic changes that have occurred since that period.

The surprising stage of maturity that the community has attained in relation to the surrounding vegetation seems to point to a long period of occupation. The growth features of the willows, the presence of a relatively well developed soil layer, and the existence of buried wood layers suggests that the willows have been growing here for long periods, either sporadically or continuously. The woody layers may be the equivalent of a woody peat found on the southeast side of "Cross Creek Valley," 2 ft. below the surface of the 20 ft. terrace (above Watts Lake) and covered with alternating layers of pebbles, silt and peat. It occurs at a point where at present there is an absence of trees, thus implying a greater extent of the "proto Cross Creek" forest than that of the present thickets in the valley. As already mentioned, a similar woody peat layer and fossil soil was discovered in an ice-cored peat mound at peat location 2, (Figure 2) in "Willow Valley". As it is usually understood that arctic peat takes a long time to form, and as more than 2 ft. of peat overlaid the woody layer, it was at first considered that the ancient forest indicated could be related to one of the older thermal maxima. That this is possibly not the case has become apparent from analyses of the pollen content of two peat deposits just over 2 ft. thick, taken at 37 ft. and 382 ft. above sea level from the southern end of Sugluk Inlet and from a radiocarbon date of 1625 ± 175 years B.P. obtained on the basal samples of peat from 382 ft. The peat was dated by Isotopes Incorporated (sample No. 1-727-J.D.I.-62-2F). Seemingly both peat deposits started to form immediately after a period when pine and spruce trees grew much further north than at the present time, as in both cases the pine and spruce pollen from the basal deposits form a higher percentage of the total tree pollen than was expected for an area 300 miles north of the tree line and about 900 miles from the nearest pine forest. Moreover, the pollen diagrams indicate a marked increase in the percentage of willow pollen upwards from the base of the diagrams. In the case of the 382 ft. deposit the willow pollen is most abundant at the 8 in. level, c. 400-500 years B.P.

Although it was impossible to produce pollen diagrams for the peat of the ice-cored peat mound in "Willow Valley" there is every reason to believe that the peat started to form at about the same time as that in the Sugluk area, as a result of a general climatic deterioration. Hence it is likely that the more extensive willow forest existed 2,000 years B.P. On this basis it is possible to theorize that the thicket community first developed during the equivalent of the so-called pine period of southern Canada but achieved its greatest dimentions during the equivalent of the Middle Ages of Europe. It is equally possible that the ice free Asbestos Hill area acted as a plant refuge during the maximum of the last glaciation thereby allowing the early recolonization of parts of "Willow Valley" by arctic plants immediately following deglaciation. The existence of a well developed substrate early in post glacial times may have permitted the development of the forest community during the hypsithermal interval and the favourable climatic situation may have allowed the forest to survive subsequent rigorous climatic changes until the present. Whether or not a few spruce and pine trees actually grew in the sheltered valleys during the 'pine period' has still to be proved.

Although it might be expected that there would be a greater boreal representation among the plant occupants, such being actually expected in view of the extraordinary environmental conditions, even before relict status was considered, this in no way invalidates the above thesis. Boreal elements, in fact, could well have been decimated in unfavourable climatic periods during the interval since the xerothermic, or simply replaced in competition by the tundra species that seem to be flourishing in the present environment. If boreal species were reduced in number reinvasion may be an extremely slow process even if conditions were currently favourably because, for one thing, all of the rivers in the intervening region to the present treeline flow in a southward direction. The communities are also so small and scattered that even if propagules were entering the region with considerable frequency, their chances of falling on favourable ground in the thickets would be very slight.

Practical considerations

The "Willow Valley" site represents a rather unique ecological situation and one that may yield much profitable information of practical value. The existing vegetation is considerably advanced in maturity in relation to the immediate surroundings. The site and the ecosystem involved are perpetuating and perhaps extending a complex group of environmental influences that may eventually permit the establishment of plants of a more boreal nature. The area should be resurveyed at intervals to determine whether the structural and floristic features developed during at least the past hundred years have advanced beyond what at present is to be found. Such information, whether it will indicate advancement or degradation, would be of significance in formulating long term climatic changes in northern Ungava. The degree to which the scope of such a project could be expanded into adjacent areas would determine the extent of useful climatic indices produced. Protection of the communities involved would have to be assured.

Because of the marked increase in growth of the tree-like willows during the 1930's and 1940's, and their spread on to the surrounding tundra, the thicket community would seem to support the idea that since the end of the nineteenth century arctic Quebec has experienced a climatic amelioration similar to that in Labrador (Wenner 1947) and other parts of the Arctic. Wenner graphically showed that the mean annual temperature at Hebron, Nain, and Hopedale, on the Labrador coast, has risen steadily since the turn of the century. In fact he calculated that at Nain the mean annual temperature rose 2°C. (3.5°F.) between 1883 and 1938. This was held responsible for desiccation of many swamps in Labrador and the invasion of such by more xerophilous vegetation, while in the Kaumajet mountains glacierettes have retreated. Similar proof of this climatic change in northern Quebec is the occurrence of a cirque glacierette, approximately halfway between Sugluk and Cape Wolstenholme, which shows evidence of recent retreat from its 6 ft. high terminal moraine. The recent nature of this retreat is attested to by the lack of vegetation, except extremely small lichens (*Rhizocarpon geograficum*), on the morainic material.

It is noteworthy that North American workers have not been specifically concerned with the quantitative investigation of arctic and subarctic thicket communities, and the factors responsible for their existence. The Russian literature abounds in sporadic reports of relic forest or thicket stands north of the treeline (Chugunov 1955; Tikhomirov and Shtepa 1956; Tikhomirov 1957; Starikov 1961; Tikhomirov 1962). Although many of these are simple factual reports of their existence, some appear to have looked critically at the reasons for their disjunct occurrence. Almost all are described as relicts although it is not clear that all are considered as phenomena of past climatic or vegetational optima, and doubtful if all may be explained on this basis. It is important that interest in these communities is developing elsewhere in arctic regions even if so far the desire is chiefly to learn of their distribution and frequency.

Several research workers in North America have attempted to deduce vegetational trends in relation to past or present trends in climatic features, from studying features of vegetation, particularly treelines (Griggs 1934; Marr 1948). Most investigators, however, seem to have forsaken such straightforward methods and are pursuing the more elaborate studies of pollen analysis and radiocarbon dating. It would seem reasonable to begin relating some of these latter measurements to critical quantitative ecological studies of the vegetation that sits on top of these stratified features, and to remember that vegetation represents the present capabilities of a group of plants of coping with a set of past and present circumstances.

Lastly, it is worth considering the practical value of understanding the climatic features responsible for the growth of thicket vegetation of this type. A knowledge of the threshold limits might permit the establishment, by artificial means, of thicket communities that might survive and flourish in the favourable microclimate that they would produce. This would be a valuable practical tool to enliven the immediate environments of towns and villages established as a result of colonizing the North.

References

Benninghoff, W. S., "Interaction of Vegetation and Soil Frost Phenomena", *Arctic*, Vol. V(1952), pp. 34-44.

Bliss, L. C., "Adaptations of Arctic and Alpine Plants to Environmental Conditions", *Arctic*, Vol. XV (1962), pp. 117-44.

Chugunov, B. V., "El'-relikt" (Spruce Relict), *Priroda*, Vol. XLIV (1955), pp. 112-13.

Geiger, R., "The Climate Near the Ground", Harvard University Press (Cambridge, 1957), 482 pp.

Griggs, R. F., "The Edge of the Forest in Alaska and the Reasons for its Position", *Ecol.*, Vol. XV (1934), pp. 80-97.

McOuat, J. F. *et al*, Murray Mining Corporation Ltd., Eng. Field Rept. no. 2 (1961), Asbestos Project, Asbestos Hill, Quebec.

Marr, J. W., "Ecology of the Forest-tundra Ecotone on the East Coast of Hudson Bay", *Ecol. Monogr.*, Vol. XVIII (1948), pp. 117-44.

Matthews, B., "Snow Conditions at Schefferville, Winter 1960-61; with special reference to the effects of wind on the pattern of snow accumulation in a muskeg area", *McGill Sub-Arctic Res. Pap.*, no. 12 (1962), pp. 65-75.

Matthews, B., "Glacial and Postglacial Geomorphology of the Sugkik Wolstenholme Area, Northern Ungava", *McGill Sub-Arctic Res. Pop.,* no. 12 (1962), pp. 17-46.

Maycock, P. F., "Plant Records New to Quebec and the Ungava Peninsula", *Can. J. Bot.,* Vol. XLI (1963), pp. 1277-79.

Polunin, N., "Botany of the Canadian Eastern Arctic, Pt. I. Pteridophyta and Spermatophyta", *Natl. Mus. Can. Bull.,* Vol. XCII (1940), 408 pp.

Polunin, N., "Botany of the Canadian Eastern Arctic, Pt. III. Vegetation and Ecology", *Natl. Mus. Can. Bull.,* Vol. CIV (1948), 305 pp.

Porsild, A. E., "The Vasular Plants of the Western Canadian Arctic Archipelago", *Natl. Mus. Can. Bull.,* Vol. CXXXV (1955), 226 pp.

Porsild, A. E., "Illustrated Flora of the Canadian Arctic Archipelago", *Natl. Mus. Can. Bull.,* Vol. CXLVI (1957), 209 pp.

Rousseau, J., "La flore de la Rivière George, Nouveau Québec", *Nat. Canad.,* Vol. XCIII (1966), pp. 11-59.

Shaw, J .B., "Climatological Summary for 1961, Schefferville (Knob Lake) P.Q.", *McGill Sub-Arctic Res. Pap.,* no. 12 (1962), pp. 131-33.

Soper, J. D., "The Blue Goose" (Monograph), Can. Dept. of the Interior, N.W.T. and Yukon Branch (1930), 64 pp.

Soper, J. D., "Solitudes of the Arctic", *Can. Geog. J.,* Vol. VII (1933), pp. 102-15.

Starikov, G. C., Reliktovaja rosca manczurskogo jasenja" (A Relict Grove of *Fraxinus Mandshurica,)* *Priroda,* Vol. L (1961), pp. 68-69.

Tedrow, J. C. F. and Cantlon, J. E., "Concepts of Soil Formation and Classification in Arctic Regions," *Arctic,* Vol. XI (1958), pp. 166-79.

Tikhomirov, B. A., "Ob obrane lesov krajnego severa" (Preservation of Wood in the Far North), *Priroda,* Vol. XLVI (1957), pp. 35-37.

Tikhomirov, B. A., "The Treelessness of the Tundra", *Polar Record,* Vol. XI (1902), pp. 24-30.

Tikhomirov, B. A. and Shtepa, V. A., "K Kharakteristike lesnykh forpostov v nizov'-yakh reki leny" (Contribution to the Knowledge of the Forest Outposts in the Lower Course of the River Lena), *Bot. Zhur.,* Vol. VIII (1956) pp. 1107-22.

Wenner, C. G., "Pollen Diagrams from Labrador", *Geografiska Annaler,* Vol. XXIX (1947), pp. 137-374.

5

The Natural Vegetation of the Southern Great Plains of Canada

F. B. Watts

This paper is concerned with a description of the nature and distribution of the natural vegetation of the southern part of the Great Plains of Canada. The area involved lies wholly within the three Prairie Provinces.

The Forestry Branch of the Department of Northern Affairs and National Resources has published an excellent description of the forest types of Canada (Halliday, 1958), but the emphasis in this paper is on the vegetation types of the great grassland formation of the Canadian West. Only very brief descriptions of the forest types which form the eastern, northern, and western boundaries of the area under discussion have been included.

In this study "natural" means fundamentally unchanged by man. The ecological role of the aborigines of Western Canada is impossible to determine with any accuracy. It is well known, however, that white settlers have radically changed the natural vegetation of the southern Great Plains as their settlement is based upon crop production and intensive grazing. These activities have virtually destroyed the natural vegetation in some areas, and have profoundly altered it in others. Much of the mixed-grass prairie and virtually all the true prairie of the Canadian West have been put to the plough, as have large stretches of the aspen grove country. Over-grazing has radically altered much of the short-grass prairie. A map of natural vegetation must therefore be a pre-white settlement or 'pre-plough' vegetation map.

Reprinted from *Geographical Bulletin*, No. 14 (1960), pp. 25-43. By permission.

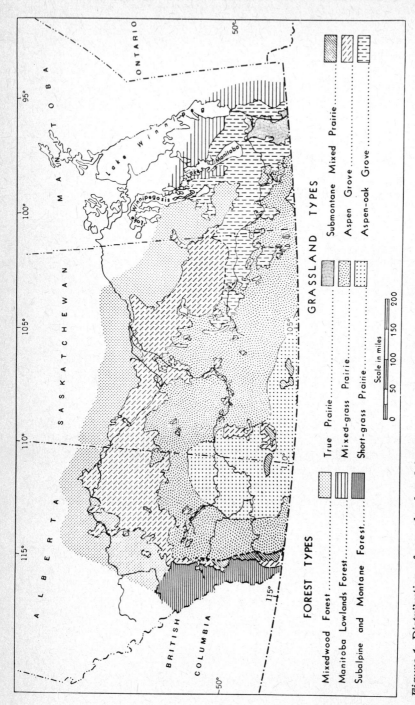

Figure 1. Distribution of grassland and forest types, southern Great Plains of Canada.

Halliday's map of forest types has, for some years, been accepted as the standard natural vegetation map of Canada (Halliday, 1958). It was constructed in areas that are now under cultivation on the basis of remnants of the original vegetation that existed at the time of mapping. Over much of Canada, the natural vegetation has been only slightly changed by man, but in the area involved in this study, man has been an ecological factor of importance. Patches of aspen cannot everywhere be taken as evidence of a former widespread aspen cover. Some tree species, specially aspen, have invaded areas where they did not exist before the advent of white settlement. However the natural vegetation zones were not static in pre-white settlement times. Aspen was invading grassland areas and spruce was invading parts of the aspen-grove country (Löve, 1959). Nevertheless, cultivation has removed grass competition and prepared a seed bed allowing aspen to invade areas formerly far beyond its range. Furthermore, so much of the natural vegetation has been removed by man that it is difficult to determine boundaries between associations on the basis of remnant patches of the original cover.

Except for a small part of southern Manitoba, the land was surveyed before white settlement took place in the Canadian West, mainly in the 1870's and 1880's. The land surveyors not only laid out the cadastral grid, but also described natural features that would aid prospective settlers. It is largely on such descriptions that this natural vegetation map is based.

The descriptions of vegetation in the townships vary in quality and detail with the various reports, but do contain much valuable information.

The surveys of the Canadian West were of the township and range variety, that is, a grid of townships was laid out east and west from fixed meridians called principal or initial meridians. Each township was laid out 6 miles on a side except where convergence of meridians narrowed the boundaries. Generally speaking, therefore, each contained 36 one-square-mile sections. As well as laying out the township grid, the surveyors described the following features in each township.

1. The vegetation visible from the boundaries of the township, plus any conspicuous feature within the township that required special investigation.
2. Surface water such as creeks, sloughs, etc.
3. Soil texture determinable by quick reconnaissance.
4. Slope conditions.

Some surveyors made mention of trappers' or hunters' trails, the presence of squatters, and included comments on wildlife. Because most surveyors were not conversant with botanical classification, the value of their descriptions is limited when used as a basis for a natural vegetation map. Among these limitations, the following are the most important:

1. Great variation in the quality of the descriptions.
2. Lack of conformity in the use of descriptive terms, especially vegetation terms.
3. No identification of grass and forb species.

Despite the variable quality in descriptions of the vegetation, it has been possible to verify this information by comparing the descriptions of the borders of adjacent townships. As each field party surveyed a strip of townships it has been possible to supplement inadequately reported information.

Some vegetation terms used by the surveyors were ambiguous; such terms as "bush" or "brush" had more than one meaning. However, once a vegetation pattern developed on the map, the meaning usually could be determined.

Within the grasslands, the surveyors frequently overstressed the infrequent trees that occurred along water courses but did not differentiate between grass and forb species. Accordingly, the reports are not satisfactory for plotting the distribution of various grassland associations, such as the short-grass prairie, and mixed-grass prairie. Some surveyors did mention grass height and the presence of certain drought-resistant species such as cactus and sagebrush, but not enough of this type of information was recorded.

Surveyors' reports for some of the northern parts of the area were not available, and accordingly a second source of information was used to fill these gaps. These were the Land Classification Surveys of the Department of the Interior completed between 1900 and 1925, with very detailed township maps in color at a scale of 40 chains to the inch. The maps portray details of land use, conditions of drainage, and natural vegetation. In each township mapped, enough of the natural vegetation is shown to classify the township or parts of it into broad natural vegetation types. Quite large sections of the mixed-wood, aspen grove boundary were mapped from this source.

The land surveys were of little help in mapping the boundary between short-grass prairie and mixed-grass prairie because no differentiation of species was made. This vegetation boundary was therefore derived from the work of more recent investigators, notably officers of the Swift Current Agricultural Station of the federal Department of Agriculture, who mapped the distribution of the short-grass prairie in great detail (Clarke *and others*, 1947).

The Classification

The classification adopted in this work is similar to that of Halliday (1958), who, in turn, adapted the basic classification of Weaver and Clements (1929) to Canadian conditions.

This classification of natural vegetation areas has been developed in three stages. Primarily two broad formations are recognized in the southern Great Plains of Canada, the grasslands and the forests. Within each of these are several associations, or large areas of natural vegetation, each with a different set of dominant plants, and therefore presenting a characteristic appearance. It is these associations that appear on the vegetation map, and which in this report are called vegetation types. A type may be in any stage of climax development, and hence at any place the dominants of the climax may be absent. In theory of course the entire area under one type is progressing towards a common climax characterized by a given group of dominants.

Within each vegetation type, there are variations in cover created by differences in exposure, run-off, soil type, site, etc. These variations are called communities, and in theory, they too are all working towards the climax.

Essentially, the different vegetation types are the result of differences in macroclimate within the broad formations, and the different communities within each formation are due to local differences in site. The communities occupy only a few square feet and therefore cannot be mapped on the scale of this study. However, descriptions of the principal community types are presented.

The method used by the writer in mapping the natural vegetation was to categorize the descriptions taken from the sources available into one of a number of natural vegetation types recognized by Halliday and others in the Canadian West. Then, by means of colored area symbols, the types were recorded on a map of the townships of the Prairie Provinces at a scale of 1 inch to 35 miles.

The surveyors almost invariably recorded the tree species. The recognition of vegetation types from these descriptions required the use of indicator tree species. For example, the mention of white spruce mixed with aspen marked the occurrence of the mixed-wood vegetation type, and the mention of clumps of aspen in the grasslands marked the presence of the aspen-grove vegetation type.

The resultant map was a patchwork of different colored symbols on which the boundaries between vegetation types stood out clearly. From the colored work map, a final black and white map was prepared.

Because the source information was gathered prior to appreciable settlement it is felt that the map closely represents the pattern of "natural" vegetation. The boundaries between vegetation types in this mapping are considered to be more accurate than would be boundaries interpolated between remnants of the original vegetation remaining after extensive cultivation had begun.

Natural Vegetation of the Southern Great Plains

The area of Western Canada south and west of the boreal forest and east of the subalpine forest contains six clearly marked vegetation types: the true prairie, the mixed-grass prairie, the short-grass prairie, the submontane prairie, the aspen grove and outliers of the boreal forest.

Each of these natural vegetation types comprises a number of communities of plants that give distinctiveness to various sites; however, each vegetation type does possess a high degree of homogeneity which is essentially the result of a set of climatic conditions which reign throughout the area under that type.

The Grassland Formation

In the southern Great Plains within a semi-circle resting on the Canada-United States border, grass was the dominant cover prior to settlement. However, the vegetation cover was far from uniform within the grassland zone; it ranged from a lush cover, shoulder high, or higher, in the true prairie of southern Manitoba, to a sparse cover a few inches high in southwestern Saskatchewan and southeastern Alberta. These differences resulted from wide differences in climate.

The True Prairie

At the time of white settlement part of southern Manitoba was covered with tall grass; this area forms a northern extension of the prairie of the American midwest. The term 'true prairie' (Weaver 1954) as used in this study sets off this natural vegetation type from the grassland associations farther west.

The small portion of the 'true prairie' of the American midwest which lay within Canada occupied part of the heavy textured soils of the Lake Agassiz plain, and covered an area of some 2,500 square miles. It lay almost wholly west of the Red River, extended north to approximately the Assiniboine River, and west to the rising ground of the Manitoba escarpment.

The 'true prairie' of Manitoba was characterized by a covering of tall grasses, few shrubs and no trees except for those along river courses. The height of the grass cover sets this association apart from the other grasslands of the Canadian West. Many early explorers commented on the grass heights in this prairie. In Palliser (1863) the statement is found ". . . level plains with long rich grass, being an Ancient Lake Bottom".

Differences in drainage, height of water table, soil, and slope result in the development of different communities in this association. On the better drained soils of the Lake Agassiz plain, the big bluestem community is the most common. "Westward, big bluestem is the most important dominant of the grasslands which occupy the broad lowland valleys of Lake Winnipeg and the Red River . . ." (Weaver, 1954). The community is dominated by the single species big bluestem (*Andropogan gerardi*).* This plant is a sturdy grass reaching a height of from 5 to 8 feet. It represents one of the two most important species found in the true prairie of North America, and, along with little bluestem (*Andropogon scoparius*), comprises some 75 per cent of the plant cover of the association. The fibrous root development of big bluestem forms a dense mass from 5 to 8 feet deep. Pallister (1864) remarked, of the Agassiz plain "It is overlaid by a great thickness of vegetable mould, varying from two to four or even five feet in depth". The very deep root development indicates the favorable soil-moisture conditions which prevail where big bluestem is dominant. The soils, very rich in organic materials, form the basis of one of the richest agricultural areas in the Canadian West.

A number of grasses of lesser importance are associated with the dominant big bluestem. Among the more important of these are: Canadian wild rye or nodding wild rye (*Elymus canadensis*), northern wheat grass or blue joint (*Agropyron dasystachyum*), little bluestem, June grass (*Koeleria cristata*) and needle grass (*Stipa spartea*).

Associated with the grasses in this community are a number of forbs; chief amongst these are: the willow aster (*Aster praealtus*),

---

*Botanical nomenclature used in this work is after H. J. Scoggan, *Flora of Manitoba*, Bulletin 140, National Museum of Canada, Dept. of Northern Affairs and National Resources, 1957.

Canada anemone (*Anemone canadensis*), tall golden rod (*Solidago canadensis*), western red lily (*Lilium philadelphicum var. andium*), and wild prairie rose (*Rosa arkansana*).

The community under virgin conditions is said to have reached a height of close to 8 feet. Remnants of it along the roadsides in southern Manitoba reach shoulder high, and give some indication of the former landscape.

Much of the Lake Agassiz plain to the southwest of present-day Winnipeg was low and wet, with a dense, fine textured soil, supporting a slough grass community of the true prairie. The slough grass or cord grass (*Spartina pectinata*) is a tall marsh grass. It makes a much poorer hay than big bluestem, but in the early years of white settlement in the Red River valley, large quantities were cut in early summer for hay. Associated with the slough grass are a number of grasses of lesser importance, among which are switch grass (*Panicum virgatum*), Canada wild rye, cord grass (*Spartina gracilis*) and northern reed grass (*Calamagrostis inexpansa*). A number of forbs were also important such as tall golden rod and Baltic rush (*Juncus balticus*).

Intermediate between the well-drained sites of the big bluestem community and the very wet sites of the slough grass community, exist the moderately wet sites of the Agassiz plain. These areas support a growth 5 to 6 feet high at maturity which is dominated by switch grass and Canada wild rye. Weaver (1954) estimates that from 20 to 30 per cent of the Red River area was covered by this community. Associated with these grasses are the big bluestem and slough grass communities as well as a number of forbs common to the other two lowland communities.

On the higher, coarse-textured ground, along the front of the Manitoba escarpment, soil water is less abundant. On these sites upland communities of the true prairie develop, the most widespread being the needle grass community. It is a community of more drought-resisting grasses dominated by needle grass (*Stipa spartea*), a grass with foliage fifteen to thirty-six inches high; in this community it is associated with other stipa grasses, little bluestem, June grass, side oats gramma (*Bouteloua curtipendula*) and western wheat grass (*Agropyron smithii*). A number of forbs are associated with these grasses on the drier sites. Especially numerous in Manitoba are: lead plant (*Amorpha canescens*), stiff sunflower (*Helianthus laetiflorus*), smooth golden rod (*Solidago missouriensis*), silver-leaf psoralea (*Psoralea agrophylla*), western red lily and wild prairie rose.

Along the river courses, on the narrow valley slopes and flood-plains in the true prairie, ribbons of forest develop. The American white elm (*Ulmus americana*), in a natural state, is confined almost exclusively to the river valleys of the prairie, and is associated with a number of other trees which occur with approximately equal frequency, namely; Manitoba maple (*Acer negundo*), basswood or linden (*Tilia americana*) and green ash (*Fraxinus pennsylvanica var. subintegerrima*). Several varieties of willows commonly form a low thicket along the borders of the streams.

The Mixed-grass Prairie

In Manitoba, the prairie to the west of the first prairie level is the so-called mixed-grass prairie. The vegetation type forms a great arc from southern Manitoba through Saskatchewan and Alberta around the dry grasslands of southwestern Saskatchewan and southeastern Alberta. The mixed-grass prairie climax is the product of a dry climate intermediate between that of the short-grass and true prairie. This grassland consists of a mixture of short grasses from 6 to 18 inches high at maturity and mid-grasses with a height of 2 to 4 feet at maturity. The dominance of the mid-grasses gives this prairie a different appearance from that of the more sparse and shorter grass cover of the drier areas of southwestern Saskatchewan and Alberta.

Almost all the grasses of the short-grass prairie are present in this vegetation type, although they occupy much less of the cover. A few of these grass types are of a xeric nature not to be found in the mixed-grass prairie.

The common shrubs and forbs of the short-grass prairie such as pasture sage (*Artemisia frigida*), broomweed (*Gutierrezia diversifolia*), silver sage (*Eurotia lanata*), Nutall's atriplex (*Atriplex nuttallii*) and hoary sagebrush (*Artemisia cana*) are uncommon and are confined to very dry sites in the mixed-grass prairie. Furthermore, a number of grass species of the mixed-grass prairie are absent, or very rare, in the short-grass prairie. These include needle-grass, northern wheatgrass, awned wheatgrass (*Agropyron trachycaulum var. unilaterale*), rough fescue (*Festuca scabrella*), little bluestem and green needlegrass (*Stipa viridula*).

There is a wide variety in site conditions within the sandgrass (*Calamvilfa longifolia*) vegetation type, hence, a number of different communities are present. On upland areas with sandy loam soils speargrass and blue gramma grass (*Bouteloua gracilis*) are dominants, whereas on the clay loams of more restricted drainage, speargrass and western wheatgrass (*Agropyron smithii*) are the most important of the grasses. On heavy clay lowlands northern wheatgrass or blue joint alone is the dominant, and in places forms pure stands. The sandy soils usually develop a grass community dominated by speargrass and sandgrass. Certain areas with strongly alkaline soils support halophytic grasses such as alkali grass (*Districhlis stricta*), Nuttall's alkali grass (*Puccinellia nuttalliana*) and cordgrass.

A number of forbs achieve considerable importance. On well-drained sites the involute-leaved sedge (*Carex eleocharis*) and the sun-loving sedge (*Carex pennsylvanica var. digyna*) are the most abundant. On the lower, moister areas near sloughs, the sedges (*Carex atherodes*) and (*Carex rostrata*) are encountered. The Baltic rush frequently borders the sloughs.

Shrubs and low tree forms add variety to the mixed-grass prairie. Western snowberry (*Symphoricarpos occidentalis*) and several species of roses are common to upland sites. On porous soils, such as those of the great sandhills of Saskatchewan, the deep-rooted chokecherry create a cover up to 15 feet high. The low bush wolfwillow (*Elaeagnus commutata*) is found in areas near sloughs, frequently backed by a shrub-form of poplar (*Populus tremuloides*).

The mixed-grass prairie displays a rich and varied flora, but possesses a unity based on the dominance and height of the grasses.

The Short-grass Prairie

A rough triangle based on the Canadian-United States border and having its apex on the Alberta-Saskatchewan border outlines the short-grass prairie of Western Canada. This semi-arid grassland is sometimes wrongly referred to as the 'Palliser Triangle'. Palliser included much of the mixed-grass prairie in the area he considered ill-suited to cultivation.

This vegetation type is dominated by short-grass species, and the mid-grass species which do occur are considerably shorter than they are in the neighboring mixed-grass prairie. The most common grass is the blue gramma grass (*Bouteloua gracilis*), which, according to a study made at the Experimental Farm at Swift Current, Saskatchewan, occupies, on the average, some 37.8 per cent of the total cover (Clarke *and others*, 1947). Common speargrass, a mid-grass, is an important constituent of this plant association which includes western wheatgrass, northern wheatgrass and June grass. The short grasses, Sandberg's bluegrass (*Poa secunda*) and niggerwool (*Carex filifolia*) are also important species. Grasses dominate the vegetation type, and form some 82 per cent of the cover (Clarke *and others*, 1947).

The sages and other xeric plants which occur only on excessively dry sites in the mixed-grass prairie in this vegetation type, assume a role of much greater importance, and the common cactus (*Opuntia polyacantha*) occurs frequently. The sparseness and shortness of the vegetation cover and the occurrence of marked xerophytic species such as pasture sage and cactus was noted by many of the land surveyors operating in this area.

Clarke, Tisdale and Skoglund measured the proportion of cover contributed by various species in several hundred square metre quadrants. They found the most abundant species of grass to be blue gramma grass and common speargrass. Others found to be important are western wheatgrass, June grass, Sandberg's blue grass, and niggerwool. These six grasses comprised 80 per cent of the cover. The most common forbs are pasture sage and dwarf phlox (*Phlox hoodii*). This information was derived from measurement on various sites, and represents an average condition throughout the vegetation type. Variations in site cause a change in composition and one can recognize several communities within the vegetation type.

On shallow soils of eroded uplands, blue gramma grass is the dominant, and common speargrass is very rare. On the deeper upland soils with better soil moisture conditions, common speargrass is the dominant. The coulee bottoms are usually lined with willows, especially the sandbar willow (*Salix interior*), and cottonwood (*Populus deltoides*) is frequently scattered along the river valleys. In poorly drained meadows or around sloughs the spike rush (*Eleocharis palustris*) and Baltic rush abound.

Most of the species involved in this vegetation type are well adapted to the aridity of the area. The dominants are low-growing perennial grasses with extensive and finely branched root systems. Plants with more exposed perennial portions such as shrubs and bushes are normally confined to sites where soil moisture conditions are better than average.

The principal non-grass forms are low-growing perennial forbs and dwarf shrubs, most of which exhibit reduced leaf surfaces, abundance of epidermal hairs and other xeromorphic features.

The annual growth cycle of most of the grasses is well suited to the climatic conditions. Most of the species begin growth early in April and develop rapidly during the relatively favorable period, April, May and June. Plant development is, in most cases, complete by July 1st. The period of marked moisture deficiency is midsummer, and by this time the grass growth is largely completed.

The grasses dry or cure when soil moisture is exhausted, and the plant is essentially at rest so far as the production of new growth above the surface is concerned.

As demonstrated by A. H. Laycock (unpub. ms.), the short-grass prairie is an area of great variability in moisture conditions. In the past, series of moister than average years have led to incursions into the area by grain growers, with disastrous results when moisture conditions returned to normal or below normal. At present, the area is devoted largely to grazing and is most suited for that use.

The Submontane Mixed Prairie

This vegetation type occupies a narrow band along the foothills of the Rocky Mountains and also covers parts of the Cypress Hills and adjacent hill country. Its presence is a reflection of better soil-moisture conditions than are present in the mixed-grass prairie. These moisture conditions are associated with the lower evaporation rates due to the cooler summers of the higher areas and somewhat higher precipitation of the foothills and Cypress Hills.

The submontane mixed prairie is sometimes termed the festuca-danthonia association after the dominant grasses, rough fescue (*Festuca scabrella*), Idaho fescue (*Festuca idahoensis*), Parry's oatgrass (*Danthonia parryii*) and wild oatgrass (*Danthonia intermedia*). Associated with these grasses, June grass and awned wheatgrass occupy minor roles. Several other grasses occur but never in abundance; among these are: nodding wild rye (*Elymus canadensis*) and marsh reedgrass (*Calamagrostis canadensis*). Blue gramma grass and common speargrass, characteristic of the short-grass prairie, are not present.

The most abundant forb is the shrubby cinquefoil (*Potentilla fruiticosa*); this species is invariably present, and, in places, provides an almost complete ground cover.

Along the coulees and in minor draws on the north slopes of hills, aspen, willows and wild roses are often abundant.

The Aspen Grove and Aspen-oak Grove

These vegetation types form a transition between the treeless grasslands and the closed boreal forest and consist of grasslands dotted with clumps of trees. The trees are principally aspen (*Populus tremuloides*) over most of the zone; however, in the southeast, the bur oak (*Quercus macrocarpa*) becomes important along with aspen. For this reason, two vegetation types are recognized: the aspen grove and the aspen-oak grove. In the Canadian West the term parkland is used for the two types.

As these types are transitional between grassland and forest they possess characteristics similar to those of the boreal forest formation and of the grasslands. The strong summer water deficiency of the mixed-grass prairie and the short-grass prairie is apparent within the parkland. The soils are dark brown to black grassland types, and the area covered by grassland is greater than that covered by trees. Accordingly these vegetation types are included within the grassland formation.

This vegetation type consists of a mixture of grasses and copses or groves of trees. The most important tree is the trembling aspen (*Populus tremuloides*), which, in places, forms virtually pure stands. Towards the margins of the boreal forest, aspen occupies an increasingly larger part of the surface, until along the boreal margin the grassland openings become small and rare. Towards the prairie margins, the tree copses are small and widely scattered.

On the drier tree sites bur oak is associated with the aspen. In places, especially along the crests of ravines, steep river slopes and shale knolls, the oak is dominant. Examples of such areas are the steep slopes of the Pembina River valley in southern Manitoba and along the shaly hills of the Manitoba escarpment. This oak occurs occasionally on alluvial flats, and on these sites attains a height of nearly 70 feet and a diameter of 3 feet. Much more typical is the scrubby form of the more xeric sites. The tree is much sought for fence posts because of its great durability, and over much of its range its numbers have been greatly reduced.

Along stretches of alluvial soils where drainage is restricted, the white elm, basswood, green ash and Manitoba maple are associated with the poplar and oak. This river flat community is found throughout the association.

The regional atmospheric climate appears to be at a balance between grassland and forest tolerance, so that locally dry sites are in grasses and less well-drained places, if not saline, are occupied by a limited development of specific native trees.

Within the aspen-oak vegetation type, the sites which favor tree growth rather than prairie growth are as follows:

(a) sites of locally moist atmospheric conditions due to higher altitude resulting in lower summer temperatures and moisture effectiveness,

(b) sites of locally humid soils or soils with more than regionally normal moisture such as found in northeast exposures of hills, ravines and river flats,

(c) in snowtraps, such as depressions and ravines,

(d) in low spots in the prairie where run-off collects and where the water table is higher, and

(e) sandy areas with moist substrata.

The dry exposures of hills (i.e. south and west exposures), in areas of thin or eroded soils and highly alkaline areas, are normally in grass.

The Aspen Grove

This association is essentially the same as the aspen-oak grove vegetation type except for the absence of the bur oak. It consists of clumps of aspen scattered over the true prairie. The same site types as in the aspen-oak grove are conducive to tree growth.

The size of the aspen varies from the prairie margins to the boreal margins of the vegetation type. On the prairie side the normal grove consists of aspen a few inches in diameter and up to 12 feet high. The trees in these groves are virtually all young trees. This is a reflection of the high mortality rate of trees near the prairie margin. Doubtless drought is a major cause of tree death, but other factors play a role. Bird (1930) points out that at the peak of their cycle, rabbits kill thousands of young aspen by girdling them in winter.

The copses of young aspen frequently have an understorey of shrubby growth composed principally of snowberry (*Symphoricarpos albus*), hazelnut, chokecherry and wild roses.

Towards the boreal forest, the percentage of the total cover represented by aspen increases greatly. Over much of its northern margin, this vegetation type might well be described as aspen forest with prairie openings. Practically pure stands of aspen cover large stretches of the country. The trees attain a height of up to 55 feet and a diameter of about 18 inches at waist level; they tend to be very closely spaced and present a branchless trunk up to 30 feet or so.

The aspen has provided fuel and fencing over thousands of square miles of the Canadian West. The species is not well suited for either purpose, but in the absence of other species has been a great boon to the prairie settler. A few good copses of aspen on a section of land made it preferred land for settlers.

An understorey of low bushes 4 to 5 feet high normally is associated with the aspen on the boreal margin of the association. The chief species involved in this understorey are: hazelnut (*red-osier*), dogwood (*Cornus stolenifera*), high-bush cranberry (*Viburnum trilobum*), roses, chokecherry, and snowberry.

Numerous herbs also occur in the understorey, principal among them being: sarsaparilla (*Aralia nudicaulis*), wintergreen (*Pyrola asarifolia*), mayflower (*Maianthemum canadense*), Solomon's seal (*Smilacina stellata*) and strawberry (*Fragaria virginiana*).

The prairie openings are usually classified as communities of the true prairie, and the chief dominants are the wheatgrasses (*Agropyron sp.*). However, others are important, principally speargrass and June grass. On some of the drier sites of Saskatchewan and Alberta, blue gramma grass is a dominant.

The Forest Formation

A number of forest types border the areas with which this study deals, or form fingers penetrating the area, or isolated forest islands within it. These forest types are: the mixedwood forest, Manitoba lowlands forest and the subalpine forest. This division of the forest is after Halliday, who divides the forest into types based on a broad uniformity of composition within each type. This does not mean that differences in site within a forest type do not involve a difference in vegetation, but on the same site type within any one class, the same vegetation response is normally apparent. Halliday recognizes several forest regions within the forest formations of Canada. Within each of these he normally discerns several forest types which may be termed associations according to the definition of the term used in this study. The forest region is a useful classification for describing the forests of Canada, but for limited areas it is a complicating factor, so in this paper the breakdown used for glasslands will be used, i.e. the formation (forest) within which a number of vegetation types or associations are recognized.

The Mixedwood Forest

In general, the mixedwood forest forms the northern boundary of the area studied. However, on higher areas, such as Riding Mountain, it penetrates far south into the prairies and aspen parkland. The occurrence of the mixedwood forest far south of the main belt is due to higher elevations which duplicate the climatic conditions along the northern margins of the parkland.

The mixedwood forest derives its name from the fact that it is composed of a mixture of coniferous and deciduous species. The two dominants are representatives of two tree types; white spruce (*Picae glauca*) and aspen (*Populus tremuloides*). Other tree species of importance are balm of Gilead or balsam poplar (*Populus balsamifera*), paper birch (*Betula papyrifera*), balsam fir (*Abies balsamea*), jackpine (*Pinus banksiana*), black spruce (*Picea mariana*) and tamarack (*Larix laricina*). It is the presence of the coniferous element which sharply distinguishes this forest type from the parkland.

Within this vegetation type, a number of communities have developed. Over much of the area repeated fire makes any discussion of climax communities a problem, but sufficient untouched forest remains to describe the communities.

On porous soils only two species, jackpine and white spruce, contribute significantly to the tree cover. The aspen, paper birch and black spruce, are poorly adapted to droughty sites and fir, balsam poplar and tamarack are entirely unsuited and never appear. Jackpine on sandy soils is frequently the dominant, and this is the only site where it assumes any great importance.

Along the southern margins of the mixedwood, the white spruce competes with prairie grasses on the sandy soils of kames, eskers, old beach ridges and deltaic deposits. The jackpine, although assuming importance within the mixedwood on sandy soils, very rarely is able to invade prairie openings on sandy soils along the southern margin of the mixedwood. Frequently single white spruce of considerable age are found in the prairie openings; these represent invasions of the grassland in wetter years. The seeds of these trees, however, were unable to germinate in normal or drier than normal years.

On deep, comparatively warm soils, the aspen is frequently dominant, and is normally associated with white spruce, balsam poplar, and birch. The aspen is a prolific producer of light airborne seed, and, sence, rapidly invades fire-cleared areas of deep, warm soils. The species, because of its pioneering ability after fire, is often called the fire tree. It matures very rapidly, and, in the mixedwood, reaches a height of close to 100 feet and attains a diameter of some 20 inches at waist height. On these areas white spruce and other important trees of the community rarely pioneer a site. They are preceded by aspen and less frequently birch. The mixedwood has suffered so severely from fire that many of the upland sites are clothed in the pioneer aspen. Frequently it may be observed, however, that young white spruce are coming up under the aspen crown, and if undisturbed by fire will become an important element in the cover, even achieving a role of dominance. On well-drained sites, the white spruce of the mixedwood reaches merchantable timber size. Heights up to 125 feet are common and diameters of 18 to 35 inches at waist height are attained.

The moderately dry sites are clothed in a poplar, white spruce, jackpine community. Jackpine is usually a lesser dominant.

Wet organic soils usually have a sphagnum, black spruce, tama-rack community. The typical bog is a sphagnum bog with an inner rim of tamarack and an outer rim of black spruce. Both tamarack and black spruce are moisture-loving species, and are very tolerant to acid organic soils.

On very moist mineral soils, such as are found on flood-plains of rivers, the balsam poplar may form pure stands.

Manitoba Lowlands Forest

This forest type occupies the eastern part of the Lake Agassiz plain, and forms the eastern boundary of the area under study. The plain has a gradual slope towards the northeast, and is crossed by low ridges at right angles to the northeast slope. Hence the surface is characterized by low parallel gravelly ridges with swampy depres-sions between. The general levelness of the Agassiz plain and the thinness of the lake deposits over the bedrock in its eastern section makes for poor soil drainage except on the gravel ridges.

Two communities repeat themselves over and over again across this plain. The depressions are characterized by sphagnum bogs rimmed with tamarack and black spruce, and the gravelly ridges have a community dominated by jackpine. In the south, a few bur oak may be associated with the jackpine and in southeastern Mani-toba an area of sand hills is clothed in almost pure stands of jack-pine. Within this area, the sandilands forest reserve, black spruce, tamarack and poplar occupy some wetter depressions. Also in the area are a few scattered red pine or Norway pine (*Pinus resinosa*). These occurrences mark the westward limit of this species.

The alluvial soils along the rivers, especially in the south, have good stands of aspen and balsam poplar.

The Subalpine Forest

In the foothills of Alberta and forming the western boundary of the area under study lies the subalpine forest. In places, this forest type joins the prairie directly, but normally a narrow zone of park-land clothes the middle altitudes of the foothills and separates it from the prairie. The subalpine forest commences at approximately 4,000 feet and reaches its upper limit at the tree line. Small outliers of this forest type exist in the higher sections of the Cypress Hills.

The dominant trees are lodgepole pine (*Pinus contorta*) and Engelmann spruce (*Picea Engelmanni*). Large sections have been burned and these are usually occupied by lodgepole pine almost exclusively.

In parts of the foothills of southern Alberta, some blue Douglas fir (*Psendotsuga taxifolia*) is associated with Engelmann spruce, and, towards the upper limits of the forest type, alpine fir (*Abies lasiocarpa*) and white-bark pine (*Pinus albicauli*) become associated. The Forestry Branch of the Department of Northern Affairs and National Resources recognizes this later association as a distinct forest type, the Douglas fir and lodgepole pine section of the montane forest region.

Summary

The foregoing descriptions of the natural vegetation types of the southern Great Plains of Canada were prepared on the basis of observations which took place over several years and from the extensive literature on the flora of the area.

The map of natural vegetation types was constructed, in large part, on the basis of verbal descriptions of the plant cover found in the reports of the original land surveyors. Further vegetation information was extracted from the maps of the land classification surveys. The information gained from the land surveyors' reports was gathered before white settlement greatly disturbed the natural flora. In those areas where the land classification maps were the chief source of information, only a small percentage of the areas had been ploughed. Since the precise ecological role of the North American Indian is impossible to determine, the patterns portrayed on the map are as close to undisturbed or natural patterns as is practicable.

Bibliography

Bird, R. D., "Biotic communities of the aspen parkland of central Canada", *Ecology*, Vol. II (1930), p. 397.
Canada, Department of the Interior, Description of the Province of Manitoba, Ottawa (1893). Descriptions of the Townships of the North-West Territories . . . between the Second and Third Initial Meridians, Ottawa (1886). Descriptions of the Townships of the North-West Territories . . . between the Third and Fourth Initial Meridians, Ottawa. Descriptions of the Townships of the North-West Territories . . . west of the Fourth and Fifth Initial Meridians, Ottawa. Descriptions of the Surveyed Townships in the Peace River District in the provinces of Alberta and British Columbia, Ottawa (1913). Abstracts from the Reports on the Townships west of the Fifth and Sixth Initial Meridians for 1912, 1913, 1914, 1915, 1916 and 1917, Ottawa (n.d.).
Clarke, S. E., and others, "The effects of climate and grazing practices in the short-grass prairie vegetation of southern Manitoba and south-western Saskatchewan, Canada, *Dept. Agric.*, Experimental Farms Serv., Publ. No. 747, Tech. Bull. No. 46 (1947).
Halliday, W. E. D., "A forest classification for Canada", Canada, *Dept. Northern Affairs and National Res.*, Forestry Br., Forest Res. Divn., Forestry Br. Bull. 89, Ottawa (1937) 1958.
Laycock, A. H., "Study of moisture conditions in the Western Provinces", Unpublished ms.
Love, Doris, "The postglacial development of the flora of Manitoba: a discussion", *Can. J. Bot.*, Vol. XXXVII, No. 4 (1959), pp. 547-85.

Palliser, John, "The Journals", Detailed Reports and Observations Relative to the Exploration by Captain John Palliser . . . during the Years 1857, 1858, 1859, 1860, London (1863).

Weaver, J. E. and Clements, F. E., *Plant ecology*, McGraw-Hill, New York (1929). *The North American prairie*, Johnsen Publishing Co., Lincoln, Nebraska (1954).

6

The Soils of Canada from a Pedological Viewpoint

A. Leahey

The word "soil" has been defined in many ways and it is being used with different meanings. The simplest definition from an agricultural viewpoint is that soil is the natural medium for the growth of land plants. From a pedological viewpoint, however, a more adequate definition is that soil is the collection of natural bodies on the earth's surface supporting or capable of supporting plants. These natural bodies may be divided into mineral or organic soils but in this paper attention will be focused almost entirely on mineral soils.

Soils have length, breadth and depth; that is, they are three dimensional bodies. Their upper limit is usually air but may be water. At the lateral margins, each soil may end abruptly but is more likely to grade into other soils, bare rock or deep water. The lower limit is the most difficult to define. One concept is that soil has a thickness determined by the depth of rooting plants. Another concept is that soil depth should be restricted to the thickness of the solum. While there are theoretical justifications for these concepts, neither is satisfactory for the mapping and classification of soils. In Canada the lower limit is usually considered for classification purposes to be about four feet.

Soils have morphological features that have developed during and by the process of soil formation. These morphological features are expressed by soil horizons which have been designated by the letters A, B and C. The A and B horizons are a reflection of the genetic forces operating on the mineral parent material; together they constitute the solum. No simple definition of the A and B horizons is possible since there are many different kinds of both horizons even in one soil. The A horizons contain most of the organic matter

Reprinted from "Soils in Canada: Geological, Pedological and Engineering Studies", *The Royal Society of Canada Special Publication No. 3*, ed. R. F. Legget (University of Toronto Press, 1961). Revised October 1968 by W. A. Ehrlich, Pedology Research Coordinator, Canada Department of Agriculture.

deposited by plants and most of the micro-organisms; they have been subject to the greatest amount of weathering and leaching of the mineral matter. The B horizons, lying immediately below the A horizons, contain most of the material leached from the A horizons and have other changes brought about by weathering and pedogenesis. The C horizons represent the relatively unweathered underlying geological deposits and are usually the parent materials of the overying sola. The C horizons have been modified to some small extent by biological activity and by receiving some mineral material, usually easily soluble-salts, leached from the A and B horizons. Soils vary widely in the nature of all these principal horizons and in the degree of expression and thickness of the A and B horizons. The depth to which soils are examined in the field nearly always includes at least the upper part of the C horizon. Thus, soil descriptions usually contain a description of the upper portion of the geological deposit or parent material of the soil.

Knowledge of Canadian soils comes largely from the work of the soil surveys which are carried out co-operatively by the Canadian Department of Agriculture, the colleges of agriculture, the provincial departments of agriculture and provincial research councils. These surveys are charged with the task of mapping, describing and classifying the soils in the agricultural and potentially agricultural regions of Canada. Since these surveys are carried out primarily for agricultural purposes, interpretation of the soils information obtained is, naturally, from an agricultural viewpoint. Experience has shown, however, that the basic information provided by the soil surveys can be used, if properly interpreted, for many other purposes.

The literature on Canadian soils is too voluminous for even brief review here. Three sources of information which are perhaps of most direct concern to geologists and engineers may usefully be mentioned. These are: (1) The soil survey reports and maps of the reconnaissance surveys: to date maps covering about 200,000,000 acres have been published so that soil information is available for most of our settled areas and for a considerable portion of the fringe areas. (2) The March-April 1960 issue of the *Agricultural Institute Review*: this issue, entitled "A Look at Canadian Soils," is devoted to papers that present a broad picture of the soils in the various physiographic regions of Canada and their classification. (3) A paper by H. C. Moss entitled "Modern Soil Science (Pedology) in Relation to Geological and Allied Science" in the *Transactions of the Royal Society of Canada, Volume* LIII; *Series III: June 1959*. Soil mapping and classification is not a static field of investigation.

This natural body known to the pedologist as soil is a mysterious body in many ways. Concepts are developed as to its origin, the significance of its morphological, chemical, physical and biological properties and its behaviour under treatments imposed by man. These concepts are limited by the sphere of knowledge at any one time and consequently, as the body of pertinent knowledge increases, concepts change. This gradual evolution of ideas affects the whole field of work generally included in the term soil survey. Thus the early soil survey publications differ markedly from those issued today as a result of evolving concepts of soil genesis and classification, accompanied by changes in terminology.

Soil Formation

The nature and distribution of Canadian soils is the result of many soil-forming factors. Some consideration of these factors is presented here as background information and to illustrate the pedological viewpoint on soils. The main natural soil-forming factors are the mineral parent material, the climate, vegetation, drainage conditions and time. Soil genesis can be viewed as consisting of two steps; (a) the accumulation of parent materials and (b) the differentiation of horizons in the profile. Climate and vegetation may be considered as the main active forces in soil formation, but their effect is conditioned by the nature of the mineral material, the moisture status, and the length of time they have been at work.

Horizon differentiation in the mineral parent material is brought about by the weathering of minerals, the accumulation and assimilation of organic matter, removal out of and transfers and transformations within the soil system, and the development of structure. While the imprint of the original parent material is clearly evident in soils, the processes of soil development have in most cases produced great changes in both chemical and physical properties. Thus the various horizons of the soil may have markedly different properties from each other and from the parent material.

Parent materials

The geological nature of soils certainly receives as much attention today as it did a half century ago when scientists thought of soil as disintegrated rock mixed with some decaying organic matter. The significance of the geological nature of soils is clearly shown by the system used in classifying the individual soils in soil survey reports. While the pedologist is mainly concerned with the geology of the upper few feet of the regolith, sometimes he must examine deeper layers and even the bedrock in seeking answers to his problems.

A large number of factors that affect the properties, classification, use and management of soils are directly related to the geology of the parent material. Some of these are particle size, degree of sorting, chemical composition and nature of the soil minerals, kind and quantity of salts, permeability and drainage, land form and topography. Hence the pedologist must be concerned with both the mineralogical nature and the mode of accumulation of the regolith. He is also concerned with the interrelations of the parent material with other soil forming factors.

Climate

In Canada, climate has both direct and indirect effects on soil formation. The indirect effect of climate which is exerted through its influence on vegetation is, with one exception, more conspicuous than its direct effect. The exception is the occurrence of permafrost which severely restricts the operation of normal soil-forming processes. The direct effect of climate has not been the subject of adequate research in this country. Certainly it would appear that the depth to which Canadian soils are leached is a function of the effective precipitation. It would also appear that climate is responsible for the geographic distribution of Dystric Brunisol (Acid Brown Wooded) soils in relation to Podzols, the occurrence of secondary podzolization in the Gray Wooded and Gray Brown Luvisol soils, and for the unique character of a group of soils on the west coast.

Vegetation

The three great vegetative regions of Canada are the grasslands in the western provinces, the forest region which covers vast areas from coast to coast and which extends well into the permafrost regions, and the tundra. The heath-covered parts of Newfoundland can be considered as a fourth vegetative region. Outside permafrost regions, these kinds of vegetation produce major differences in soils, differences which greatly affect soil classification. The effect of trees rather than tundra vegetation on soils with permafrost is however rather obscure, since present scanty knowledge indicates that the characteristics of the wooded soils with permafrost are similar to those of the tundra.

Drainage

The full effect of climate and vegetation on soil formation can only be clearly expressed on reasonably permeable parent material which can absorb the precipitation it receives without becoming water-logged. If the topography is rolling, run-off may occur and collect in the low places. In such instances, the upper part of the slopes may be more arid and the low places much wetter than is normal for the region. This results in thin sola on the drier slopes and soils developed under wet conditions in the low places. In humid regions, if the topography is level and the parent materials only slowly permeable, soils also develop under wet conditions which result in the formation of quite different soils from the well-drained soils of the regions.

Time

Soils, being dynamic bodies, progress from youth through maturity to old age. Although these stages of soil development are not entirely related to the length of time during which the genetic forces have been at work, yet it does take time for such forces to show their effect on soils. In terms of years none of the Canadian soils is very old, all of them dating from the last ice age and some of them being much younger. This youthfulness in point of years no doubt accounts for the fact that the solum of Canadian soils is thinner and less weathered than in many other countries of the world. Despite their comparative youth, many have reached a mature state of development.

Soil Classification

Soils may be classified in many ways depending on the purpose of the grouping. The pedologist must however base his classification on those features that he can observe in the soil profiles, including the mineral parent material. Furthermore, apart from the basic units of soil classification, he must be selective in the features he uses for classification purposes in order that he may be able to group soils at progressively higher levels of abstraction. In Canada, morphological features which are largely a reflection of the effects of climate, vegetation, local moisture relations and age have been selected for these higher groupings, although parent material does play a part in many instances. In other words, although soil classification in Canada is based on morphological features, concepts of soil genesis affect the selection of criteria used for the higher groupings.

Since the soil surveyor is concerned with the mapping of soils at various scales and at different levels of abstraction, as well as the grouping of soils on the basis of common or similar profile characteristics, two kinds of classification systems are used in Canada. One of these may be referred to as a mapping or geographic classification and the other a taxonomic classification. Since soils which are closely associated geographically may differ markedly in their morphological characteristics, it has not been found possible to devise one system for both purposes.

National Taxonomic System of Soil Classification

Although taxonomic groupings were in use in some provinces as far back as 1927, it was not until 1955 that the National Soil Survey Committee first proposed a national system. This proposal has been studied across Canada since then. In February 1960 the soil survey organizations accepted for official usage a revised system based on the principles established in 1955. This new national system does not as yet appear in any of the soil survey publications but it will be used in the future. Since most of the terminology and definitions now in use have been retained in the new system, those familiar with the classification followed in modern soil survey reports should have no particular difficulty in understanding it.

The taxonomic system places soils in categories at different levels of generalization on the basis of their internal characteristics. Six categories are used. These are:

Category 1: *The soil type*: this is a sub-division of the soil series based on the texture of the surface soil; hence its retention in the classification system as the lowest category is perhaps more a matter of traditional use than logic.

Category 2: *The soil series*: this is the basic unit of classification in the system since it is the natural body in the definition of soil from a pedologist's viewpoint; the series in some soil survey reports is named a "member" or an "associate."

Category 3: *The soil family*: this is a grouping of series belonging to the same subgroup on the basis of some important characteristics in the parent material; this category has not as yet been widely used in Canada.

Category 4: *The subgroup*: the subgroup is analogous with the types of profiles long recognized in Canada.

Category 5: *The great group*: this is a grouping of the subgroups on the basis of profile similarities.

Category 6: *The order*: the great groups are organized into orders on the basis of major profile similarities.

This taxonomic system will permit the study of soils at various levels of abstraction. This is shown by the fact that the large number of soil series identified in Canada to date—some 3,000—can be placed in about 156 subgroups, 22 great groups and 8 orders.

A brief description here of the eight orders and the names of the great groups may serve to show the principles on which this system of classification is based.

Chernozemic Order

Most of the soils in the grassland and park areas of western Canada are placed in this order. These soils have dark-coloured mineral-organic surface horizons and brownish, usually prismatic, subsurface and usually non-saline horizons lying on calcareous parent material. They are well saturated with bases. The sola are well drained and free of soluble salts. The order includes four great groups, the Brown, Dark Brown, Black and Dark Gray. The division into great groups is based largely on the colour of the surface soil which is a reflection of the climate and vegetation under which these soils have developed.

Solonetzic Order

The soils in this order have developed from saline parent material or under the influence of saline waters. They occur dominantly in the grassland areas of western Canada but extend into the forested regions. The dominant influence in the formation of the solonetzic soils has been the parent material. The chief characteristic of this order is the presence of a tough, finely textured B horizon which usually breaks into column-like structures or blocky aggregates that have surface coatings of organic matter. Two great groups have been recognized; the Solonetz and the Solod.

Descriptions of the Orders on Luvisolic, Podzolic, Brunisolic and Organic

Luvisolic Order

Most of the soils in this order occur west of Lake Superior. They have developed from high base status materials under forest and are characterized by an impoverished gray layer near or at the surface of the mineral soil which is underlain by a darker subsurface horizon enriched with clay. Two great groups are placed in this order: the Gray Brown Luvisol (Gray Brown Podzolic) and the Gray Wooded soils.

Podzolic Order

These soils are most common to forested areas in the Canadian Shield. They, like the Luvisolic soils, have a gray layer near or at the surface of the mineral soil but instead of an enrichment of clay in the subsurface horizon have an accumulation of organic matter and sesquioxides. This order includes three great groups: the Humic Podzol, the Ferro-Humic Podzol and the Humo-Ferric Podzol.

Brunisolic Order

For reasons associated with climate, with parent material or with age, a number of well-drained soils in the forest region do not have the leached gray horizon or the enriched subsurface horizon of the Luvisolic and Podzolic soils. The sola of these soils are dominantly brown and hence they are referred to as "Brunisolic" soils. Four great groups have been recognized: the Melanic Brunisol (Brown Forest) and Eutric Brunisol (Brown Wooded) on calcareous parent material with high base status; the Sombric Brunisol (Acid Brown Forest) and Dystric Brunisol (Acid Brown Wooded) on non-calcareous parent material with low base status. These great groups are considered to be in a youthful state of development.

Regosolic Order

A number of well-drained soils occur in Canada which lack any noticeable horizon development except, in some cases, a mineral-organic layer at the surface. Essentially these soils are composed of only slightly modified mineral parent material and this fact is indicated by the name Regosolic. There is little basis for dividing these soils into great groups as there has been little or no genetic development. Only one great group has been established.

Gleysolic Order

This order includes the poorly drained soils in which normal processes of development have been restricted. The excessive water and lack of aeration have established reducing conditions which are indicated by dull-coloured and mottled subsoils. Unlike the soils mentioned in previous orders, the Gleysolic soils may differ markedly in their profile characteristics. These have been used in setting up three great groups: the Humic Gleysols which have dark coloured mineral-organic surface horizons; the Eluviated Gleysols which have podzolic features; and the Gleysols which are in effect just wet Regosols.

Organic Order

The soils of this order occur widespread in the forested and tundra regions and occupy approximately 300 million acres in Canada. These soils developed under wet conditions and have an organic layer of a certain thickness that contains 30 or more per cent of organic matter. Three great groups, namely: Fibrisol, Mesisol and Humisol, have been established on the basis of degree of decomposition of the organic materials.

Mapping or Geographic Classification

Although the effect of climate and vegetation on soils may be fairly uniform over broad areas, local differences in parent materials and drainage have resulted in the formation of different soils closely associated geographically. Hence soil series often occur in such small areas that they cannot be used as mapping units except on very large scale maps. It is then often desirable to group soils for generalized soil maps. For these reasons, the mapping units may range from a subdivision of a series to groups of series, depending on the scale of the map and the complexity of the soil pattern.

Three terms are commonly used in Canada for the geographic grouping of soils: (1) The catena: This term is applied to the range of soils produced under different moisture relationships on the same parent material within a common climatic and vegetative region. (2) Soil complex: This term is used to designate mixed areas of soils derived from different parent materials. (3) Soil zone: This term is used for a broad geographic grouping of soils on the dominant occurrence of one great group. The boundaries and extent of the zone are largely determined by soil characteristics which can be correlated with climate and natural vegetation. Hence the zone coincides closely with major climatic and vegetative regions. From soil zone maps which have been published, it is obvious, however, that there is also a close relation between the major physiographic regions and soil zones. Soil zone boundaries do not cross major physiographic boundaries, although several soil zones may occur within one major physiographic division.

Pedologists as yet do not know enough about all the unsettled parts of Canada to divide the entire country into soil zones. Those parts not covered by soil zones may be referred to as soil regions, based on the physiography and such knowledge as is available about the soils. Most of the Canadian Shield, most of the Cordillera and the regions north of the southern limits of permafrost are referred to as soil regions.

The largest-scale map published which shows the soil zones and regions in Canada is the generalized soil map in the Atlas of Canada on a scale of 1 to 10,000,000. A soil map of Canada in a scale of 1:5,000,000 is being prepared and will be available late in 1969. More detailed information can be found in publications issued by the different soil survey organizations in Canada. In the sketch map in this paper (Figure 1), eight major soil zones and three regions are shown. Chernozemic soils are dominant in three zones, Podzolic and Luvisolic soils in three; one zone has Brunisolic soils dominant and the remaining zone has Gleysolic soils.

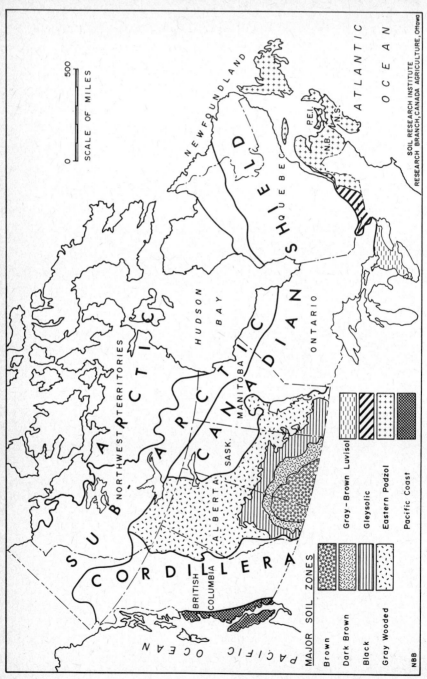

Figure 1. Major soil zones and regions of Canada.

The Chernozemic soil zones cover the grassland soils in the Prairie Provinces. The Brown soil zone lies in the most arid section, the Black soil zone in the most humid section with the Dark Brown soil zone lying between. Solonetzic soils occupy large acreages in these three zones and are in fact the dominant soils in many places. Humic Gleysol are also of common occurrence on the wetter sites.

The three zones in which Luvisolic soils are dominant are the Gray Wooded zone which covers the forested parts of the Great Plains south of the permafrost line, the Gray Brown Luvisolic zone in the Great Lakes region in southern Ontario and the Eastern Podzol zone which coincides with the Appalachian region. The predominant kind of soil in each of these zones is, of course, the great group after which they have been named. Locally, however, other soils may be dominant. In the Gray Wooded zone organic soils, commonly referred to as muskeg, cover large acreages. Other soils of significance in various parts of the zone are Gleysolic and Regosolic soils, Podzols and Black soils. The Gray Brown Luvisol zone has a common pattern of Gray Brown Luvisol soils on the well and imperfectly drained sites and Humic Gleysol soils on the poorly drained sites. Other soils of importance in some areas are Podzol, Melanic Brunisol, Regosol and Organic soils. In the Eastern Podzol zone, the main soil pattern is formed by Podzols on the better drained sites and Gleysols or Eluviated Gleysols in the poorly drained sites. Humic Podzols are of widespread occurrence in Newfoundland and occur to some extent in Nova Scotia and New Brunswick. Organic soils also occupy considerable acreages, particularly in Newfoundland.

The St. Lawrence Lowland is a zone in which Humic Gleysol soils are dominant, especially on the wide-spread fine-textured deposits. Other mineral soils which occur on moderately to well-drained sites are the Podzol, Melanic Brunisol and, to a lesser extent, Gray Brown Luvisol, Gray Wooded and Dystric Brunisol. Organic soils are of common occurrence in some localities.

The West Coast, which is characterized by mild wet winters and cool dry summers, is a zone in which Brunisolic soils (Dystric Brunisol or, to a lesser extent, Sombic Brunisol soils) are dominant. Regosols together with Organic soils are of particular importance on alluvial flood plains and deltas.

Surveys carried out to date in the areas designated as soil regions indicate that it will be possible to subdivide regions into zones when the pedologists are able to make enough observations. Many parts of these regions are exceedingly difficult to explore and it will no doubt take years to collect the necessary information. Tentative zones for parts of these regions have been shown on the atlas maps for Canada and for British Columbia. In this paper, however, these subdivisions will not be discussed.

The Canadian Shield soil region is, on the whole and as far as is known at present, dominated by Podzols interspersed with Organic soils and bare rock. In its southern fringe however the Dystric Brunisol great soil group is the main type. Several large bodies of calcareous deposits in lacustrine basins occur in this region. On these, Gray Wooded soils associated with Organic soils and to a lesser extent with Gleysolic soils form the soil pattern.

The Cordillera is a very complex region from the viewpoint of soils, due to the extreme variations in soil-forming factors which occur within short distances. Both horizontal and vertical zoning occurs. In the drier sections Chernozenic, Brunisolic (especially Eutric Brunisol), and Gray Wooded soils are dominant, while in the wetter and cooler areas Podzols and Alpine soils occur. There is also, of course, a large amount of rock and rock rubble. Organic soils are of small extent, no doubt on account of the topography.

That part of Canada in which the subsoils are permanently frozen has been divided into two regions on the basis of vegetative cover, namely the Subarctic region with forest vegetation and the Arctic with tundra vegetation. The pattern of mineral soil development in both regions is similar, in that profile development has been hindered by the presence of permafrost. There has been a little more development in the soils of the Subarctic than in those of the Arctic. Although only a few of these soils have been examined, it would seem that the mineral soils could be classified into the Brunisolic, Gleysolic and Regosolic orders, depending on their drainage and degree of development. Perhaps the greatest contrast between these two regions lies in the fact that organic soils are much more prevalent in the Subarctic region. The landscapes and nature of the surficial deposits of both regions of course vary greatly between the major physiographic regions.

7

Concepts of Soil Formation and Classification in Arctic Regions

J. C. F. Tedrow and J. C. Cantlon

Introduction

Some eighty years ago, when Dokuchaev (Margulis, 1954) distinguished five natural soil zones—tundra, podzol, chernozem, desert, and laterite—the stage was set for a systematic study of soils as naturally occurring bodies. Of these, the tundra has received by far the least attention. European investigators, notably the Russians, have made many studies of the northern regions but in North America few reports of scientific studies in the Arctic have been made by trained soil scientists. In this paper some relationships of soil-forming processes operating in the various northern regions, especially in connection with the podzolic and the so-called tundra processes, are presented; and some problems in connection with vegetation-soil relationships and the classification and mapping of soils are outlined.

In the formation of soil the most important factors that have to be taken into consideration are climate, parent material, biotic elements, relief, and time. The interaction of these five factors, operating at different intensities will produce soils with different properties. Given sufficient time, adequate drainage and depth of mineral material on the more level, stable landforms, a mature or zonal soil will tend to form. In the tropics the zonal soils will have a reddish appearance, in the prairie a dark brown to black, whereas in the northern forested regions the upper mineral horizons will have a bleached appearance. Distinct as these zonal soils are, they have at least one important feature in common, that is, they form under conditions of adequate drainage. Tundra soils, however, form under conditions of poor drainage and it may be somewhat fallacious to speak of them in terms of zonal soils as is done with podzols and chernozems.

Reprinted from *Arctic,* Vol. 11 (1958), pp. 166-79.

Soil Processes in the Northern Forest and Tundra Regions

Tundra (Tedrow *et al.* 1958) soils are those widespread, poorly drained soils of the arctic regions that are mineral in character and underlain by permafrost. Partly water-logged conditions and glei-ing are usually present in the upper mineral horizons. The organic horizon at the surface is usually several inches thick and upper horizons tend to be strongly acid in reaction. Upland tundra soils, while poorly drained, occupy the higher sites on sloping land and rounded hilltops. Meadow tundra soils occupy the lower positions, the flatter areas, and situations of very poor drainage. The pioneer work of Dokuchaev, Sibirtzev, Afanasiev, and others provided for the recognition of tundra soil in idealized, global classification diagrams. Sibertzev (Glinka, 1928; Margulis, 1954), designated tundra soil as a zonal soil in the 1890's; however, because of the paucity of information existing on tundra soils at that time he did little more than make provision for it in his schematic diagram. Marbut (1927) in his proposal categorizing major kinds of soils recognized the tundra soil as a normal soil of the cold zone just as he did the podzol, chernozem and laterite in other climatic zones. He stated:

"The normal profile. Experience has shown that in every region having what may be defined as normal relief, there is a normal soil profile. By normal relief is meant the relief that at the present time characterizes the greater part of the earth's surface, and for the purpose of this discussion, may be described as smooth, undulating or rolling, with the relation to drainage such that the permanent water-table lies entirely below the bottom of the solum."

Further, in his discussion of immature soils, Marbut (1928) states:

". . . another factor which causes some of the soils of a given region to be immature in their development is that of poor drainage. Mature soils attain maturity only under the influence of normal, good drainage. Excessive amounts of water and especially a high water-table or high ground-water prevent the development of a complete, normal profile."

Unquestionably the soil profiles that have been long recognized as tundra form under conditions of poor drainage (Neustruev, 1927). The tundra profile shows all the characteristics of gleization, and free water is commonly present up to the surface of the soil. This wet condition is greatly influenced by the presence of permafrost, usually at depths of from 1 to 2 feet. Although soil scientists point out that a zonal or mature soil can form only under conditions of free drainage, they nevertheless state that tundra soil is a zonal soil. This direct contradiction that originated over a quarter of a century ago should be done away with.

It has been suggested that it would be more appropriate to designate tundra soil as an intrazonal (hydromorphic) rather than a zonal soil (Gorodkov, 1939; Robinson, 1949; Tedrow et al., 1958).

A number of qualitative soil-forming processes operate in the several climatic regions of the earth, such as those of laterization and podzolization. These processes tend to be intensified or weakened along climatic gradients. Unfortunately, some writers imply that the podzolic process gives way northward to a special tundra soil-forming process unique to the arctic regions; or that a weak podzolic process is operating in tundra soils. Neither of these concepts is supported by facts.

Much of the misunderstanding results from the futile attempt to relate a podzol, which forms under conditions of free drainage, to a tundra soil, which forms under conditions of highly impeded drainage. A more orderly picture of relationships emerges when one compares the mature soils in the northern podzol zone with mature soils locally found in the arctic regions on well-drained sites, and the so-called tundra soils with the northern forested glei soils.

North of the zone of maximum podzolization, the podzolic process weakens but does not grade into a special type of soil formation unique to the arctic regions (Gorodkov, 1939, Tedrow et al., 1958). Instead, it continues to operate on the well-drained, stable sites (Figure 1). As mean summer temperatures become lower and precipitation decreases, the process operates at a very much reduced intensity. But it is of sufficient magnitude to bring some mineral elements into solution. These apparently recombine with the organic residues to produce the brown colour in the upper horizon. Leaching is very feeble, and no visual evidence of translocation of mineral elements is normally noted in the profile. Meinardus (1930) describes some weak processes operating in the well-drained shallow soil areas of Spitsbergen that involve leaching of divalent cations and conversion of some FeO to Fe_2O_3. Leahey (1949) mentions reddish-brown forested soils of the Yukon Territory outside the permafrost region and mineral soils within it that have a thin, reddish-brown solum. Kellogg and Nygard (1951) report subarctic brown forest soils of central and southern Alaska with various yellow and brown sola.

Arctic brown are those soils of the arctic regions that are mineral in character and form under free drainage. Their areal extent is small and is confined primarily to escarpment areas, ridges, terrace edges, and stabilized dunes. The upper mineral horizon approximates a dark-brown colour and is acid in reaction. Colours grade through various yellow-browns and grey-browns with depth. The active layer is usually deep. Arctic brown soil has been reported in Alaska north of the 71st parallel (Tedrow and Hill, 1955). In this soil the podzolic nature is so weakly developed that it can be detected only by chemical and mineralogical techniques (Drew and Tedrow, 1957). Pierre Dansereau (personal communication) supplied the authors with samples and descriptions of soils from Baffin Island that correspond to those of the arctic brown soils. This suggests that the brown soils are also present in the Eastern Canadian Arctic. At higher altitudes in the Arctic, as in the Brooks Range, the soil-forming process in the well-drained sites becomes so feeble that it is questionable whether it actually should be designated as a process. The solum in well-drained areas may be only a few inches thick. These soils resemble those assigned to polar desert by Gorodkov (1939).

Just as the very local brown surface soils of the Arctic are a northern counterpart of the podzols, so the widespread tundra soils, forming under impeded drainage, are a northern counterpart of the glei soils of the northern forested region (Figure 1). Northward of the forested areas the impermeable permafrost layer is close to the surface; this results in a very high proportion of poorly drained land. The process of gleization, although operating on great expanses, weakens in northern areas because of the reduced chemical and biological activity, short growing season, and low temperature.

In both wet and well-drained sites downslope movement combines with frost processes, tending to disrupt any orderly morphology. This downslope movement increases with steepness of slope. On slopes of 3 to 5 per cent downslope movement of soil does not appear to be a major factor. But as slopes increase to the 20 to 40 per cent level the process becomes intense. These disturbances manifest themselves in an erratic appearance of the soil profile and indirectly by the unique surface characteristics of the landscape (Washburn, 1956, Sigafoos and Hopkins, 1952) and related evidence.

Apparently, frost processes cause a certain amount of physical displacement of the mineral and organic matter. Despite the volume of descriptive literature available on the subject of frost action, virtually no quantitative measurements on rates of displacement

NORTH

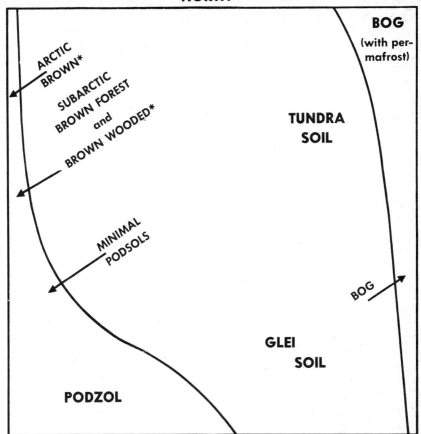

Figure 1. Podzols grade northward into arctic brown and related soils, whereas glei soils grade into tundra. The graphic generalization indicates that northward the tundra and bog soils become dominant areally whereas arctic brown soil is present only in small localized areas (Lithosols excluded).

and movement of soils are available. Until they are, one can only speculate as to the rate at which the cryopedologic processes operate. On the better-drained glei soils, such as those of the higher and gently sloping terrains, the processes of soil formation operate at an intensity sufficient for a number of genetic properties to become evident in the profile. The upper horizons display more yellow-brown and related colours near the surface, grading into duller colours with depth. If cryopedologic processes were operating at a rapid rate in these soils, colour differences would not be detected between the various upper horizons and a more homogeneous colour would be present throughout the active zone.

If the soils and soil formation processes in the arctic tundra region are examined and compared with their counterparts of temperate regions, we find that the mature, normal soil (in the sense of Marbut and earlier European investigators) is not the most extensive. The profiles of these highly local arctic brown soils reflect the full impact of the regional climate, unmodified by water-logged conditions or major frost displacement. If one chooses to equate zonality with these former unmodified conditions, then tundra soils should not be considered zonal. To assign zonal status to tundra soils equates zonality with simple regional dominance. The implied idea that the zonal profile fully reflects the impact of the regional climate must then be abandoned. On tundra soils we have the unusual circumstance that the operation of the regional climate brings about its own suppression as a soil-forming factor through the formation of the impervious frozen layer. Here minor regional differences of climate have much less effect on the soil pattern than local micro-variations in drainage.

Vegetation-Soil Relationships, Micro-Relief, and
Soil Classification Problems

Relation between soil type and vegetation. In the Arctic, as well as in most other climatic regions, the moisture status of the soil exerts a marked selective influence on the plant populations. Thus, when on the basis of profile morphology the soils of arctic Alaska are arranged into a sequence (Figure 2), representing a drainage catena (Tedrow *et al.*, 1958) the associated vegetation normally shows a characteristic sequence of communities (Figure 3). On the deep and the shallow well-drained soils, the regularity in soil-vegetation relationships, although by no means perfect, is pronounced. As the soils forming under free drainage grade to progressively more shallow ones, as in areas peripheral to rock outcrops or where the mineral substrate changes into one of unusually coarse texture, the Upland Meadow communities have less total coverage and harbour more xeric species. This trend ultimately replaces the Meadow types with Barrens types, with less than half the surface covered. Given the soil profile and the general location on the Alaskan Arctic Slope, it is possible to predict the vegetation type with a fair degree of reliability.

On soils formed under restricted drainage a somewhat more difficult problem of soils and vegetation relationships exists. Field observations show without question that on tundra and bog soils a spectrum of plant communities exists that ranges from those dominated by species associated with well-drained sites to those

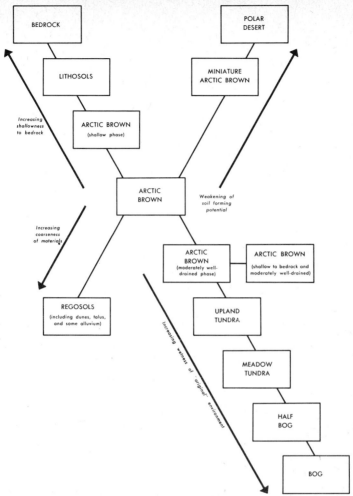

Figure 2. The genetic soils of arctic Alaska can be arranged in the form of a sequence starting with the arctic brown and progressing through more poorly drained conditions to the bog soils. A sequence of soils is also present in the more shallow areas beginning with arctic brown and continuing through progressively shallower soils to situations where bedrock is exposed at the surface.

dominated by species associated with very wet sites (Figure 3) (Cantlon and Gillis, 1957). Thus, on that portion of the catena occupied by the tundra and bog soils the reliability of predicting plant-soil relationship is poorer.

To help illustrate this situation, we may compare it with better-known vegetation-soil relationships. We find that in the moist temperate region natural vegetation is useful in inferring the stages of drainage in the soil catena. It must be remembered,

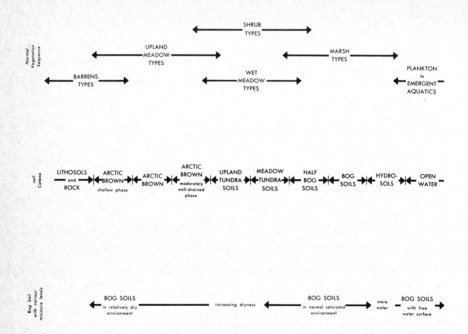

Figure 3. Vegetation-soil relationships along a moisture gradient ranging from standing water on the right to extreme dry on the left.

however, that such correlation is used for the most part with mineral soils, and very little work has been done with the vegetation differences on various organic soils. With organic soils in arctic Alaska, local differences in moisture levels produce differences in vegetation. This is true in a lower degree in the more rainy temperate region, but the total area of the drier fragments is usually insignificant. Further, in the temperate region the presence of forest lends a more homogeneous appearance, the tree layer more or less completely subjugating any micro-patterning in the understory. In the treeless Arctic, where various cryopedologic processes operate to give pronounced micro-relief, vast areas of tundra and bog soils exhibit patterns or mosaics of vegetation (Spetzman, 1951; Wiggins, 1951; Sigafoos, 1952; Churchill, 1955; Drury, 1956; Bliss and Cantlon, 1957; Cantlon and Gillis, 1957; Churchill and Hanson, 1958; among others). These patterns are due to several classes of micro-site differences but soil moisture during the growing season, and snow depth during the winter are the most frequent and conspicuous differences (Figure 4).

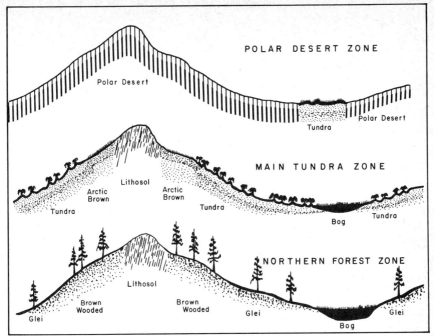

Figure 4. Diagram of soil patterns in northern areas. (From "Arctic Soils" by J. C. F. Tedrow in "Proceedings, Permafrost International Conference" 1965, 563 pp. National Academy of Sciences—National Research Council, Washington, D.C., reproduced by permission.)

Non-correspondence of profile morphology and present site conditions. In arctic Alaska bog soils normally form under naturally poor drainage, and the usual vegetation is Marsh (*Carex aquatilis,*[1] *C. rotundata, C. rariflora, Carex* spp., *Eriophorum angustifolium, E. scheuchzeri, Arctophila fulva, Dupontia fisheri, Hypnum* spp., and *Sphagnum* spp., among others) or certain Meadow types (*Sphagnum* spp., *Dicranum elongatum,* and *Aulocomnium,* with *Eriophorum vaginatum, Vaccinium vitis-idaea* ssp. *minus,* and *Rubus chamaemorus,* among many others). Subsequent frost or geomorphic processes (polygonization, headward stream erosion, and lake drainage) may produce micro-relief features that in turn increase runoff and effectively reduce the moisture content of the upper soil layers. On these better-drained bog soils vegetation becomes established that resembles communities normally found farther up the drainage catena. These are various Meadow types, ranging from Wet Meadow (*Eriophorum vaginatum* ssp. *spissum, Carex bigelowii, Dicranum* spp., *Aulocomnium* spp., *Salix pulchra, Vaccinium vitis-idaea* ssp. *minus, Betula nana* ssp. *exilis, Ledum palustre* ssp. *decumbens, Cetraria* spp., *Cladonia* spp., among others) to Dry Meadow (*Dryas integrifolia, D. octopetala, Vaccinium vitis-idaea* ssp. *minus, Salix phlebophylla,* and crustose lichens, among others). The more effective the drainage, the more pronounced the shift toward Dry Meadow, or on extreme convexities even to Barrens types with a sparse cover of lichens, mosses, *Luzula confusa,* and others. These latter communities may have many species in common with vegetation types normally associated with the well-drained mineral soils.

The creation of micro-relief features is somewhat analogous to the draining of bogs in more southerly areas by ditching or tile drains. In the temperate climates, however, profiles classed as well-drained usually have good drainage to a depth of 3 feet or more. The mesic species of the Arctic do not require such a great depth of well-drained soil, and adequate drainage and aeration to a depth of only a few inches is here sufficient to allow the more mesic communities of the Arctic to become established. The low rainfall, coupled with higher air speeds at ground level, favours xeric species on the pronounced convexities. These species are probably also favoured by the shallowness of the snow cover.

Just as there are conditions under which certain tundra and bog soils may exist in comparatively well-drained environments, so there are other conditions in which these soils, as based on profile morphology, appear to be in unusually wet environments. It is not uncommon for a mineral soil to be completely covered with water throughout the growing season, a condition favourable to the eventual formation of an organic soil. Apparently, this situation arises from formation of low-centre polygons, frost collapse, frost action in the soil, the element of time, and related factors, that cause a change in environment. Because of the short, cool growing season, however, organic matter accumulates at a very slow rate (Warren Wilson, 1957). Other situations in which the soils may be in a wetter environment than the profiles suggest are those where subsidence from thermokarst activity (Wallace, 1948; Hopkins, 1949) or stream meandering have occurred.

Normally the morphology of the soil profile is an expression of the combined factors of soil formation. If the environment changes, then the morphology should also change. Apparently, readjustment to the new environment takes place so slowly under arctic conditions that the higher water content of these mineral soils or the well-drained surface on bog soils are "semi-permanent" features of the profiles. Such lack of correspondence between the profile and present environment occurs widely and no better suggestion for their interpretation is at hand.

Soil variation and soil mapping problems. Drew (1957) discussed some of the problems involved and prepared a map of the soils of the Barrow area in northern Alaska. In flat, highly polygonized areas, a high order of variation in micro-relief features influences the moisture content of the surface soil. The elevated portions of the polygons are comparatively dry, whereas the low portions of the polygonized areas are commonly covered with water during the summer months. Thus, within distances of a few feet, a wide spectrum of soil conditions and plant species is commonly found (Wiggins, 1951). In the highly polygonized areas it would be virtually impossible to delineate and describe even in broadest terms a profile *per se* unless an abnormally large scale was used.

Somewhat akin to the difficulties met with on poorly drained sites are those frequently encountered on the steeply sloping uplands. Here, although non-sorted polygons (Washburn, 1956) are feebly expressed and perhaps locally absent, another type of micro-topography occurs. This takes the form of small, oblong mounds, ranging from a few inches up to 2 feet in height and from 2 to 6 feet long, with their long axes frequently at right angles to the contour. Irregular trenches occur between, the width of which varies from a few inches to a few feet. The soil in the trenches has a somewhat thicker organic layer and is moist, whereas the convexities have a slightly thinner layer and are drier. If slope is not excessive the differences between the mounds and the trenches are small and the entire complex falls within the range of what can be classed as upland tundra or meadow tundra soils. The vegetation on the two kinds of micro-sites show a marked difference, however, giving rise to an intricate mosaic composed of two or more groups of species (basic units in the sense of Hopkins, 1957), but which in descriptions are lumped into one "community".

On steeper slopes the micro-relief is more pronounced and the differences in vegetation between convexities and trenches strain the single "community" designation. The soil, with its excessive number of mounds and solifluction lobes, also may exceed the range usually recognized in upland or meadow tundra soils. These soils, together with such local variants as extensive areas of frost boils and stone nets, might be given special status in the delineated soil unit nearest to it in the drainage catena.

The authors believe that the soils in the arctic regions can be classified in somewhat the same manner as they are being classified in other climatic regions. In fact, delineating soil units on the well-drained sites in the Arctic is little different from doing so on their temperate region counterparts. The areas are large enough and vegetation types have a fair degree of indicator value on these sites. Delineating tundra soils on gently to steeply sloping areas can be done with facility, although there is some irregularity in the profile morphology. However, on the steep solifluction slopes and on the flat, highly polygonized areas factors in addition to profile morphology should be considered. Perhaps the independent mapping of micro-relief characteristics as proposed by Drew (1957) would suffice. Another alternative would be to describe the pattern of the soil complex based on principles set forth by Veatch (1934).

Summary

The soils of arctic Alaska can be arranged in a drainage catena in the same manner as those of other climatic regions. Mature or zonal soils (arctic brown) may be said to form only under adequate internal drainage. Tundra soils would thus not be considered mature or zonal, instead they would be intrazonal (hydromorphic). The arctic brown and related soils with brown surface horizons, tundra soils, and bog with permafrost are northern extensions or counterparts of podzol, humic glei, and bog soils, respectively.

Plant communities have been successfully correlated with soils on well-drained sites and on areas of shallow soils. Correlation between soils and vegetation on the tundra and bog soils, however, poses major problems. Non-correspondence of soil profile with current site conditions is wide-spread because of the lag in development processes. Vegetation reflects the changes somewhat earlier. If relative wetness of the site is considered together with the profile morphology a workable relationship between soils and plant communities generally exists; and if the nature of the cryopedologic features is mapped independently, suitable soil maps may be prepared.

References

Bliss, L. C. and J. E. Cantlon, "Succession on river alluvium in northern Alaska", *Am. Midl. Nat.* 58 (1957), pp. 452-69.

Cantlon, J. E. and W. T. Gillis, "Arctic plants in relation to various relief features", *Bull. Ecol. Soc. Am. 38* (1957), pp. 98-99. (Abstract of unpublished paper presented at A.A.A.S. meeting, Indianapolis, Dec., 1957.)

Corte, Arturo E., Vertical migration of particles in front of a moving plane", *J. Geophys. Res. 67* (1962), pp. 1085-90.

Day, J. H. and A. Leahey "Reconnaissance soil survey of the Slave River Lowland in the Northwest Territories of Canada", Can. Dept. Agr. Exp. Farms Ser., Ottawa (1957).

Department of Transport, Meterological Division, "Addendum to Vol. 1 of summaries for selected meterological stations in Canada", Toronto (1954).

Department of Transport, Meteorological Branch, "Climate of the Canadian July-October, Ottawa (1959).

Douglas, L. A., and J. C. F. Tedrow, "Tundra soils of arctic Alaska", Seventh Congr. Soil Sci., Madison, Wis., U.S.A., 4 (1960), pp. 291-304.

Drew, J. V., and J. C. F. Tedrow, "Pedology of an arctic brown profile near Point Barrow, Alaska", *Soil Sci. Soc. Am. Proc. 21* (1957), pp. 336-39.

Feustel, I. C., A. Dutilly and M. S. Anderson, "Properties of soils from North American arctic regions", *Soil Sci. 48* (1939), pp. 183-99.

Hill, D. E., and J. C. F. Tedrow, "Weathering and soil formation in the arctic environment", *Am. J. Sci. 259* (1961), pp. 84-101.

Kilmer, W. J. and L. T. Alexander, "Method of making mechanical analysis of soils", *Soil Sci. 68* (1949), pp. 15-24.

Lajoie, P., "Exploratory soil survey of the Fort Chimo district", Can. Dept. Agr., Unpubl. rept. (1954).

Leahy, A., "Characteristics of soils adjacent to the Mackenzie River in the Northwest Territories of Canada", *Proc. Soil Sci. Soc. Am.*, Vol. XII (1947), pp. 458-61.

"A summary report on an exploratory soil survey along the water route from Waterways, Alberta, to Aklavik, Northwest Territories", Appendix B in Gilbey, J. A. Dominion Experimental Substation, Fort Simpson, N.W.T. (1954), Prog. Rept., 1947-53, pp. 42-45.

Mackay, J. Ross, "A subsurface organic layer associated with permafrost in the western Arctic", *Geogr. pap. no. 18*, Dept. of Mines and Tech. Surveys, Ottawa (1958).

Mackay, J. R., W. H. Mathews and R. S. MacNeish, "Geology of the archaeological site, Yukon Territory", *Arctic 14* (1961), pp. 25-52.

McMillan, N. J., "Soils of the Queen Elizabeth Islands (Canadian Arctic)", *J. Soil Sci. 11* (1960), pp. 131-39.

National Soil Survey Committee of Canada, "Report of the meetings at the University of Manitoba, Winnipeg, held in March 1963", Ottawa, Mimeo (1963).

Pihlainen, J. A., "Engineering site information, Inuvik, N.W.T.", *Can. Nat. Res. Coun. Div. Bldg. Res. Tech. pap. 135*, Ottawa (1962).

Rowe, J. S., "Forest regions of Canada", *Bull. 123*, Can. Dept. of Northern Affairs and Nat. Resources, For. Br. Ottawa (1959).

Skinner, S. I. M., R. L. Halstead and J. E. Brydon, "Quantitative manometric determination of calcite and dolomite in soils and limestones", *Can. J. Soil Sci. 39* (1959), pp. 197-2.

Stewart, J. S., "Recent exploratory deep well drilling in Mackenzie River Valley, Northwest Territories", *Geol. Sur. Can. Pap. 45* (1945), pp. 29.

Tedrow, J. C. F., and D. E. Hill, "Arctic Brown soil", *Soil Sci. 80* (1955), pp. 265-75.

Tedrow, J. C. F., J. V. Drew, D. E. Hill and L. A. Douglas, "Major genetic soils of the Arctic slope of Alaska", *J. Soil Sci. 9* (1958), pp. 33-45.

Tedrow, J. C. F., and J. E. Cantlon, "Concepts of soil formation and classification in Arctic regions", *Arctic 11* (1958), pp. 166-79.

United States Department of Agriculture, "Soil classification, a comprehensive system", 7th approximation, Soil Conservation Service, (1960).

Wright, J. R., A. Leahey and H. M. Rice, "Chemical, morphological and mineralogical characteristics of a chronosequence of soils on alluvial deposits in the Northwest Territories", *Can. J. Soil Sci. 39* (1959), pp. 32-43.

8

The Characteristics of Some Permafrost Soils in the Mackenzie Valley. N.W.T.

J. H. Day and H. M. Rice

Introduction

Soils in the tundra and subarctic regions of Canada were first described in 1939 when Feustel and others analyzed samples from northern Quebec, Keewatin and Franklin districts. More recently McMillan (1960), Beschel (1961) and Lajoie (1954) described soils in the Canadian Arctic Archipelago and in northern Quebec. In the western part of the Northwest Territories only one profile (Leahey 1947) has been described under tundra vegetation, although other soils under forest, mostly unaffected by permafrost, have been described (Leahey 1954, Day and Leahey 1957, Wright *et al.* 1959).

In Alaska, Tedrow and Hill (1955), Drew and Tedrow (1957), Tedrow *et al.* (1958), Douglas and Tedrow (1960), Hill and Tedrow (1961) and Tedrow and Cantlon (1958) described several groups of soils, weathering processes, and concepts of soil formation and classification in the arctic environment. At least some of the kinds of soil they described in Alaska occur in Canada in a similar environment.

This study was undertaken to investigate the characteristics of soils in a permafrost region under different types of vegetation.

Reprinted from *Arctic*, Vol. 17 (1964), pp. 222-36. Contribution No. 93 of the Soil Research Institute, Canada Department of Agriculture, Ottawa.

The lower Mackenzie River valley is within the area of continuous permafrost (Brown 1960) and both tundra and boreal forest regions are readily accessible from the river. This paper describes soils in three localities, each with a different vegetation, the morphological, chemical, physical and mineralogical characteristics of a number of soil profiles, and the effect of permafrost and vegetation on soil development. The tundra locality at Reindeer Depot is situated on the east channel of the Mackenzie Delta at 68°42′N., 134°07′W.; the tundra—boreal forest transition locality at Inuvik is also on the east channel about 30 miles south of Reindeer Depot, at 68°21′N., 133°41′W. and the boreal forest locality at Norman Wells on the Mackenzie River lies about 280 miles southeast of Inuvik at 66°42′N., 126°51′W. In all localities permafrost is continuous and only slight differences in climate between them were found.

Methods of Investigation

The areas were visited between July 7 and 31, 1960. Observations on landform, topography and vegetation were recorded. The soil morphology was examined in dug pits and is described according to the terminology adopted by the National Soil Survey Committee (1963). The soil colours observed in the field are described using the Munsell notation.

Samples of soil from the various horizons of each profile were air-dried, ground and passed through a 2-mm sieve. Soil reaction, organic matter and total nitrogen content, cation-exchange capacity and exchangeable cations, were determined by commonly used methods (Atkinson et al. 1958). The calcium carbonate equivalent was determined by the method of Skinner et al. (1959). Free iron was determined by the Coffin (1963) modification of the method of Aguilera and Jackson (1953).

Particle-size distribution of samples of profiles 1 to 5 were calculated from the fractions prepared for mineralogical analyses, and samples of profiles 6 to 8 inclusive were analyzed by the pipette method (Kilmer and Alexander 1949) modified by using a separate sample for the determination of the organic matter-free, moisture-free, dispersed weight of sample.

The samples examined mineralogically (1 to 5 inclusive) were brought to pH 3.5 to destroy carbonates, washed free of salts, treated with hydrogen peroxide, washed, and dispersed at pH 8.0. They were then separated into sand, coarse, medium and fine silts, and coarse and fine clays by sedimentation and centrifugation. The sand and silt fractions were dried on a water-bath and the clay fractions freeze-dried (Brydon et al. 1963).

The silts were examined by X-ray powder diagrams and the

clays by oriented X-ray diffractometer diagrams and differential thermal analysis.

Climate

Meteorological records for Reindeer Depot are lacking, but are available for 6 years at Inuvik, for 22 years at Aklavik, which is about 40 miles west of Inuvik, and for 10 years at Norman Wells (Dept. of Transport 1954). Adjusted normals were prepared for Inuvik by assuming that the difference between the Inuvik and the Aklavik temperatures over a long period would be the same as during the short period for which data are available for both sites, that the ratio between the long-term averages of total precipitation at these sites would be the same as the ratio of the short-term averages, and that the proportion of the annual precipitation occurring in each month would be the same at both sites.

The data (Table I) show that Norman Wells is warmer and wetter than Inuvik. On the basis of records for coastal stations (Dept. of Transport 1959) it is inferred that Reindeer Depot has cooler summers and rather lower summer precipitation than Inuvik.

Tundra at Reindeer Depot
Landform

The area examined at Reindeer Depot is on the crest and eastern flank of the Caribou Hills, a ridge paralleling the east channel of Mackenzie River. The altitude of the ridge is over 500 feet. The landscape to the east of the ridge is generally gently to moderately sloping (2 to 9 per cent) with occasional strongly sloping (10 to 15 per cent) and very strongly sloping (16 to 30 per cent) areas. The crests of slopes are characterized by rough micro-topography; roughly circular knolls 2 to 3 feet wide are 1 to 1.5 feet higher than the separating troughs that are about 1 foot wide. The middle of a slope has rougher micro-topography and the knolls and troughs tend to be oriented down-slope. Toward the toe of a slope, the downhill face of a knoll is steeper than its uphill face. Depressions between slopes have very gently sloping, level or basin topography and some are characterized by a polygon pattern developed in peat deposits.

Vegetation

The Reindeer Depot area has been assigned to the Forest-Tundra section (Rowe 1959) but the sites sampled are more representative of the tundra. The vegetation forms a nearly continuous mat. Only an occasional willow 1 to 2 feet high is present; along watercourses and in basins protected from the wind alder 6 to 8 feet tall forms fairly dense stands. Among the dominant species are: *Betula glandulosa* (dwarf birch), *Eriophorum vaginatum* (cotton-grass), *Ledum palustris* (Labrador tea), *Arctostaphylos alpina* (alpine bearberry), *Vaccinium vitis-idaea* (mountain cranberry), *V. uliginosum* (alpine blueberry), *Empetrum nigrum* (black crow-berry), *Carex lugens* (sedge), *Lupinus arcticus* (lupine) and mosses. Other species present in minor amounts include *Salix glauca* (willow), *Castilleja raupii* (Indian paintbrush), *Cladonia* spp. (reindeer moss) and *Rubus chamaemorus* (baked-apple-berry). The vegetation is low and sparse on top of each knoll and some are bare. In the troughs the vegetation is higher and denser; there the main species are mosses and Labrador tea. In peat polygon areas, Labrador tea is dominant, with reindeer moss, mountain cranberry, and dwarf birch on the raised centre and grasses in the troughs.

TABLE I. MONTHLY AND ANNUAL AVERAGES OF DAILY MAXIMUM AND MINIMUM TEMPERATURE, MONTHLY AND ANNUAL AVERAGES OF TOTAL PRECIPITATION AND SNOWFALL.

	Jan.	Feb.	Mar.	Apr.	May	June	July	Aug.	Sep.	Oct.	Nov.	Dec.	Year
Inuvik, adjusted normals													
Mean daily maximum temperature, °F.	−11	−7	2	19	41	63	68	61	46	25	3	−7	25
Mean daily minimum temperature, °F.	−30	−26	−20	−6	22	39	45	40	30	13	−13	−26	6
Total precipitation, inches	0.51	0.43	0.35	0.49	0.44	0.85	1.19	1.35	0.96	0.78	0.65	0.45	8.45
Snowfall, inches	5.4	4.6	3.6	5.1	2.4	1.5	T	0.7	2.9	7.5	6.9	4.5	45.1
Norman Wells													
Mean daily maximum temperature, °F.	−11	−7	10	31	53	68	72	65	50	32	9	−6	31
Mean daily minimum temperature, °F.	−26	−23	−12	7	32	46	50	45	35	20	−4	−21	12
Total precipitation, inches	0.65	0.58	0.34	0.54	0.67	1.40	2.02	2.65	1.66	0.77	0.84	0.67	12.79
Snowfall, inches	6.5	5.8	3.4	4.6	1.8	0.2	0.0	T	2.8	6.5	8.4	6.7	46.7

Surficial geology and permafrost

Fine-textured glacial till covers the area to depths of 3 to 4 feet and is underlain by poorly consolidated sands, silts, and gravels (Mackay 1963) of undetermined age. The active layer is thin (6 inches) under the troughs and thick (24 inches) under the knolls, so that its basal face is a mirror image of the ground surface.

Soils

Two sites were selected to represent the main types of soils present.

⏐ The first site (profile 1) represents the ridges and upper slopes. It is a microknoll on a 4-per cent south-facing slope near the crest of a ridge about 2 miles east of Reindeer Depot. Soil profile 1 has the following characteristics:

Depth inches	Horizon	Description
3 – 2.5	1	Litter of twigs and leaves
2.5 – 0	2	Reddish-black (10R 2/1) muck.
0 – 1	3	Very dark brown (10YR 3/2) silty clay, very weak, very fine granular; pH 5.5.
1 – 7	4	Very dark greyish brown (10YR 3/2) friable clay loam; weak, fine granular; a few pebbles; boundary diffuse; pH 5.3.
7 – 14	5	Very dark greyish brown (10YR 3/2) friable silty clay; moderate, fine granular; noncalcareous; a few pebbles; pH 6.0.
14 – 21	6	Very dark greyish brown (10YR 3/2) noncalcareous clay containing a few small pebbles and stones; weak, fine granular; frozen, segregated ice lenses 0.1 to 0.2 inch thick; pH 5.8.
21 – 25	7	Colour and structure as above; pH 6.0.

The other site represents the lower slopes and is also about 2 miles east of Reindeer Depot. This site is a microknoll near the toe of a long 2-per cent east-facing slope. Soil profile 2 has the following characteristics:

Depth inches	Horizon	Description
0 – 5	1	Olive-brown (2.5Y 4/4) friable silty clay; moderate to strong, fine granular; pH 4.7.
5 – 9	2	Dark greyish brown (2.5Y 4/2) friable clay; moderate to strong, fine granular; yellowish-brown (10YR 5/6) mottles are common, fine and distinct; boundary abrupt and irregular to broken with tongues extending into horizon below; boundary marked by yellowish-brown (10YR 5/8) colour; pH 4.7.
9 – 23	3	Dark grey (5Y 4/1) amorphous silty clay; very plastic and sticky; a few small pebbles; yellowish-brown mottles (10YR 5/4) are few, fine and distinct; thickness and depth are variable because of tonguing with horizon above; pH 5.3.
23 – 28	4	Dark grey (5Y 4/1) amorphous clay; frozen, 0.1-inch lenses of ice; faint olive (5Y 4/3) mottles; pH 5.2.

Both profiles are associated with moss-covered raw peat that is frozen at a depth of 7 inches in the troughs between the microknolls.

The depressions downslope from profile 2 are filled with peat having a well-developed raised-center polygonal pattern. The top 10 inches are black muck underlain by frozen fibrous peat.

Tundra-Boreal Forest Transition at Inuvik

Landform

At Inuvik the area examined includes the gently undulating river terrace on which the settlement is located and the gently to moderately sloping upland plain to the east that rises to an altitude of about 300 feet. Both have a westerly aspect. The microtopography is rather similar to but less rough than that at Reindeer Depot.

Vegetation

The forest-tundra transition (Rowe 1959) is a continuous cover formed by the following dominant species: *Picea mariana* (black spruce), *Betula pumila* (birch), *Alnus crispa* (alder), *Salix glauca*. The continuous ground cover includes the following: *Vaccinium vitis-idaea, Ledum palustris, Hylocomnium splendens* (moss), *Rosa* spp., *Petasites frigidus* (sweet coltsfoot), *Spiraea beauverdiana*, and *Peltigera aphthosa* (lichen). The ground cover is low and sparse on the top of each knoll, higher and denser in the troughs.

Surficial geology and permafrost

In this area, fine-textured glacial till is underlain by argillite and dolomite of Devonian and earlier age, and contains more carbonates and sulfates than that at Reindeer Depot. Mackay (1963) reports that the gravelly delta of Boot Creek at Inuvik was laid down, in part, as a kame complex between ice to the west and the higher land to the east, and that a radio-carbon date of 8,000+ years for peat near the present river level at Inuvik shows that the sea-level was not higher than at present.

The active layer showed the same features as at Reindeer Depot. In the coarse-textured gravelly fan of Boot Creek permafrost was not seen in the face of the gravel pit owing to clearing and excavation, but previously the top of the permafrost layer had been at 3- to 4-feet depth (Pihlainen, pers. comm.). In late August the depth of thaw ranged from 18 to 30 inches for clayey mineral soils with peaty cover to 51 inches for gravelly soil with peaty cover (Pihlainen 1962).

Soils

Two sites were selected to represent the common soils on the upland plain, and one to represent the maximum soil development present on gravelly material.

The first site (profile 3) is about 1.5 miles east of Inuvik. It is a microknoll near the middle of a 9-per cent west-facing slope. Soil profile 3 has the following characteristics:

Depth inches	Horizon	Description
1 – 0	L	Litter of leaves and twigs, slightly decomposed at the lower limit.
	Ah	A very dark brown (10YR 2.5/2) mineral horizon high in organic matter; ranges from a trace to 0.5-inch thick; field pH 4.5.
0 – 6	Bm1	Yellowish-brown (10YR 5/4) silty clay loam; moderate, fine to medium granular; friable; boundary clear and smooth; pH 4.5.
6 – 10	Bm2	Dark greyish brown (10YR 4/2) clay loam; moderate, fine granular; slightly plastic; a few black pebbles; boundary gradual and smooth; pH 5.8.
10 – 27	BC	Very dark greyish brown (2.5Y 3/2) silty clay; a few pebbles; very weak, fine granular to amorphous; moderately plastic; boundary diffuse, smooth; pH 6.8.
27 – 38.5	Cz	Very dark greyish brown (2.5Y 3/2) amorphous clay loam; frozen, many small disseminated ice crystals; very plastic and sticky when thawed; pH 7.7.

The second site (profile 4) is about 1.5 miles east of Inuvik on a microknoll near the toe of a long 2-per cent west-facing slope. Soil profile 4 has the following characteristics:

Depth inches	Horizon	Description
5 – 3	L	Raw undecomposed leaves, twigs and moss roots.
3 – 0	F	Moderately well-decomposed mucky peat and living roots, dark reddish brown (5YR 2/2); pH 4.5.
0 – 2	Ah	Very dark brown (10YR 2/2) clay; moderate, fine granular; average thickness 0.5 inch; boundary abrupt, distinct; pH 4.8.
2 – 6	Bm	Dark brown (10YR 4/3) clay, very weak, fine granular to amorphous; slightly plastic; a few pebbles; boundary gradual, smooth; pH 6.1.
6 – 10	BC	Very dark greyish brown (2.5Y 3/2) clay; very weak, fine granular to amorphous; moderately plastic; a few pebbles; pH 6.5.
10 – 16	Cz	Very dark greyish brown (2.5Y 3/2) silty clay; a few pebbles and stones; frozen, disseminated ice crystals; structure and consistence as above; pH 6.6.

Profile 4 apparently is more poorly drained than profile 3. Both were associated with moss-covered raw peat, frozen in the troughs between the microknolls at a depth of about 6 inches.

The third site (profile 5) is on the edge of a gravel pit in the well-drained, nearly level delta of Boot Creek. Soil profile 5 has the following characteristics:

Depth inches	Horizon	Description
2.5 – 1	F	Black (5YR 2/1) matted, fibrous organic material bound together by roots; pH 4.7.
1 – 0	H	Black (10YR 2/1) well-decomposed organic material;

pH 4.7.

0 – 1.5	Ae1	Light-grey (10YR 7/2) gravelly loam; weak, fine granular; friable, slightly hard; boundary abrupt, smooth to wavy; pH 6.0.
1.5 – 3	Ae2	Light brownish grey (10YR 6/2) gravelly sandy loam; very weak, fine granular to amorphous; friable, slightly hard, boundary abrupt, smooth to wavy; pH 5.2.
3 – 4.5	Bf	Dark-brown to dark yellowish brown (7.5YR 4/4 to 10YR 4/4) gravelly sandy loam; very weak, fine granular to amorphous; stones are clean; boundary gradual, smooth to wavy; pH 5.4.
4.5 – 17	BC	Brown (10YR 4/3) very gravelly sandy loam; noncalcareous; some stones have clayey coating on underside; pH 6.7.
17 +	Ck	Brown (10YR 4/3) very gravelly sandy loam with cobbles and stones; some stones have clayey calcareous coating on underside; pH 7.5.

Boreal Forest at Norman Wells

Landform

At Norman Wells the area includes the river terrace on which the settlement is located and the slopes rising to the hills in the northeast. The aspect is southwesterly. The topography is gently sloping (2 to 5 per cent) and level and the microtopography nearly smooth.

Vegetation

The vegetation is typical of boreal regions (Rowe 1959). The continuous forest cover in well-drained localities is composed mainly of Picea mariana, P. glauca (white spruce), Betula papyrifera (white birch), with occasional Alnus spp. and Salix spp., and a ground cover of moss, rose, Arctostaphylos alpina and Cladonia spp. In poorly drained localities the dominant species are black spruce, Larix laricina (tamarack), willow, and a ground cover of moss, Labrador tea, blueberry and Carex aquatilis (sedge). Other species present in minor amounts include Castilleja raupii, Potentilla fruticosa (shrubby cinquefoil), Parnassia palustris (grass of Parnassus), Equisetum arvense (horsetail), Calamagrostis canadensis (bluejoint) and Chamaedaphne calyculata (leatherleaf).

Surficial geology and permafrost

The undulating alluvial terrace of the Mackenzie River rises to a gently sloping glacial till plain that in turn rises to a scarp composed of marine shale with local lenses of sandstone and of limestone, all of Devonian age (Stewart 1945).

The ground was frozen (July 27) at depths of 2 feet under

organic soils, 3 feet under mineral soils on inland sites with tree-moss cover, and at more than 4 feet on the terrace adjacent to the riverbank under trees and sparse ground cover. R. J. E. Brown (pers. comm.) states that this situation is general in the area.

Soils

Three sites were selected to represent the common soils of the area. Two are near the upper limit of the area in which the glacial till is covered by alluvium and the other is on alluvium.

The first site (profile 6) is located about 1.5 miles northeast of the airport and represents the best-drained soils. The slope is 6 per cent with a southern aspect. The parent material is loam alluvium over loam till. Profile 6 has the following characteristics:

Depth inches	*Horizon*	*Description*
5 – 3	L	Roots of moss, lichen and spruce needles.
3 – 0	F	Moderately decomposed woody litter; pH 6.5.
0 – 7	Bm	Brown (7.5YR 4/4) silt loam; friable, moderate, medium granular; boundary abrupt and smooth; noncalcareous; pH 7.2.
7 – 24	IICk	Dark-brown (10YR 3/3) gravelly loam; weak, fine granular to amorphous; stony below a depth of 11 inches; weakly mottled in lower part; calcareous; pH 7.5; free water below a depth of 12 inches.

At the top of the mineral soil there is a discontinuous grey layer about 0.1 inch thick. The soil is frozen below a depth of about 3 feet.

The second site (profile 7) represents the alluvial deposits of the Mackenzie River and is located about 4 miles southeast of Norman Wells near the end of D.O.T. Lake. The site is on a well-drained 3-per cent west-facing slope. The vegetation is predominantly white birch. Profile 7 has the following characteristics:

Depth inches	*Horizon*	*Description*
2.5 – 0.5	L	Litter of leaves and twigs.
0.5 – 0	H	Well-decomposed organic material.
0 – 8	Bm	Brown (7.5 YR 4/4) grading to yellowish-brown (10YR 5/4) silt loam; weak, fine granular to bedded; friable; a few pebbles; boundary wavy and smooth; pH 5.4.
8 – 10	BC	Light olive brown (2.5Y 5/4) silt loam; bedded; friable; pH 6.6.
10 – 17	Ck1	Olive (5Y 4/3) bedded silt loam; calcareous; pH 7.5.
17 – 48	Ck2	Olive (5Y 3/2 to 4/3) bedded silt loam; friable; contains old surfaces at depths of 17 and 24 inches; calcareous; pH 8.1.

There is a discontinuous grey layer about 0.25 inch thick at the top of the mineral soil (Ae). Frozen layers are absent to a depth of 4 feet.

TABLE II. CHEMICAL CHARACTERISTICS OF SOME PERMAFROST SOILS.

Horizon	Depth inches	pH	Organic Matter %	Total Nitrogen %	C/N	CaCO3 equivalent %	Free Fe2O3 %	C.E.C.	Ca	Mg	K	Na	Saturation %
								meq.* per 100 gms. soil					
Profile 1, Reindeer Depot													
2	2.5—0	4.8	—	1.56	—	—	—	—	—	—	—	—	—
3	0—1	5.5	16.5	0.53	18	—	2.8	46.2	22.2	7.4	0.4	0.1	65
4	1—7	5.3	5.0	0.14	21	—	2.8	25.0	12.8	5.7	0.2	0.1	75
5	7—14	6.0	5.2	0.17	19	—	3.0	26.1	16.9	6.9	0.2	0.1	92
6	14—21	5.8	10.6	0.31	20	—	2.4	34.9	19.0	5.9	0.4	0.1	73
7	21—25	6.0	8.1	0.22	21	—	3.3	30.7	20.0	7.3	0.2	0.1	90
Profile 2, Reindeer Depot													
1	0—5	4.7	5.0	0.14	21	—	3.5	26.0	5.9	3.3	0.3	0.1	37
2	5—9	4.7	4.9	0.16	18	—	3.8	23.9	5.3	4.2	0.3	0.2	41
3	9—23	5.3	4.3	0.15	17	—	2.5	22.8	8.2	5.9	0.3	0.1	64
4	23—28	5.2	31.2	0.71	26	—	2.7	47.5	11.6	6.9	0.5	0.1	40
Profile 3, Inuvik													
Bm1	0—6	4.5	2.9	0.12	14	—	4.6	24.5	11.0	4.5	0.3	0.1	65
Bm2	6—10	5.8	2.1	0.10	12	—	4.4	25.9	16.5	5.8	0.2	0.1	87
BC	10—27	6.8	2.4	0.11	13	—	4.7	27.9	19.0	5.7	0.2	0.1	90
Cz	27—37	7.7	1.9	0.08	14	1.7	5.0	17.2	17.5	4.0	0.3	0.1	—
Cz	37—38.5	1.7	7.7	0.08	12	—	5.3	15.4	15.9	3.0	0.4	0.1	—
Profile 4, Inuvik													
F	3—0	4.5	—	1.47	—	—	—	—	—	—	—	—	—
Ah	0—2	4.8	21.6	0.62	20	—	4.1	63.5	26.8	8.1	0.3	0.1	56
Bm	2—6	6.1	2.4	0.10	14	—	4.7	34.2	23.2	7.3	0.2	0.1	90
BC	6—10	6.5	3.0	0.12	15	—	4.4	37.3	26.3	7.8	0.2	0.1	92
Cz	10—16	6.6	2.4	0.11	13	—	4.5	29.6	22.8	6.4	0.2	0.1	100
Profile 5, Inuvik													
F	2.5—1	4.7	80.2	2.10	22	—	—	—	—	—	—	—	—
H	1—0	4.7	59.7	1.45	24	—	—	—	—	—	—	—	—
Ae1	0—1.5	5.0	2.1	0.10	12	—	10.2	24.6	11.6	3.1	0.1	0.1	61
Ae2	1.5—3	5.2	1.4	0.07	12	—	13.3	26.7	12.1	3.6	0.1	0.1	60
Bf	3—4.5	5.4	1.8	0.07	15	—	18.3	27.3	11.6	3.3	0.1	0.1	55
BC	4.5—17	6.7	2.4	0.09	15	—	11.8	25.4	17.6	4.2	0.1	0.1	87
Ck	17+	7.5	1.8	0.06	17	7.7	15.4	17.8	20.1	2.6	0.1	0.1	—
Profile 6, Norman Wells													
F	3—0	6.5		0.14	—	—	—	—	—	—	—	—	—
Bm	0—7	7.2	3.8	0.13	17	0.0	4.1	23.9	21.4	5.2	0.2	0.1	—
IICk	7—24	7.5	1.9	0.09	12	10.4	2.1	14.5	21.0	3.6	0.1	0.1	—
Profile 7, Norman Wells													
Bm	0—8	5.4	2.2	0.08	16	—	2.3	20.8	11.9	6.4	0.2	0.1	89
BC	8—10	6.6	2.3	0.11	12	—	2.3	19.2	13.8	6.5	0.2	0.1	—
Ck1	10—17	7.5	2.1	0.10	12	11.1	1.8	14.6	14.4	5.5	0.1	0.1	—
Ck2	17—48	8.1	1.4	0.09	9	15.0	2.2	13.0	22.4	11.1	0.2	0.1	—
Profile 8, Norman Wells													
H	5—0	6.9	—	1.24	—	—	—	—	—	—	—	—	—
Ahk	0—10	7.1	16.5	0.42	23	3.2	2.3	65.0	56.5	10.2	0.2	0.1	—
IICk	10—38	7.7	1.2	0.08	9	12.0	2.8	12.2	21.7	3.4	0.2	0.1	—

Milliequivalents

TABLE III. MECHANICAL ANALYSIS OF SOME PERMAFROST SOILS ON THE ORGANIC-, SALT-, WATER-FREE BASIS.

Horizon	Depth inches	Gravel <2000 μ %	Sand 2000-50 μ %	Silt 50-20 μ %	20.5 μ %	5-2 μ %	Clay 2-0.2 μ %	<0.2 μ %
			Profile 1, Reindeer Depot					
3	0—1	—	15.0	10.7	19.1	12.1	21.9	21.3
4	1—7	—	21.0	12.0	19.0	8.9	23.5	15.6
5	7—14	—	17.8	11.0	20.0	8.4	23.4	19.4
6	14—21	—	18.7	8.6	15.0	9.0	23.4	25.3
7	21—25	—	18.0	10.1	15.6	10.1	23.0	23.2
			Profile 2, Reindeer Depot					
1	0—5	—	6.9	10.9	18.2	11.7	26.1	26.1
2	5—9	—	6.4	10.1	15.0	13.6	31.2	23.7
3	9—23	—	7.7	11.8	17.0	16.4	22.4	24.7
4	23—28	—	5.4	13.7	11.3	12.3	26.2	31.2
			Profile 3, Inuvik					
Bm1	0—6	—	19.4	12.2	17.9	11.1	20.5	18.8
Bm2	6—10	—	21.6	12.4	19.6	13.1	24.8	8.5
BC	10—27	—	18.8	13.9	15.7	13.9	28.9	13.2
Cz	27—37	—	31.1	11.0	15.0	9.0	23.4	11.6
Cz	37—38.5	—	27.5	13.5	15.0	10.8	19.5	13.7
			Profile 4, Inuvik					
Ah	0—2	—	12.1	10.8	11.5	11.5	21.7	32.3
Bm	2—6	—	24.1	9.3	11.0	10.9	26.0	18.7
BC	6—10	—	15.0	10.5	16.4	10.4	34.8	13.0
Cz	10—16	—	16.9	11.7	18.9	11.2	25.5	15.9
			Profile 5, Inuvik					
Ae1	0—1.5	41	51.8	15.4	12.9	5.8	8.5	5.6
Ae2	1.5—3	28	73.5	4.9	4.5	3.7	8.2	5.5
Bf	3—4.5	36	74.0	6.0	4.2	3.9	9.0	2.9
BC	4.5—17	61	62.0	9.8	8.7	6.3	12.3	0.8
Ck	17+	70	68.4	8.4	6.7	5.1	10.6	0.9
			Profile 6, Norman Wells					
Bm	0—7	—	27.2	21.2	19.8	9.4	5.1*	17.3*
IICk	7—24	28	44.5	15.8	14.1	8.6	5.4	11.6
			Profile 7, Norman Wells					
Bm	0—8	—	20.0	35.4	19.2	5.5	3.2*	16.7*
BC	8—10	—	26.4	32.1	16.6	5.4	3.1	17.3
Ck1	10—17	—	29.7	35.6	15.1	4.5	2.5	12.6
Ck2	17—48	—	3.5	23.3	35.2	11.3	5.6	21.2
			Profile 8, Norman Wells					
Ahk	0—10	—	21.6	23.0	24.2	25.7	2.2*	3.3*
IICk	10—38	37	44.4	10.7	13.2	7.9	5.8	18.0

*Coarse clay 2—1 μ, fine clay <1 μ.

The third site (profile 8) represents the poorly drained soils in the higher upland area and is located about 1 mile northeast of the airport. The topography is level to very gently sloping and the parent material is loamy alluvium over loam glacial till. Profile 8 has the following characteristics:

Depth inches	Horizon	Description
7 – 5	L	Moss roots.
5 – 0	H	Black (10YR 2/1) granular muck; pH 6.9.
0 – 10	AhK	Black (10YR 2/1) silt loam; friable; weak, fine granular to amorphous; a few small pebbles and cobbles; boundary abrupt and smooth; weakly calcareous; pH 7.1.
10 – 38	IICk	Dark grayish brown (2.5Y 4/2) gravelly loam; mottled; amorphous; plastic; calcareous; pH 7.7.
38 +	Cz	Frozen gravelly loam; not sampled.

Chemical, Physical, and Mineralogical Characteristics of the Soils

Chemical analysis (Table II) shows that profiles 1 and 2 from Reindeer Depot have certain features not found in the other soils. The pH values are low in the surface horizons, increasing slightly with depth. The organic matter content is medium in horizons 4 and 5 and increases markedly in horizon 6. The saturation percentage in horizon 7, profile 1, suggests the possible presence of calcareous parent material below the active layer (solum). For this reason numbers were used to designate horizons, rather than the letter symbols used for the other profiles.

Profiles 3 and 4 from Inuvik also have strong acidic surface mineral horizons, but their parent materials are nearly neutral to moderately alkaline. They have lower organic matter contents in all horizons (excepting the Ah in profile 4), and lack the organic matter-rich substrata present in profiles 1 and 2.

Profile 5 from Inuvik has a well-developed free-iron profile. Although the values are very high, they clearly indicate eluvial (Ae) and illuvial (Bf) horizons.

Profiles 6, 7 and 8 from Norman Wells have strongly acidic to neutral surface horizons and alkaline parent materials. None of the profiles has an organic matter-rich subsoil as those present in profiles 1 and 2.

The mechanical analysis (Table III) show that in profiles 1 and 2 the amount of fine clay was greatest at the lowest depth, whereas in profiles 3 and 4 it was greatest at the surface. The total clay in profiles 1 and 2 tends to increase with depth whereas it tends to decrease with depth in profiles 3 and 4. In profiles 5 to 8 there is considerable textural variation with depth.

A summary of the mineralogical analysis is given in Table IV Generally there were only slight variations between horizons and between profiles. Profiles 1 and 2, and profiles 3 and 4 were very similar, and have been grouped together, even though there was only slight variation among all four. The coarse clay fraction was largely mixed-layer montmorillonite—illite, quartz and kaolinite, plus small amounts of feldspar. The fine clay fraction differed from the coarse clay in being free of quartz. Profile 5 differed from the others mainly in lacking the mixed-layer montmorillonite—illite in both clay fractions and in lacking illite and kaolinite in the fine clay fraction. The differential thermal analysis substantiated the X-ray analysis in all profiles.

TABLE IV. MINERALOGICAL CHARACTERISTICS OF SOME PERMAFROST SOILS.

	Silts	Coarse clay	Fine clay
Profiles 1 and 2	Largely quartz, some feldspar and smaller amounts of kaolinite and illite.	Largely mixed-layer montmorillonite – illite, quartz, and kaolinite plus small amounts of feldspar.	Largely mixed-layer montmorillonite – illite, with some illite and kaolinite.
Profiles 3 and 4	Largely quartz with considerable feldspar and small amounts of illite and kaolinite.	Considerable illite, some montmorillonite–illite, and smaller amounts of kaolinite and quartz.	Mostly montmorillonite-illite and a small amount of kaolinite.
Profile 5	Mostly quartz, some illite and small amounts of kaolinite.	Mostly montmorillonite, minor amounts of illite and quartz with traces of kaolinite.	Montmorillonite only

Discussion and Conclusions

Since profile 1 was located near the crest of a gentle slope and had strong, randomly oriented, microtopography and weak or absent solifluction lobes, the organic matter-rich horizon 6 is attributed to the process of differential freezing and thawing postulated by Mackay et al. (1958, 1961). Considering that the soil colour in the upper horizons was of low chroma and mottling was absent, and that the chemical data indicate a relatively limited stage of weathering, the soil is therefore regosolic in character.

Tedrow et al. (1958) have described Regosols as a group of youthful soils, usually with permafrost at from 4 to 6 feet, that lack a genetic profile. The radio-carbon date of 8,000+ years B.P. for peat at Inuvik (Mackay 1963) indicates that profile 1 is regosolic by virtue of the short time since frost action disrupted any morphological features then present and buried the organic material present in horizon 6. In the Canadian system of classification profile 1 is a Subarctic Orthic Regosol. In the system proposed in the 7th approximation (U.S.D.A. 1960) it is an Orthic Cryudent.

Profile 2, located near the toe of a long gentle slope, has developed under wetter conditions than profile 1. The chroma of 4 in the surface mineral horizon, the distribution of free iron and the lower base saturation values indicate that this profile has had a longer time since frost action buried the organic material present in horizon 4 or more favourable conditions in which to develop its morphology than profile 1. The differences in clay content with depth are thought to be inherited from the parent material. The Arctic Brown soils described in Alaska (Tedrow and Hill 1955, Drew and Tedrow 1957 and Hill and Tedrow 1961) have A horizons containing 11 to 19 per cent organic matter, whereas profile 2 has only 5 per cent at the surface and shows little variation with depth, above horizon 4. Profile 2 has characteristics more closely related to those described for the Upland Tundra group in Alaska (Tedrow *et al.* 1958, Douglas and Tedrow 1960). In the Canadian system of classification this soil is best classified as a Subarctic Gleyed Acid Brown Wooded, and as an Orthic Cryaquent in the U.S. 7th approximation.

Profile 3 has a chroma of 4 in the Bml horizon. The free-iron content and base saturation are lower in the B than in the C horizon, indicating a weak podzolic process. The low organic matter content throughout the profile is a characteristic that differentiates this soil from the Arctic Brown group. The trends in clay contents evident in Table III are thought to be inherited from the parent materials. However, the greater total clay content in the surface horizons over the subsoils, like that reported in Arctic Brown soils (Tedrow and Hill 1955, Hill and Tedrow 1961), may have resulted from frost effects (Corte 1962). In the Canadian classification scheme it is classified as a Subarctic Brown Wooded. In the U.S. 7th approximation it is an Orthic Cryudent.

Profile 4 differs from profile 3 in having a thin Ah horizon and lower chroma in the Bm horizon. It is classified the same as profile 3.

Profile 5 has well-developed eluvial (Ae) and illuvial (Bf) horizons although they are thinner than comparable horizons in Podzols in southern Canada. Tedrow *et al.* (1958) have suggested that such a soil could possibly develop in northern Alaska. Its presence at Inuvik is attributed to the permeable, gravelly sandy loam parent material. It is classified as a Subarctic Minimal Podzol in the Canadian system and an Orthic Cryochrept in the U.S. 7th approximation.

Profiles 6 and 7 have brown sola and resemble profile 3 in most respects. They are classified in the same way.

Profile 8, developed under the influence of poor drainage, has an Ah horizon high in organic matter. It is classified as a Subarctic Peaty Carbonated Rego Humic Gleysol in the Canadian system and as a Histic Umbreptic Cryaquept in the U.S. 7th approximation.

References

Aguilera, N. H., and M. L. Jackson, "Iron oxide removal from soils and clays", *Soil Sci. Soc. Am. Proc. 17* (1953), pp. 359-64.

Atkinson, A. J., G. R. Giles, A. J. MacLean and J. R. Wright, "Chemical methods of soil analysis", Can. Dep. of Agr., Chem. Div. Contrib. No. 169 (rev.), Ottawa (1958).

Beschel, Roland E., "Botany: and some remarks on the history of vegetation and glacierization". In Jacobsen-McGill Arctic Research Expedition to Axel Heiberg Island, Prelim, rept. 1959-60, McGill University, Montreal (1961).

Brydon, J. E., H. M. Rice and G. C. Scott, "The recovery of clays from suspension by freeze-drying", *Can. J. Soil Sci. 43* (1963), p. 404.

Coffin, D. E., "A method for the determination of free iron in soils and clays", *Can. J. Soil Sci. 43* (1963), pp. 7-17.

Churchill, E. D., "Phytosociological and environmental characteristics of plant communities in the Umiat region of Alaska", *Ecology 36*, (1955), pp. 606-27.

Churchill, E. D. and H. C. Hanson, "The concept of climax in arctic and alpine vegetation", *Bot. Rev. 24* (1958), pp. 127-91.

Drew, J. V., "A pedologic study of arctic Coastal Plain soils near Point Barrow, Alaska", Unpublished Ph.D. Thesis, Rutgers University, (1957).

Drew, J. V. and J. C. F. Tedrow, "Pedology of an arctic brown profile near Point Barrow, Alaska", *Soil Sci. Soc. Am. Proc. 21* (1957), pp. 336-39.

Drury, Jr., W. H., "Bog flats and physiographic processes in the upper Kuskokwim River region, Alaska", Contr. Gray Herb., Harvard Univ. 178 (1956), pp. 1-130.

Glinka, K. D., *The great soil groups of the world and their development*, (Translated by C. F. Marbut) Ann Arbor: Edwards Bros. (1928), p. 235.

Gorodkov, B. N., "Peculiarities of the arctic top soil", Isvestiya Gosudarstvennogo Geograficheskogo obshchestva 71 (10) (1939), pp. 1516-32.

Kellogg, C. E. and I. J. Nygard, "Exploratory study of the principal soil groups of Alaska", *U.S. Dept. Agr. Agricultural Monograph 7* (1951), p. 138.

Hopkins, B., "Pattern in the plant community", *J. Ecol. 45* (1957), pp. 451-63.

Hopkins, D. M., "Thaw lakes and thaw sinks in the Imuruk Lake area, Seward Peninsula, Alaska", *J. Geol. 57* (1949), pp. 119-31.

Hultén, E., "Flora of Alaska and Yukon, Parts I-X", Lunds Universitets Arsskrift, N.F., Vols. 37-46 (1941-50).

Leahey, A., "Factors affecting the extent of arable lands and the nature of the soils in the Yukon Territory", *Proc. 7th Pacific Sci. Congr. 6* (1949), pp. 16-20.

Marbut, C. F., "A scheme for soil classification", Proc. 1st Int. Congr. Soil Sci. V. 4 Comm. V (1927), pp. 1-31.

Margulis, H., "Aux sources de la pédologie", Publication de l'école nationale supérieure agronomique de Toulouse (1954), p. 85.

Meinardus, W., "Boden der kalten Region", in E. Blank (Editor) *Handbuch der Bodenlehre*, Vol. III, Berlin, J. Springer (1930), p. 550.

Neustruev, S. S., "Genesis of soils", Russian pedological investigations, Acad. of Sci. U.S.S.R., Leningrad (1927), pp. 1-98.

Robinson, G. W., *"Soils, their origin, constitution and classification"*, London, Thomas Murby and Co. (1949), p. 573.

Sigafoos, R. S., "Forst action as a primary physical factor in tundra plant communities", *Ecology 33* (1952), pp. 480-87.

Sigafoos, R. D. and D. M. Hopkins, "Soil instability on slopes in regions of perennially frozen ground", Forst action in soils: a Symposium, Highw. Res. B. Spec. Rep. 2, Natl. Res. Counc. Publ. 213 (1952), pp. 176-92.

Spetzman, L. A., "Plant geography and ecology of the arctic slope of Alaska", Unpublished M.Sc. Thesis, Univ. of Minnesota (1951).

Tedrow, J. C. F., J. V. Drew, D. E. Hill and L. A. Douglas, "Major genetic soils of the arctic slope of Alaska", *J. Soil Sci. 9* (1958), pp. 33-45.

Tedrow, J. C. F. and D. E. Hill, "Arctic brown soil", *Soil Sci. 80* (1955), pp. 265-75.

Veatch, J. C., "Classification of land on a geographic basis", *Michigan Acad. of Sci., Arts, and Letters*, Vol. XIX (1934), pp. 359-65.

Wallace, R. E., "Cave-in lakes in the Nabesna, Chisana and Tanana river valleys, eastern Alaska", *J. Geol. 56* (1948), pp. 171-81.

Warren,, Wilson J., "Observations on the temperatures of arctic plants and their environment", *J. Ecol. 45* (1957), pp. 499-531.

Washburn, A. L., "Classification of patterned ground and review of suggested origins", *Bull. Geol. Soc. Am. 87* (1956), pp. 823-66.

Wiggins, I. L., "The distribution of vascular plants of polygonal ground near Point Barrow, Alaska", Contr. Dudley Herb., Nat. Hist. Mus., Stanford Univ., Calif. 4 (1951), pp. 41-56.

9

Soil Management and Fertility– Western Canada

C. F. Bentley

Soil Management Goals

Although the technology of food production by soilless procedures has made remarkable progress in recent years, land-based agriculture will probably continue indefinitely to be the principal source of food and of many materials required by industry. This will be true for many decades at least.

The future of our nation is therefore related to the productivity of our agricultural lands. Food for today must be produced by following procedures which will ensure that there will be productive soil for tomorrow. Deterioration of agricultural lands by mismanagement, so strikingly illustrated in the Mediterranean region, must be avoided.

If Canada's future is to be wisely planned, specific objectives for soil management, water conservation, soil fertility practices and for land development in Western Canada are needed. The following goals are proposed:

(a) To maintain productivity of the land for future generations, and where practical to enhance the inherent producing ability and fertility of the soil.

(b) To meet the nation's requirements for food and industrial material by the most effective use of land.

(c) To contribute towards a better life for Canadians by enabling greater production per farm worker and to avoid unnecessary human hardship and wastage of natural re-

Reprinted from *Background Papers, Resources for Tomorrow Conference,* Vol. 1 (1961), pp. 67-73. By permission of the Queen's Printer, Ottawa.

sources in the course of developing agricultural lands not yet in use.

The abundance of agricultural land in Western Canada must not be permitted to mislead us. Western Canada has about 15 to 25 million acres of additional potentially arable land. However, a large portion is of low quality and superior soil management will be necessary if such areas are to be used for successful agriculture by people who are to enjoy a desirable level of living.

Development policies for these potential agricultural lands are of national concern. Untold human hardship and suffering as well as deterioration and wastage of natural resources will surely result again unless wise land development programs are established.[1] Planning and research must be done now, if the best interests of Canada are to be served when these lands are developed.

Soil Regions and Soil Management

To consider soil management in Western Canada, the area can be conveniently dealt with as consisting of three regions with fundamental soil differences.

(1) *The Grassland Region*

The grassland region consists of open prairies and park land areas. Humus-rich soils have developed under grass vegetation and as a consequence these soils are usually of superior fertility. The grassland region has given Western Canada a world-wide reputation for productive soils. Unfortunately, this region usually lacks in adequate amounts of moisture for optimum crop growth.

The agricultural use of the grassland soils of Western Canada has been dominated by the grain economy. This type of farming has depended primarily on a soil management practice that originated near Indian Head in the 1880's.

It was too late to till the land and plant a crop when Angus McKay and some of his neighbors returned to their farms after the Riel Rebellion. That summer, good farmer McKay cultivated his fields to kill weeds and thereby introduced a new soil management practice to the Canadian West—summer fallow. The high yields on fallowed land were a great boon to the grain economy of the prairies and thus to Canada. The agricultural development of the West, and Canada's growth as a nation, have largely resulted from that fortuitously discovered soil management practice.

However, the grain economy and summer fallowing have adversely affected much of Western Canada's *grassland* soil. Initial high fertility of millions of acres of prairie land has been lowered considerably. There is ample proof that this is the case. For example, three cropping systems have been compared continuously for about 50 years at the Lacombe Experimental Station. The comparison has shown that yields of grain crops on land cropped only to grain-grain-fallow have declined appreciably. During the same period, adjacent plots employing more suitable crop sequences have produced more grain from a similar area and in addition important amounts of hay and other crops have been produced. Soil analyses have helped explain the results obtained: there has been an appreciable decrease in the humus and nitrogen content of the soils cropped only to grain and fallow.

There are other proofs that prairie soils used primarily for grain production, frequently with bare fallow, have deteriorated. Soil fertility studies conducted in the 1930's by Dr. Wyatt and some of his colleagues at the University of Alberta[2] revealed that soils of Western Canada used for grain production had in general suffered an appreciable decrease in organic matter and nitrogen as a consequence of some 20 to 30 years of cropping. Today, because of declining soil fertility, many farmers of Western Canada find it necessary to fallow more frequently than formerly if the good yields which were previously obtained are to be produced. A more general proof of deterioration may be cited. Despite all the improvements resulting from the applications of agricultural science, average grain production per acre has not increased significantly.[3] Declining soil fertility has largely offset the benefits of improvements.

Simple explanations account for the adverse effects of summer fallowing and the grain economy on prairie soils. In general, grain farming with its frequent bare fallow has:

(a) Accelerated erosion and loss of valuable top soil—especially during the fallow years;

(b) Reduced the store of accumulated humus by acceleration of its rate of decomposition;

(c) Removed, in crops, large amounts of nutrients which have seldom been replaced;

(d) Adversely affected the excellent tilth which characterized most prairie soils when they were first cultivated.

Of course, not all grain farms have suffered these adverse effects. Where combine straws have been retained on fields and worked into the soil, erosion has been reduced or prevented, and perhaps humus content is being maintained. Moreover, fertilizer use has increased considerably during the last two decades. On some farms, fertilizers have, at least partly, balanced the removal of nutrients. However, fewer than half of the farms use fertilizer, so that fertility depletion has prevailed under the grain production system so far employed on the prairies.

The native ranges of Western Canada have also suffered considerable deterioration from agricultural use. In some areas, overgrazing has increased run-off and erosion. Desirable native species have been eliminated or reduced because of the preferential browsing of livestock. Undesirable species have invaded and/or increased in the native range lands. Shrubs and trees have spread rapidly, largely as a consequence of the elimination of prairie fires which previously helped keep these plants in check. Our grassland pastures have generally deteriorated because, for the most part, nothing whatever has been done to maintain them.[5] They have merely been used, often badly.

(2) *The Forest Region*

Soils in the forested region are rather different from soils of the prairies and most of Western Canada's potentially arable land is in this region. However, the acreage now cultivated is rather small by comparison with that of the grassland area. Forest soils generally have rather low contents of organic matter and consequently lack the general high fertility which characterizes most grassland soils. However, moisture supply in the forested region is usually more reliable than in the grassland area.

In their virgin condition, *forest* soils usually have a lower humus content than soils of the grassland region. When forested soils are cleared and used solely for grain production, the meagre humus content is rather quickly lowered and yields usually decrease accordingly. Thousands of acres of once cultivated land now abandoned in our forest areas are mute proof of this. Dr. Wyatt's soil deterioration studies provide factual information concerning the extent of the deterioration of forest soils under cultivation.

(3) *The Cordilleran Region (British Columbia)*

British Columbia, excluding the Peace River Block, is a third region differing very markedly from the other two because of its mountainous terrain and highly variable climate. The complexity of soils and climates there makes it impractical to consider soil management practices in a specific way. However, the principles of soil management to be discussed are generally as applicable in British Columbia as elsewhere in Western Canada when suitable consideration is given to the character of the soils, areas, and the crops produced.

Recommended Soil Management

Research work which has been conducted in recent decades provides a body of knowledge on which sound soil management practices for Western Canada may be based.

Experiments with crop rotations have been carried out at many locations with very favorable results. Investigational work in Alberta at Lacombe, Breton, Edmonton and Beaverlodge; in Saskatchewan at Melfort, Snowden and Indian Head; in Manitoba at Brandon, Melita and Winnipeg, has demonstrated consistently that soils of the prairie provinces give greatest production under cropping sequences which include forage crops as well as grain crops and which minimize fallowing. Moreover, such cropping systems minimize the problems of soil erosion and also greatly assist in the control of weeds. Soil tilth as well as the organic matter content of the soils have been maintained best by cropping systems which include forages as well as grains. In some instances, these cropping systems have brought about substantial improvement of inferior soils. Research work on irrigated plots at the Lethbridge Station has established that crop sequences including forage crops are also best for irrigated lands in the brown and dark brown soil zones.

Data from extensive experiments with fertilizers are available.[3] There is an authoritative publication providing recommendations for fertilizer use in each of the western provinces. However, only a small proportion of the farmers who would obtain profitable yield increases from use of recommended fertilizers are so doing. In fact, some farmers who were previously fertilizer users and who obtained substantial and profitable yield increases are no longer users, probably because they are marketing grain under a quota system.

Forage crops are undoubtedly the most overlooked aspect of good soil management in the western provinces. In spite of the advantages of cropping systems including forage crops, as mentioned in the foregoing, only about ten per cent of the cultivated land in Western Canada is used for forage crop production. Data from the Swift Current Station have shown that even on good soils in the brown zone the value of hay equals or exceeds the value of grain which can be produced. Research work at the Lethbridge and Swift Current Stations has revealed that under the semi-arid conditions in the brown and dark brown zones, beef production per acre can be very considerably increased when native range is replaced by recommended tame forage crops. More recent work at Lacombe, Alberta, and Melfort, Saskatchewan, has established that use of the rich black soils for forage production, pastured off by beef animals, can produce considerably larger net returns than use of the same land for the production of grain on fallow. Investigations at other experimental locations in Western Canada have produced rather similar data.

Production Potentials

In every district of Western Canada, the better and more successful farmers are following the soil management practices under discussion. Unfortunately, the majority of western Canadian farmers are not utilizing much of the soil management knowledge available and as a consequence, their production is far below what it might reasonably be.

The extent to which the production of western Canadian crops could be increased by the optimum use of available knowledge concerning soil fertility and management varies with different districts, climatic circumstances and soils. In almost any district of Western Canada, full utilization of present soil fertility and management knowledge would result in a ten per cent production increase. In some districts, and on rather extensive acreages, full utilization of soil management information could today increase the production by 100 per cent. The average increase possible for all of the Prairie provinces is probably in the vicinity of 50 per cent. In British Columbia, the full utilization of present management knowledge in the production of fruit and vegetables would result in a larger average increase, probably approaching 100 per cent.

In the Prairie provinces, tremendous amounts of vegetable crops could be produced if there was a market for those crops. This is particularly true in irrigated areas. The importance of including forages in the cropping sequence is very great if vegetable crops are to be produced.

It is assumed, with respect to all of the above statements concerning increases in production, that the shifts in crop sequences and production procedures would not result in an increase in the proportion of crops lost due to agricultural pests.

It is fortunate that research work conducted during the last half century or so—and especially during the last two or three decades—has provided knowledge on which soil management practices for the immediate future should be based. Few public expenditures have brought the tremendous dividends which have resulted from research work on soil fertility and management in Western Canada. However, anticipated growth of Canadian population and income will place very heavy demands on agriculture and the output per acre must increase rapidly to meet the needs. More research is needed in order to attain the goals mentioned earlier.

A few examples of problems requiring research will illustrate the practical aspects of the work.

(a) Soil moisture is generally the most important factor limiting western Canadian crop yields. So far, most of the rather limited research in this field has been conducted in the brown soil zone. Other areas merit study too.

One of the great merits of good soil management is the conservation of natural precipitation. For maximum utilization moisture should enter the soil where it falls and good soil management favours this. Reduction of moisture losses by run off maximizes crop yields by ensuring the most uniform moisture distribution possible.

Until there is made-to-order weather, crop production in the prairies will be most severely and frequently limited by soil moisture. Wise soil management should ensure that on most soils, yields are in fact primarily limited by the amount of water available to crops. That would imply optimum use of the limited precipitation available most years.

Although a few western Canadian research establishments have projects concerned with the requirement, conservation and utilization of soil moisture, the total effort is seriously inadequate. Irrigation developments are consistently accompanied by salinity problems and these too must receive increased attention if serious deterioration and/or loss of land are to be avoided. There is a lack of data concerning the amount of soil moisture lost from agricultural lands as runoff. All phases of water conservation and utilization—runoff control, minimization of water erosion, use of small reservoirs, the role of field shelter belts and tree plantings, and irrigation—require study.

Hardy varieties of winter cereals, which would make considerably more effective use of the limited amounts of moisture, would enable important increases in production if they were available.

While soil management practices and new or improved agronomic materials can enable great increases in crop production, limitations must be recognized. Even under optimum conditions, plants have definite water requirements: several hundred pounds of water are required for every pound of dry matter produced. Unless the climate of Western Canada changes appreciably, soil moisture is likely to continue as the most important factor limiting crop yields. That is why research concerned with soil moisture is so important.

(b) In spite of the widespread deficiency of nitrogen, farm use of fertilizer nitrogen has been disappointingly small. The variable and uncertain nature of yield increases, which on the average are highly profitable, has been a primary cause of this situation. Research should enable more reliable recommendations for nitrogen use.

(c) The use of sulphur supplying fertilizers in conjunction with suitable crop sequences on sulphur deficient soils frequently increases production over 400 per cent. However, many thousands of acres of sulphur deficient soil are being farmed without benefit of this knowledge because of the lack of any reliable laboratory test to determine sulphur deficiency. Research is needed.

(d) Tillage operations are usually the most expensive of crop production costs. However, the amount and type of tillage for optimum crop growth are unknown. Research might enable tremendous savings.

(e) Legumes are of fundamental importance in most recommended crop sequences. In some districts, alfalfa and Altaswede clover fail to thrive if reseeded on land which has at a previous time grown that crop. This is a serious problem which will be difficult to solve.

(f) Perhaps range and pasture lands which have never been cultivated present the greatest challenge. Control measures for trees, shrubs and undesirable species are required. Practical methods for establishing tame forages are also desired. New tame forages which can effectively extend and supplement the present grazing periods are needed. Fertility requirements, too, merit attention.

(g) In Western Canada, the amount of research work on forage crops has compared rather unfavorably with that on cereals. This situation requires rectification. As agronomists develop or import forages which recover more quickly from cutting or grazing, the value of these crops in rotations will be more widely recognized.

Space does not permit listing other examples of soil management and fertility problems which can be solved by research. Increases in production potentials as well as the effective development of millions of acres of potentially arable land depend on this work *which should begin now if wise provision is to be made for the nation's future.*

Prospective Changes

The changes now taking place in agriculture will force extensive improvements in soil management practices. The end results will be higher yields and a more intensive agriculture. These desirable shifts will probably take place as quickly as any major agricultural adjustment yet experienced in Western Canada and they are expected to be very general within the next two decades.

Several factors will account for the speedy changes forecast. Continued straight grain farming will be accompanied increasingly by inferior yields which will not be competitive with those obtained from better systems of soil management. The proportion of arable lands seeded to forage crops will increase greatly because there will be wider recognition of beneficial effects on grain production, in weed and erosion control, and on the nutritive value of grain crops which follow the forages. Perhaps the greatest impetus for these changes will come from increasing demand for livestock products, since a livestock industry requires much pasture and hay.

Today, the increasing demand for livestock products, which is expected to become much stronger in the next few decades, is providing the incentive for farmers to adopt soil management practices which will arrest, and in many cases reverse, the trend to declining production per acre. These changes represent a very happy combination of events: trends of change in demands for adjustments in crop sequences and the adoption of soil management practices which are suited to the maintenance and/or enhancement of soil fertility. At the same time, there are powerful financial incentives which are likely to be the most persuasive encouragements of all.

In short, the anticipated shift to an agricultural economy much more heavily based on livestock production promises to help implement knowledge not being utilized to a satisfactory extent at present.

In making the foregoing statements the author does not intend general condemnation of western Canadian agriculture to date! The west was opened up and developed largely on the basis of grain exports. The high inherent fertility of the virgin soils of the prairies made the type of agriculture possible. Fortunately, Canadian growth promises to offer the incentive for changes in soil management practices. The changes should arrest the decline in soil productivity which is expected, should straight grain production continue.

Soil Management and Soil Fertility Research

Soil is a dynamic resource continually changing under the influences of nature and agricultural use. Continuing research is therefore necessary as new problems constantly appear. Moreover, there is a great need for more fundamental knowledge about soil, in order to enable effective use of the innumerable individual soils that comprise agricultural land.

The practical applications of basic nuclear research, such as atomic energy and radioactive isotopes, have done a great deal to create public awareness of the returns to all citizens from fundamental scientific research. Since, on the average, expenditures on properly used fertilizers bring farmers more profits than any other purchase of similar cost made by them, there should be no niggardliness about financial support for research in soil fertility and soil management in all their ramifications.

If the goals proposed for soil management and fertility practices in Western Canada are to be attained, expansion and some reorganization of research are desirable. The following are suggested as aspects especially meriting more intensive study:

(a) Moisture conservation and utilization.

(b) Improvement of native pasture and range lands, including the control and elimination of undesirable plants.

(c) Development programs, soil management practices, and accumulation of meteorological data for potential agricultural lands.

(d) Crop quality and composition as affected by soils, climate, fertilizers, varieties, and management practices.

(e) Nitrogen problems, including symbiotic and non-symbiotic fixation, availability from organic matter and utilization of fertilizer nitrogen.

Research of the types needed is increasingly difficult and much of it requires the availability of library facilities and complex equipment. The opportunity for co-operation and consultation with research workers in other fields is also desirable. It is logical for such investigations to be centered at universities. Even if research could be done with equal effectiveness at off-campus research institutes, such establishments are barren because education of graduate students is not included as an activity. The education of such students is essential to meet the need for future scientists—a demand that will constantly expand if Canada's progress is to continue. The student-advisor relationship is a mutually beneficial one because young minds are usually stimulating to mature scientists.

There are financial advantages, too, when research is done at universities. Graduate student assistantships are among the most productive payments to research workers since such remuneration is only a small fraction of full-time salaries, even though the students often work very long hours for months on end. Expanded soil fertility work at universities would minimize expenditures on facilities since many of them are already available. Moreover, dual use of equipment and facilities for teaching and research also offers economies. University instruction should improve as a consequence of expanded research and this, too, would have wide benefits.

Isolated, inadequately equipped laboratories attempting basic research with very small staffs cannot be expected to be very productive. Scientists usually work best when there are colleagues on whom and with whom they can sharpen their wits! Universities provide such a climate.

References

1 Specific data about abandonment and depopulation of once farmed areas of south-eastern Alberta are given in *Canada Department of Agriculture Publication* No. 731, 1942. Histories of some areas of Saskatchewan and Manitoba are rather similar.
2 A. L. Brown and F. A. Wyatt, and J. D. Newton, *Effects of cultivation and cropping on the chemical composition of some Western Canada prairie soils.* Sci. Agr. 23: 229-32, 1942.
3 A compilation of crop statistics for central Alberta crop districts 6-14, for the period 1921-1950 revealed a steadily decreasing yield trend.
4 The total livestock load on the grasslands of the prairie provinces has not increased since 1920 although settlement was not complete then. The increased cattle numbers have been possible because of decreases in horses and sheep, and because beef is now marketed at an earlier age.
5 In each of the western Canadian provinces, there is an annual compilation of official data from fertilizer experiments. Provincial fertilizer recommendations are based on those results.

10

Soil Physical Properties and Erosion Control

R.Webber

The effectiveness of conservation practices for erosion control is determined in part by the physical condition of the soil surface. It has been observed that the bulk density, porosity, and aggregation of the surface soil are more important in determining surface runoff and infiltration than is the soil moisture storage capacity.[4] Raindrops alter the physical condition of the immediate surface of the soil by compaction, by the dispersion of non-stable aggregates, and by the sealing or clogging of soil pores with detached materials.[3, 11] Weakley[14] reported that water-stable aggregates significantly reduced erosion on a Sharpsburg silty clay loam. A comprehensive review of the soil properties that influence soil erosion by water was prepared by Smith and Wischmeier.[10]

Treatments and Methods

Soil erosion studies were begun in 1953 at the Ontario Agricultural College on a Guelph loam, a Grey-brown Podzolic soil developed on calcareous glacial till. Ten plots, each 15.0 by 145.0 feet in size, were established on a 7 per cent slope on the eastern side of a drumlin. Plot treatments were as follows: one plot in continuous sod, originally brome grass and alfalfa; one plot in continuous corn planted with the slope; four plots in a 4-year rotation of corn-oats-hay-hay with all crops planted with the slope; and four plots in the 4-year crop rotation with a strip-cropping program in operation. On the latter four plots, the corn or oats was planted across the slope in strips 72.5 feet wide and adjoined a strip of hay. On all plots, all residues were removed each year, no manure was applied, and fertilizers were used on each crop at levels recommended to farmers. Corn and second-year hay plots were plowed in late October of each year.

Reprinted from *Journal of Soil and Water Conservation,* Vol. 19 (1964), pp. 28-30.

Each plot was equipped with an HS-flume (0.75 foot deep), a water-level recorder, and a silt-sampling wheel.[5] A recording raingauge was located within the experimental area.

To measure the organic matter content of the soil, the laboratory methods described by Walkley[13] were utilized. Soil moisture properties were determined with methods detailed by Richards and Fireman.[8, 9] Aggregate stability was determined by the method used by Conway and Strickling[1] on a 25-gram sample of dry aggregates 2.0 to 3.0 millimeters in size.

Soil and Water Losses

Under continuous corn planted with the slope, 95 per cent of the average annual soil losses occurred during the 6-month period April to September; almost equal losses were recorded for each 3-month period (Table I). During the 10-year period, 78 per cent of the total losses occurred during 3 years: 1955, 1956 and 1962.

The insignificant soil losses under corn after 2 years of hay are attributed to the relatively high levels of soil aggregate stability and organic content on this plot, even though it was planted with the slope. Under the strip-cropping practice, the ridges and depressions left by the planting equipment and subsequent cultivation significantly increased the surface storage on the narrow plots. Soil aggregate stability and organic matter were much better on these plots than on the one in continuous corn (Table II).

Of the average annual soil losses under oats planted with the slope, 78 per cent occurred during the 3-month period April to June. During the 10-year period, the oat plot lost a total of 21.3 tons of soil per acre during the April to June period; 87 per cent of this loss occurred in May 1953 and May 1956. The oat plot was ridge-rolled immediately after the oats and the hay mixture were planted. These small ridges and the accompanying depressions were conducive to high soil losses until the vegetation covered the soil. It is believed that the stubble and the legumes and grasses in the hay mixture protected the soil after the oats were harvested. Under the strip-cropping practice, the ridge-and-depression surface retained the water and thus prevented major soil losses. This might not occur on areas larger in size than the experimental plots.

Water losses (Table I) were not significant except for the 1.08 inches of water lost during the April to September period from the continuous corn plot; this amount was 6.5 per cent of the average rainfall during that period. No estimates were made of runoff due to melting snow; only the runoff from late winter rains was recorded. Severe soil and water losses occurred in March 1956 when 2.20 inches of rain fell in a 48-hour period on an unfrozen surface under which the soil was frozen at the 4-inch depth.

TABLE I. AVERAGE ANNUAL SOIL AND WATER LOSSES DURING A 10-YEAR PERIOD, 1953-1962, BY CROPPING PRACTICE FOR 3-MONTH PERIODS, GUELPH, CANADA[a]

Cropping Practice	Jan.-Feb.-March[b]		Apr.-May-June		July-Aug.-Sept.		Oct.-Nov.-Dec.		Yearly Total	
	Water	Soil	Water	Soil	Water	Soil	Water	Soil	Water	Soil
	inches	lbs./ac.	inches	lbs./ac.	inches	lbs./ac.	inches	lbs./ac.	inches	lbs./ac.
Continuous hay	Negligible losses									
Continuous corn	0.15	800	0.44	8400	0.64	7600	T	[c]T	1.23	16800
Four-year rotation, with-the-slope planting										
Corn	0.07	T	0.04	300	0.12	800	T	T	0.23	1100
Oats	0.14	700	0.26	4300	0.15	500	T	T	0.55	5500
Hay, first year	0.13	100	T	T	T	T	T	T	0.13	T
Hay, second year	0.12	T	T	T	T	T	T	T	0.12	T
Four-year rotation, strip cropped, with the listed crop on the lower half of the plot										
Corn	0.03	[d]T	0.01	100	0.06	400	T	T	0.10	500
Oats	0.03	[d]200	0.07	800	0.04	200	T	T	0.14	1200
Hay, first year	Negligible losses									
Hay, second year	Negligible losses									

[a] Values rounded off: water to 0.01 inches, soil to 100 pounds.   [b] Erosion losses caused by three storms in 1954, 1956 and 1957.
[c] T = less than 0.01 inches of water or less than 100 pounds of soil.
[d] A rainfall of 2.20 inches within a 48-hour period on March 6 and 7, 1956, caused these losses. The soil temperature at a depth of 4 inches was 26° F. and the maximum air temperature was 35° to 39° F. for 4 days prior to the storm.

Physical Properties

Prior to the establishment of erosion plots, the land had been part of a farm devoted to the production of silage corn, oats, hay, and pasture. Manure on this farm was applied to the corn ground. The organic matter content of the soil was 4.21 ± 0.24 per cent with no apparent gradients due to position on the slope. After 10 years of use as erosion plots, the organic matter content of the surface soil had not changed significantly except under continuous corn, where it decreased to 3.1 per cent (Table II). Preservation of the original level of organic matter on the rotation plots may have been due to higher levels of fertilization and no pasturing of the hay aftermath while the area was used for experimental purposes. A build-up of organic matter on the plot that was in continuous sod did not occur; this may reflect insufficient nitrogen fertilization for a sward dominated by grasses during the latter years of the tests. The organic matter content of the soil in an undisturbed fence row on the experimental area was 6.5 per cent.

The highest levels of soil aggregate stability and organic matter content were reached under continuous sod, the lowest occurred under continuous corn (Table II). In the rotation plots, aggregate stability values differed little under corn or oats but were greatest under second year hay.

The differences in the moisture retained at 0.33-bar and at 15-bars under the different treatments probably are not significant (Table II).

TABLE II. PHYSICAL PROPERTIES OF GUELPH LOAM AFTER 10 YEARS UNDER DIFFERENT CROPPING PRACTICES

Cropping Practice	Organic Matter	Aggregate Stability	Moisture Retentivity at	
			0.33 bar	15 bars
	percent	percent >0.5 mm.	percent	percent
Continuous sod	4.4	84.7	24.2	8.8
Continuous corn	3.1	21.6	21.6	7.3
Four-year rotation, with-the-slope planting				
Corn	4.0	57.8	22.5	8.3
Oats	4.2	60.7	24.5	8.4
Hay, first year	4.3	55.8	23.6	8.7
Hay, second year	4.1	71.4	22.9	8.2
Four-year rotation, strip cropped				
Corn	4.1	52.3	22.9	7.3
Oats	4.2	55.9	22.6	7.7
Hay, first year	4.0	60.9	23.0	7.6
Hay, second year	4.4	74.0	23.2	8.3

Soil Porosity

The volume of air-filled pores at a tension of 60 centimeters of water is used frequently as a criterion of soil aeration and drainability. The data in Table III indicate that all plots except the one in continuous sod exhibited signs of soil compaction or that soil pores were clogged by detached material.[3, 11] The volumes of air-filled pores at 20 and 40 cm. tensions were low in the continuous corn plot, a condition reflected in the low percentage of water-stable aggregates (Table IV). In a previous study of these plots,[2] the volume of air-filled pores at 60-cm. tension from cores taken at the 2- to 5-inch depth were nearly double the values reported in Table III.

The earlier study of these plots[2] also revealed that increases in the organic matter content and the porosity at 60 cm. tension did not produce significant increases in the moisture retained at 0.33 atmosphere of pressure. Jamison[6] reported similar results; he indicated that a decrease in the moisture retained at 0.33 atmosphere and an increase in the 60-cm. porosity were due to structural improvements in a soil.

The bulk density of the soil under continuous sod was 1.25 ± 0.06 g./cm.^{3} and under continuous corn it was 1.35 ± 0.06.

TABLE III. VOLUME OF AIR-FILLED PORES AT FOUR TENSIONS IN THE SURFACE 2 INCHES OF SOIL

| | Volume of Air-Filled Pores | | | |
| | Tension, Centimeters of Water | | | |
Cropping Practice	20	40	60	80
Continuous sod	6.1	9.2	11.4	15.3
Continuous corn	0.0	3.0	6.0	10.1
Four-year rotation, with-the-slope planting				
Corn	3.8	8.0	10.7	15.7
Oats	2.6	5.8	7.9	15.6
Hay, first year	3.9	7.4	9.0	13.2
Hay, second year	2.9	4.9	7.7	11.0

[a]Test samples were 2- by 2-inch cores.

Nature of Eroded Material

Massey and Jackson[7] proposed the use of enrichment ratios to show the concentration of soil fertility constituents in eroded material relative to that in the plot soil. Samples of the plot soil obtained in late August were analyzed and the results were used to calculate enrichment ratios. The P_2O_5 included the dilute-acid soluble and adsorbed forms, extracted with HCl (0.1N) and NH_4F (0.05N) solution; replaceable K_2O was extracted with H_2SO_4 (0.05N) and NH_4OAc (0.01N).

The enrichment ratios for organic matter did not show marked differences due to cropping practices (Table IV). The ratios for phosphorus and potash under rotation corn and oats were greater than under continuous corn. Total soil losses under rotation corn were composed of individual losses of small amounts; on only two occasions did soil losses in excess of 1 ton per acre occur as the result of a single storm. It has been reported that losses of small amounts of soil over a period of time as opposed to large losses at one time favor the removal of material higher in nutrient composition than the plot soil.[12]

A particle-size analysis of material eroded by one storm in July 1962 from the continuous corn plot showed enrichment ratios of 1.6 for material less than 2 microns in size, 1.5 for the 5μ material and 0.68 for material coarser than silt, 50μ. The eroded material contained less sand and more fine material than the plot soil; similar data were reported by Stoltenburg and White.[12]

Summary and Conclusions

This study involved measurement of soil and water losses on plots on a 7 per cent slope near Guelph, Canada, for 10 consecutive years. The principal soil treatments were continuous cropping with corn and with hay and rotation cropping with and without the practice of strip cropping. Major soil losses were confined to two treatments: continuous corn and oats in rotation, both planted with the slope. Erosion on the continuous corn plot resulted in significant decreases in organic matter content, aggregate stability, and the volume of air-filled pores at low tensions of water. Minor soil losses under corn in rotation and planted with the slope resulted in small changes in these properties.

The soil and water losses under oats in a rotation of corn-oats-hay-hay planted with the slope were attributed to a ridge-rolling practice used in establishing grasses and legumes.

These results indicate: (a) that a crop rotation including a hay or pasture crop is important in maintaining the organic matter content and the stability of soil aggregates, and (b) that a significant erosion hazard is associated with ridge-rolling with the slope to aid the establishment of small seeds.

TABLE IV. ENRICHMENT RATIOS FOR ORGANIC MATTER, PHOSPHORUS, AND POTASH UNDER CONTINUOUS CORN, ROTATION CORN, AND OATS

Fertility Constituent	Enrichment Ratios and Standard Deviations		
	Continuous Corn	Rotation Corn	Oats
Organic Matter	1.46±0.16	1.41±0.23	1.53±0.50
P_2O_5	1.60±0.29	2.04±0.39	2.52±0.25
K_2O	1.59±0.25	1.93±0.35	2.02±0.08

References

1 Andrew W. Conaway Jr., and Edward Strickling, "A comparison of selected methods for expressing soil aggregate stability", *Soil Sci. Soc. Am. Proc.* 26 (1962) pp. 426-30.

2 John DeVries and L. R. Webber, "Field capacity of a soil as affected by previous cultural treatment", *Can. J. Soil Sci.* 42 (1962), pp. 13-16.

3 F. L. Duley, "Surface factors affecting the rate of intake of water by soils", *Soil Sci. Soc. Am. Proc.* 4 (1939), pp. 60-64.

4 C. B. England and E. H. Lesesne, "Effects of single crop covers on runoff", *J. Soil and Water Cons.* 17 (1) (1962), pp. 11-12.

5 L. L. Harrold and D. B. Krimgold, "Devices for measuring rates and amounts of runoff", *Tech. Pub. 51*, Soil Conservation Service, Washington, D.C. (1943).

6 V. C. Jamison, "Changes in air-water relationships due to structural improvements of soils", *Soil Sci.* 76 (1953), pp. 143-51.

7 H. F. Massey and M. L. Jackson "Selective erosion of soil fertility constituents", *Soil Sci. Soc. Am. Proc.* 16 (1952), pp. 353-56.

8 L. A. Richards and M. Fireman, "Pressure plate apparatus for measuring moisture sorption and transmission by soils", *Soil Sci.* 56 (1943), pp. 395-404.

9 L. A. Richards "Pressure membrane apparatus, construction, and use", *Agr. Eng.* 28 (1947), pp. 451-54.

10 Dwight D. Smith and Walter H. Wischmeier, "Rainfall erosion", Advances in Agron. 14 (1962), pp. 109-48.

11 Kamil Sor and A. R. Bertrand, "Effects of rainfall energy on the permeability of soils", *Soil Sci. Soc. Am. Proc.* 26 (1962), pp. 293-97.

12 N. L. Stoltenberg and J. L. White, "Selective loss of plant nutrients by erosion", *Soil Sci. Soc. Am. Proc.* 17 (1953), pp. 406-10.

13 A. Walkley, "A critical examination of a rapid method for determining organic carbon in soils", *Soil Sci.* 63 (1947), pp. 251-64.

14 Harry E. Weakly, "Effect of HPAN soil conditioner on runoff, erosion and soil aggregation", *J. Soil and Water Cons.* 15 (4) (1960), pp. 169-71.

11

Soil Erosion in Western Canada

J. H. Ellis

Introduction

Soil erosion in Western Canada, as elsewhere, can be observed in varying locations, in varying forms, and varying in frequency of occurrence and in degree of severity.

In respect of soil erosion, Western Canada is by no means a regional unit. In Manitoba, Saskatchewan and Alberta, climate, vegetation, soils, land use, and consequently the form and degree of erosion, range in horizontal zonation from the extensive open plains of the semi-arid grasslands region, through prairie and aspen grove, to the boreal forest region in the north and east, and to the sub-alpine forest region in the west. In British Columbia, climate, vegetation and soil range in vertical zonation from dry inter-mountain valleys and montane forest plateaus, or from the coast littoral through Columbia and Coast forest regions, to sub-alpine forest, alpine tundra, and the snow-capped peaks of the mountain ranges.

With such a variety of conditions, it is difficult to give much of the detailed information that may be desired in the space here allotted. Consequently, an attempt has been made to give a few references from which more detailed information can be obtained, and to present herein a general concept of soil erosion: (I) on "Crown lands"; (II) in the main agricultural area east of the Rockies; and (III) in the mountain region of the West Coast province.

Reprinted from *Agricultural Institute Review,* March/April (1954), pp. 36-39.

The Soil Erosion Problem

(I) *On "Crown Lands"*

The lands not held as farms in the respective western provinces, (according to the 1951 census), constitute 87.4 per cent of Manitoba; 59.5 per cent of Saskatchewan; 72.1 per cent of Alberta; and 98 per cent of British Columbia. Thus in the four provinces there are 553.5 million acres of virgin land that are not under agricultural jurisdiction. Included in this acreage are the National Parks (which are the responsibility of the Government of Canada); the Provincial Parks and Forest Reserves; the lands within provincial boundaries that are the responsibility of the respective governments; and small areas, under private or corporate ownership, alienated from the Crown but not listed as farm lands.

These virgin areas are largely, but not entirely, Crown lands and in the main are located in the forested zones. Under virgin conditions the soil deterioration most to be feared is the destruction of organic soils, and of the "A_0" or leaf mat of forest soils, by fire. However, soil erosion may be accelerated through destruction of vegetation by uncontrolled pulpwood and logging operations or, if permitted, through overgrazing and browsing by wild life; but as long as native vegetation is maintained and preserved, the soils of virgin areas under the jurisdiction of government departments and departmental officials are not likely to suffer widespread or accelerated damage from wind or water erosion. No new government or other machinery is required to combat soil erosion in such areas. The real need is for the public and the respective legislative bodies to show appreciation of their own officials (whose duty, and desire, it is to guard against exploitation and destruction of forests and wild life), and to extend to such officials the support necessary for the enlargement of their efforts.

(II) *In the Main Agricultural Area East of the Rockies*

To ensure a common understanding of the problem of soil erosion and its control on farm lands in the three provinces east of the Rockies, consideration should be given to the following pertinent facts:

(a) *Effect of Limitations in Land Use*:

Of the 96.8 million acres of cultivated farm land in Canada, 71.8 million (or 74 per cent) is located in the provinces of Manitoba, Saskatchewan and Alberta. One-seventh of this cultivated land could support the total urban and rural population of 2.5 million living in these three provinces.

Except for the development of ranching in the open plains of the semi-arid brown soil region, and of the irrigation projects in southern Alberta, agriculture in the prairie and aspen-grove region in the West was initially developed, and continues largely to be maintained, through recognition of the suitability of prairie soils for the production of high quality grain, and through ability to dispose of grain and its products through export or outside markets. On the cultivated lands of the grassland region, the development of diversified and pastoral agriculture to supply domestic markets has been limited mostly to the requirements of a limited urban population. Thus the utilization of at least six-sevenths of the cultivated farm lands in these provinces is determined more by the agricultural products that export and outside markets will take than by the agricultural products the resident population can consume. This economic limitation in land use, in such an extensive agricultural region (where the total population of all the cities is considerably less than one million), has imposed a type of fallow-grain culture on this region which, during the last 60 to 80 years, has augmented and accelerated the erosion naturally induced by the peculiarities and vicissitudes of climate.[1]

(b) *Predisposing Climatic Factors*:

It must be recognized that soil erosion by wind was active in the grassland areas of the West long before agricultural development was initiated or before human culture became a contributing factor. Throughout the plains region, even where soils are of silty or clay texture, micro-undulating topography, resulting from low dune formation, is not uncommon. In solonetzic soil areas, blowouts[2] (or local micro-relief depressions with scanty vegetation) indicate sites where, subsequent to dessication of the "A" horizon, soil has been removed by wind. In a Saskatchewan sand-dune area under native vegetation of Bouteloua, Koeleria, Artemisia, and ground cedar, the writer has observed as many as three buried soil profiles, each separated from the respective overlying or underlying soil by two to three feet of wind-blown sand. Such buried soils are mute evidence of excessively severe droughts, during which the retarded native vegetation failed to prevent soil erosion, and the deposition of wind-blown drift was the result.

---

[1] R. L. Erdman, "Effect of wind erosion on the composition and fertility of some Alberta soils", *Sci. Agr. 22* (1942), pp. 533-45. H. C. Moss, "Some field and laboratory studies of soil drifting in Saskatchewan", *Sci. Agr. 15* (1953), pp. 665-79.
[2] J. Mitchell, H. C. Moss and J. S. Clayton, *Saskatchewan soil survey report No. 12* (1944), p. 59.

In the semi-arid brown steppe region, the native vegetation (unlike the turf-forming prairie grasses of the Blackearth zone, or the close sod of cultivated grasses in humid regions) is of bunch-grass type with bare ground between the tufts.[3] When normal growth of vegetation is inhibited by periodic droughts, or destroyed by overgrazing and insect pests, and when winds of sufficient velocity move over the open plains, surface soil material from between the dormant tufts of grass and herbs can be, and frequently is, removed as clouds of dust.

Such evidence of the combined effects of wind and drought on local sites under varying conditions in the past, together with the widespread soil drifting and dust storms that occurred in the "dirty thirties", and which will not readily be forgotten, emphasize the wind erosion hazard to which this area is regionally and naturally exposed.

Erosion by water is also a naturally-occurring phenomenon resulting from summer rainstorms and spring run-off. Evidence of erratic and abnormally high floods that have occurred periodically in the past as the result of climatic conditions, rather than as the result of recently introduced culture, can be seen in soil profiles and in historic records. The soil survey maps of the respective provinces show appreciable acreages of juvenile and immature soils, in the vicinity of large and small streams, which are in the process of development on natural levees, flood plains, deltas, overwash and stream outwash. These deposits reflect river floods that have occurred over long periods of time. Prior to the general development of agriculture, which did not begin on the prairies until after 1870, three historic Red River floods, each higher than the disastrous flood of 1950, are recorded as occurring in 1826, 1852, and 1861. Such excessive run-off, resulting in river floods, is likely to occur in the grassland region whenever a wet autumn and an early winter with severe and continued frosts is followed by heavy snowfall during the latter part of the winter, and by higher than normal rainfall subsequent to a late and sudden spring thaw.[4]

Although soil erosion in the forested zone of the West may be considered, in general, as basically similar in form (even if regionally different in degree) to soil erosion in Eastern Canada, soil

---

[3] S. E. Clarke, J. A. Campbell and J. B. Campbell, "An ecological and grazing capacity study of the native grass pastures in southern Alberta, Saskatchewan and Manitoba", *Can. Dept. of Agri. Tech. Bull. 44* (1942).

[4] R. H. Clarke, "Notes on Red River floods", *Man. Dept. of Mines and Natural Resources* (1950).

erosion in the grassland zones may be considered as in a somewhat different category.

The approach to an understanding of the soil erosion problem, in the semi-arid to sub-humid grassland regions, is not through the lamentations and hysterical recriminations of the prophets of gloom, but by recognition of the facts that must be faced. The real problem here is how to control soil erosion where grain growing is, and for a long time will continue to be, a major enterprise, supplemented by diversified agriculture as a minor form of land use, under the peculiarities and vicissitudes of a continental climate which naturally predisposes to widespread periodic erosion by wind and a periodic erosion by water

(c) *Causes of Erosion and Principles of Control:*

WIND EROSION: It is not necessary to encloud wind erosion with mystery. The essential facts are simple. With dry conditions as a prerequisite, soil erosion by wind is caused by a force (i.e., wind or moving air currents) in action against objects (i.e., soil particles and aggregates) of such size and in such condition that their mass is not sufficient to resist the action of the force. Consequently the fundamental approach in combating wind erosion is either (1) to reduce the force, or (2) to increase the mass (or size) and the stability of the structural aggregates. If neither of these objectives can be accomplished, then the alternative is (3) to cover the soil materials so that they are not exposed to the erosive force.[5]

WATER EROSION: The causes and the principles of control in the case of soil erosion by water are also simple. Elaborate experiments are not required to prove that, if water falls or snow melts faster than it can penetrate into or percolate through the soil, surplus water will accumulate on or above the soil surface; and unless it is retarded, such surface water will flow to lower levels and become a moving force. Soil and soil materials are objects that can be moved when they are exposed to this force. Therefore the fundamental approach in combating water erosion is three-fold, i.e., (1) to reduce the force by getting as much of the precipitation as possible into the soil on which it falls; (2) to further reduce the force of flowing water by reducing the speed of the run-off, and

5 J. H. Ellis, "Soil conservation and soil deterioration", Soils Subject Division papers, Agricultural Institute Conference, Lethbridge (1947). A. E. Palmer, "Soil drifting problem in the Prairie Provinces", *Sci. Agr.* 16 (1936), pp. 264-65. A. E. Hopkins et al., "Soil drifting in the Prairie Provinces", Can. Dept. of Agr. Pub. (1946), p. 568.

(3) to protect the inevitable intermittent water runways with perennial vegetation, and the cultivated fields with some form of cover.[6]

The foregoing may seem a too simple summary of the causes of soil erosion and the principles of its control, but in the West, the underlying principles are simple. The real difficulties arise when attempts are made to select and apply methods of control that are practical and usable, and that are in harmony with regional environment and with land-use limitations.

CONTROL PRACTICES: Of the wind erosion control practices that are gradually coming into use, or that could be used more generally, a few examples only can be given. Methods of reducing wind velocity at ground level include: Cropping in strips, with a surface cover of trash on the cropped and fallow land; the growing of cover crops for the protection of soil in the absence of trash or crop residue; the use on fallow fields of tall-growing annuals, such as corn or sunflowers, at intervals, in single or double rows; and, in restricted areas, the planting of trees for field shelterbelts.

The most practical method of providing the cultivated fields of the prairies with a protected cover, and one that is being more and more extensively used, is to maintain a trash cover of combined-straw and stubble. However, during a series of dry years, the straw produced may be inadequate to give the needed protection, but in moist seasons an excessive amount of straw can cause problems in the use of tillage and seeding machinery that demand solution.

Field shelterbelts of utility trees are the most effective for protection from wind, but their use is limited to sites with sufficient moisture for the support of tree growth (as in the Blackearth zone, or in local sites with moist sub-soils in the drier soil zones). It should be noted that Field Shelterbelt Associations were initiated as one of the Prairie Farm Rehabilitation activities on groups of farms at Lyleton in Manitoba; at Conquest and Aneroid in Saskatchewan; and at Porter Lake in Alberta.[7] Individual farmers elsewhere also have undertaken private programs of field shelterbelt plantings; and, where they can be grown successfully, planting of suitable utility trees for field shelterbelts, flanked by tall-growing

---

[6] W. D. Albright, "The menace of water erosion in the Peace", *Sci. Agr. 19* (1939), p. 241. J. A. Toogood and J. D. Newton, "Water erosion in Alberta", *Univ. of Alta. Bull. No. 56* (1950).

[7] P.F.R.A., "A record of achievement", Can. Dept. of Agr. (1943), p. 29.

shrubs or shrub-like trees, should be extensively developed as community projects.[8]

In the aspen-grove region, use can and should be made of the native woods, supplemented by suitable tree plantings for the protection of cultivated fields from wind; and when lands are cleared in the forested areas, strips of native trees and shrubs should be retained for the protection of the cleared strips which (if possible) should be long and narrow, and 'on the contour'.

Although the grassland soils are generally characterized by good micro-structure, the various types of macro-structures vary with tillage and with variations in moisture and weather conditions. This necessitates care in the choice of tillage machines, and in the time and speed of tillage operations. Considerable interest is now being directed to tillage machines that will work under and through trash or that will leave the surface roughened without undue pulverization.[9]

Single-grained soils that do not have or which, because of removal of fine components, have lost the capacity to form effec- tive structural aggregates under proper tillage, together with trun- cated soils and eroded sites on knolls, etc., should be retired to grass or other perennial crops. In some areas a system of alternate grain growing and grazing on land temporarily retired to grass may provide a satisfactory land-use program. Droughty areas, and coarse textured sandy soils with low water retention capacity in the plains region, should be, and over a considerable area are being, withdrawn completely from fallow-grain culture. The establishment of community and municipal pastures on lands not suited to con- tinued arable culture has been an active program under P.F.R.A. during the last two decades. Fifty-seven of such pasture units[10] are now in operation in Saskatchewan and Manitoba; and in Alberta large tracts are administered under the Alberta "Special Areas Act".

In local parts of the West, some lands have been cleared that are too steep for continued arable culture. These lands should be put into woodlot or seeded permanently to alfalfa or grass. On lands

---

[8] J. H. Ellis, C. B. Gill and F. W. Broderick, "Farm forestry and tree culture projects for the non-forested regions of Manitoba", Man. Dept. of Agr. Pub. Branch (1945).

[9] A. E. Hardy, "The use of tillage machinery in soil drifting areas", *Sci. Agr.* *16* (1936), p. 281. K. W. Hill, "Soil drifting, its cause and control", Can. Dept. of Agr. Pub. (1953), p. 896.

[10] Report on Prairie Farm Rehabilitation and related activities, 1952-53, Can. Dept. of Agr. (P.F.R.A. Branch, Regina).

that are not too steep for arable culture but where erosion by water is a factor, the following practices have been initiated and are slowly being adopted: The smoothing and seeding down of water runways and the conservation of unproductive destructive gullies to productive and protective waterways; the stripping of slopes with strips of grass, at intervals, parallel to a master contour to act as buffer strips to ensure strip cropping and cultivation crosswise of the slopes; alternate cropping of the stripped areas so that no long slope is all in fallow or bare cultivation at the same time; the use of trash coverings of straw and stubble on the cropped and fallowed strips; the use of rotations which include periodic seeding down to grass-legume mixtures on lands with broken or hilly topography; the smoothing and seeding down of roadside ditches; and the installation of road culverts with adequate capacity, and adequate soil protection at culvert outlets. In addition, it cannot be too strongly stressed that diversion of creeks and intermittent water runways should only be undertaken after careful study and in consultation with responsible water resources officials.

(III) *In the Mountain Region of the West Coast Province*

In the mountain region of the West Coast Province, climate, terrain and culture, which are major factors in determining erosion, are all in marked contrast to the contributing factors in the western plains. Under a range of climate that varies from the moist Pacific Coast to the dry interior, solifluction, soil creeps and earth slides are natural local hazards; and reference need be made here only to the disastrous floods that occur occasionally on the flood plains of the Fraser and other rivers.

With a population of 1.16 million, (of which nearly one-third live in Vancouver, New Westminster, and Victoria), the West Coast Province, due largely to rough terrain, has only 1.5 million acres of land under cultivation, and part of this is in the Peace River block east of the mountains. About 20 per cent of the arable acreage of the province is devoted to the intertilled crops largely concentrated on the smaller-sized farms, and much of the land adapted to tree fruits, small fruits, vegetables and seed production is irrigated.[11]

The importance of soil erosion in British Columbia is shown by the following excerpts from more detailed information supplied to the writer by courtesy of D. G. Laird.[12] In giving credit and ex-

---

[11] J. C. Wilcox, "Soil conservation and land use in British Columbia", *Agr. Inst. Rev.* 2 (1947), p. 401.

[12] D. G. Laird and associates, "Problems related to the soils of British Columbia", 3rd. B.C. Nat. Res. Conference (1950).

pressing appreciation to Dr. Laird for the information, it should be noted that the writer takes full responsibility for any errors in interpretation or quotation here presented.

"The ravages of accelerated erosion are only too apparent in British Columbia." Here, "erosion by wind is of little or no consequence", but "that caused by water is responsible for serious damage. Clearing of native vegetation, without regard to topography, natural water reservoirs and natural drainage systems, is one of the major factors contributing to erosion in this province". In regard to virgin lands it is pointed out that "the disastrous effects of forest fires upon timber resources is perfectly obvious, but what is not so readily appreciated is that fire may impair the productive capacity of the soil". Also "during logging operations on slopes, the establishment of roads and snaking of logs sets up ideal conditions for the initiation of gullies".

In reference to erosion in the dry interior it is noted that "constant overgrazing is primarily responsible for serious damage to soils of the range country. About 1.5 million acres are involved", and "grasshopper epidemics, too, contribute to the denuding of grazing slopes and make them ideal for subsequent erosion".

"Erosion is a problem encountered under irrigation. Application of irrigation water by the furrow method leads to gullying, but when systematic surface cultivation is practised the evidence of erosion is usually obliterated. . . . The application of irrigation water throughout the Okanagan has resulted in ground-water movement such that hillside slipping of silt banks along the Okanagan Lake has resulted in an annual loss of valuable property. Of the remedial measures which have been investigated, sprinkler irrigation holds the most promise. . . . Approximately 30 per cent of the orchards in the Southern Interior are irrigated in this fashion. . . . The absence of tillage, combined with cover crops and sprinkling, where practised, have reduced erosion almost to zero".

"Throughout the Southern Interior, in non-irrigated areas devoted to intertilled groups, erosion is observed in clean cultivated orchards and in areas devoted to intertilled crops. . . . Cropping and tillage practices require detailed study looking to improvements whereby erosion may be reduced".

What To Do; and How

It has been pointed out that the management of Crown lands, and consequently soil erosion on such lands, is under the jurisdiction of the respective government departments and officials.

However, the lands aliented from the Crown have passed under the use, supervision and jurisdiction of a host of private individuals and corporate owners. It is particularly in these alienated lands, where the soils are under arable culture, that soil deterioration has become serious. Legislation for the control of natural phenomena such as soil erosion on freehold land is futile. Alberta, Saskatchewan and Manitoba each have Acts relating to soil drifting, but as nature pays little attention to them, they are relegated to shelves where such legislation is filed.

In any attempt to develop a logical soil erosion program (on lands that are freehold and farm operations are the responsibility of the respective farm operators), the first step is to ascertain the specific erosion problems and the control practices required to meet these problems; and the second step (supposing that, in cases where, suitable soil erosion practices are not followed) is to determine how the necessary practices may be introduced and adopted on the farms. The first step is well under way, and as a result of the observations and studies made during the Federal-Provincial Soil Surveys, specific soil problems and their geographical distribution are being ascertained; and it might even be conceded that the soil scientists who live and work in the West are not unfamiliar with methods of control.[13] As far as the second step is concerned, it must be recognized that the management of fields on freehold farms is the business, the privilege, and the responsibility of the respective farm managers and operators. Consequently, the management and operational practices carried out on the farms of Western Canada depend on (1) the knowledge, (2) the will, and (3) the ability of the individual managers and operators. Thus, if sponsored programs of soil erosion control are to be effective, they must be channelled along the three lines of action:

First—Education: To spread the knowledge of what to do and how to do it.

Second—Inspiration: To kindle the desire on the part of each farm operator to undertake and put soil erosion practices into effect, and to undertake all that he can do by his own efforts.

Third—Assistance: To help organized groups and individuals with technical assistance and leadership where necessary or where farm operators have not the ability to undertake certain district projects.

---

13 J. H. Ellis, "A summary of soil conservation problems and soil conservation activities for specific areas in Manitoba", Proc. Man. Agron, Conf. Man. Dept. of Agr. (1950).

12

Soil Erosion in Eastern Canada

N. R. Richards

Eastern Canada covers a land area of slightly less than one million square miles. The extent to which erosion has affected this area is governed by soil factors such as topography and texture, by climatic factors, particularly the amount and intensity of rainfall, and by the land use. Although quantitative surveys have not been conducted on a broad scale to assess the status of erosion in this area, yet investigational work carried on at Experimental Stations has shown that under certain cropping practices losses of soil occur. Controlled experiments conducted at Ottawa and Guelph have indicated that the amount of loss is determined largely by the texture of the soil, the per cent slope, and the crop grown. These experiments also showed that soil losses can be reduced to a minimum through cropping practices, by maintaining a close-growing cover on the land for as large a proportion of the time as possible. Because accurate quantitative estimates of soil erosion in Eastern Canada are not available, a review of the factors that influence suspectibility to erosion, namely, climate, soil and present land use, will assist in appraising this important problem.

Climate

The amount of precipitation and its distribution in Eastern Canada contribute in no small part to the problem of erosion. Studies and observations indicate that the total rainfall for a period is of less importance than the intensity with which the rain falls. The violent storms of short duration that occur in Eastern Canada in early spring and during the growing season cause serious soil losses on sloping land, particularly if it is without crop cover. Climate determines to a large extent the crop that can be grown in a particular area. In some areas soil losses will be increased because climate favours the growing of crops that in turn cause greater erosion.

Reprinted from *Agricultural Institute Review*, March/April (1954), pp. 40-43.

In the agricultural areas of Ontario the precipitation ranges from 28 to 35 inches per year. In Quebec, agriculture is confined largely to the more southerly regions bordering the Ottawa and the St. Lawrence Rivers where the climate is similar to that in the adjoining areas of Ontario. The climate of the Maritime Provinces is influenced by the Labrador current and the cold winds which sweep down from the interior of northern Quebec. Annual precipitation in the Maritime Provinces averages 40 to 50 inches per annum, although along the southern coastline of Nova Scotia the precipitation is 10 inches greater. Newfoundland has a humid climate with short cool summers. The Island has abundant precipitation, having the equivalent of about 40 inches of precipitation per annum. About one-half of the precipitation occurs during the growing season. During the part of the year the entire area of Eastern Canada is frozen, erosion is reduced to a minimum.

Soils

The soils of Eastern Canada have developed under a humid climate and under forest vegetation. The areal extent of the major soil zones is shown on the small scale soil map in Figure 1.[1] Within each zone the dominant soils have similar profile characteristics as a result of the influence of similar climate and vegetation. These characteristics have an important bearing on the land use, the problems of management, and the productivity of the different soils. The susceptibility to erosion is closely related to the productivity of the soil. If a soil does not contain plant nutrients in sufficient quantities to support dense vegetative growth, the erosion problem is greatly increased.

The Grey-Brown Podzolic soils occur in Ontario and Quebec. The northern boundary of these soils is sharply demarcated by the geological boundary of the Canadian Shield. Typically, the Grey-Brown Podzolic soils have developed under deciduous trees. The soil parent materials are of glacial origin and derived from sedimentary rocks with an admixture of igneous and metamorphic rocks from the Precambrian Shield. The natural fertility levels are medium, and good results are obtained from applications of manures and fertilizers. Many of the Grey-Brown Podzolic soils are susceptible to sheet and/or wind erosion. The degree to which erosion has affected them depends on the per cent slope, the texture of the soil, and the cropping practices followed.

---

[1] P. C. Stobbe and A. Leahey, Pub. 748, Canada Department of Agriculture (1943).

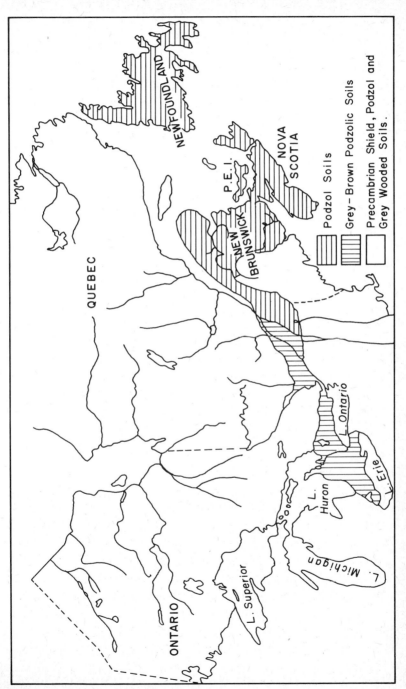

Figure 1. Generalized soil map of Eastern Canada.

Podzol soils occur in the agricultural areas of Quebec, and throughout the Maritime Provinces and Newfoundland. Leahey estimates that the soils contained in this zone occupy about fifty million acres.[2] Owing to the rough terrain in parts, coarse texture and low fertility, however, only nine to ten million acres can be classified as arable land, even under good management practices. These soils are more highly leached than the Grey-Brown Podzolic soils and the fertility levels as well as the organic matter content are usually low. In most instances Podzols have developed under coniferous trees. When the coarse-textured soils were cleared and used for agricultural purposes, however, the fertility was insufficient to produce adequate cover to protect the soils from the ravages of wind erosion. The Podzol soils are more susceptible to both wind and water erosion than the Grey-Brown Podzolic soils. Soil management practices that include the use of lime, fertilizer and manure, and hay and pasture crops in the rotation form the basis for erosion control on the Podzol soils.

The soils of the Precambrian Shield are for the most part of the Podzol or Grey Wooded type. Sufficient information is not available at the present time to indicate the distribution of these soils in Eastern Canada. Leahey suggests that most of the Precambrian Shield consists of rough lands with large areas of bare rock or extensive deposits of muck and peat. Generally the agricultural lands are confined to river valleys, to some of the smoother ridges along the southern edge, and to extensive lacustrine deposits.

Extensive lacustrine deposits occur in the Lake St. John and Abitibi districts of Quebec and the New Liskeard, Cochrane-Hearst and Rainy River districts in Ontario. Some of the soils developed from the lacustrine deposits are fairly good for agricultural purposes, but poor natural drainage, together with varying thickness of muck and peat on the surface of the mineral soil, limits the usefulness of others. At the present time only a small portion of the total land area is used for agriculture. The prevailing climate does not permit the growing of a large proportion of row crops. Although the fine-textured soils erode easily, particularly on slopes of more than 2 to 3 per cent, soil losses are reduced to a minimum when the rotation contains a large proportion of hay and pasture crops.

The topography of the majority of the Grey Wooded soils in Eastern Canada is slightly undulating. However, in those areas

---

[2] *Agricultural Institute Review, Vol. 1, No. 5* (May (1946).

where the topography is rolling or where the land has been dissected by stream courses the erosion problem is serious. Only a very small proportion of the Podzol soils in the Precambrian area are used for agricultural purposes.

Large areas of poorly drained mineral soils, muck, and peat occur in association with the Grey-Brown Podzolic, Podzol and Grey Wooded soils. The topography of these soils is level to depressional and there is no problem of erosion. Of the area in Eastern Canada used for agricultural purposes possibly 35 to 40 per cent is in this category.

Topography and suspectibility to erosion are closely related. The topography of much of the area adjacent to Lakes Erie, Ontario and Huron is strongly undulating to rolling. Water erosion is a considerable problem on these sloping lands unless cropping practices are followed that maintain a close cover for as large a proportion of the time as possible. With the exception of the lowlands west of a line joining Quebec City and Lake Champlain, the Appalachian and Acadian regions occupy practically all the part of Canada lying southeast of the St. Lawrence. The Appalachian region is confined to Eastern Quebec. In the Acadian region, which includes the provinces of New Brunswick, Nova Scotia and Prince Edward Island, much of the area is strongly rolling to hilly. The topography is such that, when the soils are cleared and used for agricultural purposes, erosion becomes severe unless fertility and cropping practices are followed that will reduce it to a minimum. The land forms and topography of Newfoundland are similar to those of the Maritime Provinces.

Present Land Use

The use that is being made of land determines to a large degree the extent to which erosion affects an area. At one time the entire land area of Eastern Canada, exclusive of rock and water, supported a tree cover that reduced the obstacle of erosion to a minimum. According to the 1953 Forest and Forest Products Statistics,[3] of a total land area in Eastern Canada of 959,414 square miles, 645,452 square miles is still forested. Under such a protective cover of trees erosion is not a problem.

The soils in Eastern Canada that may be eroded are those that have been disturbed by man in the production of food for humans and livestock. According to the 1951 census, there are 24.3 million

[3] *Forestry Branch Bulletin 106*, Canada Dept. of Resources and Development (1953).

acres of improved land in Eastern Canada, which is less than 4 per cent of the total land area. This includes land used for field, garden and orchard purposes. Thus it would seem reasonable to assume that this is the land which is used for growing cultivated crops and on which erosion is most serious, depending on the type of farming followed. Areas of specialization are not well defined, and it is unusual to find all farmers in a given area producing the kind of product for which the area is known. The majority of the farming in Eastern Canada falls into some system of livestock or livestock combination. Livestock farming requires large acreages of hay and pasture to provide forage the year round. Effective erosion control programs can be developed most easily around rotations that include a large proportion of hay and pasture. There are, however, areas of specialization where row crops such as corn, potatoes, soybeans and tobacco are grown extensively. Space does not permit a review of the wide diversity in the type of crops grown in Eastern Canada. In Ontario cash crops are of great significance in southwestern counties. Corn and soybeans are being grown extensively even on rolling land. Potatoes are an important crop in more than a half-dozen areas in the Province. In a large proportion of Quebec the agriculture is dairy specialty or dairy combination. Often dairying is combined with the harvesting of forest products. In the Rouville and Montreal areas dairying is combined with the production of apples, market garden crops, livestock, tobacco and potatoes on an extensive scale. Prince Edward Island and the area in Carleton and Victoria Counties in the Upper St. John Valley of New Brunswick favour the intensive production of potatoes. In nearly all parts of Prince Edward Island, especially in the East Point and Kings County area and the Lake Traverse area, potatoes provide the major proportion of farm income. Dairy specialty areas are found in the St. John-Sussex area in southeast New Brunswick, the Truro area in the mainland of Nova Scotia, and the Sydney area in the northeastern part of Cape Breton Island. Agriculture in Newfoundland is limited. Soil and climate are not favourable and usually the farms are small. Agriculture appears to be somewhat supplementary to the other primary industries. Dairying is the dominant type of farming carried on in Newfoundland.

The most comprehensive appraisal of soil erosion in Eastern Canada is obtained from a review of the soil survey data for the various Provinces. Although the prime purpose of soil survey is not to determine the extent to which erosion has affected our soils, it does provide a sound appraisal of the susceptibility of soils to this obstacle. The erosion map was compiled at the Ottawa headquarters of the National Soil Survey of Canada in 1950 for the Food and Agriculture Organization of the United Nations. Statistical information concerning the loss of productivity by erosion is scanty. Possibly the most complete picture concerning erosion is shown on the map (Figure 2). An attempt has been made to assess erosion on the lands disturbed by man. All areas where 10 per cent or more of the land is occupied by farms have been placed in the class "Lands Disturbed by Man".

The erosion classes were defined on a loss of productivity basis as follows:

(1) *None or slight erosion*—Loss in productivity due to erosion less than 10 per cent.

(2) *Moderate erosion*—Loss in productivity due to erosion between 10 and 35 per cent.

(3) *Severe erosion*—Loss in productivity due to erosion more than 35 per cent.

A large percentage of the land in Eastern Canada, because of rolling topography and texture of the soil, is susceptible to erosion. However, the degree to which erosion has affected the area has not reached alarmingly serious proportions. This is due in no small part to the livestock or combination livestock farming that is practised in most areas. Where such a type of farming is practised, rotations usually include a large proportion of hay and pasture crops that are well suited to reducing soil losses and controlling erosion.

The most serious erosion often occurs in areas where large amounts of row or cash crops are grown. Soil losses in these areas are high, particularly when sound soil management and erosion control practices are not followed. Losses can be reduced and erosion effectively controlled in these areas through the use of diversion ditches, strip cropping, and diversion terraces, provided that adequate fertility levels are maintained in the soil.

Although the degree to which erosion has affected Eastern Canadian soils in general cannot be considered severe, nevertheless, it may be very serious on individual farms. Occasionally only a small acreage of high quality land occurs on a farm. To procure an adequate income the farmer may find it necessary to use land on which the susceptibility to erosion is high. This problem becomes more serious if the soil and climate permit the growing of crops that are not well suited to erosion control.

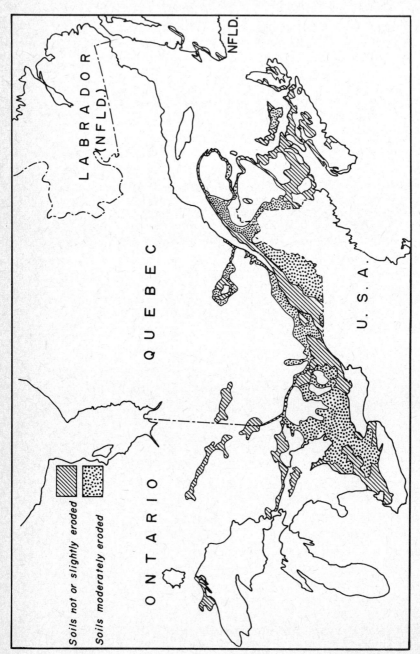

Figure 2. Soil erosion on lands disturbed by man.

Of greater importance than the loss of soil through erosion are the low fertility levels that exist in many soils, particularly in Eastern Canada where a large proportion of the soils are highly leached and inherently low in fertility. This inherent lack of plant food has contributed greatly to the degree to which erosion, particularly wind erosion, has worn away cultivated soils. The first requirement of an affective erosion control program is the building and maintaining of adequate fertility levels in the soil, so that sufficient vegetation cover can be produced to protect the soil from both wind and water erosion.

Soils have always been and always will be exposed to the obstacle of erosion. Under natural forest cover erosion seldom occurs, but under cultivation it may become a serious problem. By the application of efficient land use and sound soil management practices which must include maintenance of adequate levels of fertility, and by cropping practices suited to the land, soil losses can be reduced to a minimum.

13

On the Origin of the Mammalian Fauna of Canada

C.C. Flerow

It has been known for quite a long time that the faunal composition of the Palearctic is very similar to that of the Nearctic. This is especially true with respect to the mammalian faunas of Northeastern Siberia and Canada, as many zoogeographers and paleogeographers have noted (Baker, 1920; Romer, 1933; Colbert, 1937; Stirton, 1951, Jelinek, 1957; Zeuner, 1959). With the exception of a few purely American endemics, such as American porcupines, raccoons, and American deer, most of which are descended from South American groups, the mammal species in Canada are of Asiatic origin. Recent paleontological research has demonstrated not only similarity of the present Palearctic and Nearctic faunas but also their very great similarity throughout a considerable part of the Anthropogene Period.

The Pleistocene mammals of Siberia and northwestern North America are well known (Scott, 1937; Frick, 1937; Simpson, 1947; Gromov, 1948; Hibbard, 1958; Vangengeim, 1961). Therefore, after a few general remarks, I shall pass on to a review of the factors that determined the formation of the present-day mammalian faunas of North America.

The skeleton of a vertebrate animal gives a very complete idea of the organism, and permits one to reconstruct the functional importance of individual parts of the animal as well as its general structure and biology. Because they are represented in abundance and variety in modern faunas and in many fossil faunas, mammals

Reprinted from *The Bering Land Bridge*, ed. D. M. Hopkins, Stanford University Press, 1967, pp. 271-80.

provide extremely rich material for the understanding and reconstruction of extinct communities. Many mammal species are strictly associated with definite environmental conditions, so that they are very important for interpreting landscapes of the past. The great variety of biological types represented, and of ecological niches occupied, make mammals perfect indicators of landscapes. The intimate interrelationships that exist between herbivorous mammals and the flora permit one to make a more reliable judgment concerning the vegetation that existed when a certain species was living. One must not forget that the slightest change in the composition of the vegetation serving as food, or in the method of food procurement or mode of movement of a mammal species, is reflected by evolutionary changes in the bony structure. All of these factors make mammals, as compared with other animals, among the best objects of study in paleogeographic reconstructions. For this reason, mammals provide extensive and abundant data concerning the role of Beringia in the faunistic history of North America and eastern Asia, and serve as an excellent basis for the interpretation of the factors in the development of the modern faunal complexes in these two regions.

A determination of routes, directions, and rates of dispersal is essential to an analysis of penetrative migrations of complete faunas. In establishing the routes, we simultaneously distinguish the obstacles, many of which result from geological transformations, that hinder migration of either the entire fauna or of some of its components. It is necessary, therefore, to determine the tempo or rate of migration of separate species as well as of entire faunas. It is quite obvious that dispersals across Beringia at times of intercontinental connection between Asia and America differed for different species, as each overcame the obstacles in its individual way. For example, elephants, bison, musk-oxen, sheep, and many species of deer crossed from Asia into North America comparatively easily. Saiga and yak, on the other hand, were unable to disperse past Alaska, the obstacles beyond proving to be insuperable for them; these inhabitants of open country did not enter the mountainous and forested areas of Canada. Woolly rhinoceros, musk deer, and squirrels were also unable to overcome the barriers they found on their way; since they were forest dwellers, the open, treeless country was impassable.

The Bering Land Bridge

Recent studies lead us to assume that the Bering Land Bridge has appeared and vanished repeatedly during the Cenozoic Era

(Hopkins, 1959 and this volume; Flint and Brandtner, 1961; Saidova, 1961). The earliest Cenozoic connection across this bridge took place during the Paleocene, at a time when there was a double link with America—eastward from Asia and westward from Europe. However, the animal migrations that took place at that remote time are of little importance for the understanding of the later history of the fauna and of the formation of the present-day faunal complexes. It is now definitely established that the Indo-Malayan, African, and Neotropical faunas had acquired their present character by the end of the Pliocene Epoch, while the Palearctic, Nearctic, and Alpine faunas were formed only during the Anthropogene. Consequently, my discussion will be confined to tracing Anthropogene events that affected mammals in Eastern Asia and North America.

Repeated migrations of mammals from Asia into North America took place during the Pleistocene across a Beringian isthmus that formed and disappeared several times. Saidova's study of benthonic foraminifera in the bottom sediments of Bering Sea and the North Pacific indicates that synchronous uplift of the ocean floor and lowering of sea level have brought the Beringian isthmus into existence at least three times during the Pleistocene; the earliest of these events corresponds to the Kansan or Mindel Glaciation (Saidova, 1961, and this volume).

During times of Anthropogene emergence, it is assumed that the Bering Land Bridge was an area of wide plains with low hills and sparse woodlands, affording an opportunity for numerous mammals to migrate from Asia to North America (Flerow and Zablozkii, 1961). This environment was such that most northern species of mammals could migrate across the land bridge, with the exception of those animals that inhabit forested mountains. The musk deer, whose ancestors lived in warm, humid, forested areas and probably migrated north and became adapted to cold climates and forested mountains as early as the second half of the Pliocene, is an example of a mammal that did not succeed in crossing the Bering Land Bridge. Neither the musk deer nor the squirrel (*Sciurus*) has migrated even to Kamchatka, since Kamchatka is separated from their main area of development by an expanse of open, treeless country. Conversely, the fact that the Rocky Mountain goat (*Oreamnos*) is derived from Asiatic ancestors suggests that those ancestors were adaptable to the plains of the Bering Land Bridge and that this goat was transformed into a true Alpine form only recently, at the beginning of the Pleistocene. The absence in Alaska of the woolly rhinoceros (*Coelodonta antiquitatis*) is also explained by the nature of the Bering Land Bridge. Rhinoceroses were confined to forest-steppe and forest areas that had a shrubby undergrowth. The woolly rhinoceros apparently did not inhabit open steppes; it would seem that this animal could not feed on harsh steppe grass, but browsed on trees, shrubs, and other soft fodder. Their remains are much rarer in the north of Eastern Siberia than in the south, where they are very numerous. Evidently in the northern part of their range in Eastern Siberia, they found the necessary food only in narrow belts along the rivers.

Nature of Faunal Dispersal

As already mentioned, when speaking of the migration of entire faunas, one must realize that it is not the fauna that is moving; instead, we are observing a movement of biocoenotically related complexes of organisms. Both now and in the past, orographic, ecological, and morphological barriers played a major role affecting the dispersal of terrestrial animals. Some species of a faunal complex can expand into new territories and adjust themselves to new conditions relatively easily; others move slowly and have to reconstruct their ecology and morphology quite appreciably. Forms that have lived for a long period in the area of their origin can change little and only slowly when physical geographic conditions change slightly. On the other hand, that part of the population that migrates early into areas of contrasting conditions often begins to change rapidly as it adjusts itself to the new environment. The resulting morphological lability—the ability of the organism to acquire new adaptations rapidly—is a decisive factor in determining potentialities for migration and expansion into new areas. In other words, the more easily the organism is able to adjust itself to varying conditions, the more readily it can expand its range.

The prior presence in a new territory of ecological analogues is of great importance. For example, the numerous forms of Antilocapridae that developed in North America during the Miocene and the greater part of the Pliocene were full analogues of the deer of Europe and Asia, and occupied biotopes in North America that corresponded to those occupied by deer in the Old World. With the extinction of the majority of genera and species of Antilocapridae during the second half of the Pliocene came an explosive development and dispersal of deer in America (Flerow, 1950).

The main mass of migrants moved from Asia to America, and only a few moved from America to Asia. Most of the "Americans" achieved but limited penetrations into northeastern Asia, and only reindeer, musk-oxen, and a few others established large territories in northern Asia and Europe. The explanation for this east-west imbalance seems to lie in the fact that the principal ecological niches in Asia were already occupied by an abundant and varied mammalian fauna. The thermophile forms that had inhabited the forests of North America at the beginning of the Pleistocene were pushed southward with the appearance of the continental ice sheet in Canada. When the ice sheet disappeared, the American endemics were unable to adjust rapidly enough to reoccupy the newly de-glaciated area. This permitted Asiatic immigrants to disperse explosively.

Composition and Relationships of the North American Fauna

The present fauna of North America has a dual affinity to the Palearctic fauna. One component consists of species very similar to or even conspecific with species in Eastern Siberia; in some cases identical subspecies are present in both regions. Another component consists of taxa undoubtedly closely related to Asiatic forms but differing specifically or even generically.

Close study shows that a substantial part of the first group consists of taxa characteristic of northern latitudes in North America, including Alaska and part of Canada. The northern group includes the forest bison (*Bison priscus athabascae*), snow sheep (*Ovis nivicola*), musk-ox (*Ovibos moschatus*), moose (*Alces alces americanus*), New World elk or wapiti (*Cervus elaphus canadensis*), brown bear (*Ursus arctos middendorffi*), ermine (*Mustela erminea richardsoni*), weasel (*Mustela nivalis rixosa*), wolverine (*Gulo gulo luscus*), wolf (*Canis lupus*), red fox (*Vulpes vulpes*), lynx (*Lynx lynx*), arctic hare (*Lepus timidus*), lemmings (*Dicrostonyx torquatus, Lemmus sibiricus*), and voles (*Microtus oeconomys, Clethrionomys rutilus*).

The second and less closely related group, on the other hand consists of taxa distributed chiefly in the southern part of North America. The ranges of the species included in this group extend either across southern Canada and the United States or through the Rocky Mountains south of Alaska. The second group includes the plains bison (*Bison bison*), bighorn sheep (*Ovis canadensis*), Rocky Mountain goat (*Oreamnos montanus*), grizzly bear (*Ursus horribilis*), black bear (*Ursus americanus*), American badger (*Taxidea taxus*), skunks (*Mephites* and others), coyote (*Canis latrans*); swift and kit fox (*Vulpes velox, macrotis*), bobcat (*Lynx rufus*).

As I suggested earlier, this dual similarity is explainable by differences in the glacial history in North America and Northeastern Siberia. Glaciation in Northeastern Siberia has consisted only of relatively small ice sheets and local alpine glaciers, and vast areas remained that were inhabited by a varied mammalian fauna, including the bisons. On the other hand, enormous areas in North America, including all of Canada, were subjected to glaciation for a lengthy period of time (Flint, 1947), and these areas were unsuitable for mammal life. Asiatic mammals that had migrated to North America before the maximum glaciation were cut off from their original homeland and lost all connection with it. Furthermore, they were pushed southward to the area of the present United States and were forced into new environments quite different from the northern landscapes. This resulted in rapid evolution and the acquisition of specific adaptations to the new conditions. During the retreat and disappearance of the continental glaciers in Canada, a new migration of Asiatic mammals across the Beringian isthmus took place. This history of immigration, evolution in isolation, and renewed immigration is illustrated by the history of sheep and bison, and explains the twofold degree of similarity to Asiatic mammalian faunas.

The sheep that migrated to America prior to the maximum glaciation were closely related to the living Asiatic argali (*Ovis ammon*). During the glaciation, they were forced southward and there evolved into the distinctly different American bighorn sheep (*Ovis canadensis*), which retains, however, many features of its Asiatic ancestor. Later, another Asiatic species, the Siberian snow sheep (*Ovis nivicola*) entered North America and dispersed southward along the Rocky Mountains to northern British Columbia. Its modern range includes areas on both sides of Bering Strait but does not merge with that of *Ovis canadensis*.

An even more striking illustration of the effect of the differences between Siberian and North American glaciation is provided by the history of the bison (Skinner and Kaisen, 1947; Flerow and Zablozkii, 1961). The early stages in the history of the bison are not yet clearly understood. However, an Asiatic origin is indicated by the fact that the earliest records of the genus are represented by *Bison sivalensis* (Falconer) Lidekker in the late Pliocene Siwalik deposits of India and by *B. paleosinensis* Chardin and Piveteau in the late Pliocene Nihowan fauna of China. During early Pleistocene time, bison dispersed into the temperate zone of Asia and Europe. At this time, short-horned forms, including first *B. tamanensis* Vereshchagin and the later *B. priscus schoetensaki* Freudenberg, are found in southern Europe as far north as the north Caucasus (Predkavkazie). By middle Pleistocene time, bison apparently disappeared completely in southern Asia but became widely distributed across Europe, northern Asia, and northern North America as a large, long-horned form, *B. p. crassicornis* Richardson. During this long period, extending from the end of the Mindel Riss Interglaciation into the beginning of the Riss–Würm Interglaciation, landscape conditions were more or less uniform, the range of bison was continuous across Holarctica, and no substantially different species appeared.

Bison priscus crassicornis migrated from Asia to America before the Riss (or Illinoian) Glaciation. During this glaciation they were forced southward out of Canada to the present area of the United States, where they evolved into the giant species *B. latifrons* Harlan. This southern population was completely isolated from the northern group, which continued to live in Asia, Beringia, and Alaska. The ancestor of the modern plains bison, *B. alleni* Marsh then developed in the southern part of the United States, and this form evolved into the steppe bison of the Wisconsin Glaciation (*B. bison antiquus* Leidy) and finally into the living post-Pleistocene *B. bison bison* Linnaeus.

To the north, in Alaska and Siberia, the long-horned bison (*B. priscus crassicornis*) persisted through much of the late Pleistocene, but by the end of the Wisconsin (or Würm) Glaciation, bison began gradually to become smaller throughout Holarctica. Their horns became shorter, as well, and the long-horned *B. p. crassicornis* was replaced by the short-horned *B. p. priscus* Bojanus, which was equally holarctic in distribution and which also failed to produce distinct local forms.

With the withdrawal of the Wisconsin ice sheet, bison again penetrated into Canada from Alaska and Beringia to the northwest. However, like other late Pleistocene Asiatic immigrants, the northern bison dispersed only into the MacKenzie River basin and failed to reach the Hudson Bay region and eastern Canada. These areas probably were cleared of ice later than other parts of Canada and therefore remained unsuitable for such mammals as bison, moose, and wapiti. The presence of Hudson Bay also affected the climate and created very severe environments.

At the end of the Würm (or Wisconsin) Glaciation, the range of bison began to shrink and disintegrate, and by the beginning of the Holocene was completely disrupted. Bison became extinct over enormous areas and persisted only in parts of Europe, Eastern

Siberia, Alaska, Canada, and the United States. The isolated populations began to differentiate, resulting in the wisent (*Bison bonasus*) of Europe, the large wood bison (*B. priscus athabascae*) of Eastern Siberia, Alaska, and Canada, and the plains bison (*B. bison bison*) of the United States. Further isolation in Europe produced a reduction from the moderate horn length of the ancestral wisent (*B. bonasus major* Hilzheimer) to the short-horned Lithuanian bison (*B. b. bonasus* Linnaeus) and Caucasus bison (*B. b. caucasicus* Satunin). *B. b. major* was once present in the Caucasus and in Transcaucasia, but later its range diminished, and *B. b. caucasicus* persists only on the western half of the main ridge of the Caucasus.

Eastern Siberia, Alaska, and Canada were inhabited by the big *B. priscus athabascae* Rhoads, but a very small, short-horned endemic race evolved in an extreme northern part of Eastern Siberia isolated from the general range of the species by mountain ranges. This subspecies occupied lowlands adjoining the Arctic Ocean in the Lena, Indigirka, and Kolyma River basins and became extinct during the post-Würm thermal maximum.

In Canada, the post-Pleistocene history of bison has been one of range reduction and extinction similar to that in Eurasia. The history follows the same pattern seen in musk-ox (*Ovibos moschatus*), which became extinct throughout Palearctica and were preserved only in North America and Greenland, where the periglacial conditions to which they were adapted are still present. Even in North America, the musk-ox gradually disappeared west of the MacKenzie River and retreated eastward nearer to the glaciated areas, a process that has continued into historic time. Similarly, the range of forest bison shrank eastward, and the species finds its last refuge in the forests of the Great Slave Lake region of Canada (Seton, 1886, 1912, 1927; Flerow in Adlerberg *et al.*, 1935; Raup, 1935; Soper, 1939, 1941; Fuller, 1962) in an area of severe climatic conditions in which small patches of prairies are present in the taiga forest. These prairie patches apparently approach the character of the cold forest-steppes that were once widely developed in Siberia, Alaska, and Canada at the end of the Pleistocene and during the early Holocene. All features characterizing this big Canadian wood bison indicate its very close morphological affinity with the extinct Pleistocene and early Holocene species of the so-called "primary bison," *Bison priscus* (Rhoads, 1898).

We can say confidently that the typical Pleistocene mammals of northeastern Asia were unable to survive the period of the Holocene thermal maximum and the resulting change in the vegetation.

The formation of *Sphagnum* associations (muskegs) in northern regions deprived most species of large herbivorous animals (including horses, oxen, and many species of deer and antelope) of their main source of forage. Rhinoceroses and mammoths became extinct at the same time and probably for the same reason. Only the muskox and the wood bison survived this crisis in America, persisting in areas where remnants of Pleistocene landscapes were preserved. These "living fossils," once contemporaries of the mammoth, survived to the present time as the last representatives of the Pleistocene fauna.

References

Adlerberg, G. P., B. S. Vinogradov, N. A. Smirnov and C. C. Floerow, *Zveri Arktiki* (Arctic mammals), Leningrad (1935), p. 579.

Baker, F. C., "The life of the Pleistocene or Glacial Period", *Univ. Ill. Bull.*, Vol. XVII, no. 41 (1920), p. 476.

Colbert, E. H., "The Pleistocene mammals of North America and their relations to Eurasian forms", p. 173-184 in G. G. MacCurdy, ed., *Early Man,* Lippincott, New York (1937), p. 363.

Flerow, C. C., "Morfologiia i ekologiia oleneobraznykh v protsesse ikh evoliutsii" (Morphology and ecology of deerlike animals and processes of their evolution), Akad. Nauk SSSR, Materialy po chetvertichnomu periodu SSSR (Data on the Quaternary Period) Bull. 2 (1950), pp. 50-69.

Flerow, C. C., and M. A. Zablozkii, "O prichinakh izmeneniia areala bizonov" (On the reasons for the change in the range of bison), *Bull. Moskva Ob-va Ispytatelei Prirody Otd Biologii*, Vol. XLVI, (1961), pp. 99-109.

Flint, R. F., *Glacial geology and the Pleistocene Epoch*, Wiley, New York, (1947), p. 589.

Flint, R. F., and F. Brandtner, "Climatic changes since the last Interglacial", *Am. Jour. Sci.*, Vol. 259 (1961), pp. 321-28.

Frick, C., "Horned ruminants of North America", *Am. Mus. Nat. Hist. Bull.*, Vol. LXIX (1937), p. 669.

Fuller, W. A., "The biology and management of the bison of Wood Buffalo National Park", Canadian Wildlife Serv., *Wildlife Mgmt. Bull. Ser. 1*, no. 16 (1962), p. 52.

Gromov, V. I., "Paleontologicheskoe i arkheologicheskoe obosnovanie stratigrafii kontinental 'nykh otlozhenii chetvertichnogo perioda na territorii SSSR" (Paleontological and archaeological bases of the stratigraphy of continental deposits of the Quaternary Period in the territory of the USSR), Akad. Nauk SSSR, Tr. Geol. Inst., Bull. 64, Ser. Geol. No. 17, (1948), p. 519.

Hibbard, C. W., "Summary of North American Pleistocene mammalian local faunas", *Papers Michigan Acad. Sci., Arts, and Letters*, Vol. XLIII, (1958), pp. 3-32.

Jelinek, A. J., "Pleistocene faunas and early man", *Papers Mich. Acad. Sci., Arts, and Letters*, Vol. XLII (1957), pp. 225-37.

Raup, H. M., "Botanical investigations in Wood Buffalo Park", *Nat. Mus. Canada Bull. 74*, Biol. Ser. 20 (1935), p. 174.

Rhoads, S. N., "Notes on living and extinct species of North American Bovidae", *Proc. Acad. Nat. Sci., Philadelphia*, Vol. XLIX (1898), pp. 483-502.

Romer, A. S., "Pleistocene vertebrates and their bearing on the problem of human antiquity in North America", pp. 49-81 in D. Jenness, ed., *The American aborigines, their origin, and antiquity*, Toronto Univ. Press (1933), p. 396.

Saidova, H. M., "Ekologiia foraminifer i paleogeografiia dal'nevostochnykh morei SSSR i severo-zapadnoi chasti Tikhogo Okeana" (Ecology of foraminifera and paleogeography of the Far East Seas of the USSR and the northwestern part of the Pacific Ocean), Akad. Nauk SSSR, Inst. Okeanologii, (1961), p. 232.

Scott, W. B., *A history of land mammals in the Western Hemisphere*, 2nd ed., Macmillan, New York (1937), p. 786.

Seton, E. T., "The ruminants of the Northwest", *Proc. Can. Inst.*, Ser. 3, Vol. XXI, no. 4, fasc. 3, (1886), pp. 113-17. *The Arctic prairies*, Constable, London (1912), p. 415. *Lives of game animals*, Vol. III, Doubleday, Doran, New York (1927), p. 780.

Simpson, G. G., "Holarctic mammalian faunas and continental relationships during the Cenozoic", *Geol. Soc. America Bull.*, Vol. XVIII, (1947), pp. 613-88.

Skinner, M. F., and O. C. Kaisen, "The fossil Bison of Alaska and preliminary revision of the genus", *Am. Mus. Nat. Hist. Bull.*, Vol. LXXXIX, Art 3, (1947), pp. 123-356.

Sopers, J. D., "Wood Buffalo Park; notes on the physical geography of the Park and its vicinity", *Geogr. Rev.*, Vol. XXIX, (1939), pp. 383-99. "History, range, and home life of the northern bison", *Ecol. Monogr.*, Vol. XI (1941), pp. 347-412.

Stirton, R. A., "Principles in correlation and their application to later Cenozoic holarctic continental mammalian faunas", *Rept., 18th Internat. Geol. Cong. (London)*, 1948, pt. 11 (1951), pp. 74-84.

Vangengeim, E. A., "Paleontologicheskoc obosnovanie stratigrafii Antopogenovykh otlozhenii severo vostochnoi Sibiri" (Paleontological basis of the stratigraphy of the Anthropogene deposits of Northeastern Siberia), Akad. Nauk SSSR, Tr. Geol. Inst., Vyp. 48, (1961), p. 182. In Russian; English translation of parts available from Am. Geol. Inst.

Zeuner, F. E., *The Pleistocene Period; its climate, chronology and faunal successions*, Hutchinson, London (1959), p. 447.

14

Effects of Fire on Barren-Ground Caribou and their Forest Habitat in Northern Canada

G. W. Scotter

The numbers of barren-ground caribou (*Rangifer tarandus groenlandicus*) on the mainland of northern Canada have decreased drastically during the present century up to about 1959. In 1906, Seton (Hoare, 1927) estimated that "Cutting in half the estimates of explorers who went before me, and making a most conservative estimate there are not less than thirty millions of these caribou letting the wind blow through their whiskers in that northern country." In 1927 Hoare wrote that "It is doubtful if at the present time there are three millions, that is only one-tenth of Seton's 1906 estimate of thirty millions of caribou, left on the mainland in the Northwest Territories." An estimate by Anderson (Hoare, 1930) agreed with Hoare's. A 1950 estimate based on aerial censuses (Banfield, 1954) placed the number at 670,000. A recount during 1955 resulted in an estimate of about 270,000 animals, a decline of over 50 percent in about five years. Although many believe that early estimates, such as Seton's, were highly exaggerated, a drastic decline in population since about 1900 is certain.

The destruction of winter rangelands by fire has been suggested by several writers as one possible cause for the decline of the caribou herds. This study evaluates the effects of fire on four key wintering areas within the coniferous forest, or taiga, of northern Canada. It was begun by the writer for the Canadian Wildlife Service in 1959 as part of an intensive caribou research project.

Reprinted from Proceedings, *Thirty-Second North American Wildlife Conference,* ed. J. B. Trefethen (1967), pp. 246-59.

Some of the primary objectives of the study, as reported here, were (1) to determine what portion of the winter range has burned out and whether the amount has increased in recent years, (2) to determine the effects of fire on the usable standing crops of terrestrial forage and arboreal lichen, and (3) to determine the effects of fire on range use by barren-ground caribou and moose (*Alces alces*).

The Study Areas

The winter range of barren-ground caribou is restricted largely to the coniferous forest belt of northern Canada. It covers approximately 295,000 square miles in northern Manitoba, northern Saskatchewan, northeastern Alberta, and the District of Mackenzie (Figure 1). Rather than commence an extensive study over such a large expanse, key wintering ranges were chosen for more intensive study. Presumably, data collected on these study areas would be applicable to wintering areas throughout the coniferous forest of northern Canada. It was desirable that the study areas be important or key winter ranges and that they contain burns of various ages. In addition, the areas had to be as accessible as possible, since travel was limited to airplanes and boats. With assistance from federal and provincial biologists with previous experience in caribou research, four areas, ranging from 5,000 to 8,000 square miles, were chosen (Figure 1).

The forest on the winter range is largely coniferous, with deciduous trees occuring in disturbed regions. The major tree species are black spruce (*Picea mariana*), white spruce (*Picea glauca*), jack pine (*Pinus banksiana*), white birch (*Betula papyrifera*), tamarack (*Larix laricina*), and quaking aspen (*Populus tremuloides*).

Methods

Survey of History and Extent of Forest Fires

Information on the history and extent of forest fire on the winter range of barren-ground caribou was obtained in three ways. The first was by a review of literature pertinent to caribou and caribou ranges. Second, fire control reports on forests within the winter range were obtained from various government agencies in Alberta, Saskatchewan, Manitoba, and the District of Mackenzie for the period 1961 through 1964. The reports provided data on numbers, sizes and causes of fires which were controlled. Lastly, vegetation cover maps of the northern Saskatchewan study area were prepared by interpreting recent aerial photographs. Forests and burned areas were classified as 1 to 15, 16 to 30, 31 to 50, 51 to 75, 76 to 120, or exceeding 120 years of age. The area of each age class was determined from the cover maps by using a dot-grid overlay. The average annual destruction by fire was determined by dividing the acres in an age class by the number of years in that class.

Determination of Fire Effects on the Standing Crop of Forage

Effect of fire on the standing crop of usable forage was determined in forest stands from each of the four study areas. A stand consisted of a spruce forest, or a seral stage of white birch or jack pine which precede the spruce, on an upland site within one of six age classes and with similar floristic composition and cover throughout. Forest stands were divided into six age classes extending from 1 to 10, 11 to 30, 31 to 50, 51 to 75, 76 to 120, and in excess of 120 years. Each stand was sampled using the weight-estimate method of forage inventory (Pechanec and Pickford, 1937; and Campbell and Cassady, 1955).

The usable standing crop was measured for 126 forest stands distributed among 38 locations on the four study areas. In each stand 5 sites, each 100 feet square in area, were chosen for sampling. When possible, one site was selected on the north, south, east, and west slopes and the fifth on a level area. The positions of the sites were chosen so that they were, as nearly as possible, representative of the slope or level area under consideration. Sites were placed from 0.1 mile to 2 miles apart, depending on topography and size of the forest stand.

Sixteen randomly selected sample plots were located within each of the 5 sites. The sample plots at a site were stratified so that four fell into each quarter of the square. The sample plots were circular and covered 9.6 square feet.

Usable standing crop was determined by clipping and weighing, or estimating, the grams of forage in the circular plots. Forage was removed from the plots and separated into species or groups before being weighed on a spring scale. Actual and estimated weights were recorded to the nearest 5 grams of green weight.

Weight of the current growth was recorded for forbs, grasses, grasslike plants, and deciduous shrubs. Leaf growth was removed from evergreen shrubs, such as mountain cranberry (*Vaccinium vitis-idaea* var. *minus*) and common Labrador tea (*Ledum groenlandicum*). Lichen growth was removed to the level where decomposition of the podetia was first observed. Decaying portions of podetia have a pungent odor and probably are not preferred by caribou. Bryophytes were not included since they are probably not eaten by barren-ground caribou except incidentally with other forage.

The green weights obtained in the field were converted to air-dried weights. Daily collections of samples were made from each major forage species; then 100-gram samples were stored at room temperature until no fluctuation in weight could be detected. Lichens, in particular, could be compared only on an air-dried basis, since moisture content varied from 20 to 85 percent depending on weather conditions. Prior to actual field work a training period was held for the purpose of checking estimates against actual weights. Also, field estimates were checked daily throughout the season.

Usable standing-crop data were considered with respect to the barren-ground caribou's winter food habits. Shrubs and lichens were assigned high, moderate, or low values as caribou winter food, primarily on the basis of information gathered from Loughrey (1952), Banfield (1954), Kelsall (1957, 1960), and Scotter (1967).

Figure 1. A map of northern Canada showing the distribution of summer and winter ranges of barren-ground caribou and the locations of major study areas.

This information was supplemented by summer observations of plants which had been grazed during the previous winters and by winter observations. Assigned values were based on plant abundance and utilization by barren-ground caribou and not on nutritive content. The high, moderate, and low values compare only the forage within a group.

The standing crop of arboreal lichens was determined in the northern Saskatchewan study area by using the following method: Four black spruce and four jack pine trees, each one representative of its forest stand, were selected as sample trees. After felling and measuring, the trunks were divided into 10-foot sections. Lichens were removed by hand from the trunk and branches of each section, and the relative abundance of different species noted. The masses of lichens were placed in cotton bags, air-dried at approximately 72°F., and weighed. An estimate of the number of trees per acre was made at each site by taking five wedge prism readings and measuring the diameter of all trees viewed in each 360° horizontal sweep. Standing crops of arboreal lichens above and below the 10-foot level were calculated in pounds per acre.

Determination of Range Use by Caribou and Moose

Within each 9.6-square foot circular plot used for calculating the standing crop of usable forage, pellet groups were counted to compare the use by barren-ground caribou and moose in each forest age class. When six or more winter pellets of one type were found in a plot, they were recorded as a pellet group. Kelsall (1957) regarded six or more pellets as a group because barren-ground caribou generally drop their pellets while moving, leaving a point of concentration and several widely scattered pellets. Each pile of summer moose droppings was considered a group. Pellet groups per stand were converted to pellet groups per acre.

Results

History and Extent of Fires on Caribou Ranges

Historical Review.—Journals of early explorers and their modern-day counterparts confirm that in earlier times forest fires were prevalent throughout the winter range of barren-ground caribou in northern Canada. During his third venture in search of copper in 1771-1772, Hearne observed burns near the Coppermine and Slave Rivers. Near the Slave River in January 1772, Hearne (Mowat, 1958) noted that "During the preceding summer they [Athapascow Indians] had set fires to the woods, [and] notwithstanding the deep snow, and many months which had elapsed, the fires were still burning in many places. . . ." He also recorded that Indians departed for new camp-sites leaving fires unattended. In their journals, covering a period from 1774 to 1792, Hearne and Turnor (Tyrrell, 1934) frequently mentioned forest fires. In 1796 Thompson (Tyrrell, 1916) commented on forest fires in northern Saskatchewan. Pike (1892) stated that barren-ground caribou ". . . seldom come in large quantities to the Mackenzie River, where they used to be particularly numerous in winter. This is in a great measure accounted for by the fact that great stretches of the country have been burnt, and so rendered incapable of growing the lichens so dearly beloved by these animals."

After spending more than 30 summers in northern forests, Bell (1889) stated ". . . from a very extensive personal knowledge of the conditions of the forests of Northern Canada, I am able to state the fires have become more and more frequent as we approach the present time. . . . The areas of the 'brules' of different dates may be said to be greater in proportion to their recentness."

From observations made in 1914 and 1920, Harper (1931) stated that "Unfortunately a considerable part of the country appears to have been swept time and again, and with disastrous effect, by forest fires, some of which are set purposely by the Indians in order to temporarily improve the hunting." Fire-destroyed forests were recorded by Camsell and Malcolm (1919) in the Mackenzie River basin in the Northwest Territories. Dogrib Indians told Harper (1932) that caribou had avoided the lower Taltson River for several years because of forest fires there. Irregular barren-ground caribou migrations were caused by burned-over sections of land, according to Hornby (1934). Anderson (1938) stated that ". . . the destruction of the winter forage of lichens by fire may have been the prime cause of extended movement." In Manitoba, barren-ground caribou were known to have been deflected by recent burns north of The Pas, which caused them to extend their movements to the southwest. Clarke (1940) reported that smoke from fire on the winter range near Yellowknife during July of 1936 was so thick that aerial photography was impossible. Kelsall (1960) calculated that 29 percent of the land area had been burned on an important wintering range for barren-ground caribou between Great Bear Lake and Great Slave Lake. In discussing the vegetation of northern Manitoba, Ritchie (1960) wrote ". . . the proportion of mesic sites occupied by stable or mature vegetation is remarkably small— as little as 5 percent in areas that the writer had examined, although this figure is probably lower than the average. If it was established with certainty that the vegetation found in undisturbed sites of Forest-Tundra and Open Coniferous Forest areas is essential for these animals [barren-ground caribou] as winter range, then the apparent impoverishment of vegetation by fire, together with slow recovery, might well be an important factory in their ecology." Larsen (1965) also commented on the unchecked fires in northern Manitoba.

Devastation by fire has not been limited to forests within the winter range of barren-ground caribou in northern Canada. Fire also has been mentioned as a contributing factor in declines of caribou and reindeer (*Rangifer tarandus tarandus*) in other parts of North America. In their study of Alaskan wildlife, Leopold and Darling (1953a) commented, "To ignore range limitations for caribou is to ignore the crux of the problem. One fire easily could undo the work of decades in protecting a local caribou population from men and wolves." They concluded that forest fires have eliminated or placed serious restrictions on caribou herds. Leopold and Darling (1953b) believed that accelerated burning had particularly adverse effects on caribou since they are members of a climax biota. Fire was considered by Palmer (1926) to be the greatest enemy of reindeer herds in Alaska. In two unpublished reports Palmer (1940, 1941) described the effects of fire on caribou range in interior Alaska. Darling (1954, 1956), Skoog (1956), and Buckley (1958) have also commented on the relationship between fire and caribou in that state. Raup and Denny (1950) reported that almost all forest stands along the southern part of the Alaska highway show modifications by fire. Since the late 1890's an estimated 80 percent of the forests and rangelands in Alaska have burned (Robinson, 1953). Lutz (1956), in reviewing the history of fire in coniferous forests in Alaska, observed that most forests showed evidence of fire in their history.

In Wells Gray Park, British Columbia, the decline of woodland caribou (*Rangifer tarandus caribou*) has been attributed mainly to fire (Edwards, 1954). In the eastern Rocky Mountains of Alberta, Cormack (1953) found many burnt-over areas. Much of this area was formerly within the range of woodland caribou.

In Ontario, Quebec, and Labrador the effects of fire on caribou have not gone unnoticed (Hind, 1863; Low, 1897; Allen, 1942; Manning, 1946; de Vos, 1948; Rousseau, 1951; Moisan, 1955; Cringan, 1957, 1958; Banfield and Tener, 1958). Low (1897) reported that in interior Labrador fires, which occurred annually and often burned throughout the summer, had destroyed one-half of the forested area during the preceding 25 or 30 years. According to Fernow (1912), only 100,000 acres, or 2 percent, of the 5,000,000 acres of forested area in Nova Scotia were virgin or semi-virgin timber. Fire was largely responsible for this destruction. It may be more than co-incidental that the last woodland caribou on the mainland of Nova Scotia was reported killed about 1912 (Anderson, 1938).

Fire Control Reports.—During a 4-year period extending from 1961 through 1964 fire control reports for the portion of winter range within their region were obtained from government agencies in the District of Mackenzie and the Provinces of Alberta, Saskatchewan, and Manitoba. Total known destruction during that period was 7,822 square miles, or approximately 2.7 percent of the winter range of 295,000 square miles. That is a rather alarming total when no records are available from vast portions of the winter range.

According to the records, 72 percent of the fires were believed to have been caused by lightning. Changes in the summer weather pattern in recent decades may have resulted in more lightning strikes or in conditions more suitable to the spread of fire. As would be expected, most man-caused fires occurred near the centers of population.

Cover Maps.—As revealed by the forest cover maps which were prepared by the interpretation of recent aerial photographs, average fire destruction in the 1 to 15, 16 to 30, 31 to 50, 51 to 75, 76 to 120 year age classes was 20,779, 14,080, 15,040, 14,310 and 6,599 acres per year, respectively. In the 1 to 15-year age class fire destruction increased 1.4 times over the 16 to 30, 31 to 50, 51 to 75-year age classes, where the annual rate of fire destruction was almost constant, and 3.1 times over the 76 to 120-year age class. Destruction rate in the 16 to 30, 31 to 50, 51 to 75-year age classes was 2.2 times greater than in the 76 to 120-year age class. These increases coincide with mining activity and white settlement. The possibility that some forests may have been burned more than once during the interval was not considered. Multiple burning would increase the area of young forests and reduce the area of more mature forests.

As revealed by the historical review and fire control reports, the ecological relationships between forest fires and barren-ground caribou have existed for a long time. However, the cover-map data on forest age classes suggest that the amount of destruction in recent years has increased.

Effects of Fire on the Forage Supply

The relationship of forest fires to barren-ground caribou is complex, but one of the most obvious effects on the winter range is the reduction in the amount of forage available. Both terrestrial and arboreal forage plants are affected. Among the forage plants, lichens generally are regarded as the principal winter food of caribou (Banfield, 1954; Kelsall, 1960). Nearly 60 percent of their winter forage is composed of those plants, according to data obtained from rumen samples collected in northern Canada (Scotter, 1967).

TABLE I. AVERAGE STANDING CROP OF USABLE AIR-DRIED FORAGE, IN POUNDS PER ACRE, IN UPLAND FOREST BY AGE CLASSES.

Forage Type	Pounds of Forage per Acre by Forest Age Classes					
	Age Classes in Years					
	1-10	11-30	31-50	51-75	76-120	120+
Grass and grass-like plants	35	8	1	1	3	2
Herbs	68	9	2	3	4	7
Shrubs						
High value	14	124	189	169	248	253
Moderate value	10	8	2	3	4	6
Low value	45	95	83	107	101	92
Subtotals	69	227	274	279	353	351
Lichens						
High value	1	15	147	319	291	560
Moderate value	1	39	76	84	97	129
Low value	1	50	89	66	35	36
Subtotals	3	103	312	469	423	725
Others 1	2	T	—	T	T	T
Total pounds of forage per acre	177	348	589	752	783	1085

1 Others include club mosses and fungi.

Terrestrial Forage.—Average air-dried weight of the usable standing crop ranged from 177 pounds per acre in the 1 to 10-year class to 1,085 pounds per acre in the oldest age class (Table I). Grass, grasslike plants, and forb yields were highest in the 1 to 10-year age class, but in subsequent age classes never exceeded a few pounds per acre. Shrub production was low in the first age class, but was reasonably consistent throughout the remaining age classes. The standing crop of lichens increased consistently from 3 pounds per acre in the youngest age class to 469 pounds per acre in the 51 to 75-year age class. The amount of lichens was slightly less in the next age class because of moderate to heavy use by caribou of many forest stands. Despite similar use in the oldest age class, the standing crop of usable lichens increased to 725 pounds per acre.

More important than the increase in the standing crop of lichens was the increase of high-value lichens. The high-value group included the so-called "reinder" lichens, such as *Cladonia alpestris, C.*

mitis, and *C. rangiferina.* Average standing crop of high-value lichens varied from 1 pound per acre in the 1 to 10-year old class to an average of 560 pounds per acre in the class exceeding 120 years of age. Moderate-value lichens reached their peak abundance in the oldest age class, and low-value lichens attained their maximum in the 31 to 50-year age class. Although there were variations within each age class, lichen abundance was related to maturity of the forest. Older forests occasionally produced less forage than younger forests in the same age class because of variations in tree density, soil type, caribou utilization, and other factors.

The destruction of lichens is critical because of their slow succession, their slow growth rates, and their importance as winter forage for barren-ground caribou. Fire appears to be as destructive to the major forage lichens as to the mature conifers, when the rate of recovery is considered. It usually takes from 70 years to more than a century for the major forage lichens to recover to their former abundance and composition, according to observations made during this study. Part of that time is required for the return of suitable biological conditions for lichen growth, part for the succession of lichens through a number of seral stages, and part because of the slow rate of growth of the major forage species. The average growth rate obtained by the major forage lichens, as determined from a number of sample sites in three of the study areas, ranged from about 3 to 5 millimeters per year depending on the species (Scotter, 1963).

Arboreal Forage.—Forest fires on the winter rangelands of barren-ground caribou not only destroy terrestrial vegetation, but the arboreal lichens as well. In northern Saskatchewan, the standing crop of arboreal lichen within 10 feet of the ground was estimated to be 605 pounds per acre in mature black spruce and 339 pounds per acre in mature jack pine (Table II). Standing crop on many other segments of the winter range of barren-ground caribou

TABLE II. STANDING CROP OF ARBOREAL LICHENS IN BLACK SPRUCE AND JACK PINE FORESTS IN NORTHERN SASKATCHEWAN, EXPRESSED IN POUNDS PER ACRE (AIR-DRIED WEIGHT)

| Forest Type | Pounds of Arboreal Lichen per Acre (Air-dried Weight) | | |
	Below 10 Foot Level	Above 10 Foot Level	Total
Black Spruce	605	464	1069
Jack Pine	339	1490	1829

appeared to be less than those figures. Lichens on fallen trees and lichens above the 10-foot level which are dislodged by wind or snow increase the amount available in many areas.

Arboreal lichens may be an important food source for caribou, particularly as emergency food during periods of deep or ice-crusted snow (Scotter, 1962). Destruction of these extremely slow-growing plants by fire must be considered a serious loss of winter caribou forage. As a forage source *Alectoria, Evernia,* and *Usnea* are thought to be the most important of the arboreal lichens.

Effects of Fire on Range Use by Caribou and Moose

An important indirect effect of fire in the boreal forest is the change of a climax community—with its cover of trees, shrubs, bryophytes, and lichens—into a tangle of fallen snags and exposed soil, and later into a fireweed-grass-shrub community. Fire alters plant cover both in kind and quantity. These changes subsequently modify wildlife populations.

TABLE III. AVERAGE NUMBER OF CARIBOU AND MOOSE PELLET GROUPS PER ACRE IN FOREST STANDS BY AGE CLASSES

| Kind of Pellet Groups | Pellet Groups per Acre by Forest Age Classes | | | | | |
| | | | Age Classes in Years | | | |
	1-10	11-30	31-50	51-75	76-120	120+
Caribou pellet groups	18	133	248	497	633	722
Moose pellet groups	18	47	26	10	14	3

The densities per acre of barren-ground caribou and moose pellet groups for the various forest age classes are summarized in Table III. In forests over 120 years old, 722 caribou pellet groups per acre were found compared with only 18 per acre on the 1 to 10-year age class. There were 47 moose pellet groups per acre in the 11 to 30-year age class and only three per acre in forests over 120 years old. Moose apparently prefer habitats less than 50 years old, but barren-ground caribou favor those more than 50 years of age.

Barren-ground caribou feeding patterns were noted in northern Saskatchewan and the southern Mackenzie District during the winter by aerial observations. Feeding craters, which were dug in the snow by barren-ground caribou, were easily observed from the air. Visual impressions of the frequency and distribution of those feeding craters in the forest age classes agreed with the pellet-group counts. Such craters were confined largely to mature forests. Occasionally trails and feeding craters in recent burns were caused by animals crossing from one mature forest to another.

In some areas of North America, such as the Kenai Peninsula of Alaska, forest fires have resulted in improved moose ranges and subsequently higher moose populations (Leopold and Darling, 1953a, 1953b). A large moose population, however, was not evident in the four study areas. Some preferred moose browse plants, such as willows (*Salix* spp.) were present in only small amounts in the post-fire vegetation. White birch, a good moose food, was abundant in many of the younger forest stands which had been disturbed by fire.

Conclusions

Although damage by fire to winter range of caribou occurred before the white man came to North America, the increased rate of forest destruction by fire accompanying settlement and exploitation, as well as possible changes in the summer weather pattern, has contributed to the loss of habitat for barren-ground caribou. Fires adversely affect the standing crop of both terrestrial and arboreal forage utilized by the caribou. Lichens appear to be more seriously affected by fire than other forage plants because of their slow growth rates.

In considering only two big-game species, fire appears to reduce the quantity of winter range for barren-ground caribou and improve it for moose on upland forests of the study areas. Based on the pellet group data collected during this study, the biomass of caribou per acre of mature forest appears higher than that of moose on early subclimax forests on upland sites. Thus in terms of meat production, the upland forests may be best suited to barren-ground caribou use.

Referring to the winter range of caribou in interior Alaska, Leopold and Darling (1953a) wrote ". . . fire had played so dominant a part in destroying the lichen range that we feel quite safe in attaching to that one factor the major blame for caribou decrease." Research data from northern Canada may not justify the same bold conclusion. Data are insufficient to determine the extent to which forest fires have influenced directly the recent decline of the barren-ground caribou population. With the effect of fire on the standing crop of forage, plant succession, and animal use there can be little doubt that forest fires have been one of the principal causes of the decline. Regardless of the reason for the recent decline, the present winter range, with its vast fire-destroyed areas, will not permit a large increase in numbers for several years. The reduced carrying capacity of the winter range does not appear to be the factor limiting the caribou population at the present low levels, however. And yet it may well have been the factor which caused the reduction of caribou numbers until men, wolves, and other factors were effective in maintaining the population at low levels. More prevention and control of forest fires would seem desirable in light of the small caribou population and the long-term destruction of winter range by fire.

References

Allen, G. M., "Extinct and vanishing mammals of the Western Hemisphere", *Am. Com. Intern. Wildl. Protection. Spec. Publ. No. 11* (1942), p. 620.

Anderson, R. M., "The present status and distribution of the big game mammals of Canada", *Trans. N. Am. Wildl. Conf. 3* (1938), pp. 390-406.

Banfield, A. W. F., "Preliminary investigation of the barren-ground caribou", Canadian Wildl. Serv. Wildl. Mgmt. Bull. Ser. 1, 10A pp. 1-79, 10B pp. 1-112 (1954).

Banfield, A. W. F., and J. S. Tener, "A preliminary study of the Ungava caribou", *J. Mammal 39* (1958), pp. 560-73.

Bell, R., "Forest fires in northern Canada", *Proc. Am. Forestry Congr.* (1889), pp. 50-55.

Buckley, J. L., "Effects of fire on Alaskan wildlife", *Proc. Soc. Am. Foresters* (1958), pp. 123-26.

Campbell, R. S., and J. T. Cassady, "Forage weight inventories on southern forest ranges", *Southern Forest Exp. Sta. Occasional paper 139*, (1955), p. 18.

Camsell, C., and W. Malcolm, "The Mackenzie River Basin", *Canada Dept. Mines, Geol. Survey, Mem. 108* (1919), p. 154.

Clarke, C. H. D., "A biological investigation of the Thelon Game Sanctuary", *Nat. Mus. Canada Bull.*, No. 96 (1940), p. 135.

Cormack, R. G. H., "A survey of coniferous forest succession in the eastern Rockies", *Forestry Chronicle 29* (1953), pp. 218-32.

Cringan, A. T., "History, food habits and range requirements of the woodland caribou of continental North America", *Trans. N. am. Wildl. Conf. 22* (1957), pp. 485-501. "Influence of forest fires and fire protection on wildlife", *Forestry Chronicle 34*, (1958), pp. 25-30.

Darling, F. F., *Caribou, reindeer and moose in Alaska*, Oryx 2 (1954), pp. 28-85. *Pelican in the wilderness*, Allen & Unwin, London, (1956), p. 380.

de Vos, A., "Status of the woodland caribou in Ontario", *Sylva 4* (1948), pp. 17-23.

Edwards, R. Y., "Fire and the decline of a mountain caribou herd", *J. Wildl. Mgmt. 18* (1954), pp. 521-26.

Fernow, B. E., "Forest conditions of Nova Scotia", *Canada Comm. Conserv.* Canada (1912), p. 93.

Harper, F., "Physiographic and faunal areas in the Athabaska and Great Slave Lakes region", *Ecology 12* (1931), pp. 18-32. "Mammals of the Athabaska and Great Slave Lakes region", *J. Mammal 13* (1932), pp. 19-36.

Hind, H. Y., *Exploration in the interior of the Labrador Peninsula, the country of the Montagnais and Nasquapee Indians*, Vol. I, Longman, Green, Longman, Roberts, and Green, London (1863), p. 351.

Hoare, W. H. B., "Report of investigations affecting Eskimo and wild life, District of Mackenzie, 1924-1925-1926", Northwest Territories Branch, Canada Dept. of Interior (mimeo) (1927), p. 44. "Conserving Canada's Musk-oxen", Canada Dept. of Interior (1930), p. 53.

Hornby, J., "Wild life in the Thelon River area, Northwest Territories, Canada", *Canadian Field-Nat. 48* (1934), pp. 105-11.

Kelsall, J. P., "Continued barren-ground caribou studies", *Canadian Wildl. Serv., Wildl. Mgmt. Bull.* Ser. 1, 12 (1957), pp. 1-148. "Co-operative studies of barren-ground caribou 1957-58", *Canadian Wildl. Serv., Wildl. Mgmt. Bull.* Ser. 1, 15 (1960), pp. 1-145.

Larsen, J. A., "The vegetation of the Ennadai Lake area, N.W.T.: Studies in subarctic and arctic bioclimatology", *Ecol. Monographs 35* (1965), pp. 37-59.

Leopold, A. S., and F. F. Darling, *Wildlife in Alaska,* Ronald Press Company, New York (1953), p. 129. "Effects of land use on moose and caribou in Alaska", *Trans. N. Am. Wildl. Conf. 18* (1953), pp. 553-62.

Loughrey, A. G., "Caribou winter range study, 1951-52", unpubl. Rept. in files of Canadian Wildl. Serv., Ottawa (1952), p. 30.

Low, A. P., "Report on explorations in the Labrador Peninsula along the East Main, Kosoak, Hamilton, Manicuagan, and portions of other rivers, in 1892-93-94-95", *Geol. Survey of Canada Ann. Rept. for 1895*, Vol. 8L (1897), p. 387.

Lutz, H. J., "Ecological effects of forest fires in the interior of Alaska", *U.S. Dept. Agr. Tech. Bull. 1133* (1956), p. 121.

Manning, T. H., "Bird and mammal notes from the east side of Hudson Bay", *Canadian Field-Nat. 60* (1946), pp. 71-85.

Moisan, G., "The caribou of Gaspé: A preliminary study of range conditions and herd status", Unpubl. M.S. thésis, Cornell Univ., Ithaca, New York (1955).

Mowat, F., *Coppermine journey,* McClelland & Stewart Limited, Toronto (1958), p. 144.

Palmer, L. J., "Progress of reindeer grazing investigations in Alaska", *U.S. Dept. Agr. Bull. 1423* (1926), p. 37. "Caribou versus fire in interior Alaska", Unpubl. Rept. in files of U.S. Fish and Wildl. Serv. Juneau, Alaska (1940), p. 5. "Caribou versus fire in interior Alaska", Unpubl. Rept. in files of U.S. Fish and Wildl. Serv. Juneau, Alaska, (1941), p. 13.

Pechanee, J. F., and G. D. Pickford, "A weight estimate method for the determination of range or pasture production", *Am. Soc. Agron. 29* (1937), pp. 894-904.

Pike, W., *The barren ground of northern Canada*, Macmillan and Co., New York (1892), p. 300.

Raup, H. M., and C. S. Denny, "Photo interpretation of the terrain along the southern part of the Alaska highway", *U.S. Geol. Survey Bull. 963D* (1950), pp. 95-135.

Ritchie, J. C., "The vegetation of northern Manitoba v. Establishing the major zonation", *Arctic 13* (1960), pp. 211-29.

Robinson, R. R., "Forest management and protection on the Alaskan public domain", *Proc. Alaska Sci. Conf. 4* (1953), pp. 92-94.

Rousseau, J., "Basic principles for the protection of the barren ground caribou and reindeer breeding in Quebec", *The Province of Quebec Assoc. for the Protection of Fish and Game Ann. Rept. for 1951* (1951), pp. 28-35.

Scotter, G. W., "Productivity of arboreal lichens and their possible importance to barren-ground caribou" (Rangifer articus), Arch. Soc. 'Vanamo' 16:2 (1962), pp. 155-61. "Growth rates of Cladonia alpestris, C. mitis, and C. rangiferina in the Taltson River region, N.W.T.", *Canadian J. Bot. 41* (1963), pp. 1199-1202. "The winter diet of barren-ground caribou in northern Canada", *Canadian Field-Nat. 81* (1967), pp. 33-39.

Skoog, R. O., "Range movements, population, and food habits of the Steese-Forty-mile caribou herd", Unpubl. M.S. thesis, University of Alaska College, Alaska.

Tyrell, J. B., *David Thompson's narrative of his explorations in western America, 1784-1812*, The Champlain Soc., Toronto (1916), p. 582. *Journals of Samuel Hearne and Phillip Turnor between the years 1774-1792*, The Champlain Soc., Toronto (1934), p. 611.

15

Some Observations on Animals, Landscape and Man in the Bow Valley Area: c. 1750-1885

J. G. Nelson

This essay is concerned with: (1) the large variety and number of animals in the Bow Valley area in early European days; (2) some of their effects on the landscape; (3) the decline of the beaver and the bison as a result of the fur trade and other aspects of white settlement. The Bow Valley area is not precisely defined but can be thought of as the plains-foothills-mountain transition zone between approximately the Red Deer and the South Saskatchewan Rivers.[1] 1750 is chosen as the beginning date because the essay is based on historical evidence and the earliest accounts of any significance to the Bow Valley area date from about 1754. 1885 is selected as the terminus because, by that time, the bison had been eliminated as a wild animal not only in the study area but

---

Paper presented to the Canadian Association of Geographers, Calgary, 1968.

---

[1] A more precise definition of the study area has not been attempted mainly because it was not considered vital to the purposes of the essay which was originally prepared to give information on aspects of the recent landscape history of the Bow Valley and surrounding country to those attending the Canadian Association of Geographers meetings in Calgary in late May and early June, 1968. The findings set forth in this essay probably would hold in many other parts of the northern plains area, although such things as the Hudson's Bay Company's conservational attempts do not seem to have had parallels on the American side of the border. At any rate the drawing of fine areal distinctions is for another time and place.

the Great Plains as a whole. Other animals also had become less numerous, the natives had been assigned to reserves and a new phase in white settlement and landscape history had begun.

The essay is divided into two basic parts. The first briefly outlines white exploration and settlement to about 1885, in the process giving background information on chronology, the development of the fur trade and on historical sources. In the second part these sources are used to describe the variety and number of animals, some of their effects on the landscape, and the decline of the beaver and the bison.

Exploration and Settlement: c. 1750-1885

The earliest descriptions of the Bow Valley area derive from the fur trade. Canadian traders from Montreal moved onto the plains of present-day Manitoba in the 1730's and 1740's, interrupting the pre-existing flow of fur to English posts on Hudson Bay. As a result the Hudson's Bay Company sent men out to bring the natives and their fur to the "Bay". One of these men, Anthony Hendry, was the first to enter the Bow Valley area, reaching a point about 100 miles north of present-day Calgary in 1754.[2] Another, Matthew Cocking, did not travel far west of the present Saskatchewan-Alberta border, but his observations, and those of others like him, are often of value to the student of the landscape history of the Bow Valley area.[3]

By the 1790's a string of competing English and Canadian fur trade posts had been constructed along the North Saskatchewan River valley into what is now Alberta. The first white traders known to have actually reached the Bow River valley travelled from these posts. The earliest trips for which written records are available were made by David Thompson and Peter Fidler, who wintered with the Piegan, members of the Blackfoot group of native peoples, in 1787-88 and 1792-93 respectively.[4]

Travel by white traders to the Bow Valley area seems to have been comparatively rare between about 1800 and 1832, although

2 L. G. Burpee, ed., "The Journal of Anthony Hendry, 1754-55", *Proceedings and Transactions of the Royal Society of Canada*, 3rd series, I (1907), Section II, pp. 307-54.
3 L. G. Burpee, ed., An Adventurer from Hudson's Bay, The Journal of Matthew Cocking, From York Factory to the Blackfoot Country, 1772-73, *Proceedings and Transactions of the Royal Society of Canada*, 3rd series, II (1908), Section II, pp. 89-121.
4 R. Glover, ed., *David Thompson's Narrative,* Toronto, (1962) and Peter Fidler, "Journal of a Journey Overland from Buckingham House in the Rocky Mountains in 1792 and 1793", *Hudson's Bay Company Documents,* National Archives, Ottawa; see also J. G. McGregor, *Peter Fidler: Canada's Forgotten Surveyor, 1769-1822,* Toronto, (1962).

trapping was carried on by the natives who took their furs to posts such as Rocky Mountain House on the North Saskatchewan River. The journals of Alexander Henry, commander of this post in 1810, refer to natives who came to trade from the Bow Valley and areas further south. Indeed in the spring of 1810 a party arrived with furs which they had taken from some Americans attacked in the Missouri Valley country.[5]

A major change in the character of the fur trade occurred in 1821 when, after many years of intense competition, the North West Company of Montreal amalgamated with the Hudson's Bay Company. But a new rivalry was developing between Canadian-based traders and others operating in the Missouri Valley. The Americans, Lewis and Clark, travelled up the Missouri and across the mountains to the Pacific in 1804 and 1805. Thereafter increasing numbers of traders moved up the river, with transitory posts being established on the Yellowstone and the headwaters of the Missouri by 1810. However the Missouri traders had much trouble with the natives, notably the Piegan and other Blackfeet who controlled and hunted in the country between the Missouri and the Bow Rivers.[6]

Firm trade relations were finally established with the Piegan by the American Fur Company in 1830, diverting some of the native trade from the English posts along the North Saskatchewan. This competition led the Hudson's Bay Company to construct Piegan Post, which is believed to have been the first trading post to operate in the Bow Valley. The post was built in the summer of 1832, in the foothills along the Bow River, about 40 miles west of present-day Calgary, being abandoned in less than two years, apparently because of trouble with the natives and low returns relative to expense.[7]

With the abandonment of Piegan Post no fur trade or other settlements are known to have been maintained in the Bow Valley until the 1870's. Rather, for many years after 1834, the natives traded with both the Hudson's Bay Company and the American Fur Company on the North Saskatchewan and the Missouri respectively.

---

5 E. Coues, ed., *The Manuscript Journals of Alexander Henry and David Thompson,* Minneapolis (1965), p. 735.
6 See D. L. Morgan, *Jedidiah Smith and the Opening of the West,* Lincoln (1964), and R. E. Oglesby, *Manuel Lisa and the Opening of the Missouri Fur Trade,* Norman (1963).
7 See J. E. A. McLeod, "Piegan Post and the Blackfoot Trade", *Canadian Historical Review,* XXIV, 3 (1943), pp. 273-79.

Missionaries, artists and others began to come to the western plains area in the 1830's and 1840's, but relatively few penetrated the Blackfoot country and the Bow Valley area.[8] Among the exceptions were two missionaries, Father de Smet, a Jesuit, who passed quickly through the upper Bow Valley and nearby areas in 1845, and the Reverend Rundle, a protestant, who worked for a number of years in the vicinity of the North Saskatchewan River and made several visits to the Bow Valley in the 1840's.

By the 1850's the governments of Britain, the United States and Canada were interested in the settlement and development of the northern Great Plains and sent scientific exploring expeditions into the area. Members of the British expedition, notably the leader, John Palliser, and the natural scientist and physician, James Hector, passed through the Bow Valley several times during the years 1857-60.[9]

References are made in the reports of the British exploring expedition to American wanderers on the Canadian plains. Such men had begun to move north after the discovery of gold in present-day Montana and other nearby parts of the United States in the 1850's and early 1860's. One group is said to have prospected every stream from the Marias to within about twenty miles of Edmonton in 1862.[10] More or less contemporaneous with these prospectors were American traders who built a number of posts north of the border in the late 1860's and early 1870's.[11] The grip of the Hudson's Bay Company on the western plains clearly was weakening and in 1869 it sold most of its land holdings to Canada.

Permanent white settlement appears to have begun in the Bow Valley in the early 1870's with the construction of a trading post by the Americans and a mission by the McDougall's, Canadian protestants who worked for many years in the vicinity of the North Saskatchewan Valley and left a written record of considerable value to the landscape historian.[12] In 1874 the Canadian North

[8] See J. Warkentin, *The Western Interior of Canada*, Toronto (1964).

[9] See I. M. Sprye, *The Palliser Expedition*, Toronto (1963) and United Kingdom, *The Journals, Detailed Reports and Observations Relative to the Exploration by Captain Palliser of that Portion of British North America, which in Latitude, lies Between the British Boundary Line and the Height of Land or Watershed of the Northern or Frozen Ocean Respectively, and in Longitude, Between the Western Shore of Lake Superior and the Pacific Ocean During the Years, 1857, 1858, 1859 and 1860*, London (1863).

[10] G. L. Berry, *The Whoop-Up Trail*, Edmonton (1953), pp. 39-40.

[11] Berry, *op. cit.*, and P. F. Sharp, *Whoop-Up Country*, Helena (1960).

[12] *The Calgary Herald*, January 24, 1968. Reporting a talk by H. Dempsey, Archivist, Glenbow Foundation, Calgary and J. McDougall, *On Western Trails in the Early Seventies*, Toronto (1911).

West Mounted Police built a post in the Bow Valley and the town of Calgary began to grow around it.[13] Ranchers and other settlers came into the area in increasing numbers. The Blackfeet were assigned to reserves in the late 1870's. The railroad arrived in 1883. The bison was eliminated as a wild animal, other animals considerably reduced and a new phase in white settlement and landscape history began.

Animal Life, Landscape and Decline: c. 1750-1885

In the following paragraphs, descriptions by men such as David Thompson and Peter Fidler are used to show the abundance and variety of animal life in the Bow Valley area in early European days. Attention is then directed to the bison and the beaver and the landscapes associated with them. Finally the decline of the beaver and the bison is considered, as are the causes for this and the attempts at conservation by the Hudson's Bay Company.

The Kind and Number of Animals

At the outset it should be recognized that the number of animals of various kinds living in the Bow Valley area in early European days cannot be estimated accurately. As one difficulty in this regard, at least some of the bison and other animals migrated into and out of the area in accordance with climatic changes, grass fires and other influences so that animal numbers varied seasonally or over a period of years. As another difficulty, the historical sources do not always lend themselves to precise quantitative analysis so that the bison population of the American plains has been variously estimated at 20 or 30 or 40 million in the years not long before or after the coming of the white man. On the other hand the historical sources do give a vivid impression of many animals frequenting the Bow Valley and nearby areas prior to their depletion and eventual elimination in the course of white settlement.

Many early descriptions refer to the large number and variety of animals. For example, on September 13, 1754, Anthony Hendry was travelling from the North Saskatchewan toward the Red Deer Valley and saw "many herds of buffalo grazing like English cattle". Three days later the animals were so numerous that Hendry and his companions were "obliged to make them sheer out of the way". At this time the wolves were also so plentiful as to be "without number".[14]

---

13 Sir Cecil Denny, *The Law Marches West*, Toronto (1939), pp. 84-86.
14 Burpee, *op. cit.*, (1907), pp. 332-33.

Buffalo, deer, antelope, wolves and other animals were observed moving in large associated groups, one obvious reason being that predators such as the wolf fed on the young, infirm and old animals. While in the Bow Valley in 1787, David Thompson described one such association. The herds of bull bison came first, followed by the cows and then by "small herds of doe and red deer" and by wolves and foxes.[15] Such masses of animals placed heavy pressure on the grass and forage; the animals observed by Thompson were said to have come north from the Missouri country after eating "the ground bare of grass" in that quarter.

On his return to the North Saskatchewan from the Bow country in 1793, Peter Fidler saw incredible numbers of bison and also recorded evidence of heavy grazing and consequent movement of animals. For example, on February 13th, while near the Red Deer River, he observed so many buffalo that from "the north to the south the ground is entirely covered by them, . . . I am sure there was some millions in sight as no ground would be seen for them in that compleat semi-circle and extending at least 10 miles." On March 20th, while still in the same area, he saw great numbers of the animals cross the Red Deer River; "they have eat all the grass up is the cause of their crossing".[16]

Aside from heavy grazing, the bison and associated animals affected the landscape in other ways. The ground was often marked with deep trails or paths, especially near stream and river valleys. These were frequently referred to by travellers; for example, while near the junction of the North and South Saskatchewan in 1808, Alexander Henry observed "deep beaten paths, where the buffalo ford the river".[17] The bison also disturbed the ground by wallowing, that is by rolling in the dust or mud, apparently for a variety of reasons, including the desire to escape insect attacks when the winter pelage was lost in spring. The resulting depressions, which not uncommonly were about forty feet long, fifteen feet wide and a foot deep, could extend over very large areas. When Matthew Cocking was somewhere in the triangle between the North and the South Saskatchewan in 1772 he stated that: "All over the Country where buffalo resort are many hollow places in the ground . . .". He attributed them to the agitation of the bulls in the rutting reason.[18] Later travellers often did not understand the origin of the wallows. For example, while carrying out original surveys not

---

15 Glover, *op. cit.*, p. 48.
16 Peter Fidler, *op. cit.*, references can be traced by date.
17 Coues, *op. cit.*, p. 490.
18 Burpee, *op. cit.*, (1908), p. 108.

far from the Bow River in 1882, O. J. Klotz described some "inferior" soil, "full of depressions six to twelve inches in depth, as if washed away, and more or less destitute of vegetation. Of the origin of these depressions I have been unable to find a satisfactory explanation."[19]

The bison also deposited large quantities of dung, other organic debris and bones upon the landscape. The bones were copious enough to provide employment for thousands of natives, Metis and early white settlers who sold them for manufacture into fertilizer and for other purposes in the 1880's. The dung was laid down in sufficient quantities to serve as fuel for the camp-fires of generations of Indians and fur traders and many settlers as well. An impression of the organic productivity of the bison can be gleaned from the writings of Isaac Cowie, a Hudson's Bay Company man, who fell in with a large number of the animals north of the Qu 'Appelle River, in present-day Saskatchewan in 1869.

"Our route took us into the midst of the herd, which opened in front and closed behind the train of carts like water round a ship, . . . The earth trembled, day and night, . . . as they moved . . . over the inclinations of the plains. Every drop of water on our way was foul and yellow with their wallowings and excretions."[20]

The foregoing makes it clear that one can think in terms of a bison landscape, marked by numerous associated animals, short grass, deep ruts or paths, wallows, and also by great quantities of dung, bones, and organic debris. The extent to which erosion occurred in the ruts and other land forms created by the bison is a matter for further study. How extensive such a landscape actually was in the Bow Valley is unknown. Early settlers often found wallows, paths and so forth, but little information has been collected on their location and extent.

The Beaver Landscape

Another animal which was exceedingly plentiful in the middle and late eighteenth century was the beaver. Like the buffalo, this animal was a major force behind the creation of a distinct type of landscape. The beaver built innumerable dams and re-organized the drainage over large areas. Ponds and swamps were widespread. These drainage changes also had their effect on vegetation, with marsh growth attracting certain animals, for example the moose.

19 *Canada Sessional Papers (No. 23)*, Annual Report of the Department of the Interior for the Year 1882, Ottawa, (1883), p. 37.
20 I. Cowie, *The Company of Adventurers*, Toronto (1913), p. 137.

This beaver landscape is clearly described in the journals of Anthony Hendry and was probably widespread in the eighteenth and nineteenth centuries in the plains-foothills fringe, although, again relatively little information has been collected on the Bow Valley in particular. While Hendry was about thirty miles southwest of the present town of Red Deer, on October 22, 1754, he described the country as "Level land with poplars; a great many Creeks and ponds, with plenty of Beaver houses". The next day, the natives killed two moose, one buffalo and ten beaver, but Hendry complained that they might have killed two hundred if they had wished, "but they only killed a few for cloathing and for Beaver feasting; Buffalo being their chief food at present. The ponds here are surrounded with Beaver houses; and numbers along the Banks of creeks; . . ."[21]

To quote another example, on December 10, 1754, Hendry was travelling with natives near the fringe of the foothills' forests and the plains. The land was level with "ledges of woods and ponds of water". The group saw plenty of moose but did not disturb them. On December 14 moose and elk passed in herds within two hundred yards of their tents. On the 16th a great many moose were seen. On the 19th they were out on the plains and observed plenty of wolves, elk and moose.[22]

The Beaver: Depletion and Attempts at Conservation

The beaver and other small fur bearing animals were the first to show depletion. Indeed the migration of posts along the North Saskatchewan was in part a reflection of this and in part of the relatively fresh fur territory just ahead. To what level animal populations would be trapped and traded under these circumstances is uncertain, but hunting pressure likely would not proceed close to the point of extinction so long as there was fresh territory upstream. Statements to the effect that the fur traders could ruin a country in seven years or so must be taken as meaning a reduction to some low level beyond which it would pay to move to new ground.[23]

In the preceding paragraph, the words "relatively fresh territory" are used advisedly because many fur trade posts had a very large trade area and so indirectly affected the beaver and other animals of regions hundreds of miles away. For example the Black-

---

[21] Burpee, *op. cit.*, (1907), p. 340.
[22] Ibid., p. 344.
[23] See the introduction, A. S. Morton, ed., *The Journal of Duncan McGill-ivray: 1794-1795*, Toronto, (1929).

foot Indians regularly traded at Edmonton House, undoubtedly coming from at least as far away as contemporary southern Alberta. They also came from the Missouri country to Rocky Mountain House with furs. As a result of such trade, many areas seemingly would be considerably reduced in beaver before a trading post ever was actually established nearby.

The effect of the competitive trapping of many years becomes clear in correspondence between Governor George Simpson and headquarters in London following the amalgamation of the two companies in 1821. In a letter dated July 16, 1822, Simpson stated that many parts of the country undoubtedly were exhausted of valuable furs but not to such a low ebb as might generally be supposed.[24]

To increase returns over the years, Simpson advocated "extending the track" or expansion in some areas, a traditional policy of the Hudson's Bay Company, and also the "nursing" of other regions, a procedure not favoured hitherto.

Simpson linked these two policies in sponsoring the Bow River Expedition of 1822-23. The expedition consisted of over one hundred men and was to explore the South Branch, or Bow, as it then was often called, in order to determine whether a series of posts could be built and operated profitably along the valley and if possible over the Rockies into the Columbia Basin. If the expedition were successful, Simpson planned to abandon and nourish the North Saskatchewan. As he put it:

> "the loss in that Department this year is very heavy little short of 4,000 and we have it in contemplation to abandon it altogether next season in the event of the South Branch Expedition coming up to our expectations . . . By withdrawing those heavy establishments the country will in the course of a few years recruit and become rich in valuable fur bearing animals which are now from the length of time it has been trapped nearly extinct . . ."[25]

However, the Bow River Expedition was not successful for a number of reasons, including inadequate planning and preparation, and trouble with the natives. The expedition also was unsuccessful in finding large quantities of fur and so in paying its way. Probably many areas near the South Branch had already been trapped by natives and Metis for many years, the furs having been taken to posts in the north.

---

24 George Simpson, Official Reports to the Governor and Committee in London, 1822, Hudson's Bay Company Documents, microfilm, (Reel 3 M 42) National Archives, Ottawa, letter to the Governor and Committee from Simpson, York Factory, July 16, 1822.
25 Ibid.

After 1821 the Northern Council of the Hudson's Bay Company introduced a number of management policies which aimed to conserve the beaver for future use. In 1824 a resolution was passed to the effect that the natives be discouraged from beaver hunting in the summer and they be convinced of the injurious effect of this practice to themselves and the country at large. By 1826 a system of sustained yield also was being attempted. The returns for 1823, 1824 and 1825 were averaged. A reduction was then made, presumably for safety's sake, and a yield set, which was not to be exceeded by the 1826 Outfit. For example, in the Saskatchewan, Lesser Slave Lake and Assiniboine District of which the southern plains and the Bow Valley were a part, 7,800, 6,493 and 6,896 beaver were traded in 1823, 1824 and 1825 respectively for a total of 21,189 animals. The average for the District was 7,063: this was reduced by one-fifth, or 1,412 beaver skins, with the result that no more than 5,651 were to be produced in the Saskatchewan, Lesser Slave Lake, Assiniboine District in 1826.[26] For years thereafter a figure of 5,550 beaver was set for the District.[27]

These attempts at conservation do not seem to have worked very well, particularly in the Saskatchewan District where the growing competition of Americans raised the same basic problems as had existed in the days of strife between the North West and the Hudson's Bay Companies. Conservational practices were sacrificed in order to attract the plains tribes and if possible to drive the Americans from the field. In 1833, the Council of the Northern Department exempted from conservation regulations those posts competing with the Americans. Resolution 92 of that year states:

> "that Gentlemen in charge of Districts and Posts accept (sic) such as are exposed to opposition, exert their utmost efforts in discouraging the hunting of Cub Beaver and beaver out of season, and that no Beaver traps be issued from the Depot, except for sale to the Piegan Indians and that in any cases where an unusual proportion of Cub or unseasoned Beaver appears the same will be particularly represented to the Governor and Committee".[28]

As has been noted earlier, Piegan Post, the first European settlement of any consequence in the Bow Valley, was constructed and operated for two years in order to compete with the Americans for the Piegan trade. The journals and account books of the post give a good picture of the landscape of the Bow Valley in the early

---

26 "Minutes of the Council of the Northern Department", *Hudson's Bay Company Documents*, microfilm (Reel 1 M 814) National Archives, Ottawa, Resolution 131, 1826.
27 Ibid., Resolution 119, 1827, and Resolution 92, 1830.
28 Ibid., Resolution 92, 1833.

1830's. The personnel lived off the country and seem to have secured most of their subsistence within a day or so of the fort. Their kill also indicates the wide variety of wildlife in the Bow Valley at the time. Between the 11th of August and the 9th of September, 1833, for example, eight bison, seven moose and four red deer or elk seemed to have been taken along with some fish. On September 6th, one of the men went to work a beaver house he had found on his last excursion. He returned on the 7th with two large beaver. On September 29, the hunters brought in a moose and five mountain sheep. On November 30, the hunters went out only to return the next day with the meat of nine large and six small red deer or elk.[29]

The accounts for Piegan Post in 1832-33 give a good idea of the variety of animal life and the level of the beaver population in the Bow Valley area. Among the animals listed in the returns are 23 large grizzly bears, 10 cub grizzly, 666 kit foxes, 41 red foxes, 4,500 muskrats, 1,116 wolves, 377 prime buffalo robes, 300 common robes, 30 large moose skins, 81 large red deer skins, 22 small red deer skins and 498 buffalo tongues. In addition, the list shows 343 large beaver and 200 half beaver, as well as several hundred beaver cuttings.[30]

In the late 1830's and the early 1840's the beaver as well as other animals continued to be killed by Indians pulled in two directions, north toward Rocky Mountain House and Fort Edmonton and south toward the Missouri country. At this time the demand for beaver was dropping because of the introduction of substitutes in the making of beaver hats. Nevertheless, the furs were still valuable and the Hudson's Bay Company continued to try and conserve them. Even so, by 1840, the Chief Factor at Fort Edmonton, John Rowand, wrote to Governor Simpson as follows:

> "There is so many unforeseen difficulties to contend with it is not easy to conjecture how matters will turn out in these difficult times. I can only say with truth that we refuse nothing in the shape of Furs, as for the Beaver it is, I am sorry to say, getting preciously scarce indeed.

---

29 J. E. Harriott, "Piegan Post and Rocky Mountain House Journal, 1833-34", *Hudson's Bay Company Documents*, Microfilm (Reel 1 M 16), National Archives, Ottawa.
30 "Bow Fort Account Book (Piegan Post) 1832-33", *Hudson's Bay Company Documents*, microfilm (Reel 1 M 433) National Archives, Ottawa.
31 H. A. Dempsey, "A Letter from Edmonton", *Alberta Historical Review*, Vol. XI, no. 1, pp. 723-24, cited in A. R. Byrne, *Man and Landscape Change in the Banff National Park Area Before 1911*, Studies in Land Use History and Landscape Change, National Park Series No. 1, The University of Calgary, (1968), p. 49.

How can it be otherwise this poor old worn out District encroached on from all sides not only by our American opponents but also by Indians and Half Breeds from other Districts."[31]

By 1841 the Council of the Northern Department was prepared to take even more serious measures to try to preserve the beaver. The gentlemen in the districts were strictly enjoined to discourage the hunting of the animal by every means in their power. No more than half of the beaver collected in 1839 were to be brought to the posts during the next three years. It was also noted that the gentlemen had disregarded such regulations in the past; this time those who did so could be retired from the service. Special payments also were authorized for those natives who did not kill beaver, but rather other small fur bearing animals.[32]

However, the previous regulations again did not apply at Edmonton, Carlton and other posts where the traders were in competition with the Americans. Thus, areas such as that near the Bow were open to uncontrolled trapping which undoubtedly reduced the beaver to low levels. Relatively little reference is made to these animals by visitors of the 1840's, 1850's, 1860's and 1870's. In discussing the foothills region in general in 1845 de Smet personifies the beaver landscape, but refers to the animal itself in a rather passive way.

"A large portion of the surface of the country is covered with artificial lakes, formed by the beavers. On our way we had frequent occasion to remark, with wonder and admiration, the extent and height of their ingeniously constructed dams and solid lodges. These are remains of the admirable little republics, concerning which so many wonders have justly been recorded. Not more than half a century ago, such was the number of the beaver in this region that a good hunter could kill 100 in a month's space.[33]

The Decline of the Bison

The story of the virtual elimination of the buffalo is better known than that of the beaver, but mainly on the basis of the American example. The observations of travellers such as Rundle suggest little evidence of depletion in the 1840's in the Bow Valley area. While returning from the south in 1841, Rundle saw enormous numbers of buffalo in the 100 miles or so between the Bow and Red Deer Rivers; the herds being in sight "nearly the whole of the time".[34]

---

[32] Minutes of the Council of the Northern Department, *op. cit.*, Resolutions 90, 91, 92, 1841.

[33] J. P. De Smet, *Oregon Missions and Travels in 1845-46,* New York (1847), pp. 184-85.

[34] R. T. Rundle, A Journal Composed of Notes, Diaries, Notes and Lists of Marriages and Baptisms, 1840-48, photocopy, Glenbow Foundation, Calgary, April, 1841.

Yet certain of the forces for depletion had been at work for many years, notably the long continued pressure of the fur trade. The animals were not hunted so much for robes and hides in the late eighteenth and early nineteenth centuries as later, although an attempt was made to start a Buffalo Wool Company in the Red River Colony about 1820, and hundreds of robes were included in the returns of establishments such as Piegan Post. However, a heavy and continuous toll on the bison seems to have been exacted for subsistence from the very beginning of the fur trade. The meat of the bison, whether fresh, dried, pounded or as pemmican, provided most of the energy for the trade, although large numbers of other animals and fish were a part of the diet too.

To appreciate the toll levied for subsistence, one should have some knowledge of the oft-times gargantuan appetite of the traders. At Fort Qu'Appelle, on the river of that name, during the late 1860's,

> "the daily allowance for each child was one-quarter, and for a woman one-half that for a man, which was twelve pounds fresh buffalo meat or six pounds dried buffalo meat, or three pounds pemmican, or six rabbits, or six prairie chickens, or three large white fish, or three large or six small ducks . . . with a weekly allowance of tallow or fat (besides potatoes, milk, sometimes berries) . . . Daily to feed the establishment required in the form of fresh meat, the tongues, bosses, ribs and fore and hind quarters of three animals, for the head, neck, shanks, and insides were not worth freighting from the plains to the fort. The product of three buffalo in the concentrated form of pemmican was equivalent to the daily issue of fresh meat . . ."[35]

During this period about 53 men, women and children were living at Fort Qu'Appelle, as well as 30 dogs using the equivalent of 20 men's rations.

The Qu'Appelle example should not be considered as unusual. At Pembina Post in southern Manitoba, 17 men, 10 women and 14 children, along with 45 dogs, consumed the meat of 147 buffalo during the period of September 1, 1807-June 1, 1808.[36] About 600 to 800 buffalo were used each year to feed personnel at Fort Union, near the Missouri-Yellowstone junction, in the early 1830's.[37] Occasionally, however, even fur trade appetites exceeded the bounds of common or official acceptance. For example, the Chief Trader at one post was fined when consumption reached 1,444 lbs. of fresh, 3,363 lbs. of dried and 1,343 lbs. of pounded meat, along with 667

---

35 F. G. Roe, *The North American Buffalo,* Toronto (1951), p. 854.
36 Ibid., p. 854.
37 Maximilian, Prince of Wied, *Travels in the Interior of North America, 1833-34,* Cleveland (1906), p. 382.

pounds of grease and 33,162 fish during the period September-June 1823-24. The post was home for 36 persons, 16 of whom were children. In addition 900 lbs. of dried provisions were used for winter journeys.[38]

In addition to the use of a great many bison at the hundreds of establishments that existed for various lengths of time during the eighteenth and nineteenth centuries, buffalo were also killed to provide dried meat and pemmican for shipment to other posts; for example, those in the north where animals were not so plentiful. Large number of animals also were killed by travellers who took only what they required at the moment and moved on. Much waste also occurred as many animals were wounded and left to die.

Native peoples killed large numbers of bison as well. To assess their role in depletion, in comparison to the European or to other influence, is not the intent here. Some have attempted to attribute the decline of the bison to one influence or another, be it the natives or otherwise. Suffice to say that these people played their part in depletion along with other factors. In doing so they often seem to have been doing nothing more than following traditional hunting practices. For example, in 1754, Anthony Hendry described a very large kill from enormous numbers of bison grazing south of the North Saskatchewan River. The Indians are said to have killed a "great many Buffalo; only taking what they choose to carry."; this apparently being chiefly tongues, for Hendry later said he was well stocked with them.[39] In a later example during 1883, when the bison were all but gone as a wild animal, Sitting Bull led a band of Sioux out "to hunt the buffalo as in days past". They found what seems to have been the last herd of 1,000 not far from the Black Hills "and in two days of hunting . . . wiped it out to the last animal".[40]

The Metis or mixed bloods also were an important force for depletion. These people had been increasing in number since the European first appeared in the west. Many of them eventually came to live around the fur trade posts. They often were sent to subsist on the plains for the summer, many posts being abandoned for those months, while furs were carried by canoe to the depots and supplies were brought in for the following winter's operations. Over the years the main body of Metis settled in the Red River and the Assiniboine Valleys near present-day Winnipeg. By 1843,

---

[38] Minutes of the Council of the Northern Department, *op. cit.*, Resolution 132, (1825).
[39] Burpee, *op. cit.*, (1907), p. 333.
[40] R. K. Andrist, *The Long Death,* New York (1964), p. 334.

about 571 Metis families lived in the area, this number increasing to 816 or approximately 6,000 people by 1856. Many of these people went to the plains every summer, hunting bison as far away as the Yellowstone River and the land between the North and South Saskatchewan Rivers. Hundreds of other Metis wandered freely on the plains, visiting the settlements only occasionally.[41] Both the Red River and the plains Metis killed large numbers of bison each year. To illustrate, in June, 1840, 620 men, 650 women and 300 children left the Red River area with 1,210 carts. They are said to have returned with an average of 900 pounds of buffalo meat per cart or about 1,100,000 pounds overall.[42] How many buffalo this represented is a question. An estimate of recovery might range from 75 pounds to 300 or 400 pounds per animal. Whichever figure is used, the result is thousands of buffalo.

The earliest known reference to bison depletion in the general vicinity of the Bow Valley is found in the reports of the Palliser Expedition. In the summer of 1859, while crossing from the Cypress Hills to the Rockies, James Hector met and talked with some Stoneys at the junction of the Highwood and the Bow a few miles from Calgary. The Chiefs told him that every year it was more difficult to keep from starving. The buffalo could not be depended on as before. They were said to be present "only in large bands", so that when "one tribe of Indians are hunting them the other tribes have to go without until the band migrates into their country".[43]

In the late 1860's and the 1870's a number of changes led to the elimination of the bison from the southwestern plains. Most important was the entrance of the American traders. These people induced the Blackfoot and other plains tribes to hunt the bison for robes and hides in return for alcohol and other goods. Technological change in the 1870's led to greater demand for hides and further intense pressure on the bison. Previously many skins were collected with the hair on to be used for various purposes: carriage robes, overcoats, gloves, hats and the like. Other skins were collected without hair, having been prepared and tanned by native women. The leather was rather soft, however, and could not be used readily for heavy duty purposes such as machine belts. But in 1871 a young Vermonter shipped 50 skins east to his brother

41 H. Y. Hind, *Narrative of the Canadian Red River Exploring Expedition of 1857 and of the Assiniboine and Saskatchewan Exploring Expedition of 1858*, 2 vols., London, Vol. 1, (1860), pp. 179-81.
42 Roe, *op. cit.*, pp. 403-404.
43 United Kingdom, *The Journals . . . by Captain John Palliser, op. cit.*, p. 145.

in New York. The brother sold them to a tannery, which experimented and produced a superior leather, useful for shoes, saddles and other purposes. In a word, the leather was competitive with cow-hide in quality and the demand for bison hides increased rapidly thereafter.[44]

As a result, the hunters began to kill the bison solely for its hide, leaving the rest of the carcass to waste away on the plains. The hide men operated largely in the United States where they often killed more than 100 animals in a day and thousands in a summer hunting season. They also moved north into contemporary southern Alberta, where their activities were observed by members of the Mounted Police in the 1870's.[45]

The toll exacted for hides is impossible to estimate with any accuracy. In 1874 George McDougall thought that more than 50,000 robes had been traded from the natives each year for a number of years and sent to Fort Benton on the Missouri.[46] Other robes were also shipped east to Fort Garry at this time. On June 14th, 1876, the Manitoba Free Press reported that the total trade sent to Fort Benton as a result of native hunting during the winter of 1875-76 was "fully forty thousand robes", exclusive of other pelts, "amounting to several hundreds, such as elk, beaver, wolf, bear, etc."[47] The beaver obviously had become a small item in the trade and the bison was to be soon; for the 40,000 robes did not include the "unprecedented good trade" on the Montana side of the border. The Free Press concluded that the buffalo would not persist for many years longer.

Large numbers of bison were observed in or near the Bow Valley until about 1878. In the winter of 1874-75, while returning from a missionary meeting in Edmonton, John McDougall encountered numerous buffalo in the vicinity of present-day Calgary and the Bow Valley to the west. During the next several days he and others killed many of the animals.[48]

In the next five to ten years a great many pressures built up in the Bow River country. More and more native people were pushed into the southwestern plains of Canada and nearby areas of the United States as settlement proceeded on all sides. The work of

---

[44] Andrist, *op. cit.*, p. 179.

[45] Denny, *op. cit.*, pp. 59-60.

[46] J. McDougall, *George Milliard McDougall: Pioneer, Patriot and Missionary*, Toronto (1902), p. 198.

[47] J. McDougall, "Letters from the West", *Alberta Historical Review* Vol. XV, no. 3 (1967), p. 10.

[48] J. McDougall, *op. cit.*, (1911), p. 236.

the fur traders and hide hunters continued. Some Americans are said to have deliberately favoured a policy of exterminating the buffalo as they sought to bring the natives under control and, like the Canadians, claim their land. According to Andrist, a number of American Generals "had taken the position that the quickest way to tame the roving Indians and keep them on the reservations would be to hurry up the extermination of the buffalo".[49] Ranchers also began to move into the area in the late 1870's and saw the buffalo not only as a means of subsistence, but as an animal that competed with cattle for range or carried them off as part of the wild herds. The railway, with its hungry force of thousands of labourers, also took its toll.

And working along with the previous cultural changes were the natural influences that had long killed large numbers of bison and probably held their annual rate of increase to about 18 per cent.[50] Included were the wolves, the grizzly bear, disease and hard winters. Prairie fires also killed large numbers of bison, although how frequently is not clear. Rundle came across many burned carcasses while near the Red Deer River valley on May 14th, 1841.[51] Many bison also drowned each year, particularly in the spring, while trying to cross the weak ice of the Missouri, the South Saskatchewan and other rivers and streams in the region. Such natural controls became proportionately more and more important as the herds of bison were reduced in number and confined in area, so that what had been a minor winter kill for millions of animals over a vast range became a threat to the survival of the species.

In his report for 1878, the Commissioner of the North West Mounted Police stated that "the best authorities in the North-West are of the opinion that the buffalo as a means of support, even for the Indians in the southern district, will not last more than three years". According to him, extensive prairie fires burned over "nearly all the country out from the mountains, the favourite haunt of buffalo", during the winter of 1878. As a result of this and "the mild weather, the herd did not come into their usual winter feeding ground;" but remained out on the plains. This caused hunger and famine for the Blackfeet who were forced to take "long journeys of seventy and one hundred miles" to secure food. The Sioux Indians also came up from the south to hunt and are said to have eventually killed immense numbers of animals and prevented "the

49 Andrist, *op. cit.*, p. 183.
50 Roe, *op. cit.*, p. 505.
51 Rundle, *op. cit.*, references can be traced by date.

Northern Indians from securing their usual supplies".[52] Following this kill the Sioux are said to have driven "the large eastern herd south". The Commissioner predicted that "It is a matter of reasonable doubt whether the herd will ever return in anything like the same number as heretofore".[53] In his report for the next year, 1879, the Commissioner commented that he had had little thought that his prophecy would be so literally fulfilled. But such proved to be the case.

> "Once during the summer a very large herd crossed the line east of Cypress Hills and smaller bands have come into the country, in some instances making their way north to the South Saskatchewan. The main herd, hemmed in by nearly all the Indians of the North-West and Montana, remained south of the Milk River about the 'Little Rockies' and the 'Bear Paw', extending, I believe, across the Missouri into the 'Judith Basin'."[54]

So the buffalo were reduced to one large herd which was wiped out in 1883 in the United States. No observations of large numbers of bison are known for the Bow Valley area after 1879. The last recorded observation of more than a few animals may have been made by the surveyor, O. J. Klotz. During the field season he met several small herds of buffalo "between the Saskatchewan and the Bow River".[55]

Summary Statement

By about 1885, then, the beaver had been reduced to a relatively low level. The bison herds were gone. The various landscapes associated with these animals were retreating or disappearing. The causes have been outlined and obviously are numerous and interconnected. A basic cause, particularly for the beaver, was competition, first between the Canadian Companies and the Hudson's Bay Company, and later between the Hudson's Bay Company and the American Fur Company and free traders. The competition worked against the effective introduction of sustained yield and other conservational practices, which were considered by the Hudson's Bay Company after the amalgamation of 1821, not for ecological or environmental reasons, but because they were good business and in the long term interests of the Company. In the end, however, the effects of white settlement must be given due recognition. As

---

52 *Canada Sessional Papers (No. 52)* Appendix D, Report of North-West Mounted Police for 1878, Ottawa, 1879.
53 Ibid., p. 23.
54 North-West Mounted Police Force Commissioner's Report, 1879, Part III, p. 3. From collected reports of North-West Mounted Police, Glenbow Foundation Library, Calgary.
55 *Canada Sessional Papers (No. 23)*, Annual Report of the Department of the Interior for the Year 1882, Ottawa (1883), p. 38.

Fuller has put it "There were many factors involved (in the disappearance of the bison) . . . but the overriding factor is that the bison is not compatible with the raising of livestock or grain growing. Without the hide-hunters the bison would have held on a little longer, but only until the plains were fenced".[56]

Over the years following 1885, agriculture, industry and population growth led to a kaleidoscope of urban areas, roads, railroads, mining operations, irrigation projects and other attributes of the contemporary landscape; a great contrast with the Bow Valley as it was seen as late as 1875 by Cecil Denny, one of the Mounties who founded the fort from which Calgary grew.

> "We crossed the Bow River a little above the mouth of the Elbow, finding a good ford at this place. The view from the hill on the north side of the Bow, when we reached it at the beginning of September, 1875, amazed us. Before us lay a lovely valley, flanked on the south by rolling hills. Thick woods bordered the banks of both streams; to the west towered the mountains with their snowy peaks; beyond the Elbow stretched another wide valley, and heavy timber further west along the Bow. Buffalo in large bands grazed in the valleys, but of man we saw at first no sign."[57]

---

[56] W. A. Fuller, "Emerging Problems in Wildlife Management", *Background Papers, Resources for Tomorrow Conference,* Ottawa, Vol. II (1961), p. 884.
[57] Denny, *op. cit.,* p. 83.

16

The Fur Trade and the Fur Cycle: 1825-1857

I. M. Cowan

It has long been realized by those interested in the history of the fur trade that the number of furs reaching the fur sales from year to year varied considerably. Much interesting light is shed upon these fluctuations by the note-book, now in the Provincial Archives, in which James Douglas, with characteristic thoroughness and care, tabulated year by year, from 1825 to 1857, the fur returns of the posts and trading districts in the area west of the Rocky Mountains.

Besides the summarized returns from New Caledonia (roughly the area now known as the Omineca district, northern British Columbia), the Columbia district, and the Northern Department, there are detailed figures from Fort Langley, Fort Victoria, Fort Vancouver, Fort McLoughlin, Fort Rupert, Thompson's River (Kamloops), Fort Colville, Fort Nez Perces, Fort Nisqually, Fort Simpson, Fort Durham, and Stikine, as well as a statement of the furs collected by the steamship *Beaver* along the coast of what is now British Columbia, and the results of the Snake River expeditions.

Due to unsettled conditions in the West, many of the returns are not complete throughout the full period mentioned. Several of the posts, such as Fort Victoria and Fort Rupert, were founded subsequent to 1825; while others were only maintained for a short time and then for various reasons abandoned and dismantled. Of those for which the longest unbroken series of records are available, I

Reprinted from *The British Columbia Historical Quarterly,* Vol. 11 (1938), pp. 19-30.

have summarized the figures from Forts Nez Perces, Colville, Thompson's River (included in New Caledonia subsequent to 1841), Fort Vancouver, Fort Langley, and New Caledonia. From these data the accompanying graphs have been prepared.

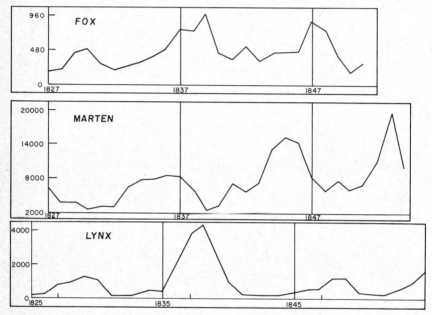

Figure 1. Graphs illustrating abundance of fox, marten and lynx, animals which exhibit the 9-10 year periodicity.

With certain minor exceptions, we are probably safe in assuming that the fur traded at each of these posts was drawn, for the most part, from a more or less circumscribed area in its vicinity.

Few have given much thought to the cause of these fluctuations. Some have accepted them as a matter of course and not paused to analyse. Others have perhaps blamed changes in personnel within the Hudson's Bay Company, rising or falling fur prices, the dictates of fashion, or perhaps abnormally severe or open winters, for the rise or fall in the tide of furs reaching the metropolitan centres of the world. While it is doubtless true that these factors did exert an influence of sorts, the fundamental mechanism rests in the animals themselves.

In so far as the fur returns have been the only records kept of the abundance of any kind of North American mammal over a period of years, we are more cognizant of the features of the pulse of abundance in fur-bearing animals than in other types. However, precisely the same phenomena are found in almost all, if not all, of the mammals inhabiting the temperate regions of the world, from the mouse to the moose. In fact, to the casual observer the alternating periods of scarcity and abundance are oftentimes much more evident in the case of certain of the smaller types of animals than in the larger, more elusive fur-bearers. Any orchardist in the rural districts can vividly recall certain winters in which the field-mice existed in hordes, and did considerable damage to his fruit trees by removing the bark around the butts. Similarly, any one familiar with the region generally referred to as the Great Northern Forest —which, to be specific, extends south in our Province well into the Cariboo district—will tell you of years in which rabbits were everywhere, of years in which rabbits were completely absent.

In 1932, for instance, in 4 miles along the Cariboo Highway a few miles north of Quesnel, I counted upwards of 150 rabbits feeding on the edge of the road, and these conditions obtained throughout the entire northern section of the Province. Two years later, in the same district, not a rabbit was to be seen. Four years later a week's trapping produced but four individuals. The casual observer, trusting to his memory alone, does not appreciate the periodicity involved in these fluctuations. To the biologist, however, it is well known that mice, especially of the group generally known as the voles or field-mice, reach a period of abundance on the average about every 4 years. It so happens that rabbit conditions have been recorded over a period of 174 years in Canada; and it has been shown by R. Macfarlane, D. A. MacLulich, Ernest Thompson Seton, C. G. Hewitt, and others, that they reach a period of abundance on the average every 9.7 years.[1]

The basic mechanism of this rhythm of periodic abundance and scarcity is simple. Animals increase in geometrical progression. A pair of snowshoe rabbits, for instance, having two litters of 4 young each per year will, in 5 years, have increased to 31,250 individuals— neglecting deaths in the meantime. Actually the number of young per litter may be double that we have postulated, with corresponding effect on the rapidity of increase of the population.

---

1 R. Macfarlane, "Notes on mammals collected and observed in the Northern Mackenzie River district, etc." *Proceedings*, U.S. National Museum, XXVIII (1905), pp. 673-764. Ernest Thompson Seton, "The Arctic Prairies," New York (1911), C. G. Havitt, "The Conservation of Wildlife in Canada," New York (1921). D. A. MacLulich, "Sunspots and abundance of animals," *Journal of the Royal Astronomical Society of Canada*, XXX (1936), pp. 233-46.

Both environmental factors and others within the animal are involved in this cycle. For instance, it has been shown by Hamilton[2] that, in field-mice, with numerical increase the litters come more frequently, the litters become larger, and the breeding season is prolonged. Favourable weather conditions may also contribute by eliminating the heavy winter-kill, or by reducing the juvenile death-rate which may result from wet weather when the young are very small. All these factors serve to build up, in a short space of time, the vast hordes of animals we have remarked upon.

Under the conditions of acute overcrowding attendant upon this saturation point, disease spreads rapidly, and in the short space of a few months the animals may become almost absent. No single disease accomplishes this cataclysmic decrease. In the rabbit, tularæmia has been identified as one cause of death; there is a high incidence of infection with the pus bacillus *Staphylococcus aureus,* which, accompanied by almost complete absence of Staphylococcus antitoxin in the blood of the snowshoe rabbit, often becomes fatal; and there is frequently heavy infestation with tapeworms of at least two species—notably *Multiceps serialis.* MacLulich finds that the most serious parasite is a threadworm, probably *Obeliscoides,* which lives in the stomach by sucking blood.[3] These worms were the apparent cause of death in six out of seven captive animals that died of "natural causes."

The rabbit-tick *Haemaphysalis leporis-palustris* and the woodtick *Dermacentor andersoni* are often extremely abundant on the head, neck, and ears of the rabbits, and probably act as vehicles for the spread of some diseases. In mouse plagues, mouse septicæmia (*Bacillus murisepticus*) and a toxoplasm infection of the brain have been found to be the most important, if not the sole disease responsible. Similar ailments may yet be found in rabbits, as the story is as yet largely untold.

Some authors have sought to establish correlation between periodicity in the rabbits and lynx with periodicity in sun-spots. A recent examination by MacLulich of the records of these mammals for a term of 174 years has conclusively shown that no such correlation exists. Between 1751 and 1925 there were 18 rabbit cycles, averaging 9.7 years, and in the same years 15½ sun-spot cycles, averaging 11.1 years. Even if fortuitous coincidence had suggested correlation

2 W. J. Hamilton, Jr., "The Biology of Microtine Cycles," *Journal of Agricultural Research,* Vol. LIV, no. 10, May 15 (1937), pp. 779-90.
3 D. A. MacLulich, "Fluctuations in the Number of Snowshoe Rabbits," *Forestry Chronicle,* Univ. of Toronto (1935), pp. 283-86.

between these cycles, the 3- to 4-year cycle of smaller rodents, such as the field-mouse, would remain to be explained.

Inasmuch as the smaller mammals, such as mice, squirrels, and rabbits, between them supply the bulk of the food of our carnivorous fur-bearers—and all the Canadian fur-bearers except the beaver and muskrat fall into this class—it is only to be expected that such great increases would have an effect on the numbers of the fur-bearers dependent upon them.

Such has been shown to be the case by Seton, Hewitt, and many others. During periods of abundance of rabbits, food is easily obtained and the carnivores are well fed, have larger litters of young, avoid the trappers' baits, and do not succumb to starvation during the winter. Their numbers show a corresponding annual increase. However, when the rabbits disappear in one of the periodic epidemics which kills them by the million, the predator fur-bearers are hard put. Those most closely dependent upon a particular food source are the first to suffer. The more adaptable, more omnivorous types will be affected later or not at all. The dependent species wander widely, and often migrate to new territory in search of food. In the meantime many of them die of starvation, many others fall victim to the trappers' baits. Those that survive are ill-nourished and either fail to breed, or at best produce very much smaller litters. In many of the fur-bearers, then, an increase in the fur returns indicates not merely a larger animal population, but also an acute food shortage which makes the animals easier to trap.

It follows that the rapidity of onset of this shortage, subsequent to the disappearance of the rabbit, will naturally indicate the extent of the dependence of any carnivorous fur-bearer upon the rabbit for its food supply. Proof of this is seen in the fact that the marten and lynx have been shown to be the most closely dependent upon the rabbit for food; and fluctuations in the numbers of these animals follow most closely those of the rabbit.

All the biologists above mentioned, in studying the fluctuations in numbers of fur-bearers, have worked with figures compiled at the fur sales. These figures comprise the returns for Canada as a whole, and represent accordingly but average conditions over the thousands of square miles of terrain involved. Inasmuch as the furs came from varying distances under widely different conditions of transportation, those appearing in one sale not only represented in many instances the fur-catch of two winters back, but often included furs resulting from two or more trapping seasons, and the figures have to be discounted accordingly. Therein lies the value of Douglas's note-book. To my knowledge this is the first instance in which authentic annual returns for specific forts over a more or less homo-geneous area have been available for study. It is consequently of interest to examine these, not alone for evidence of the basic truths already outlined, but also to investigate the local nature of the attendant phenomena.

Unfortunately there are no figures available representing the rabbits years in our region. However, as there is conclusive evidence that a close association exists between these and the fluctuations of lynx and marten, we can approximate the dates of such with a fair degree of accuracy. Judging by the lynx and marten returns, it is safe to assume that rabbit peaks occurred in British Columbia in or near 1827, 1835, 1845, and 1853.

Having derived our rabbit years thus, it is of little avail to com-pare them with the years of abundance of lynx and marten. Suffice it to say that the lynx was most abundant in 1828, 1836, 1846, and 1855 in British Columbia as a whole. However, the Hudson's Bay Com-pany returns did not distinguish between the true lynx (*Lynx cana-densis*) and the bobcat (*Lynx fasciatus*), two animals which live under totally different conditions. The lynx, a dweller in the north-ern forest, is closely dependent on the rabbit. The bobcat, a south-erner frequenting the heavy coastal forests and the sage-brush plains alike, lives on rabbits when such are abundant, but has a variety of alternative food sources to fall back upon. It is not surprising, there-fore, to find that the returns from Fort Langley and Fort Vancou-ver, where "lynx" would be largely bobcat, shows a different series of peaks than those of New Caledonia; *viz.*, 1831, 1840, 1850, and 1856 at Langley, and 1833 and 1854 at Fort Vancouver. In these two localities the rabbits never undergo the extreme fluctuations in num-bers characteristic of the north. Correspondingly, we note that the lynx population is more stable, ranging from a low of 2 in 1833 to a high of 46 in 1845 at Fort Vancouver, and a low of 8 and a high of 423 at Fort Langley, in contrast with a low of 43 and a high of 4,246 in New Caledonia. This same series of figures illustrates nicely the change that takes place as one proceeds from the colder to the warmer regions, progressing as one does so from the violently fluctu-ating populations of the north (where lynx increase 100 times from lowest ebb to highest), through an intermediate increase of 50 times in the intermediate latitude of Langley to a relatively stable popula-tion (an increase of but 20 times) at Fort Vancouver, 300 miles far-ther south.

In Canada as a whole it has been found that the marten does not respond to a period of rabbit scarcity as rapidly as does the lynx, which indicates that the marten is a more versatile hunter. Yet for some reason, over the short period of years covered by the present returns, there is a closer correlation between marten and rabbit than between lynx and rabbit. In other words, the highest number of marten were trapped in the winter prior to that in which the greatest number of lynx were trapped, *i.e.,* in 1826, 1836, 1845, 1853. The intervals between peaks are here 10, 9, and 8 years, with an average of 9 years duration.

With the disappearance of rabbits in the northern woods, the marten, as do the lynx, undertake extensive mass movements. That these are motivated by lack of food can hardly be controverted. In the case of the lynx, the earlier lean years of each rabbit depression are often marked by their appearance in territory not usually inhabited by them. It is of passing interest to note that the "no-rabbit" years see a wave of horned owls and goshawks sweeping out of the north over the rest of North America, birds which under better food conditions would have wintered in the boreal forests.

Though the mink feeds aquatically to a greater or less degree, depending on local conditions, the parallelism between its peak years, 1825-26, 1837 (as the mean of two minor peaks), 1845, and 1855, and those of the marten already given, would suggest a common dependence on a single food source—the rabbit. The above peaks for mink show an average interval of 9.7 years—precisely that demonstrated for the rabbit.

The fur returns from Fort Victoria, while including a small percentage of furs from the mainland, as evinced by the presence on the list of fisher, fox, lynx and badger, species not occurring on Vancouver Island, are no doubt largely indicative of conditions on this extensive and effectively isolated island.

We have here the opportunity of examining the pulse of abundance in mink and marten independent of the influence of rabbit fluctuations, as Vancouver Island has these fur-bearers but no indigenous rabbit population. Fort Victoria returns show marten peaks in 1842, 1852, 1855, and 1857, a rhythm entirely independent of that on the adjoining mainland. The fluctuations in the number of marten on Vancouver Island are very possibly correlated with corresponding changes in abundance of mice and squirrels, their chief food. Though figures are lacking, it is well known that these forms of mammal life undergo waves of increase and decrease similar to those of the snowshoe rabbit, but with a shorter period, averaging about 4 years. On the other hand, the mink on Vancouver Island is largely an aquatic feeder, so that parallelism between the mink and marten suggests something more abstruse than mere fluctuation of food supply as the controlling agent.

The red fox, with its colour phases, the cross-fox and silver fox, undergoes marked periodic fluctuations. Though the fox feeds on almost any animal matter, and even under certain conditions eats quantities of berries and other vegetation, it is dependent upon the rabbit to a sufficient degree that its cyclic behaviour parallels that of the rabbit. Periods of maximum abundance appear in 1829, 1838, 1846, and 1857—average periods of a little over 9 years.

The fisher is one of the largest of the weasel family, and is of particular interest to the fur-trader because it possesses the most highly valued pelt within that family. It is never as abundant as its smaller relative, the marten, and by reason of its larger size and certain special psychological adaptations, it has a wider choice of food. For instance, this animal is famed as one of the few daring regularly to kill and eat the lowly porcupine. As a result of its scarcity, the fisher did not display the pronounced fluctuations seen in the more abundant species. Nevertheless, 1829, 1838, and 1847 appear in the fur returns as years of greatest abundance. These, it will be noticed, display a 2- to 3-year lag when compared with our computed rabbit years of 1827, 1835, and 1845. Hewitt, comparing the records over a much longer period, found 9.7 years to be the cyclic period for the fisher, running 4 years after the peak rabbit years. He thought that this indicated a rhythm independent of that of the rabbit, and consequently an inherent periodicity quite apart from any food source; but this has yet to be demonstrated in any of our carnivores. It is more logical to conclude that the fisher represents the maximum lag of any animal sufficiently dependent upon the rabbit to be affected by its disappearance. It takes from 2 to 4 years for the fisher to deplete the other available food sources, and the effect of the rabbit depression is therefore deferred rather than immediately operative.

The food of such animals as the wolf, wolverine, and bear may include large numbers of rabbits during peak years; but no relation can be traced between fluctuations in their numbers and the rabbit cycle. They feed upon rabbits simply because the latter are easily obtainable, but are so omnivorous that other food sources are adequate to tide them over the lean period between "rabbit years" without material decrease in their numbers. It is true that more wolves and wolverine are taken in the "no-rabbit" years than at other times; but that is largely because, in their search for alternative food, they take the trappers' bait more readily.

The returns covering black, brown, and grizzly bear are of interest, not because they exhibit periodicity, for they do not, but because of the extraordinary degree of correspondence between the number of black and brown bear taken, and the number of grizzlies taken in the same years. It is hard to visualize the co-ordinating mechanism of such a correspondence between animals of such entirely different habits. It may simply be a reflection of weather conditions as they influence hunting conditions.

Living as it does for the most part on ground-squirrels, mice, and insects, the 5-year cycle of abundance of the badger (peak years 1832, 1837, 1841, 1846) may quite plausibly be regarded as governed by the periods of maximum and minimum abundance of the small rodents which provide the mainstay of its existence.

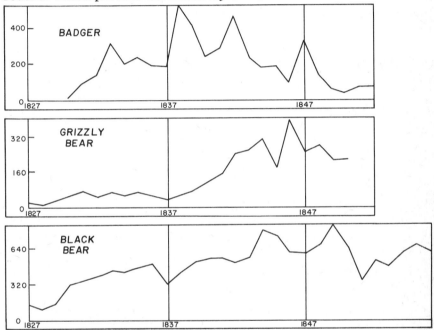

Figure 2. Graphs illustrating abundance of badger, grizzly bear and black bear. The first exhibits a 4-5 year periodicity, the latter two show no periodicity.

In the muskrat we encounter quite a different rhythm of abundance. This marsh-dwelling rodent is very much at the mercy of weather conditions—low water in the fall accompanied by little snowfall and hard frosts, or extensive spring floods, decimate the muskrat colonies. Nevertheless, there does seem to be an indication of periodicity in its numerical fluctuation. Records show years of abundance to have been 1827, 1833, 1838, 1842, 1845, and 1852. Periods of 6, 5, 4, 3, and 7 years, averaging 5 years, are suggestive of the 3- to 4-year cycle characteristic of many of the smaller rodents.

The record of beaver trapped depicts a sad story of extermination —so much so that any normal periodicity which might have been reflected in the fur returns was completely eliminated. In the high year of 1832, 21,290 beaver were trapped. From that year, however, the take fell steadily downward to a low point in 1840, when but 4,474 pelts were traded in the entire area now comprising British Columbia, Washington, and parts of the Yukon Territory and Oregon.

My data for otter and racoon give no indication of periodicity. This is only to be expected. The otter, largely an aquatic feeder, has a constant and more or less assured food supply. Especially is this the case on the coast. The racoon, like the bear, is an omnivorous feeder, and as such is not calculated to exhibit a periodicity activated by any one food supply.

I have examined the present data carefully for any evidence of a regular sequence in the succession of peak years associated with geographic location. By reason of the varied nature of the fauna and flora in the region under consideration, the marten and the mink are the only fur-bearers which are found throughout the area, and which at the same time exhibit a 9- to 10-year periodicity. In these two animals there is a tendency for the maximum to be reached one to two years earlier in the northern interior than in the Great Basin. Except in this instance there seems to be no regular sequence.

To conclude, it is evident from the fur returns recorded by Douglas that at least three main types of biological influence were involved in the early fur trade. In the first place, there was the influence of certain rodents, some of which themselves yielded furs of considerable value, which fluctuated violently in numbers, with a periodicity of about 4 years in some species, about 10 years in others. Secondly, associated with these were dependent flesh-eaters, whose numbers fluctuated in response to the scarcity and abundance of their rodent prey. Lastly, there were other fur-bearers, whose diet, while preferably carnivorous, nevertheless was flexible enough to make them independent of any one source of food. The latter underwent numerical fluctuations from year to year, but these did not conform to any regular cycle.

Though much undoubtedly depended upon the skill and industry of the individual fur-trader and trapper, it is thus clear that fundamental biological factors, beyond man's control, did much to determine the success or failure of their enterprise.

17

Wolf Control In Canada

D. M. Pimlott

The wolf poses one of the most important conservation questions of our time. Will the species still exist when the twentieth century passes into history? Or will man have exterminated the wolf as a final demonstration of his "conquest" of the wilderness and of wild things that dare to compete or conflict with him?

The fear engendered by contact of man with wolf, the apparent competition for game animals and the conflicts arising from wolf predation on livestock, have been the important factors in the war which man has waged on wolves. The struggle has been such an emotional one that it is almost impossible to sort out fact from fiction in historical and much contemporary writing. Unfortunately, the old stories—particularly those pertaining to attacks on people —are still uncritically quoted even though present-day experiences indicate that wolves do not consider people suitable prey.

Many contemporary newspaper reporters are also uncritical in their reporting. When a good wolf story comes along, the main concern seems to be to get it on the wire service rather than to verify the facts. As a result, Canadian newspapers have had a number of "good" wolf-human stories in recent years which have had little or no basis in fact. They have, however, helped to perpetuate the Little Red Riding Hood fable that has been the bane of the wolf's existence for many centuries.

In the less spectacular but still emotional problem of predation on livestock and game animals, precise facts are often even more difficult to establish. Wolves live to a large extent on big-game

Reprinted from *Canadian Audubon,* Vol. 23, (1961), pp. 145-52.

animals. In areas where livestock are raised by ranchers or farmers, sheep and cattle are often killed by wolves. These facts have been the basis of bounty systems and other forms of intensive control that have cost taxpayers millions of dollars in this century.

Unfortunately there has been little inclination to investigate beyond the simple fact of the killing of game or livestock. In game areas, for example, *the case for or against wolf control should be based on the influence that the killing has on the game population,* not on the fact that the killing occurs. In many areas of Canada, moose are becoming, or have become, too numerous for their own food supply. In such areas the killing of a moose by a wolf is beneficial, not harmful. The payment of wolf bounties or the salary of a predator control officer in such an area is a waste of money. It is, in fact, a crime cloaked under the misnomer of "conservation" or "wildlife management".

Throughout North America, the war on wolves began when the continent was first settled. The campaign began to reach a high degree of efficiency in the United States in 1915 and 1916, when control of wolves on livestock ranges was organized under the Biological Survey of the Federal Government. In the intervening years the control program has been extended to other carnivores and to rodents. There is now a large organization (the Branch of Predator and Rodent Control) in the U.S. Fish and Wildlife Service which co-operates with state organizations on control work. The efficiency of their efforts is suggested by the fact that the only areas, excluding Alaska, where healthy timber wolf populations occur in the United States are in the Superior National Forest in Northern Minnesota and Isle Royale National Park in Lake Superior. Neither area has had the benefit of Federal Government predator control operations.

In Canada, things have not developed so quickly. Until the 1950's bounty systems were used to encourage the destruction of wolves and/or coyotes in all provinces except the Maritimes, which have no wolf or coyote populations.

Wolf and Coyote Bounty Systems

The Ontario wolf bounty system can be traced back to the 18th century. It was broadened to include brush wolves (coyotes) after they colonized many parts of the province in the first half of this century. In British Columbia, bounty payments were first made in the early 1900's; in Alberta and Saskatchewan the records date back to 1899.

The cost of the bounty system has been high. Ontario has spent over $1,000,000 during this century, British Columbia approximately the same amount from 1922 to 1956. The cost to Saskatchewan increased rapidly during the 1940's, with the Provincial Government paying out $225,000 during the last ten years that bounties were paid on both wolves and coyotes. In the latter two cases the figures quoted represent only a part of the bill, for additional sums were (and in Ontario still are) being paid out by county or municipal governments.

In the western provinces particularly, climbing costs and mounting public pressures for larger bounties or supplemental programs gave rise to a strong movement, within governments, to dispense with the bounty system. The transition from the bounty system to governmental control programs was slow, resulting in a number of years when there was a duplication of the two systems. In British Columbia this overlapping period extended from 1948 to 1955, in Alberta from 1951 to 1955, in Saskatchewan from 1950 to 1954 and in Manitoba from 1949 to 1955. The Canadian Predator Control Conference, which was held in Calgary in 1954, passed a resolution recommending that all provinces consider the possibility of simultaneously abandoning the bounty system. This provided the final stimulus needed for the western provinces to dispense with it.

In the east, Quebec and Ontario have moved much more slowly. Quebec now combines bounty payments with a governmental control program. Ontario remains the last stronghold of the bounty system. There have been no major revisions of the system in recent years and as yet there has been no combination of bounties and governmental control, except in experimental work.

Predator Control Organizations

The change-over from the bounty system to governmental control programs has resulted in considerable variation in the control of coyotes and relative uniformity in the control of wolves. I will deal principally with the latter.

British Columbia formed a predator control organization in 1947. It has now achieved divisional status, as the Predator Control Division, in the Game Branch of the Department of Recreation and Conservation. It constitutes by far the most ambitious approach to predator control in Canada, and was probably modelled after the United States organization mentioned earlier. It has 12 permanent staff members and this year has a budget of approximately $112,000.

No comparable organization has been formed by any of the other provinces or by the Yukon or the Northwest Territories. In all cases, control of timber wolves is undertaken by an organization with more general duties. In Saskatchewan, for example, the wolf control program is conducted by the Fur Management Division, while coyote control is undertaken by the Game Management Division, both of the Department of Natural Resources. Neither division has any employees whose sole job is predator control. In 1960 Manitoba employed one full-time and four part-time professional hunters in the southern part of the Province.

A predator control officer (supervisor) for the Northwest Territories was appointed by the Canadian Wildlife Service in 1957. This position no longer exists. The program now comes under the direction of the Superintendent of Game. Although a number of predator control officers are employed on contracts, no permanent positions have been established.

Control Methods and Programs

Wolf and coyote control in Canada is conducted almost entirely by the use of poisons. The two generally used are strychnine and compound "1080" (sodium fluoroacetate). Strychnine has a relatively fast action, and animals that are killed are usually found close to the bait station. Compound "1080", on the other hand, is deadly but slow-acting. Wolves that take "1080" bait usually travel many miles before they die. Because of this, the results of programs in which "1080" is used can only be indirectly appraised.

This compound was developed during World War II and has now come into wide use in all types of pest and rodent control programs throughout the world. It has an especially high toxicity for members of the dog family and so is generally favoured in the control of foxes, coyotes and wolves, when recovery of the carcass is not considered to be important. Other factors favouring its use are its tastelessness, its lack of odour and its high solubility in water. The last is considered particularly desirable since it simplifies the preparation of baits.

Except in the Northwest Territories, aircraft are used in establishing a high percentage of poison-bait stations. In some cases, particularly in British Columbia, the baits are simply dropped from the aircraft in flight. In other cases the aircraft lands on a lake and a marked bait station is established, with the baits frozen into the ice. This procedure is usually followed in strychnine programs where at least part of the appraisal is done on the basis of the number of animals killed.

A part of the strong campaign in Western Canada for wolf and coyote control was brought about by the spread of rabies. This disease first reached epidemic proportions in the Northwest Territories.

Alberta made a particularly intensive effort to prevent the spread of rabies. During 1953 and 1954, 170 trappers were hired to ring the settled area of the province with 5,000 miles of traplines and poison stations. At the same time poison was being distributed to landowners in the settled areas by the Pest Control Program of the Department of Agriculture. Between 1951 and 1956 a fantastic amount of poison was distributed: 39,960 cyanide guns, 106,100 cyanide cartridges and 628,000 strychnine pellets. In addition "1080" bait stations were being established. This program expanded from 25 bait stations in 1951 to 800 in 1956. During the period it was estimated that 246,800 coyotes were killed.

It appears that no estimate was made of the number of desirable wild animals that were killed.

In British Columbia, initial emphasis was on the use of strychnine and cyanide guns. After experiments in 1952, "1080" came into wide use. The number of "1080" stations increased from 768 in 1953 to 2,101 in 1955; it gradually declined until 1960 when 1,200 were established.

In Manitoba, the wolf control program has three distinct phases: control adjacent to or within the fringe of settlement, control in more remote areas, and control on barren-ground caribou winter range. Much of the work in the first phase is done through ground operations, while in the other two it is primarily conducted by the use of aircraft.

A complete accounting of control methods is not given for Manitoba. In the program in remote areas, and on barren-ground caribou range, 341 strychnine baits were placed in 1959-60. Since both predator hunters and conservation officers use poison in other phases of the program, 500 is probably a conservative estimate of the total number of baits placed. There was a known kill of 800 wolves in the various programs.

The Saskatchewan program is quite similar to the one in Manitoba, although no specific mention is made of work on the fringe of settlements. In 1958-59, 294 baits were placed in the wolf control program. There was a known kill of 176 wolves.

In the Northwest Territories, the principal objective of wolf control is to reduce predation on barren-ground caribou. In this area, the setting of poison baits by predator hunters has proven to be more successful and less costly than the use of aircraft. Because of the high cost per wolf killed, a recommendation has been made to discontinue the use of aircraft in the program.

In 1957-58 a total of 564 poison baits were placed. No complete accounting is available for subsequent years. The cost of the program since 1955-56 to the present time has ranged from $25,000 to $48,000, representing between $23.00 and $73.00 per wolf killed.

Wolf Control and Wildlife Management

The changeover from the bounty system to methods of governmental control has had some alarming aspects from a conservation viewpoint.

In the late 1940's and early 1950's, when the western provinces were striving to bring the bounty system to an end, we frequently spoke of the bounty system as the great evil—the greatest conservation monstrosity of our time. We led ourselves to believe that the discontinuance of the bounty system would bring us into some sort of utopian state. We were a little hazy about the future, however; we were certain that at the very least this gigantic waste of conservation funds would end. We sent men to be trained in the United States and we planned, and began to conduct, extensive poisoning programs. *We did not, however, institute a single wolf or coyote research program to determine the significance of predation on livestock or on game populations.*

In denouncing the bounty system, we said that it did not actually control wolves and that it did not concentrate effort where it was really needed. Both points were valid. However, we usually failed to point out that animals were being killed in vast areas where no killing—no control—was justified.

A familiar phrase in our vocabulary in discussing the future was (and still is), "Control when and where needed". Lacking the background information of intensive research on wolves and their prey, how are we to recognize "Where needed"? With a few exceptions, control seems to have become "When and where *wanted*". In addition, the bill for predator control has been high. In British Columbia it soon exceeded the greatest sum that had ever been expended on bounty payments.

In Ontario there was enough doubt, enough questioning about the advantages of the new over the old (extensive poison control programs versus the bounty system), that very little was done to bring about the elimination of the latter. Finally, in 1957, a wolf and coyote research program was instituted to provide background knowledge for management programs.

This year at the Federal-Provincial Wildlife Conference, I stated the basic attitudes on wolves which exist in the Ontario Department of Lands and Forests, as:

1. The use of the term wolf control, and wolf control as such should be discontinued. The goal should be wolf management—management connotes, (i) control when and where needed (not when and where wanted) or (ii) protection of varying degrees, depending on specific conditions of game populations and range or on livestock damage.

2. A detailed knowledge of the ecology and population dynamics is as important to predator management as it is to the management of any game species, hence intensive research is of vital importance.

3. Predators have many positive values, some economic, some aesthetic. A concerted effort is necessary to establish the two-sided nature of the predator question in the public mind.

4. The bounty system is not necessarily the greatest evil. Unless directed to where specific need has been demonstrated, governmental control programs may constitute a greater abuse and a greater waste of public funds than the bounty system constitutes.

Do present Canadian wolf control programs constitute a better form of wildlife management than did the bounty system? Where do the dangers lie? What is the bright side of the picture? These are some of the questions I will try to put into focus.

Neither space, nor available information will permit a detailed analysis of the situation for the entire country. I will concentrate mainly on the programs that are being conducted in British Columbia and on the winter range of barren-ground caribou. The latter is done mainly in the Northwest Territories, but laps over into Saskatchewan and Manitoba. These are, in fact, the only two areas where there is enough information available to make an appraisal possible. In other areas the information is so limited that it is sometimes possible to raise the questions but rarely find answers.

British Columbia: In other sections I gave some of the background on the British Columbia organization and its program. I will briefly review the facts. The Province has a permanent predator control organization with 12 permanent staff members and an annual budget exceeding $100,000. Compound "1080" is widely used in both wolf and coyote control. Much of the bait-setting in northern areas is done with aircraft. In 1955, 2,101 major poison stations were established. In 1960, 1,200 were in use. Extensive poisoning is done in remote northern areas as well as in the cattle range of the central interior.

The two situations just mentioned, control on cattle-game range, and control on game ranges, need to be kept clearly in mind. The necessity for action and the political pressures associated with the two are quite different. In this comparison with the program in the Northwest Territories I will speak mainly of wolf control on moose range.

Moose are the most important prey of wolves over large areas of British Columbia. The writings of Dr. James Hatter and his associates tell a most interesting story of the build-up of the moose herd in the central part of the Province, where moose were unknown prior to 1900. The herd increased very rapidly in the wake of large forest fires, and by the 1930's heavy winter mortality was being reported due to starvation from overbrowsing and winter ticks.

In the northern part of the Province (D Division of the Game Commission), comprising approximately 200,000 square miles, much less was known about the moose and about the condition of its food supply. However, during the early 1950's moose were said to be increasing, and by the spring of 1953 they were found dying in one part of the Division. By 1956 it was reported that there was a heavy moose population in the area. Two years later, moose winter ranges in most sections of the Province showed excessive browsing. At the same time in the Prince George area, where intensive wolf poisoning had been done, the moose range was severely overbrowsed.

During this same period, when moose were increasing in numbers to the point of causing great destruction of their own food supply, wolves were being intensively poisoned throughout the Division. There were 768 "major" poison stations in 1953, and although the exact number was not published, probably more during the next two years. The program was still being expanded.

This history of intensive wolf control in the face of an increasing moose population that was increasing too quickly raises many questions about the need for, and the wisdom of, the poisoning campaign conducted in northern parts of British Columbia. I believe that to a large extent, the program cannot be justified. I consider that it constituted a greater abuse of conservation principles and a greater waste of public funds than the bounty system which it complemented and later replaced.

If this is true, why was such a program carried out? The proceedings of the British Columbia Game Conferences are quite enlightening. The records of the conference discussion show that there were a number of "pressure groups" acting—stockmen on the southern fringe, trappers and guides throughout the area. In addition, there were members of the Game Commission staff who were convinced that wolves constituted the greatest danger that game herds faced. In 1947, for example, the inspector for D Division stated that wolves were plentiful throughout the Division and were a greater menace to game than disease, hunters and other predators combined. In the face of this strong body of opinion it was necessary to be very efficient in the control campaign so that bounties on coyotes and wolves would be abolished. I question that the end result justified the means.

The Tundra Wolf-Control Program: The barren-ground caribou have declined very drastically during the past quarter century. Dr. Frank Banfield of National Museum tells a stark story of overexploitation and waste by Indians and Eskimos. The decline has continued during the past decade. The caribou population was estimated at 670,000 in 1949. A resurvey only six years later indicated that there were less than 300,000. At the time of the 1949 study the annual crop of calves was estimated at 145,000, while the total mortality was placed at 178,000! Of this number, 100,000 were estimated to have been killed by humans and 34,000 by timber and tundra wolves.

It is obvious from the figures that humans are a primary cause of the decline of the caribou herd. In the face of these facts, an intensive wolf control program was undertaken on the wintering range of the caribou. At the same time, educational work began with the native people in an attempt to persuade them to modify their hunting practices, to spare does and to eliminate wasteful cacheing practices.

What have the results been? It appears that the wolf control program is being successful—at any rate the wolf population seems to have been reduced; the educational program has meet with only limited success. A large Indian band, in a key location in the Northwest Territories, is completely unconvinced of the need and virtually refuses to co-operate. In other areas there has been some success. The annual picture is that *the human kill of caribou approaches or exceeds the reproduction of the herds*. The caribou crisis continues. The barren-ground caribou may become extinct.

With this situation in mind, was intensive control of tundra and timber wolves justifiable? I consider that it was. Many factors are involved. Human psychology is one of them. Throughout the world people believe that wolves constitute a serious menace to game populations. The possibility of obtaining co-operation by the native people would have been even less if wolf control had not been undertaken.

A second factor is that the number of caribou killed by wolves in any year could possibly mean the difference between a decline and an increase in the herds. A final factor, in my view at least, is that as long as control of tundra wolves is judicious it will have little or no effect on their status decades hence. Their numbers are so closely related to those of the barren-ground caribou that their ultimate fate hinges more on the caribou than on control. If the caribou survive and continue their migrations, the tundra wolves will survive. For this reason, intensive, short-term control of tundra wolves can conceivably benefit the wolves themselves.

In summation I believe that control of the wolves that prey on the barren-ground caribou constitutes a valid approach to wildlife management.

What about wolf control programs in areas other than northern British Columbia and on barren-ground caribou range? Can they justifiably be called "wildlife management", or are they largely "demand" programs? As I stated before, the available information on the control programs that are being conducted and on the status of game and the condition of their food supplies is so limited that it precludes any form of detailed appraisal. There are, however, a few straws in the wind that can be discussed.

The Cattle-Game Range of British Columbia: This is the central interior area of the Province where moose have been overbrowsing their range and periodically dying of starvation since the 1930's. Demands for wolf control by stock raisers in this area are so strong that conviction seems to have developed that it must be retained as a wolf-free area. This is done regardless of the status of the associated game populations. In addition to intensive control within cattle range, it is considered necessary to maintain a 40-mile protective zone around the areas.

What are the economics of this situation? Are wolves such a serious menace to cattle that they must be eradicated? I cannot answer the questions, although it is obvious that the answer to the second question is "yes" so far as British Columbia authorities are concerned. The most disturbing thing is that there is no evidence of any study having been done on the pattern of wolf predation on cattle or on the economics of the situation. In Northern Ontario, where small farms are intimately associated with forest, the cattle predation that occurs suggests that intensive specific control, rather than extensive general control, will produce a satisfactory answer to predation problems. The one thing that is most apparent is that the question of control of wolves on the cattle-game ranges of British Columbia warrants far more serious study than it has been given.

Alberta: The rabies control program conducted between 1952 and 1956 on both agricultural and forested areas was a colossal effort to destroy all animals that might spread the disease. The threat of rabies was considered so serious that the program was under the direction of the Veterinary Services Branch of the Alberta Department of Agriculture. One aspect of the program, as I mentioned earlier, was the employment of 170 trappers, for a two-year period, to maintain 5,000 miles of trap and poison lines. It was stated that they were provided with every known device to kill predators.

Was such an extensive program really necessary? The Alberta authorities consider that it was. In a report on the program, the officers in charge stated that until there is much more information available on the migration of wild animals, rabies control of animals in forested areas will be empirical.

A rabies outbreak began in Ontario in 1954 and probably reached epidemic proportions the same year. During the intervening period, no concerted attempt has been made to control animals that might spread the disease. Since the outbreak began, rabies has been diagnosed in approximately 2,365 animals. Only 12 of these involved wolves or coyotes, although both species live close to human habitations in many parts of the Province. This certainly suggests that wolves have not been much affected by rabies. Intensive control of wolves to prevent the spread of the disease would have been of questionable value. Wolves and rabies in Ontario cause me to wonder about the need for Alberta's intensive wolf and coyote control program.

Manitoba and Saskatchewan: Both Provinces disavow any intention of exterminating wolves. Certainly the intensity of the kill in the northern halves of the two Provinces does not suggest that the present programs are likely to achieve that end in remote areas. The question at the moment pertains more to the necessity of the program.

The annual reports of both Provinces indicate that big-game populations have been increasing steadily, and in the case of moose particularly, quite rapidly.

The Manitoba reports from 1957 through 1960 all refer to the fact that the moose population is not being hunted up to potential. Some of the reports refer to the danger of overpopulations in remote areas. The 1960 report stated that moose in the northern portion of the interlake area had reached an optimum level. In the same report in the section on Predatory Animals the following paragraph appears:

"Some difficulty was experienced in cleaning out a remnant population of four timber wolves in the Sleeve Lake district of the Interlake area. These animals had survived a continuing extermination program and had learned to avoid snares, traps and poison baits set for them. They were eventually all destroyed in the spring of 1960."

This paragraph stands in stark contrast to one which appeared in the 1959 report:

"Predator control has not been pressed to the point of extermination. Such a policy would be contrary to all concepts of good farm and game management. For these reasons the present program is aimed toward predator control through selective killing when and where needed."

What is one to believe? Why were the Sleeve Lake wolves exterminated? Why is it necessary to place 300 to 400 poison baits a year in remote areas when dangers of over-populations of moose exist? Do Conservation Officers, who have been provided with strychnine kits, simply kill wolves because they are present in their areas? If not, on what criteria do they make their decisions? Saskatchewan reports also point out that moose are plentiful wherever habitat is suitable, and that they are underharvested in inaccessible areas. In 1958-59, 231 poison baits were placed in remote parts of the province. This excludes the Athabasca Region, which is part of the barren-ground caribou program. How many of these baits are performing a valid function? To what extent is this a "demand" program?

In Terms of the Future

Ontario and Quebec: Moose are very abundant in northwestern Ontario and have now reached huntable densities over most of the Province's moose range. With the possible exception of the southern part of the range, and of the most accessible areas elsewhere, the present kill could be much greater. However, as yet no winter mortality resulting from malnutrition has been reported.

The white-tailed deer picture is more complex. In the eastern part of Ontario, hunting is very heavy and may limit the population in many areas. The influences of periodic deep snows, wolf predation and changing forests are all intermingled. Research programs are being conducted to determine the role of the various factors.

Under Ontario's Bounty Act wolves are killed indiscriminately, although it is known that their presence in many parts of moose range is beneficial. From 1,000 to 1,500 wolves are killed each year. The Bounty Act is a legislative matter and can only be amended by legislative action. The present big-game and wolf research programs are beginning to provide the background knowledge necessary for the establishment of management programs. This could result in the eventual repeal of the Bounty Act.

Little can be said about wolves and big-game in Quebec. This Province has done almost nothing to initiate research and management programs on game species. No information is available on the status of moose or deer or on present wolf control work being conducted in the Province. The little information I obtained was acquired by personal contacts and through newspaper accounts.

What does this all mean in terms of the future?

A bright side of the picture is, that of all the areas that are now concerned with wolf control only British Columbia has formed an organization with the prime responsibility of controlling predators. This is encouraging, because organizations that have a diverse responsibility are not nearly as likely to fight to retain the status quo on predator control. There is also more likelihood of freedom of expression. An interesting sidelight to this point is also provided by British Columbia. Prior to the formation of the Predator Control Division, big-game workers questioned in their writings the need for intensive control of wolves. No comments were made by members of the group after wolf control became the function of a specific division. As the paucity of formal predator control organizations is a bright side of the present picture, so, a future danger is that more such organizations will be formed, as the demand for game and for land increases.

Another encouraging aspect is that all provinces, with the exception of Quebec, now have big-game research programs established. Since wolves live primarily on big-game, the results of this research will provide a much more realistic understanding of where control is needed. This is certain to influence wolf control operations eventually.

The wolf research programs in Ontario and in the Northwest Territories are also encouraging signs. They indicate that wolf predation is no longer being accepted at face value. We are no longer simply asking, "Do wolves kill deer?" We are seeking the answers to what the killing means in terms of the deer or moose or caribou populations.

Scare programs constitute a very real danger to timber wolves. If the remainder of the country were to adopt the approach of Alberta in attempting to eliminate rabies, timber wolves could conceivably be extirpated over large areas. Their gregarious habits make them particularly susceptible to intensive control of this nature.

The greatest danger to timber wolves lies in the future—in the latter part of this century—when large areas of big-game range are no longer inaccessible, when the annual hunting kill has finally approached the production of the herds. What will our attitude be then? Will we be willing to share deer, moose and caribou with the wolves, or will area after area, like Manitoba, report, "These animals had survived a continuing extermination program and had learned to avoid the snares, traps and poison baits set out for them. **They were all destroyed in the spring of 1964.**" The answer is likely to be in the affirmative unless a much greater segment of the populace comes to appreciate the positive aesthetic and practical values of the wolves.

References

Annual Reports, Alberta, Department of Lands and Forests; British Columbia, Game Commission, Department of Recreation and Conservation; Manitoba, Department of Mines and Natural Resources; Ontario, Department of Lands and Forests; Quebec, Department of Fish and Game; Saskatchewan, Department of Natural Resources, (1954).

Banfield, A. W. F., "Preliminary investigation of the Barren-Ground Caribou, Part I, Former and present distribution, migrations and status, Part II, Life history ecology and utilization", *Wildl. Mgt. Bull. Ser. 1*, No. 10A and 10B, Dept. Northern Affairs and Nat. Res., (1956). "The caribou crisis", *The Beaver*, Spring (1956).

Cowan, I. McT., "Predation", *Proc. B.C. Game Conv., 1* (1947), pp. 34-44.

Hatter, James, "Preliminary report on moose investigation in British Columbia", *Proc. 1st Ann. B.C. Game Conv. Pp.* (1947), pp. 20-28; "Progress report on moose investigations in central British Columbia", *Proc. 2nd Ann. B.C. Game Conv. Pp.* (1948), pp. 23-31; "The status of moose in North America, Trans. *N.A. Wildl. Conf. 14* (1949), pp. 492-501; "Some trends in the hunting and harvest of moose and mule deer in British Columbia," *Proc. 6th Ann. B.C. Game Conv. Pp.* (1952), pp. 57-63.

Hatter, J., D. J. Robinson, P. W. Martin, L. G. Sugden, E. W. Taylor and W. G. Smith, "Inventory and valuation of wildlife resources of British Columbia", *9th B.C. Nat. Res. Conf. Trans.* (1956), p. 56.

Mair, W. W., "Predation—problems and plans of British Columbia Game Commission thereon", *Proc. B.C. Game Conv., 4* (1950), pp. 88-95; "The predatory animal programme in British Columbia", *Proc. B.C. Game Conv., 5* (1951), pp. 70-74.

Pimlott, D. H., "Wolf Control in Ontario—Past, Present and Future", *Pres. 25th Fed. Prov. Wildl. Conf.*, Ottawa (1961).

Sessional Papers, Northwest Territories Council.

West, G. A., "Why we control predators", *Proc. B.C. Game Conv., 7* (1953), pp. 109-12.

18

Ducks and the Great Plains Wetlands

D. A. Munro

If you were to draw a line from Edmonton through Prince Albert to Winnipeg you would trace the northern boundary of North America's most important duck breeding grounds. Continue the line southward from Winnipeg to take in the western half of Minnesota, trace it to the west and north to take in the eastern half of South Dakota, then follow the Missouri River to Great Falls, Montana, and move northwestward along the Rocky Mountain foothills to Calgary and Edmonton. You have enclosed the area where 50 per cent of all North America's ducks breed. The larger part of the area lies in Canada. This Great Plains wetlands region is only about 10 per cent of the continent's total duck breeding area, but 70 to 80 per cent of the hunters' most favoured species, mallard and pintail, are produced there. The Great Plains wetlands region is the only significant breeding area for redhead, canvasback, and ruddy duck. Of all North American ducks, only a few—notably the eiders, oldsquaw, wood duck, and black duck—breed there only rarely or not at all.

Many people think of the prairies as a uniform, featureless expanse of grass or grain, here and there relieved by one or two grain elevators and the occasional curling rink. Nothing could be farther from the truth.

Reprinted from *Canadian Audubon,* Vol. 25 (1963), pp. 105-11.

Prairie topography varies from level through rolling to hilly. The major rivers have carved deep valleys or coulees across the land. The effects of the ice ages are prominent. Glacial moraines and outwashes are extensive. Numerous poorly drained depressions were formed by the melting of chunks of ice within the moraines. This is "knob and kettle" country to the physiographer, "pothole country" to the waterfowl biologist. Following the ice age, several large glacial lakes formed on the lower levels of eastern Saskatchewan and Manitoba. When the lakes disappeared, the prairies' few really level areas of heavy clay and silt were left behind.

Topography is not the only variable feature of the prairies. The soil zones of the region lie roughly in concentric arcs centred about a point at the middle of its southern boundary. From the centre outward the zones are brown, dark brown, black, and grey wooded. Soil textures vary from fine silt to coarse sand. Alkalies are common in the drier parts of the region. The deep clays of the glacial-lake plains are relatively free of stones, but moraine and outwash areas may contain gravel and boulders.

The climate of the prairies is characterized by cold winters, hot summers, and low, but extremely variable, precipitation. Average precipitation is lowest in southern Alberta and southwestern Saskatchewan (the well-known Palliser Triangle within which annual precipitation is less than 15") and increases toward the northern and eastern limits of the region. Average annual precipitation at Edmonton is 17.46" and at Winnipeg, 20.83". Throughout the region almost half the annual precipitation occurs in May, June, and July. That part of the region which is driest is also that in which there is the greatest variability in precipitation between years.

There are two major ecological zones within the Great Plains wetlands region. These are the grasslands, which correspond roughly with the Palliser Triangle, and the aspen parklands which lie to the north and east (see Figure 1). The boundary between the two zones, like most natural boundaries, is a shifting, imprecise area rather than a sharply defined line. Both the grasslands and the aspen parkland may be divided into sub-zones and communities.

Potholes, which are filled by surface drainage from their immediate surroundings and usually lose water mainly by evaporation, are the most important wetlands for breeding ducks. In the wetter years, some potholes may form parts of intermittent watercourses, overflowing from one to the other. Potholes may vary in size from fractions of an acre to several hundred acres.

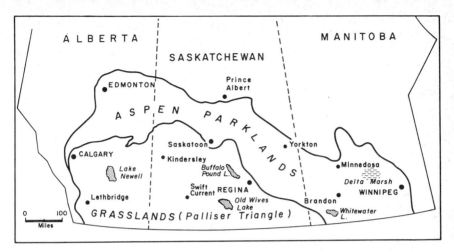

Figure 1. The Great Plains Wetlands.

Other types of prairie wetlands are the marshes and lakes. These differ from potholes in that they are usually larger, and occur in flattened basins or plains. Many provide extensive habitat for breeding ducks and other waterfowl, but are most notable as concentration areas for moulting birds and staging areas for migrants.

In years of favourable water conditions there may be as many as 150 potholes per square mile in morainic areas of particularly irregular topography. In May 1955, there were over six million water areas in the southern Prairie Provinces. The potential number in the region, the number which would be filled if all parts of the region were equally blessed with soil moisture, snowfall, and spring rains in one season, must be well over eight million. That potential is probably never realized.

It is, of course, the variation in precipitation which results in variations in amounts and distribution of surface waters. Winter snowfall, the speed of the spring thaw, and early spring rains are particularly important. The amount of surface water is highly variable. For example, in southeastern Saskatchewan the index of water areas was 1,335,000 in 1955, but only 49,000 in 1961. I will mention later some of the effects of these changes in water distribution on vegetation and waterfowl distribution.

Many of the water areas or wetlands about which we have been speaking exist only seasonally. On the average there is a 32 per cent reduction in numbers of water areas throughout the region between May and July. This seasonal decline continues through the summer. As might be expected, it is most pronounced

in southern Alberta and southwestern Saskatchewan, least pronounced in Manitoba. Occasionally, the number of water areas in
southern Manitoba has actually increased between May and July
because of heavy rains in June.

As an aid to their continuing studies of factors affecting the
fortunes of waterfowl, biologists have devised a number of systems
for classifying prairie wetlands. A simple classification based on
permanency, and helpful in understanding the importance of the
different types of wetlands to ducks, is as follows:

Sheet water—very shallow, usually enduring for only a few days
in early spring, supporting no wetland vegetation, used by waterfowl for loafing and feeding on waste grain.

Temporary potholes—many contain as much as 18 inches of
water, endure usually for less than six weeks, support sedges,
cattails, and bulrushes; used as breeding areas by ducks and are
highly productive when in the vicinity of more permanent water
areas to which broods can move.

Semi-permanent potholes, marshes and lakes—may contain as
much as five feet of water and may not dry up for several years;
support both emergent and submergent vegetation; serve as the
most important brood rearing areas.

Permanent potholes, marshes and lakes—contain more than five
feet of water and rarely, if ever, dry up; support emergent and
submergent vegetation in the shallows; individual areas are highly
variable in capacity to support water fowl; most important as
reservoir areas in dry years.

The Pothole Community

Why is the Great Plains wetlands region so favoured as a
breeding area for ducks? Other areas are as well-watered, and
the waters are more permanent. The answer probably lies in a
combination of circumstances. Certainly the distribution of prairie
water, in numerous small bodies which are separated, yet close to
each other, favours the build-up of large populations of animals,
such as ducks, which space themselves out in response to their
territorial requirements. Another favourable circumstance is that
the variability of potholes in size and vegetation serves to meet
the changing habitat requirements of ducks at different stages
of their breeding cycle. Somewhat the same conditions are provided by the lakes of the Canadian Shield and the extensive sub-
Arctic and Arctic tundras and muskegs. Those, however, have
mainly acid waters of low fertility, and are much less productive
of the basic food organisms which must form the foundation of

any ecological pyramid of numbers. The prairie potholes are not only numerous and densely distributed, they are highly fertile and support a rich flora and fauna. They are generally shallow and become warm by late spring. The floral and faunal characteristics of prairie potholes vary not only between potholes at any one time but, also, for any one pothole, over the course of a year and from year to year.

There is a classical concept of succession, or continuing change, in the vegetative components of wetlands. The components of each stage vary from region to region as well as with local conditions of soil, and amount and quality of water. Essentially the progression is from open water to water choked with submerged plants, to water with emergent plants, to wet meadow, and finally to a growth of shrubs or trees. The final stage is known as the "climax", and the intervening ones are termed "seral". The intermediate stages are those which are most attractive to waterfowl. Any, and often all, stages can be found arranged in roughly concentric zones in one location. Ecological succession in prairie potholes is not the relatively orderly affair it is in areas of greater humidity and less variable climate. Because of annual variations in rainfall, and the resultant fluctuations in amount and distribution of surface water, succession rarely proceeds to the climax stage in any individual pothole. In the course of 20 years, succession may stop, regress, and readvance three or four times. This circumstance has, over the years, doubtless favoured the continued existence of wetlands in the successional stages most attractive to waterfowl.

Soil erosion, as well as climatic variation, has an effect on ecological succession. Many prairie potholes are surrounded by tilled fields, from which soil is removed by wind and water at a fairly rapid rate. Much of the soil removed from the more elevated areas naturally finds its way to the depressions which often are, in fact, the potholes. There has been no study of the rate of sedimentation in prairie potholes, but it seems obvious that it must be quite rapid in some areas.

Bearing in mind that there is probably no such thing as a typical prairie pothole, let us consider in greater detail the plant and animal components of a pothole community.

Plants, whether plankton, floating forms, submergents, emergents, or terrestrial forms growing near the potholes, are of tremendous importance to waterfowl. Planktonic algae are significant primarily as the basic fodder for small invertebrate animals. They are the first link in the pothole food chain.

The most common floating plants in parkland and grassland potholes are the filamentous algae and the duckweeds (*Lemna*). The duckweeds are important themselves as food for some species of ducks. Both duckweeds and filamentous algae also harbour various invertebrate animals. Sometimes, duckweeds cover the surface of the water so thoroughly that lack of light inhibits the growth of rooted aquatic plants below.

The most important of the submerged plants in prairie potholes are the pondweeds (*Potamogeton sp.*) The leaves, tubers, and particularly the seeds of a number of species are important as duck food.[1] The distribution of various submerged plants is related to depth, salt-content, and muddiness. Some species are more tolerant with regard to these variables than others.[2]

The most commonly found "deep-water" emergents are cattail (*Typha latifolia*), softstem and hardstem bulrush (*Scirpus validus* and *S. acutus*), whitetop (*Scolochloa festucacea*), and sedges (*Carex spp.*).

The widespread and familiar cattail is of some value as nesting cover for redhead, canvasback, ruddy duck, and coots. It is not a useful duck food plant, and is often an undesirable competitor of some of the more valuable emergents. It is a hardy and successful plant, difficult to eradicate. Mowing or heavy grazing at certain stages, flooding to a depth greater than four feet, and the use of herbicides will control it. Herbicides should, of course, be used with care by someone familiar with their characteristics and effects. The bulrushes and sedges are useful for both food and cover for ducks. As with other groups, distribution of the various species is governed by their tolerance of environmental conditions.

Shallow water emergents include the smartweeds (*Polygonum*), another important duck food, particularly in the grassland areas.

---

[1] Sago pondweed (*P. pectinatus*) is a particularly valuable plant. Water milfoil (*Myriophyllum*), hornwort (*Ceratophyllum*), ditchgrass (*Ruppia*), water-celery (*Vallisneria*), and stonewort (*Chara*) are other common genera.

[2] On small impoundments in south-eastern Alberta, Lloyd Keith found *Potamogeton pusillus* and *P. pectinatus* largely restricted to waters less than 2.5 feet deep. *P. Richardsonii* was dominant in the depth zone from 2.5 to 3.5 feet, and *P. Friesii* and *Chara* were most abundant in waters from 3.5 to 7.5 feet deep. *Myriophyllum exalbescens* and *Ceratophyllum demersum* exhibited a much broader depth tolerance than most pondweeds. *Ruppia occidentalis* and *P. pectinatus* are halophytic; *P. Richardsonii* and *Ceratophyllum demersum* are relatively intolerant of salinity. All these considerations have some bearing on the quantity and quality of duck food produced and thus may be significant in relation to the carrying capacity of water areas for waterfowl.

Burreeds (*Sparganium*), arrowheads (*Sagittaria*), spikerushes (*Eleocharis*), rushes (*Juncus sp.*), and reed (*Phragmites communis*) are common plants of the water's edge.

Woody plants—primarily willows nearest the water, and then aspen—wholly or partially enclose the shoreline of potholes in the parkland zone, and willows may form interrupted margins along the edges of grassland sloughs.

The surroundings of prairie potholes have been so much influenced by man that it is useful to refer to them at least partly in accordance with their use by man. Thus we may speak of arable land in grain or summerfallow, pasture—lightly grazed, pasture— heavily grazed, hayland, and woodland. Some of the most important species of waterfowl, notably mallard and pintail, and, to a lesser extent, blue-winged teal, baldpate, shoveller, and gadwall may nest a considerable distance from water. The existence of nest cover in areas surrounding potholes is, therefore, of great importance. Uncropped grasses, sedges, and weeds along fence rows and roadsides, clumps of buckbrush or snowberry (*Symphoricarpos*), wolf willow (*Elaeagnus*), and rose (*Rosa*) are much used as nesting cover. Aspens (*Populus tremuloides*) provide nesting sites for the hole-nesting ducks—buffleheads and goldeneyes. Local topography, microclimate, soils, and use of the land, all affect the distribution of cover plants.

The invertebrate animals inhabiting potholes are of major importance as duck food. They are particularly valuable in the spring when plants and their seeds are less available to ducks, and they provide the protein-rich diet which growing ducklings need. The importance of animal food for ducks was under-estimated for many years because relatively few animal remains were found in the ducks' gizzards. This was because the soft animal material becomes unrecognizable more rapidly than the hard-covered seeds of plants. Recently Nolan Perret has shown that specialized collecting methods and examination of gullet contents give a more accurate picture of duck feeding habits and place the animal component of the ducks' diets in proper perspective.

Within the potholes there is a varied and interesting invertebrate fauna. It is an exciting experience to examine the haul from a plankton net drawn through the waters of a prairie slough. Crimson, bulbous water mites (hydrachnids), and delicate, pinkish, water fleas (*Daphnia*), fat, grey-green amphipods (*Gammarus*), and insect larvae of various sizes, shapes and shades, notably chironomid larvae, are often caught in a single sweep of the net.

Snails are common among the weed beds, and their empty shells often form windrows on the shores. Invertebrates are far more abundant in prairie potholes and lakes than they are in the lakes and ponds of other parts of the country. A precise comparison is not possible, but it is likely that most potholes contain over 10 times as many invertebrate animals per unit volume of water as do the lakes to the north and east of the prairie.

How do ducks fit into the prairie pothole community?

It is clear that the pothole is the focal point of the ducks' activity. Records of duck distribution and water distribution obtained during 15 years of extensive aerial survey show a strong positive correlation.

The pothole is more important to some species than to others. Canvasback, redhead, and ruddy ducks establish territories on the potholes, obtain all their food there, and build their nests over water in the emergent vegetation. Lesser scaup sometimes build their nests on dry land, but rarely stray far from the water. Mallard, pintail, baldpate, gadwall, blue-winged teal, and shoveller all establish territories which include part of the pothole, but their nests may be as much as a mile away. Mallards obtain a good deal of their food away from the potholes, from patches of sheet water in spring, from grain fields in late summer and autumn, but they court and loaf on the potholes. Pintail also feed in the fields to a significant extent. The other surface-feeding ducks feed in the fields infrequently, if at all.

Studies of the duck food available in and around potholes suggest that lack of food would be most unlikely to limit the abundance of ducks or give rise to competition between the species of ducks. Strangely enough, there have been few thorough studies of the feeding habits of prairie waterfowl, particularly during the critical period in the spring of the year when natural food supplies are lowest. Thus some questions must remain unanswered for the time being. As in other closely related groups of animals, differences in feeding habits preclude the possibility of competition. Diving ducks tend to feed in deeper water than the surface feeders. The larger surface feeders such as mallard, pintail, gadwall, and baldpate can feed in deeper water than the smaller ones, such as the teal. Among the surface feeders there are those which feed in the fields whenever grain is available.

The sight of a drake rising from his loafing spot to drive off a pair of the same species is a common springtime sight at any prairie pothole. It is a manifestation of territorialism and is direct evidence that there is some sort of competition for space among prairie waterfowl. Although it seems obvious that territorial fighting is the means by which the individuals of a species space themselves out within the available habitat, territorial requirements are not inflexible. Alex Dzubin studied territorial behaviour of mallards in two areas, the well-wooded Minnedosa pothole country of southern Manitoba, characterized by a high density of small potholes, and the Kindersley grasslands where water areas are larger and more widely separated. Dzubin found mallard nests to be spaced out just as much at Kindersley as at Minnedosa, but Kindersley mallards seemed much more tolerant of crowding at the loafing areas on the pothole edges. Nest dispersion probably favours survival of a species since it reduces the impact of predators, but it can be disadvantageous in dry years when some potholes dry up between the time of laying and hatching.

Predation

Predation seems to play an important role in the lives of prairie waterfowl, although it is difficult to evaluate. Destruction of eggs by crows, magpies, skunks, and ground squirrels is probably more significant than predation upon young or adult birds. Rates of clutch loss based on individual nest histories have frequently been found to exceed 50 per cent. One of the difficulties in evaluating the effect of egg predation lies in the fact that the observer can never be certain that his own activities have not influenced the behaviour of both predators and ducks. Moreover, much remains to be done in evaluating the compensatory effects of re-nesting by hens which have lost their first clutch. Although there have been fewer intensive studies of waterfowl production in the grasslands, biologists suspect that egg predation is less significant there than in the aspen parklands. Certainly the trees of the parklands are a necessary element in the breeding habitat of the crow, one of the major predators. Predators respond to changes in distribution and abundance of potential prey species. In the mid-1950s, when ducks were particularly abundant, there was an obvious increase in numbers of both marsh hawks and Swainson's hawks in the grasslands. Contrary to previous experience, both species were found to be taking nesting female and young ducks. Sportsmen in the Prairie Provinces have for years shot large numbers of crows and magpies, apparently with very little effect on their populations. Whether a program of control directed at those species could significantly reduce their numbers, and, if it did, result in improved waterfowl productivity, remains a matter for speculation.

Duck Diseases

One of the more obvious population depressants is botulism, a poisoning caused by the bacterium *Clostridium botulinum*. In rich, warm, saline waters the bacteria produce a toxin which may be ingested by birds while feeding. The toxin causes malfunction of the central nervous system, and, among other things inhibits the function of the salt gland. Normally the salt gland enables the birds to excrete salts in excess of the capacity of the kidneys. This is a necessity with birds which inhabit the alkaline sloughs and lakes of the southern prairies. Failure of the salt gland causes poisoning of the birds by salt. Botulism outbreaks generally occur in the large, shallow prairie lakes in late summer. Numbers of birds involved in some outbreaks have been estimated as follows: White-water Lake, Manitoba, 1949—75,000 deaths; Delta Marsh, Manitoba, 1958—50,000 deaths. Lake Newell, Old Wives Lake, and Buffalo Pound Lake are other areas where conditions favour periodic outbreaks of botulism. (See Figure 1.)

The occurrence and effects of other intoxications, diseases, and parasitic infections are not well known in any quantitative sense, although various collections of animals parasitic on ducks have been made from time to time. Infection by *Echinuria*, a nematode, may be a serious mortality factor for ducklings in some areas. The presence of certain species of algae results in waterfowl poisoning. An investigation of the role of ducks as carriers of western equine encephalitis is now under way.

Effects of Cultivation

Man's effects on the biotic processes centred around prairie potholes have been most significant. In 60 years the Canadian prairies have become one of the world's most important agricultural regions. Hard wheat, durum wheat and barley are the crops which provide food for ducks. Oats and flax, and the relatively small acreages of mustard and sunflowers are not important to waterfowl.

During the past 60 years there have been profound changes in vegetation and surface water distribution. These have been due not only to agricultural practices, but also to better control of fires. This has led to more tree growth and an expansion of the parkland zone.

John Lynch has determined that with the Great Plains wetlands region 38 per cent of the land is clean farmed, and the ground cover is either grain, stubble, or weeds. Twenty-four per cent of the land is moderately farmed, with small patches of woodland or unbroken grassland interspersed with land in crop or summer-fallow. Pasture and mixed pasture and crop land account for 34 per cent of the land. Thus to greater or lesser degree the hand of man is felt practically throughout the continent's prime waterfowl breeding area.

Quite apart from such associated activities as pothole drainage, brush clearing, and weed burning, the growing of grain and the consequent provision of large amounts of grain as food has certainly had an effect on those species of waterfowl which have been able to adapt to grain as a food. Unfortunately, we know nothing specific about the population levels of ducks in the pre-agricultural era so we cannot say whether there has been a change in populations related to the change in feeding habits. Grain is now a major item in the food supply of mallard, and it is obviously present in excess of the birds' requirements during the period the birds are in the prairies. Nolan Perret's work has shown that availability is the key factor in food selection by mallards in spring and early summer. He found that in the Minnedosa pothole area male mallards fed heavily on waste grain in early spring; females, which spent more time on potholes and were less mobile, used grain to a lesser extent.

Crop Damage

The use of grain by adults and young of both sexes in late summer and autumn is extensive and conspicuous. In season when rainfall delays the harvest and the grain may lie in swath for several weeks, ducks feeding on the grain, fouling it, and knocking it out of the heads may cause severe losses to farmers in certain areas. Canadian Wildlife Service surveys of duck damage to crops indicate that in 1962 about one prairie farmer out of eight suffered damage by ducks. The mean value of damage was estimated to be $194, but over one-third of the farmers responding to questionnaires reported losses greater than $200. Duck damage seems to have decreased in the past several years due to favourable harvest seasons and declining duck numbers. Nevertheless, substantial numbers of farmers continue to incur a significant loss of income because of ducks.

Experimental and developmental work by the Canadian Wildlife Service, the provincial game agencies, and the National Research Council have been carried on for some years. An automatic exploder for frightening ducks from unharvested fields has been perfected and is now being commercially manufactured in Saskatoon. Proper ways to use the exploders have been worked out. It seems certain that the next step is the provision of food and feeding space in the form of "lure crops", in conjunction with the use of exploders by individual farmers. Investigation of the effectiveness of lure crops of different grain varieties at various sorts of locations is continuing. Insurance against wildlife damage to crops is available in Saskatchewan and Alberta.

Pothole Drainage

Activities associated with grain growing have been generally detrimental to waterfowl. Drainage of potholes, which some people have termed "permanent drought", is a particularly dangerous threat. Pothole drainage is increasing in parts of the prairies, particularly within the parkland zone. Even from the agricultural viewpoint, drainage has its pros and cons. The trend toward increased stock-raising to complement or replace grain-growing means that surface waters will become more valuable. Not only is some water storage provided by the pothole, but in times of drought, last year's pothole becomes this year's hay meadow, if it is not broken by the plough. But on some farms potholes are economic liabilities. Ultimately, those who value waterfowl will have to seek means of converting those liabilities into assets. The Canadian Wildlife Service has used public funds to take easements on potholes in a pilot project area. The easements provide that in return for a sum related to the value of the surrounding land, the farmer agrees not to drain or fill potholes on his property or burn the vegetation around them. If this approach proves useful and acceptable, it will be desirable to extend it throughout the area where potholes are otherwise of little benefit to farmers.

Land Clearing

Clearing of brush and trees reduces nesting cover and changes the patterns of soil moisture distribution, evaporation and transpiration. A tree-rimmed pothole is a snow trap. Complete clearance of pothole margins generally results in reduced water levels in the spring. On the other hand, potholes with partially open shorelines provide more of the loafing space which ducks require.

Weed burning reduces nesting cover and sometimes destroys nests.

Stock raising is generally more compatible with waterfowl production than grain growing. Construction of stock-watering dams, which usually have shallow edges at least part way around, is quite beneficial in expanding waterfowl habitat. The typical steep-sided dugout is less useful. Some attention is being given to modifying the design of dugouts to provide at least one gently sloping edge. Haying on temporary sloughs is not detrimental to waterfowl unless the hay is cut too early, but reclamation of semi-permanent potholes and sloughs to provide more land for fodder production is a loss to waterfowl. Light grazing of slough edges is probably beneficial by controlling the density of cattails. Heavy grazing is detrimental.

Highway construction has both beneficial and adverse effects. Some ditches and many borrow pits[3] act as artificial potholes, but the sorts of ditches which are built along many modern highways serve as main canals to which can be led feeder canals from nearby potholes. Better highways lead to greater driving speeds, which in turn seem to result in more birds being killed by cars. Telephone and hydro wires cause the death of some ducks.

Value of Prairie Wildlife

Man not only makes a living on the prairies, he must also live there. Over 100,000 prairie dwellers hunt ducks and geese each fall. The number varies with the supply of ducks. Well over a million hunters in other parts of Canada and the United States are to some extent dependent on prairie duck production. Not only prairie residents but visitors to the prairies, both in ever increasing numbers, are finding that it is the living communities of the prairies which give them much of their beauty and dramatic interest. The sages, pasque flower, black-eyed Susan, yellow lady's slipper, western red lily, and cactus, each in its favoured site, brighten the native grasslands in spring and summer. The large, vociferous waders, such as the avocet, willet, godwit and long-billed curlew, as well as the less noisy but ever-active midsummer flocks of phalaropes, ring-billed and Franklin's gulls, black and common terns, the several grebes and a host of other avian inhabitants of the wetlands and wetland edges provide colour, sound and movement to thrill all but the most blasé. **These are the things that are becoming important to mid-century Canadians.**

Recreations such as bird watching, looking for wild flowers, and hunting benefit not only the individual but also the economy. Expenditures on travel, and on the purchase of special equipment, to mention only two items, generate business wherever they are made. Thus it is clearly in the interest of the nation to understand the workings of our living communities and seek to manage them so that they may be used by all who wish to do so for many years to come.

---

[3] Borrow pits are depressions formed when soil, gravel, etc., are taken for use in the construction of nearby roads and highways.

The processes of life in a community have often been likened to a web, but the simile is too limited. A web is visible, its functions can be located, its dimensions measured. As yet we cannot see or evaluate all the interactions of living forms in the Great Plains wetlands region. We cannot even speak with certainty of the effects of our own activities. Then too, life's patterns change. What may be true of ducks in times of drought may not apply when water is plentiful. We are continually changing the face of the land. The animals and plants with whom we live respond to our activities by changes in their habits, distribution, and abundance.

Thus our understanding of waterfowl and wetlands, indeed of any of the living creatures of the prairies, will never be complete. But we can assume that research will lead to greater understanding that will enable us to manage the land and the life on it so that North Americans will continue to enjoy, in such fashion as they may choose, the spectacle of wildlife in the Great Plains wetlands region.

19

Insecticide Applications and their Effects on Wildlife

A. de Vos

The significance of the direct and indirect effects of pesticides on wildlife is not clearly understood. Also, it is apparent that the problem is not simple. Following intensive studies of one pesticide, and after obtaining information on lethal dosages, direct and chronic effects, biotic changes, and development of diagnostic tests to detect the cause of death of game birds and mammals, one may find that new insecticides have been developed and studies must start all over again.

Mammals and birds, fish and other aquatic vertebrates are most sensitive to insecticides. Fish have died after applications of 0.25 pounds per acre of DDT in oil, whereas cold-blooded terrestrial vertebrates have tolerated amounts up to 1 pound per acre. Birds have tolerated up to 3 pounds, and most mammals up to 5 pounds per acre, with little or no apparent immediate effect. Most of the newer insecticides that are commonly applied to wildlife habitat are more toxic to vertebrate animals than is DDT.

The Patuxent Wildlife Research Centre Laboratory Studies and Toxicology of the U.S. Fish and Wildlife Services in Maryland has conducted tests on captive bobwhite quail and ring-necked pheasants for some years, and more recently on mallard ducks, blackbirds, starlings and small mammals. These tests are designed to determine quantities of common pesticides which will produce acute

Reprinted from *Canadian Audubon*, Vol. 23 (1961), pp. 47-51.

or chronic poisoning, and to furnish information on the effects of repeated or prolonged exposure to sublethal dosages. Appraisals are complicated by the fact that effects of a chemical vary with the species of animal, dosage rate, duration of exposure, time of year, sex, age, vigor, and nutritional status of the individual.

Feeding of low levels of insecticides prior to or during the breeding season produced adverse effects upon the reproductive capacity of quail. Production, fertility or hatchability of eggs were reduced, and unusually high percentage of chicks were crippled or defective. Viability of the apparently normal chicks was reduced, and mortality of the young birds during the first six weeks of life was above normal. Examination of the distribution of insecticides in tissues following varying degrees of exposure indicated variation from compound to compound and from species to species.

Direct Effects of Insecticides on Field Populations of Wildlife

Direct intoxication in the field is influenced by the particular habitat, chemical, dosage rate, formulation, species involved, and a host of other ecological considerations.

Repeated applications during one season of a dosage of 1 pound per acre of DDT for forest insect control are hazardous to treetop-inhabiting birds. When a single dosage is increased to 3 pounds per acre there is no observable effect on adult birds, but there is considerable mortality among nestlings.

Numerous reports indicate that wildlife mortality has occurred as a result of treatments for Dutch elm disease control. Dosages in this type of treatment vary from one to 5 pounds of DDT per tree. In unsprayed communities in Wisconsin, songbirds numbered 409 pairs per 100 acres, while in sprayed communities populations ranged from 31% to 90% lower. There were 50 times as many robins in the average unsprayed community as in the most heavily treated community. In towns that had been using DDT for 3 years, about 35% of the robin population alive on April 26 had disappeared by June 6. Similar results for the robin have been reported in Michigan.

Much field work has been concentrated upon appraising the effects upon wildlife of granular applications of heptachlor and dieldrin for the control of fire ants in the southern parts of the U.S.A. No exact quantitative figures are available on the effects of this program on mammals, but all studies indicate some mortality of game and small mammals.

All studies except one show severe mortality of birds following treatment. Data from all studies reveal a virtual elimination or serious reduction of ground-feeders and other low-strata species on treated areas, and little effect on the higher-strata or treetop species. Also, birds of limited home range or territory may survive on small untreated tracts. Chemical tests of birds and mammals found dead revealed significant amounts of insecticides in their tissues.

The bobwhite quail has received special study, and several investigations in at least three states give quantitative findings which enable rather precise predictions of the fate of quail on treated areas. Treatment results in virtual elimination of the species on treated areas, with gradual repopulation during the first year after treatment, but with some mortality, and with depressed populations persisting into the second year.

Dosage rates of DDT of 6 pounds per acre used in orchards must cause some mortality among birds. The use of endrin as a rodenticide has been increasing. Effects of these treatments on wildlife have not been determined, however, on a quantitative basis.

The effects on wildlife of treatments of aldrin or heptachlor at 0.125 to 0.25 pound per acre, chlordane at 0.5 to 1 pound per acre, and toxaphene at 1 to 1.5 pounds per acre in programs to control grasshoppers, and as bait used (in bait at about one tenth the dosage) to control Mormon crickets, have been studied. Parts of treated areas received as many as three overlapping doses in the same season. Insufficient quantitative data have been collected so far. Aldrin in bait form has been shown to kill a few birds and up to 70% of mice present. In marsh areas, aldrin reduced duck production up to 33%. Treatment of 1.5 pounds per acre of toxaphene caused death of 20 birds of 7 species on a 1,600-acre plot. All but one dead bird contained significant amounts of toxaphene. Bird counts indicated a marked drop among insectivorous species.

Indirect Effects of Insecticides on Wildlife

Direct mortality, however, serious and spectacular, is not the only danger to wildlife from insecticides. Indirect mortality or loss of reproductive potential may result from consumption of minute amounts of poisonous chemicals over a period of time.

In laboratory studies certain compounds are found to be additive, while others are synergistic. Some food organisms are relatively resistant, and may store toxicants.

I have already referred to experiments with adult quail and pheasants unaffected by minute amounts of toxicant in their feed, may become deficient in reproductive potential. Penned quail whose diets contained DDT at the rate of 3 ounces per ton of food produced eggs whose fertility was reduced 30%. They produced 33% fewer chicks per hen and 80% more cripples than did quail on diets uncontaminated by DDT. More than 90% of the chicks from treated birds died within 6 weeks, even though pesticides were not fed to the chicks themselves. In other pen tests, woodcock, which had first been fed DDT with little apparent effect, were more susceptible to dieldrin than uncontaminated birds.

Earthworms have been shown to be relatively resistant to pesticides, to be able to store toxicant in tissues, and to poison vertebrates feeding on them.

To control a gnat, Clear Lake, California, was treated in 1949, 1954 and 1957 with DDD at 0.01 to 0.02 parts per million. The summer breeding colony of western grebes disappeared soon after the first treatment, apparently from eating contaminated fish.

In November, 1957, hundreds of wintering grebes died. Both the breeding and wintering populations have been affected through the fish the birds consumed. Samples of tissue from fish and grebes contained very high concentrations of DDD, up to 1,600 parts per million in grebes and 2,500 p.p.m. in fish.

The Toxicity of Some Recently Developed Insecticides to Wildlife

Some of the more recently developed hydrocarbon insecticides, including aldrin, dieldrin, endrin, toxaphene and lindane, are much more toxic than DDT, and offer a considerable hazard to wildlife, particularly to birds. The effects of these insecticides on wildlife generally have been inadequately tested. Dieldrin at applications as low as 0.2 pound per acre caused mortality among songbirds. Chlordane at 0.5 pound per acre caused some losses among birds. When aldrine is applied at the rate of 1 pound per acre, one square foot of ground surface will contain enough chemical to potentially kill 2 adult quail, 20 young quail, or 5 young pheasants.

In Germany, application of 0.4 kg. of lindane per hectare caused nestling birds in a treated area to gain weight much more slowly than in an untreated area. In the same country an application of a mixture of 0.2 kg. of dieldrin and 0.2 kg. of lindane per hectare resulted in a complete kill of broods in a forest of 25 hectares. Dieldrin, toxaphene, aldrin and endrin all have deleterious effects on reproduction.

Aldrin and dieldrin are considerably more toxic to mammals than lindane, chlordane and toxaphene. Dieldrin sprayed at 1 pound per acre in California orchards has killed rabbits and hares; when sprayed at 3 pounds per acre it caused extensive deaths of rabbits and rodents in Illinois.

Chlorinated hydrocarbons are also causing great concern because of their long-time stability. Inadequate research has been done about accumulations of these insecticides in the soil.

Among the systemic insecticides, schradan has lethal effects on mammals and birds, as proved by recent experiments in England.

Some of you may wonder by now: what is he worried about? What does it matter if some birds and mammals fall by the wayside on the road to progress? Isn't it the important thing to step up agricultural production so that we can feed all the hungry mouths of the world?

It is impossible, in this space, to compare the recreational and aesthetic values of wildlife, with the need for stepped-up food production. Let it suffice that there is an ever-increasing number of naturalists and hunters who enjoy the values of wildlife.

It is also interesting to point out that there is a direct correlation between human population densities and appreciation for wildlife, at least among civilized nations. Certainty, so far as I am concerned, there is an ever-increasing problem, and it is high time that more was done about it. This is recognized in the U.S.A., where the Bureau of Sport Fisheries and Wildlife has a substantial budget for studies on the effects of pesticides on wildlife.

Recommendations for Safeguarding Wildlife Values During Pest Control

With the knowledge now available it will be possible in some cases to predict in advance the degree of direct effects on wildlife which will take place with any given application. In many other cases this cannot be done, and even less can be predicted about the indirect effects on wildlife. The following suggestions are made to reduce damage to wildlife:

1. *Before* insecticides are used, the effects on different kinds of animals and on animals living in different habitats should be studied in the area to be treated.
2. Only minimum quantities of chemicals and a minimum number of applications necessary to achieve adequate control of pests should be made.
3. Whenever possible, chemicals should be applied at the seasons of the year when damage to wildlife will be least.
4. Particular caution should be observed in respect to applications of the highly toxic chlorinated hydrocarbons.
5. The minimum possible area should be treated. Serious effects are more likely to result from treatments over large areas.

6. Tightening of federal and provincial legislation covering use of insecticides should be recommended. The public needs protection from over-zealous or irresponsible control groups.

For the future, research should be pressed in two directions: the development of more specific chemicals and more specific methods of application, and the development of biological and environmental controls.

Entomologists and wildlife biologists in the United States and Europe are quite ready to acknowledge that insufficient research has been done regarding the effects of insecticides on wildlife. But at least they are doing something there. In Canada no satisfactory research is in progress at the moment, and no special funds are available for this type of research. This is a highly undesirable situation. We should not rely on the findings of other countries, because of the different species of animals, the different habitats and climatic conditions of this country.

It is a tragic state of affairs that professionally trained biologists employed by companies which sell insecticides are sometimes better up-to-date in this country than the professors who are supposed to teach and do research on the subject. The obvious advantages of this state of affairs to the industries, do not need further emphasis. High-pressure salesmanship will take care of this situation.

We cannot afford to fall behind any further on this matter, and therefore I wish to make a strong plea for funds to be made available to study insecticides-wildlife relationships and for the appointment of specialists on the subject either by institutions of higher learning or by the governments concerned. I also wish to suggest the enactment of legislation that prohibits, or provides penalties for, improper or excessive use of toxicants that directly or indirectly may injure wildlife. Legislative action, comparable to the Magnuson-Metcalf bill which was passed by the U.S. Congress in 1958, should be suggested to undertake continuing studies of the effects of pesticides on wildlife.

References

Cannon, N. and G. C. Decker, "Insecticide residues as hazards to warm-blooded animals", *Transactions of 24th North American Wildlife Conference* (1959), pp. 124-32.

De Witt, J. B. and J. L. George, "Pesticide-Wildlife Review", U.S. *Fish and Wildlife Service, Circular 84*, (1960).

Eng, R. L., "Two-summer study of effects on bird populations of chlordane bait and aldrin spray as used for grasshopper control", *Journal of Wildlife Management, 16* (1952), pp. 326-38.

Genelly, R. E. and R. L. Rudd, "Effects of DDT, toxaphene, and dieldrin on pheasant reproduction", *The Auk, 73* (1956), pp. 529-39.

George, J. L., "Effects on wildlife of aerial application of strobane, DDT and BAC to tidal marshes in Delaware", *Journal of Wildlife Management,* *21* (1957), pp. 42-52.

Hickey, J. J. and L. B. Hunt, "Songbird mortality following annual programs to control Dutch elm disease", *Atlantic Naturalist,* Vol. XV, no. 2 (1960), pp. 87-92.

Leedy, D. L., "Pesticide-wildlife problems and research needs", *Transactions of 24th North American Wildlife Conference,* (1959), pp. 150-65.

Mitchel, R. T., "Effects of DDT upon survival and growth of nesting songbirds", *Journal of Wildlife Management, 17* (1953), pp. 45-54.

Robbins, C. S., "Effects of five-year DDT application on breeding bird populations", *Journal of Wildlife Management, 15* (1951), pp. 213-14.

Rudd, R. L., and R. E. Genelly, "Pesticides: their use and toxicity in relation to wildlife", *Department of Fish and Game, State of California, Game Bulletin No.* 7, p. 209.

Scott, T. G., et al., "Some effects of a field application of dieldrin on wildlife", *Journal of Wildlife Management 23 (4),* (1959).

Stickel, L., "Wood mouse and box turtle populations in an area treated with DDT", *Journal of Wildlife Management, 10* (1951), pp. 216-17.

Stickel, L. F. and P. F. Springer, "Pesticides and wildlife", *U.S. Fish and Wildlife Service, wildlife leaflet 392,* (1957), p. 12.

Wallace, G. J., "Another year of robin losses on a university campus", *Audubon Magazine 62 (2),* (1960), pp. 66-69.

20

Remarks on Eskimo Sealing and the Harp Seal Controversy

D. C. Foote

Most inhabitants of the North today are employed full time or part time in the harvesting of biological resources. Until World War II, earnings from the production of renewable resources in nearly every major region of the circumpolar North exceeded incomes from non-renewable-resource based industries. In general, the most important producers have been the commercial fisheries of subarctic waters, followed by furs of wild and domesticated land mammals, again predominately from subarctic areas. Since the heyday of European and American northern hunting in the eighteenth and nineteenth centuries, however, the economic importance of marine mammals has often been highly underrated.

One reason that marine mammals are usually relegated to a secondary economic role is that many species have been decimated by decades of overexploitation. The walrus has been nearly exterminated in the northeastern Atlantic and drastically reduced in numbers in the northwestern Atlantic and northern Pacific. The Greenland and white whales, in both oceans, reached such low population levels that international prohibition of hunting was instituted. Similar international agreements also saved the sea otter and northern fur seal from extinction. Recently, concern for the steady decline of Greenland or harp seals in the White and Barents seas led the Soviet Union and Norway to proclaim a five-year closed season in these areas and restricted hunting in Jan Mayen waters.

Reprinted from *Arctic*, Vol. 20 (1967), pp. 267-68.

In order to protect the breeding of the harp seal population in the Gulf of St. Lawrence, Canada has taken steps to strengthen conservation practices. Also at Canada's request, seals are now considered one of the responsibilities of the International Commission for the Northwest Atlantic Fisheries.

In the twentieth century, the two northern marine mammal species considered most important, in terms of cash value, have been the newborn harp seal, or "whitecoat," and the northern fur seal. But direct income to northern native peoples from the harvest of these animals has been negligible. In the first case, harp seal pups are taken almost exclusively by nonaboriginal hunters, and in the second case, comparatively few native people receive wages from the government-controlled fur seal industry. To the average Eskimo hunter of Alaska, Canada, or Greenland, therefore, cash income from the sale of marine mammal products has been minimal and usually much less than that earned from terrestrial animals such as the fox, land otter, muskrat, wolf, wolverine, or polar bear.

Beginning in about 1962, advanced techniques in the preparation of hair-seal pelts and the increased use of sealskins in clothing, especially in Europe, combined to create a rapidly expanding market for skins from all seal species. For the first time, the ringed seal, or jar, of the far north reached market values which made Eskimo seal hunting highly lucrative. For example, in eastern Baffin Island, young ringed seals sold for $4.00 per skin in 1955 and $17.50 in 1963. Mature ringed seals increased in value from $1.50 to $12.25 during the same period. Exceptionally good skins often sold for well over $20.00 in Alaska and Canada during 1963 and 1964. Average sealskin prices in Greenland, carefully controlled by the government, rose from $2.80 in 1958 to $8.30 in 1965.

Response to the improved market for hair seals was widespread throughout the North. In the Northwest Territories, the number of sealskins traded increased from 10,470, valued at $48,689 in 1961-62, to 46,962 skins worth $691,707 in 1963-64. In Alaska, the number of pelts sold increased from 15,000 in 1962 to 60,000 in 1965. Alaskan hair-seal production in 1965 was valued at $1,000,000. In Greenland, the seal harvest increased from 52,763 in 1954 to over 76,000 in 1964. The average value of skins produced in Greenland in 1963 and 1964 was about $800,000 per year.

Starting in 1964, individuals associated with the Society for the Prevention of Cruelty to Animals, especially in New Brunswick and Quebec, became increasingly concerned with the manner in which newborn harp seals were killed in the annual Gulf of St. Lawrence and Newfoundland hunt. These critics contended that seal pups were skinned alive. Evidence in the form of television films and eye-witness accounts were widely disseminated in many parts of western Europe and eastern North America. A book, *The Last Seal Pup*, by Peter Lust also focused attention on the purportedly inhumane killing of whitecoats.

Results of the campaign to prevent cruelty in the harvest of harp seal pups have ranged far beyond the killing grounds of eastern Canadian waters. The highly charged emotional overtones of the issue apparently caused the average female consumer to boycott all sealskin products. By the spring of 1967, the market for sealskins in Switzerland had dropped to 5 per cent of its former level, sales in West Germany were down by 50 per cent and one quarter of the Greenlandic skins placed on auction in April went unsold. Although world sealskin prices have dropped since 1965, the most catastrophic decline has come, not in whitecoat and fur-seal pelts, but in other species, especially the ringed seal. During the summer of 1967, most buyers in Alaska refused to purchase ringed-seal skins at any price; in Canada, the Hudson's Bay Company announced that it would buy pelts at $2.50 each in order to prevent total economic collapse in many northern areas, and in Greenland the Royal Greenland Trade Department has had to review its price structure, which was originally set on 1965 market values.

It is ironic that the efforts to prevent inhumane killing of new-born harp seals have had their greatest impact on seal hunters who use the most humane killing methods and who seldom, if ever, encounter a harp seal pup. These sealers are the Eskimos of Alaska, Canada, and Greenland. Because they hunt with high-powered rifles the seal is usually killed instantaneously with a head shot. Ecological conditions and migratory habits of the harp and other seal species cause the composition of the average Eskimo seal take to be 90 per cent or more ringed seals. The irony of the situation is further emphasized by the fact that retail market reaction has been strongest against skins which the consumer can obviously identify as seal. Both the whitecoat and fur seal provide high quality pelts that undergo specialized tanning and dying processes to produce a finished product quite unlike the stereotyped version of a sealskin. The appearance of the ringed seal and other hair seal species, however, remains unchanged as a result of tanning. These skins, therefore, are easily rejected by prospective buyers influenced by any stigma surrounding sealskins in general.

To a great many Eskimos in the northern Western hemisphere the drop in sealskin prices has been a calamity. It has meant destruction of a viable industry badly needed in an economically depressed region. In 1956, for example, the Eskimo population of Cumberland Sound earned a total of $14,526 from furs and white-whale hunting. This gave an average per household income of $115. In 1964, the estimate value of the area's fur take was $163,573, or about $1,434 per household. At Clyde River, in northern Baffin Island, the total value of furs traded in 1957 was $3,678, or about $111 per household; in 1964, a total of $28,000 worth of furs were sold, giving an average income of approximately $609 per household. The increased value of furs in both areas can be attributed almost exclusively to higher sealskin prices.

Although the final outcome of the depressed sealskin market is difficult to forecast, there are indications of its probable impact on many Eskimo groups. In Greenland, it has been estimated that one quarter of the population stands to lose its livelihood, with no alternative in sight. This figure is probably much higher in most parts of arctic Canada and in coastal northern Alaska. To a number of Eskimo hunters, the present situation is critical because they have already invested profits from the seal hunt in modern equipment. In eastern Baffin Island, for example, most hunters used their earnings of the early 1960's to purchase low-calibre high-powered rifles with telescopic sights, outboard motors, canoes or flatbottom boats, and motorized snow machines. The Cumberland Sound region in 1962 had only 1 native-owned snow machine. By 1964, the number had increased to 17 and in 1966 there were 36 machines in use. During the summer of 1953, the Clyde River area Eskimos had only 2 small, unpowered wooden boats and one 18-foot canoe with an outboard motor. In 1966, the same region was serviced by 25 canoes, 27 outboard motors, and 1 large, powered whaleboat. Broughton Island, in 1961, had 2 canoes and 3 whaleboats, whereas in 1966 the community had 9 canoes, 12 rowboats, and 6 whaleboats.

Modernization of the Eskimo seal-hunting industry has meant an increase in operating costs. A study of gasoline, motor oil, and ammunition expenditures for the period August 1965 through July 1966 for eastern Baffin Island showed the cost per sealskin sold, for all species, was $6.29 in Cumberland Sound, $5.45 at Broughton and Padloping Islands, and $4.46 at Clyde River. It is clear from these figures that the present value of sealskins in no way covers basic operating and depreciation costs.

The controversy over killing methods of harp seal pups has produced consequences far beyond those intended by the well-meaning persons who first publicized the issue. But if accusations are true that television films were intentionally falsified in order to create public outrage, then the campaign to prevent cruelty to animals has been doubly tragic. At the moment, the individual who has suffered most is the isolated Eskimo seal hunter of the Arctic who can no longer earn enough from a basic way of life to utilize his newly acquired equipment and support his family.

21

The Polar Bear: A Matter for International Concern

V. Flyger

The polar bear is an international resource of the frozen arctic seas. This is the essence of the initial statement of accord issued by the delegate of the First International Scientific Meeting on the Polar Bear. Delegates from Canada, Denmark, Norway, the U.S.S.R., and the United States met in Fairbanks, Alaska, for one week in 1965 to discuss and make recommendations for the intelligent conservation of this animal. It was the consensus that: (a) polar bear harvests should be conservative; (b) females and cubs should be protected at all times; (c) the nations surrounding the polar basin should engage in research to learn more about this animal; and (d) information concerning polar bears should be exchanged promptly.

There are several reasons for the recent build-up of interest in polar bears. For one thing, they are not as numerous in some areas as in the past and they have disappeared entirely from others. Conservationists have become alarmed at the increasing harvest by hunters in Alaska and have objected to the unsportsmanlike hunting carried out from aircraft in Alaska and from shipboard in Svalbard. The use of set-guns in Svalbard has also received unfavourable comment.

The reason for the decline in numbers of polar bears over the past 100 years is not entirely clear. It is true that the polar ice cap has receded and that the consequent disappearance of pack ice has caused bears to become a rare sight in areas such as southeast

Reprinted from *Arctic*, Vol. 20 (1967), pp. 147-53.

Greenland and Iceland. Pack ice is the habitat of the polar bear and the seals which are his food, so naturally, as the ice goes, so go the bears. But this cannot be the whole explanation for the general decrease; on some arctic islands, excessive hunting has definitely eliminated the animal or has sharply reduced his numbers. However, the overall picture is not clear, and the polar bear, perhaps the world's largest carnivore, may go the way of the world's largest mammal, the blue whale, if the nations bordering the polar basin cannot agree on a management policy for him. The blue whale is now close to extinction—a disgraceful reflection on the nations that have allowed it to happen by permitting selfish interests to govern their actions. Although it is the nations bordering the polar seas that demonstrate the greatest interest in the polar bear, he actually belongs to everyone. Surely the peoples of the world would want to assure this great animal a permanent place on the globe, not because he is something for hunters to shoot, but because he is a symbol of the Arctic and a worthy companion of mankind.

Frequently, those people harvesting animals (whales and deer, for example) assume exclusive rights to their prey and actively resent others taking even a passive interest. This attitude was evidenced by an incident that occurred in the spring of 1966. Five polar bears were killed in a research project which had the ultimate goal of preserving the species. Although they were not killed for pleasure and their deaths were truly regretted by the scientists concerned, hunters hearing of the incident greatly resented it because these five animals would no longer be available for them to shoot. Of course, the scientists could have kept the deaths of the bears a secret, but that would not have been consistant with their obligation to be honest in reporting their results.

Polar bears have considerable commercial value. Their hides, depending upon size and condition, have a retail value of between $300 and $800 apiece. Hunters pursuing polar bears for sport in Alaska or Norway may bring up to $1,500 or $2,000 into either of these countries for each bear shot, in the form of revenue from licences, food and lodging, guide fees, and other expenditures. Hunters travelling to Alaska and harvesting 300 or more bears bring into the state something like $500,000 every year. Because polar bears are one of the more easily exploited resources of the Arctic, serious consideration must be given to the economic aspect in any management plan concerning this species.

The annual worldwide harvest of polar bears is approximately 1,200, according to reported kills; unreported kills probably do not exceed 300 animals. Biologists have estimated the number of polar bears in existence to be in the range of 15,000 to 20,000. The annual harvest of about 1,500 animals, therefore, is somewhere between 5 per cent and 10 per cent of the population. According to the experts, such a harvest is not excessive; but the experts can be wrong! Some people may remember that one of the world's foremost whale biologists maintained for many years that there was no indication of a decline in whale stocks. This man's opinion weighed heavily in negotiations concerning whales; so heavily that today some of our whale species are almost extinct. The public surely would not wish to risk the possibility of the polar bear's extermination.

Although it is known that polar bears wander great distances, little is known about their population dynamics or movement patterns. Probably their constant journeying makes it impossible for local races to develop, and they mix too much to permit the development of racial strains. However, because the animal is highly mobile and observes no national boundaries, it is possible that excessive harvest in one or more sections of the Arctic could endanger the entire stock.

Local groups of polar bears are often distinct from each other with respect to age and sex composition. For example, the bears shot west of Kotzebue are larger and older than those shot in the Point Barrow or Point Good Hope regions, and the proportion of males among them is higher. We can only guess at the reasons for such variations, but they are probably due to differences in migratory habits between the sexes and between young and old bears.

Polar bears can be controlled on a practical basis if we possess knowledge of their population dynamics, and ascertain the importance of their migratory habits. Until recently, the only information available was that gathered by Eskimos, hunters, trappers, and arctic travellers, and this was so mixed with folklore that it was almost impossible to separate fact from fantasy. A standard method of collecting data from bears harvested by hunters and trappers should be used so that information gathered in one area could be compared with that gathered in other areas. Such data could yield the age-sex composition of the annual kill, which would be valuable in controlling the polar bear harvest.

Conservationists are rightly concerned over the possible immoderate harvest of the animals and object, in some cases, to the manner in which they are killed. Actually, if a portion of an animal population can be harvested, it matters not how they are harvested, unless the method is a cruel one. However, the potential of the animals to give maximum recreation and aesthetic pleasure is not realized if the animals are hunted as they are at present. All true sportsmen recognize this, and their attitude is reflected by two of America's outstanding sports clubs: the Boone and Crockett Club and the National Rifle Association. Both have removed polar bears from their list of animals that can be submitted as trophies. These organizations are dedicated to the highest sporting standards, and their action will certainly have some effect on hunting in Alaska.

In Alaska, hunters fly out with a guide in small ski-equipped aircraft from several points and search for polar bear tracks. Upon finding tracks, one plane flies on ahead and the hunter and his guide land, get out of the plane, and hide behind a pressure ridge. The other plane drives the bear towards the men waiting on the ice, and when the bear comes within close range it is killed with a high-powered rifle. The hunter usually gets back into the warm airplane while the guide skins the bear, and they then return with the hide and skull, leaving the carcass on the ice.

In Norway, hunters depart from Tromso in sealing vessels. These vessels work through the loose pack ice around Svalbard, and when polar bears are sighted, the ships approach as close as the hunters wish. All a hunter has to do is to pick up a rifle and shoot the bear while it is swimming in the water or running over an ice floe. The dead bear is hauled on board using the ship's boom, and the crew skins the animal. As in Alaska, only the hide and skull are saved and the rest of the animal is discarded.

The above-described methods of hunting polar bear are certainly not sportsmanlike, and serious consideration should be given to improving the ways of hunting the animals for recreation. One possibility is to encourage the use of bows and arrows. Although only one or two bears have actually been killed by bow and arrow, this method offers considerably more sport. The archer must be nearer the bear and frequently, upon being hit, the animal attacks and must be shot with a rifle at close quarters by the guide. Another exciting type of hunting is the Eskimo's method, which involves dogs and a long chase over the ice.

But the most exhilarating way to hunt is with a gun that fires a syringe filled with an immobilizing drug. With this weapon the animal is not killed, but is merely drugged into unconsciousness for a short period. In contrast to hunting, where the excitement ends with the squeeze of the trigger, most of the fun here begins after the syringe-gun trigger is pulled.

I have experienced many types of hunting, but nothing matches that of catching a live animal. I recommend this as one of the most rewarding sports anywhere in the world. Now modern science and technology have given us new tools and instruments to add to the sportsman's enjoyment, and the time is ripe to switch from lead bullets to projectile syringes.

Catch-them-alive hunters could bring back photographs as evidence of their prowess and, at the same time, contribute to science by marking the polar bears with ear tags before releasing them. Naturally, some of the animals would be killed, because the method is not yet foolproof; but the annual toll would be greatly reduced.

To insure minimum mortality, it would be necessary to give considerable training to the guides. Although many hunters have greatly exaggerated opinions of their own ability, very few know much about their quarry or the out-of-doors; they get their bear because of the knowledge and efficiency of their guide. For this reason, the use of syringe guns would necessitate the training of the guides only.

The present regulation of polar bear harvesting by individual governments is variable and impractical. For example, Alaska tries to exert control by requiring a licence to hunt and then restricting the number of licences sold. The bears are shot on the high seas and all the licence does is permit the hunter to bring his trophy into the state. A hunter could actually shoot as many polar bears as he wished as long as he brought back only one trophy. Perhaps some enterprising hunters will test this possibility in court by shooting bears and returning home without going through Alaska. Anyone with enough money could charter a ship and hunt bears off the ice outside of any country's territorial limits and violate no laws.

In Canada and Greenland, only natives are permitted to hunt polar bears. Hunting for sport is entirely forbidden and non-natives may shoot only in personal defence. At some DEW Line sites there are signs warning the operating personnel: "If you shoot a polar bear in self-defence, remember, he has a better lawyer than you have." All polar bear hunting is forbidden in the U.S.S.R.

They may, however, be taken for zoological gardens under special conditions.

Polar bears can be managed and studied only through co-operation between nations, especially those bordering the polar seas. A treaty would be necessary, and perhaps the harvest could be regulated by the United Nations or by one of its specialized agencies. Action on this matter must come soon and must be decisive if it is to insure that this big animal will remain one of the inhabitants of the earth. Financially-interested countries must not be the only ones concerned, because the whole world has a stake in the polar bear. Perhaps the best initial step would be to establish a commission with a permanent secretary, made up of representatives from nations bordering the polar basin and other interested states. UNESCO might be the appropriate agency to appoint the commission, so that the educational, scientific, and cultural aspects would be stressed rather than the political.

Adequate practical research can only be carried out in an effective and efficient manner if all the nations surrounding the polar seas collect similar types of data on all aspects of the problem and work together in studying them and acting upon them. Of course, research would turn up many more questions than it answered, but this is one of the advantages of such work. It would also be highly desirable to establish a series of biological stations throughout the Arctic from which research on the polar bear and on other problems could be conducted by scientists regardless of nationality. This would be an excellent opportunity to train students in polar biology and to acquaint young scientists with their colleagues from other countries.

Recent technological developments now make it possible to study the movements of polar bears by the use of transmitter-receivers attached to collars around their necks. Telemetry studies on other animals, including black and brown bears, have contributed to an understanding of the habits of these animals, but because of the inhospitable environment in which the polar bear lives, it is not possible to employ the tracking systems used with other species. However, with a polar-orbiting satellite, signals could be picked up from polar bears and relayed back to a tracking station on earth. With such a technique, theoretically, the movements of about 100 bears could be checked every 2 hours for a period of 6 months, and precise information could thus be obtained on how this animal lives in its forbidding environment. The radios could also transmit data on blood pressure, heart beat, respiratory rate, and internal and external temperatures. This information would also make it possible to relate the activities of the polar bear to conditions in the Arctic such as storms and their location.

Close co-operation among nations bordering the polar basin is also necessary in order to take the fullest advantage of satellite tracking. Bears could be fitted with these transmitter-receivers throughout the Arctic and followed for the life of the satellite (6 months), regardless of where they travel. A number of bears carrying such devices would certainly cross international boundaries, and it would be necessary for scientists of all nations to understand completely the nature of this work. Of course, the data received from these bears should be available to all participants.

If the peoples of the world feel that the polar bear should be preserved, they must take immediate steps to ensure its preservation. They must decide whether they are willing to permit hunters and trappers to assume the responsibility of controlling the animal. If they are not willing to do so, an international agreement on research and control would seem to be necessary.

Calling a total halt to the harvest of polar bears it not recommended at this time. It would be unfair to hunters, because there is no clear evidence that the harvest is at present excessive. Furthermore, if the bear were to receive absolute protection, it would be difficult, if not impossible, to put the animal back on the list of species permitted to be hunted. The experience of various game departments with other species supports the wisdom of this.

The polar bear is part of the world's heritage and has an aesthetic value probably far in excess of his economic value to hunters. Nevertheless, both values must be considered if and when an international regulating body is formed to set management policy and to co-ordinate research on the polar bear. The important thing, now, is to set the wheels in motion for the formation of the international commission mentioned above. The First International Scientific Meeting in 1965 was a good beginning, but it was not enough; a permanent body is needed. The polar bear definitely merits international concern—and action.

22

Emerging Problems in Wildlife Management

W.A. Fuller

A wildlife problem arises when man impinges on wildlife or its habitat, or when wildlife impinges on man or his works. In order for problems to emerge, there must be some change in one of the relationships involving people, wildlife, or their respective habitats. In other words, *emerging* implies a dynamic rather than static situation. It then becomes necessary to identify the dynamic element. It is obvious that the increasing human population of Canada is a dynamic force that is creating and will continue to create wildlife problems.

The first category of wildlife problems includes those where wildlife endangers man or damages his interests. No doubt the first example of this sort coincided with Champlain's settlement in 1608. After the first crop was planted there were undoubtedly birds, and perhaps mammals as well, on hand to share in the harvest. As settlement progressed and agriculture gained in importance, *problems* of damage arose more and more frequently. They remain with us today.

A second category of wildlife problems includes those of preserving essential habitat. The early settlers made much use of wildlife, but there were not enough people to make serious inroads on wildlife populations or to cause much deterioration of wildlife habitats. At the same time and quite fortuitously, the small-scale clearing of the forest actually improved the habitat of most forest species of game, and a slight pollution of lakes and streams by erosion of the land may have improved fish habitats by making available increased supplies of inorganic nutrients. This early situa-

Reprinted from *Background Papers, Resources for Tomorrow Conference*, Vol. 11 (1961), pp. 881-88. By permission of the Queen's Printer, Ottawa.

tion was one in which a very small human population lived in essential harmony with nature. As the increasing human population made more intensive demands on resources, breaking and clearing of land and pollution of waters went beyond the point of benefiting wildlife, and resulted in habitat deterioration and destruction. These processes continue and thus we still face problems of habitat maintenance.

The third category into which wildlife problems fall centers around the need to regulate the harvest in order to perpetuate the supply. With a few notable exceptions, there was until recently insufficient hunting pressure to cause direct reduction of game populations. Since the end of the Second World War, however, the number of hunters and fishermen wishing to share in the wildlife harvest has increased at a phenomenal rate. There now seem to be enough hunters and fishermen, at least in some parts of Canada, to have a direct controlling influence on populations of many species of game and game fish. Direct pressure of this sort seems certain to increase in the future.

Wildlife problems in the fourth category may be educational, political, sociological, or philosophical. They cut across all of the others and are interwoven with them in complex ways. Primary problems in this category are the establishment of standards of value and their dissemination. Thus we become concerned with wildlife, not so much in the material sense, but as an abstraction —as a component of our *whole life*.

Problems of Damage

On rare occasions an encounter between a person and a wild animal results in injury or death to the person and a subsequent outcry in the press. The most dangerous combination is the grizzly bear and the careless tourist in the western National Parks, but occasionally even a well armed hunter is overcome by his intended prey, perhaps a *gentle* deer. With more and more people entering the woods as tourists or novice hunters, there may be more contacts of this kind and more editorial outbursts for eradication of all bears and abolition of the sport of hunting. Will these intemperate outcries be resisted? I think they will, but the responsibility to reduce the chance of death and injury remains.

Less dramatic, but more hazardous to human welfare are the many diseases and parasites of animals transmissible to man. Scourges such as bubonic plague (black death) are no longer of serious concern, although foci of infection are still with us in ground squirrels and feral rats. Rabies appears to be enzootic in members of the dog and weasel families in several parts of Canada, and migratory bats may be important in reinfecting northern areas from more southerly reservoirs of the disease [20]. Several strains of the virus-causing equine encephalitis have been recovered from a variety of birds including grouse, pigeons, owls, hawks, shore birds, blackbirds, and sparrows [13]. Encephalitis was of considerable concern to public health officials in Saskatchewan in 1938 and 1941, and the potential for further outbreaks still exists. Spotted fever and tularemia are also known from Canada, though never in epidemic proportions. All of these diseases will bear watching, but there is no apparent reason why any of them should increase in importance in the future.

In Indian and Eskimo societies, where much wild game and fish is consumed without thorough cooking, parasites of animal origin are common enough to be of concern to public authorities. Thus, hydatid disease, caused by the tapeworm (*Echinococcus granulosus*), was found in about six per cent of northern Indians[21]; broad fish tapeworm (*Diphyllobothrium latum*) was widespread in Indians and Eskimos admitted to tuberculosis sanatoria[26]; and trichinosis (*Trichinella spiralis*) in the Arctic is considered by Connell[7] to be "a major public health problem for which there appears to be no immediate practical solution."

I do not foresee this phase of the problem increasing in severity. On the contrary, improved sanitation and decreasing dependence on wild game should combine to produce a lowered incidence of these and other animal-borne parasitic diseases of man.

In summary, wildlife does not pose a threat to the continuance of *Homo sapiens* as a species but nature still bears a sting for those individuals who would court her carelessly.

What I have just been discussing are direct interactions between wildlife and man. There are also many situations in which wildlife affects us indirectly through our forests, crops, or livestock.

We now know that climax forest shelter little game. Creating openings in those forests by fires or logging sets off a complex series of changes in the vegetation. The early stages create ideal conditions of food and cover for several forest game species which may reproduce so fast that they effectively stop all forest regeneration. As recently as 1955 the Newfoundland Royal Commission on Forestry[14] failed to recognize that damage to young conifers by moose was of serious proportions. Such damage is now (1960) causing concern both to the Game Branch and to large timber operators in the Province. In Nova Scotia and New Brunswick, large populations of white-tailed deer may be expected to depress forest reproduction, and in both regions ungulate damage will be supplemented by snowshoe hare damage, particularly in years of hare abundance.

Wildlife affects livestock (including poultry) in two ways— raptorial birds and carnivorous mammals prey on it directly, and herbivores, from mice to moose, compete with it for food. Reducing losses from predators requires improved husbandry, combined in some cases with reduction of the numbers of predators. Experience has taught us, however, that control of animal populations, whether predator or game, is not as simple as it once appeared to be.

Competition for food between big game and domestic animals is severe in some parts of Alberta and British Columbia. On privately owned lands, the needs of livestock should generally have priority. It is questionable whether the same priority should be given to livestock on public ranges. This competition is unlikely to diminish. A carefully worked out policy for the management of public ranges in the public interest is needed.

Probably the most important conflict between wildlife and man arises through destruction of agricultural crops. Both game and non-game species are involved. In Canada, the most pressing current problem is duck damage to grain. The Canadian situation was reviewed by Mair[19] and Leitch[16]. Non-game birds are another cause of damage to grain, vegetables and fruits. Thus, according to a recent review[11], 20 species of birds were found to damage 10 agricultural crops in 20 states of the United States. The most serious depredations on both grains and fruits were caused by one or more species of blackbird. In Canada, too, blackbirds cause troublesome problems.

Mammals are not blameless in this respect. Mice, rats, and ground squirrels may do extensive damage, especially to stored grains; mice and rabbits kill fruit and ornamental trees by girdling; moose and elk play havoc with hay stacks.

In theory, big game damage to forests and crops can be controlled by adequately harvesting the game species, but several problems arise here. The first is how does one induce hunters to take a harvest on relatively inaccessible lands? Second, what constitutes an adequate harvest? What density of a given species of game is compatible with the minimum acceptable level of forest reproduction? Research and experimentation oriented toward solution of these problems must be pursued more energetically.

Losses of livestock and agricultural crops could obviously be eliminated by eradication of the offending species. But is this an acceptable, even if feasible, solution? Clarke[5] says that Canadians accept and value wildlife. If this is so, and I believe it is, then some other solution must be found. On the other hand, attempts to control the numbers of wild animals have often run into difficulties, some predictable, others not. For example, reduction of coyote numbers to reduce predation on livestock has often been followed by plagues of crop-destroying mice. Often, too, the economic loss from the mice exceeded that originally attributed to the coyotes. Do we know for sure that this is a cause and effect relationship? If so, can we devise means for keeping the mice in check? If it is necessary to control or reduce wild animal numbers, can we devise methods more efficient (and humane) than the use of guns, traps, and poison? The use of repellents is increasing. Another promising approach might be through altering the physiology of the animal rather than outright killing. The active ingredient in the *poison baits* of the future may be something which inhibits reproduction.

In summary, wildlife damage of many kinds has been with us for a long time. However, our concern over the damage sustained has varied according to the offending species. In general we have persecuted predators of poultry and livestock, but have shown a good deal of tolerance toward many of the herbivores that attack forest, field, or orchard. In the future, though, as the need to feed, clothe, and shelter increasing numbers of people forces us to make more intensive use of the land, we will have to concern ourselves more with losses caused by the wildlife that shares the land with us.

Problems of Habitat

It is axiomatic that wildlife needs a place in which to live. Equally true, but less obvious perhaps, each species of wildlife has its own special requirements of habitat. This dependence has arisen through a long evolutionary history. Thus, white-tailed deer, coyotes, pheasants, and carp can thrive in close association with agriculture. Mule deer, wolves, spruce grouse, and rainbow trout cannot. A third generalization is that wildlife, like trees and agricultural crops, is a product of the land. In some cases the interests of the farmer or forester parallel those of the wildlife manager; in others they do not. Before attempting predictions, let us look briefly at some of the conflicts that have already arisen.

The oft-told story of the disappearance of the bison may serve as our first example. There were many factors involved that need not concern us here, but the overriding factor is that bison is not compatible with the raising of livestock or grain-growing. Without the hide-hunters the bison would have held on a little longer, but only until the plains were fenced.

Agriculture is crowding out another great migratory resource in a slightly different way. I refer, of course, to the drainage of duck-producing potholes to raise crops that are often surplus from an economic viewpoint[16].

Forestry, by its very nature, alters wildlife habitats. Forests disappear altogether, or the composition of the forests changes. The effects on wildlife are a mixed blessing. The creation of openings in the forest and the abundance of young growth, following a logging operation, certainly benefit the white-tailed deer. This species will remain the major component of our big game crop. These same changes in habitat, however, have pushed the woodland caribou farther and farther back into the wilderness. Forestry also affects fish in various ways. Removing the trees that shade a stream leads to a rise in water temperature that may render a stream unsuited to some species, notably the trouts and chars. Bad forestry practices, such as clear cutting and destruction of ground covers, lead to increased erosion, and this in turn gives rise to silt-laden streams no longer suited to the production of fish.

Both forest and agricultural crops are beset by insect pests. To combat these, the chemical industry has developed some effective sprays that can be spread over immense areas by the use of aircraft. This problem, too, has such significant implications for wildlife that a separate paper[8] has been devoted to it.

The development of hydroelectric power may have far reaching effects on wildlife, particularly fish [2, 15].

One of Canada's newest major industries is the petroleum industry that blossomed in Alberta in 1947. In the intervening 13 years, almost 700,000 miles of exploration and seismic trails have been bulldozed through the forests of Alberta in the search for oil (Heustis, *personal communication*). Thus 1.5 to 1.8 million acres of wildlife habitat have been altered rather drastically. Worse still, there have been cases of rival companies pushing through parallel roads only a few yards apart, thus unnecessarily doubling the amount of destruction.

People, too, need living space. In the postwar years, many of our cities have known the phenomenon of *urban sprawl*. My own home in Edmonton, for example, sits on land that was a lake until after World War II. J. Dewey Soper (*personal communication*) remembers trapping muskrats in that lake in his youth. Nor are people content to sit at home; the automobile has given us a civilization on wheels. Just how important a factor this is may be appreciated from the following quotation[12]: "Modern traffic, like a many-bedded river, has torn wide gashes through today's central cities and has carried beyond the city large chunks of urban enterprise which now will never return to the centre . . . in some cities traffic takes up twice as much land as is given to all other forms of human occupancy . . . this ratio, as high as it is, is still not high enough—it must increase."

Finally, there is the gigantic problem of pollution of lakes, streams, and even the oceans with industrial wastes. Larkin[15] deals with the effects of pollution on fish. Waterfowl and sea birds are probably the classes of wildlife next most vulnerable to pollution, especially when the pollutant is oil. Giles and Livingstone[10] reported heavy losses in sea-bird colonies off the coast of Newfoundland. On both our coasts, the problem is a particularly difficult one because in some cases the oil is dumped, or ships' bunkers are flushed, beyond our territorial limits. Wind and currents combine to sweep the oil toward shore.

Turning now to the future, I think we may anticipate some new areas of conflict.

At present two tremendously large regions of Canada are barely touched by economic activity—the Pre-Cambrian Shield and the arctic tundra. These act as very large preserves for some species of game. What will happen when the world's insatiable demand for paper makes it economically feasible to harvest the scrubby pines and black spruce of the Pre-Cambrian? Of more immediate concern, will the search for oil in the Arctic result in destruction of the tundra on the same scale as the destruction of Alberta forests? If so, can the tundra, usually thought of as a rather fragile biome, withstand such destruction?

Finally what of nuclear power? Will we dump radioactive wastes into our rivers? How many trout streams will be used to cool a reactor? How much wild land will be fenced off around each reactor site to protect the public from accidental exposure to harmful radiation?

The present situation may be summed up, by saying that various forms of economic activity have created, and are creating, pressures on wildlife habitat. As a result, habitat for many forms of wildlife is shrinking. The increasing human population of Canada will continue to act as a spur to economic activity. One may confidently predict, therefore, that the pressures of those activities on wildlife habitat will continue to increase. The important questions are whether the pressures will be irresistible, and whether they can be modified so that their impact on wildlife is not entirely destructive.

Problems of Harvest

How to obtain a harvest that just balances productivity is now, and always has been, the central problem of the art of wildlife management. The harvest problem may be considered under two headings—over-harvest and under-harvest. At first sight over-harvest might appear to be the more serious. However, examples in which wildlife populations have been exterminated by over-harvest alone are rare. The near extermination of the bison is one of the best, although the bison was doomed by the advance of agriculture anyway. The timber wolf, too, has been steadily reduced in numbers because of relentless persecution by man. In many other cases, over-harvest has been only one factor working in combination with other factors, chiefly habitat destruction, which is discussed in a later section. This seems to be true of the barren-ground caribou and the whooping crane for example.

Under-harvest usually results in one or more undesirable effects. By definition there is waste of part of the game crop. If an over-abundance of a game species occurs close to agricultural crops, crop damage frequently results. Most serious, however, is the extreme case in which the animals literally eat themselves out of house and home. Many years may then elapse before the habitat recovers sufficiently to support a harvestable stand of game again.

The control of over-harvest poses several difficulties, some biological and some essentially political. The political problems of securing suitable restrictive legislation and adequate enforcement staff lie beyond the scope of this paper. They are dealt with by Munro.[23] Perhaps the chief biological problem is the difference in sensitivity to exploitation exhibited by different species of wildlife. Thus we have a somewhat paradoxical situation in waterfowl management where some species, notably mallards, are so abundant that they cause important crop losses, while other species, notably canvasbacks and redheads, are faced with local extermination. In a different situation—the great boreal forests—it is well known to trappers that marten and fisher can be easily caught and quickly eradicated, whereas the red squirrel cannot be exterminated by trapping alone. A final example may be drawn from the fishery field, where there seems to be no practical limit to the angling pressure that the warm water species can withstand. There is a definite limit, however, to the amount of angling that the slow-growing trouts and chars of the cold mountain streams can stand.

The problem is most acute when scarce and abundant species occur in close proximity, as with the waterfowl. To harvest mallards and protect redheads it is obviously necessary for the hunter to know one species from the other. Does this foreshadow the day when prospective hunters will be required to pass a test on their knowledge of wildlife?

Under-harvest is always associated with one of two things. The first is difficulty of access to the game crop. In the case of ungulate populations this is caused by lack of roads, coupled with the disinclination of the modern hunter to leave his automobile and travel on foot. To mention only two examples, this factor is at the root of the moose problem in Newfoundland forests and an overpopulation of elk in parts of Alberta. In the case of small game the deteriorating relations between the sportsman and the landowner are more often to blame. Essentially this is a social problem; it will be discussed, along with problems of values, in part four of this paper. Fishermen too have access problems. Lake Simcoe, within easy reach of the dense population of fishermen in Metropolitan Toronto, contains an overabundance of harvestable fish. However, the lake is ringed by privately-owned land so that only a handful of fishermen can actually get access to the water during the summer. The anomalous situation has developed wherein fishing pressure is heavier in January than on a sunny Sunday in July, simply because in January the public has free access to all parts of the lake on the ice. (C. H. D. Clarke drew this example to my attention.)

The second general cause of under-harvest is based on some of our attitudes toward wildlife. I am thinking particularly of the *buck law* school of thought. It has been demonstrated again and again that adequate harvests cannot be obtained when only adult males are hunted, yet opposition to harvesting females and young, particularly of ungulates, continues. The fisheries people in general have had more success in ridding themselves of such ancient shibboleths. Thus minimum sizes and daily possession limits have gone by the boards in many fertile lakes where overpopulation of some species has been demonstrated.

For many Canadian species of small game, fur-bearing mammals, and upland game birds, periods of great abundance alternate with periods of scarcity. Thus, problems of securing an adequate harvest may be replaced by the problems of preventing over-harvest in a short space of time. Biologists recognize the phenomenon and can usually predict the year of maximum harvest, but administrators and sportsmen are often too cautious to raise bag limits in time to cash in on the periodic bonanzas.

What now of harvest problems in the future? Clarke's[5] analysis of the increased numbers of hunters and fishermen in Canada in recent decades gives reason for apprehension, if not alarm. He shows that the number of hunters and fishermen increased by a factor of three or four while the population of Canada was doubling. Alberta has had the greatest increase. The number of hunting licences sold in 1958 was greater by a factor of 10 than the average number sold yer year in the first 44 years of this century.[22] There seems little reason to doubt that the population of Canada will continue to increase, but it is less certain that the more-than-proportionate increase in hunters and fishermen will continue as well. If this trend does continue, however, problems associated with over-harvest may assume a dominant role.

Problems of Values

Sociological problems arise out of differences in our attitudes toward wild things. Clarke[5] has examined our attitudes in some detail, but their importance is such that I must refer specifically to several here.

A basic dichotomy arises because most species of wildlife have both negative and positive values, and seldom is the line clear-cut. Few mammals contribute more in a positive way than the beaver, and certainly none has contributed more in the past, yet even the beaver has negative values when its activities lead to washed out highways. At or near the other end of the scale are the raptorial birds and the large predators such as the wolf. Most people see in the swoop of a hawk or the howl of a wolf only a threat to either their economic well-being or their favorite sport. Only those with an *ecological conscience*[18] perceive, in those events, the drama of evolution. When and how are we to protect and preserve our large wild predators? Will Canada be richer or poorer if they are lost?

There is a secondary dichotomy even among those who stress the positive values of wildlife. The hunters and trappers are consumptive users of wildlife whereas bird watchers, camera-hunters, and just plain native lovers are nonconsumptive users. Furthermore, even the consumptive users are divided into factions. For example, there are the *bucks only* school and the *any deer* school; the pot hunter and the trophy hunter; the treblehook fisherman and the dry-fly addict.

I believe that those who value wild things are in the majority, but unless they set aside their differences and pull together they are in danger of losing out to the minority by default. Will we see a united front for conservation of wildlife in the next 20 years? How can we help to bring it about?

If wildlife conservation is to serve all the people we must modify the widespread belief that economics alone determines all land use. Leopold[18] has branded this "the fallacy that economic determinists have tied around our collective necks." Regardless of any peregrinations of the gross national product, Canada will be irreparably poorer if, as a result of economic pressure, we lose a single species of our native wildlife. Who will teach ordinary Canadians about the esthetic values of wildlife? Will we recognize those values before we lose them in the face of economic *progress*?

In many cases people should know better are engaging in bad conservation practices. I can do no better than quote with approval from a recent writer,[4] a polymer chemist by profession.

> "Ignorance of a similar kind is found in technology, philosophy and science. For example, it may be discovered that a certain spray will be extremely effective in killing mosquitoes, or their larvae. Wholesale spraying, then, of parks, fields, streams, does indeed kill off the mosquitoes, but also the birds and fish which, had they been fostered, might have done a reasonably good job in the first place. (Solutions which pertain to be absolute—"to kill off *all* the mosquitoes"—should on principle be avoided, or in any event, thoroughly scrutinized.) This kind of error lies in mistaking analysis for all there is, or in looking at a complicated system with a very low-level-of-abstraction viewpoint, narrowly restricted. The proper functioning of analysis, synthesis, and reduction to practice would lead one to think of the whole situation. This is what ecologists are trained to do, and a well-trained ecologist would not commit such mistakes."

If the scientists themselves cannot reach agreement, can we expect to get the message across to the general public?

Canada, like the United States, owes a great deal to its early pioneers. Those pioneers treated the wilderness as something to be conquered, and with their energy, fortitude, and indomitable will, conquer it they did. For most Canadians now the frontier exists only on television, yet it is surprising how much our attitudes toward wildlife are still coloured by the pioneer tradition. Witness, for example, the titles of two recent books—*Men Against the Frozen North*[3] and *Three Against the Wilderness*[6]. Stefansson refuted Calder as long ago at 1921 with *The Friendly Arctic*[24] and a reading of Collier's book discloses that the wilderness treated him very well and that he is in fact very much on the side of the wilderness. One can only presume that the titles were intended to attract a wide readership by appealing to the remnants of our pioneer spirit. Thus we keep alive the idea that the wilderness is an enemy. This may promote book sales, but hardly provides the background for good conservation.

Finally, there is evidence of an enormous indifference toward wildlife. It probably has its roots in the attitude that, since wildlife belongs to everyone, it is the responsibility of no one. This theme has been elaborated by the Editor of *The Atlantic*, an ardent fisherman who writes poetically about the New England States, the Maritime Provinces, and Newfoundland. I should like to quote from a recent editorial.[25]

> "As everyone who is interested in water knows, it is the devil and all to keep a good river alive. . . The river I most love, the Northwest Miramichi, has—or had—in its upper water an exceptionally deep and beautiful pool, at a curve in the river known as Black Pool, because of the shade cast over it by a giant, century-old pine. Prospectors camped at the point, and wanting a quick way to cross the stream, simply felled the tree to provide their foot-bridge; the chunks of it which protruded were sawed off and dumped into the pool. The metallurgists in charge of the party and the French Canadians saw nothing but efficiency in this desecration."

To me, such small acts of personal indifference are more frightening than the large, impersonal acts of many corporations and cities. The individual may understandably be indifferent to pollution of the St. Lawrence, for, after all, what can one person do to stop that? On the other hand, indifference of a few individuals led to the desecration of Black Pool. I think we must attack the problem on an individual level and perhaps, if we succeed in instilling a sense of ownership of wildlife into individuals, more corporations will develop an *ecological conscience*.

Discussion and Conclusion

In the next few decades the problems in wildlife management are not going to change in essence. They will manifest themselves in new places as man's activities are extended into hitherto unexploited areas. They will intensify as more and more people cluster in our present centres of population. More than anything, we need to anticipate our problems and develop the will to meet them in good time.

Earlier in this paper I referred to possible destructive influences on the tundra. It seems to me that this example epitomizes our future problem. There seem to be two basic unknowns. First, if the tundra community is damaged, can it recuperate and if so, how long will it take? Second, whether or not the damage is permanent, will we allow the tundra community to be squeezed out of existence by burgeoning economic pressures such as the search for oil or, far into the future, perhaps, tundra agriculture.? The answers to the first group of questions can come only through basic, ecological research.[9] For problems of the second kind, involving attitudes toward wild things, the only hope is in educating all Canadians to an appreciation of their natural heritage.

What is required then is a double-barreled attack—first to acquire new knowledge and second to see that what we know now and may come to know is widely disseminated. So far we have been better at learning than teaching. One example will have to suffice. Game managers have long since proved the inefficiency of bounties for the control of predators, yet bounties are a perennial item on the agendas of Fish and Game Association Conventions and they still figure in the budgets of some Game Departments. What we need, therefore, is not less ecological research, but more, much more, emphasis on education. Other branches of science are faced with the same problems.[1] Nor are the two types of problems unrelated. A public that wants to preserve our wildlife heritage will more actively support ecological research, and accept research findings, than a public that doesn't know, therefore doesn't care.

The aim of education in this field is to develop an *ecological conscience*. This implies recognition that wildlife is part of the land community with which we must live in harmony rather than in a state of war. As a part of the land community, wildlife should receive consideration in all programs involving land use. The contribution of wildlife must be considered in esthetic as well as economic terms, and in some cases, at least, the esthetic values should be recognized as truly priceless.

The task is formidable, but not without hope. As Aldo Leopold has said: "to promote perception is the only truly creative part of recreational engineering."

References

[1] Ashby, E., "Dons or Crooners?", *Science, no.* 131 (1960), pp. 1165-70.

[2] Boan, J. A., *The Significance of Reservoirs in Recreation*, Paper prepared for 1961 Resources for Tomorrow Conference.

[3] Calder, R., *Men Against the Frozen North,* George Allen and Unwin Ltd., London, (1957), pp. 279.

[4] Cassidy, Harold G., "The problem of the Sciences and the Humanities. A diagnosis and a prescription", *American Scientist*, no. 48 (1960), pp. 383-98.

[5] Clarke, C. H. D., *Wildlife in Perspective,* Paper prepared for 1961 Resources for Tomorrow Conference.

[6] Collier, Eric, *Three Against the Wilderness*, E. P. Dutton, and Co. Ltd., New York (1959), pp. 349.

[7] Connell, F. H., "Trichinosis in the Arctic: a review", *Arctic*, no. 2 (1949), pp. 98-107.

8 Cottam, C., *Pesticides and Wildlife*, Paper prepared for 1961 Resources for Tomorrow Conference.

9 Cowan, E. McT., *Research in Relation to Management Needs*, Paper prepared for 1961 Resources for Tomorrow Conference.

10 Giles, Lester A., Jr. and J. Livingstone, "Oil Pollution of the Seas", *Trans. North Am. Wildl. Conf. 25* (1960), pp. 297-303.

11 Giltz, Maurice L., *The nature and extent of bird depredation on crops*, *Trans. North Am. Wildl. Conf. 25*, (1960), pp. 96-99.

12 Haskell, Douglas, "More Land Said Needed for Traffic", *Edmonton Journal*, October 19 (1960).

13 Johnson, H. W., "Public health in relation to birds. Arthropodborne viruses", *Trans. North Am. Wildl. Conf. 25* (1960), pp. 121-33.

14 Kennedy, H., D. R. Cameron and R. D. Goodyear, *Report of the Newfoundland Royal Commission on Forestry*, Queen's Printer, St. John's (1955), pp. 240.

15 Larkin, P. A., *Effect of Man-Made Changes on Fish Environment*, Paper prepared for 1961 Resource for Tomorrow Conference.

16 Leitch, W. G., *Problems of a Mobile Resource—Migratory Waterfowl*, Paper prepared for 1961 Resources for Tomorrow Conference.

17 Leopold, Aldo, *Game Management*, Charles Scribner's Sons, New York, (1933), pp. 481.

18 Leopold, Aldo, *A Sand County Almanac*, Oxford University Press, New York, (1949), pp. 226.

19 Mair, W. W., "Ducks and Grain", *Trans. North Am. Wildl Conf. 18*, (1953) pp. 111-17.

20 Martin, R. L., "A history of chiropteran rabies with special reference to occurrence and importance in the United States", *Wildlife Disease*, 3, (1959), pp. 1-75.

21 Miller, Max J., "Hydatid Infection in Canada", *Journal of Canadian Medical Association*, 68 (1953), pp. 423-34.

22 Mitchell, George J., *Alberta's Upland Game Bird Resource*, Queen's Printer, Edmonton (1959), p. 27.

23 Munro, D. A., *Legislative and Administrative Limitations on Wildlife Management*, Paper prepared for 1961 Resources for Tomorrow Conference.

24 Stefansson, V., *The Friendly Arctic*, The Macmillan Co., New York (1921).

25 Weeks, Edward, "The Peripatetic Reviewer", *Atlantic*, 206 (1960), pp. 114-15.

26 Wolfgang, Robert W., "Indian and Eskimo Diphyllobothriasis", *Journal of Canadian Medical Association*, 70 (1954), pp. 536-39.

23

Maintaining the Wilderness Experience in Canada's National Parks

J. S. Marsh

Introduction

Land use problems are growing in the National Parks, as is recognition of the need to "manage" parks and wilderness. There are external pressures tending to reduce the area of parks and wilderness and pressures and management problems within wilderness areas. It is essential to consider how such pressures and problems relate to recreation and how, in the future, the Canadian National Parks can provide for recreationists seeking a high quality of wilderness experience.

The term "National Parks" is taken to embrace all parks designated as such and presently included in the system administered by the National and Historic Parks Branch, Department of Indian Affairs and Northern Development, Canada. These parks are varied in size, character and history yet have many important common characteristics. Many include unique or classic examples of scenery, flora and fauna. Though man's impact has not been excluded[1] they owe a good deal of their present character to the policy of landscape preservation that has prevailed with varying intensity over a number of decades. They lie at one end of a landscape spectrum that has at the other end the largely artificial environment of the modern city. Some parts of the parks, through isolation and neglect, have retained a primeval character almost unaltered by

Paper presented to the conference on *The Canadian National Parks: Today and Tomorrow*, Calgary, 1968.

[1] A case study of man's impact is: A. R. Byrne, "Man and Landscape Change in the Banff National Park Area before 1911", *Studies in Land Use History and Landscape Change*, National Park Series 1, Calgary (1968).

man. Other, larger areas have undergone some, often subtle, changes but the absence of such permanent features as housing, roads and industry has left them unspoiled. For the purposes of this paper areas within the parks that exhibit these characteristics may be termed "wilderness".[2] On this basis large sections of the National Parks can still be defined as wilderness though it must be remembered that landscapes having wilderness qualities grade gradually into those without making a precise delimitation of the wilderness very difficult.

Wilderness areas in the parks fulfill a number of functions, *e.g.,* as wildlife sanctuaries, floral preserves, and natural science research areas. However, the character, accessibility and management of many areas in the parks have made recreation the most obvious and significant land use. The types of recreation that can be undertaken in a wilderness area are restricted, usually non-facility oriented and include hiking, riding, man-powered boating, cross-country skiing and snowshoeing, fishing, camping, mountaineering, nature study, photography and painting. Such activities may be grouped under the term "wilderness recreation".

The people that engage in such recreation react to wilderness and enjoy what may be termed a "wilderness experience". The nature and quality of this experience varies with the individual, and is influenced by a number of factors such as the character of the area, the type of travel and activities involved and the person's socio-economic and cultural background. There are variations in the individual's concept of what constitutes wilderness and what detracts from or heightens the recreational experience. However, the sustained, repeated and increasing use of wilderness in the National Parks, and studies of wilderness users, indicate that the parks serve to provide most wilderness users with a satisfying, high quality experience.[3]

---

[2] The problem of defining wilderness is discussed in: The Wildland Research Centre, University of California, Wilderness and Recreation—A Report on Resources, Values and Problems, pp. 25, 26. Study Report 3, Outdoor Recreation Resources Review Commission, Washington, D.C., (1962).

[3] Studies of wilderness use anad users in Canada include: G. B. Priddle, "Recreational Use and 'Wilderness' Perception of the Algonquin Park Interior", Unpublished M.A. Thesis, Clark University, (1964); G. D. Taylor, "A Survey of Visitors to Wells Grey Park, British Columbia", *Forest Chronicle 36* (1960), pp. 346-54; J. Thorsell, "Waterton Lakes National Park Visitor Use Survey", Part 2, Wilderness Recreational Use, National and Historic Parks Branch, Ottawa (1967); J. Thorsell, "An Analysis of Mountaineering and Ski Touring Registrations, Banff National Park, 1966-67", *Recreational Research Report 32*, National and Historic Parks Branch, Ottawa (1967); J. Thorsell, "A Trail Use Survey, Banff and Yoho National Parks, 1967", *Recreational Research Report 33*, National and Historic Parks Branch, Ottawa (1968). Many other reports exist for areas in the U.S.A.

This paper is intended to indicate some of the problems and possibilities involved in providing for high quality wilderness recreation or a wilderness experience in Canada's National Parks in the future.

Problems

Despite a long-standing policy of land use control and preservation there are certain actual or potential land uses likely to change the parks and reduce the area of wilderness.

Resource-based industries such as lumbering and mining were established in areas that subsequently became parks. Their influence on the landscape was often quite marked and continued within the parks well into the era of preservation. In Banff, Yoho and Glacier National Parks quite considerable areas were operated or reserved as lumber berths.[4] These lumber berths may still be utilized today, and the possible impact of this activity demands that such a potential land use within the parks should not be overlooked. Mining and quarrying also have occurred within many parks. For example, in Banff Park coal mines were operated at Anthracite and Bankhead as late as 1904 and 1923 respectively.[5] Indeed, for a while, such features were regarded as an interesting and valuable aspect of the park. Although present legislation prohibits prospecting and the staking of claims in the parks, existing valid claims must be seen as a possible land use pressure in, and threat to, the parks and wilderness.

Park lands have also been used for grazing livestock as is the case in Riding Mountain National Park.[6] Currently, this is a localized and minor land use pressure, but it is a precedent, and its expansion—perhaps in the form of game ranching, might influence park wilderness areas.

The potential of the western cordillera for water storage and power development was recognized early and reservoirs and hydro plants were constructed in some parks. For example, in Banff Park, Lake Minnewanka was dammed and used for power production.[7]

---

4 For Banff see: Byrne, *op. cit.*, p. 93.
5 R. C. Scace, "Banff: A Cultural Historical Study of Land Use and Management in a National Park Community to 1945", *Studies in Land Use History and Landscape Change,* National Park Series, no. 2, Calgary (1968), p. 17.
6 D. A. Blood, "Range Relationships of Elk and Cattle in Riding Mountain National Park, Manitoba", *Canadian Wildlife Service, Wildlife Management Bulletin,* Series 1, 19 (1966).
7 R. C. Scace, et al., "Proposed Itinerary and notes for Rocky Mountains Field Trip, Sunday and Monday, May 26 and 27, 1968", pp. 14-16. Prepared for Canadian Association of Geographers Conference, The University of Calgary, Calgary (1968).

Such water bodies may sometimes be attractive foci for recreation but they can also be a threat to the quantity and quality of the park wilderness. As demands for water and power continue to increase, further pressure to develop sites in the parks can be anticipated.

Since the establishment of trails in park areas there has been a continued expansion of routeways in and through most parks. In Banff, Yoho and Glacier Parks the building of the C.P.R. in the 1880's resulted in major and permanent land use and landscape changes.[8] Construction involved clearing and earth removal and was accompanied by widespread fires and game depletion. More recently roads, and associated features like car parks, gravel pits and service stations, have become major and expanding uses and modifiers of park land. Although route development decreases, subdivides and modifies the area of park wilderness, expansion of the network seems inevitable. The Trans-Canada highway has been doubled for much of the distance between Calgary and Banff Park. With increasing traffic in the park a similar expansion of the Trans-Canada westwards through the park, can be expected. There is also a strong possibility that more scenic access roads will be built for example, in the Cascade and upper Red Deer valleys of Banff Park.[9] The likelihood, and influence, of such route expansion on the park wilderness should not be underestimated.

The agency administering and operating a park invariably requires land for office buildings, stores, maintenance depots and housing. Even when limited in extent such areas are often unsightly as, for example, the maintenance yards at Lake Louise and Rogers Pass. When centralized a townsite may develop and expand as shops and community facilities are required. Such development is especially likely when the town also serves as a visitor centre.[10] Thus, there are townsites, such as Banff, Jasper and Waterton, within the parks. The expansion and multiplication of administrative centres, visitor centres and recreational facilities poses a great threat in maintaining the area and quality of park wilderness. Recreation in the mountain parks began with the arrival of C.P.R. and the development and promotion of a tourist spa at Banff. From the beginning, recreation was facility oriented and as tourism increased places of accommodation and entertainment, trails, roads and services multiplied. Today the demand for facilities, such as

---

[8] Byrne, *op. cit.*
[9] Fire roads already exist in the Cascade Valley and lower Red Deer valley, Banff Park.
[10] Scace, *op. cit.*

motels, campgrounds, ski lifts, and access roads continues. In satisfying such demands, the area and quality of wilderness have always been sacrificed.

In the early years of the parks mechanized transport was relatively inflexible and restricted to a limited number of prepared routeways. Access to areas away from rail and road was on foot or horseback. Today wilderness areas are vulnerable to invasion by more flexible machines, notably trail-scooters, ski-doos, power boats, planes and helicopters. Such machines, through wear and tear, pollution and noise, can soon damage wilderness areas and the wilderness experience. Some legislation exists to restrict such pressures but precedents have been established and this potential threat to wilderness and wilderness recreation does not seem to be fully appreciated. For example, use of ski-doos has been permitted recently in sections of Banff Park. This may only be an experiment, but a precedent has again been established, conflicts with cross-country skiers have occurred and the impact on wildlife is scarely known.

There are a large number of existing and possible land uses in the National Parks. Individually such uses may seem insignificant but in total they exert formidable pressure. In competing for land within the parks they place particular pressure on the size and quality of the wilderness areas. Legislation and management techniques have not yet proved adequate to resolve conflicts and to guarantee protection of high quality wilderness areas. Precedents have been established in permitting certain uses, yielding to and encouraging others, that are not compatible with wilderness conservation.

As a result, since the establishment of most National Parks, there has been a progressive diminution of the wilderness area. This trend seems likely to continue until public pressure or legislation halts it. Not only will the area of wilderness be less but it will be distributed in smaller units as routeways and recreational developments expand. The remaining wilderness will contain land that is largely unsuitable for other purposes, e.g., high mountains, rocky shores, and its value as wilderness recreation land may also be limited.

Certain areas will no longer be viable ecological units and their size will render them more susceptible to external influences, such as noise pollution.[11] Even if external pressures are restrained, and

---

[11] In Banff Park, railway engine whistles can be heard up to ten miles away sometimes. In Glacier Park, trucks crossing Rogers Pass can be heard several miles away, as can the gravel extraction operations.

large areas reserved, maintenance of wilderness for a high quality recreational experience will depend upon the solution of many internal pressures and problems. Most National Park wilderness areas have a number of functions, *e.g.*, floral and faunal sanctuaries, typical ecological units, natural science research areas, education and recreation areas. In large wilderness units conflicts between such uses may be minimal but in smaller units, especially where recreational use is intense, problems may arise.

The preservation of endangered plant and animal species may pose many problems where wilderness recreation is intense and unrestricted. The current survival of the whooping crane can be partially attributed to the fact that it breeds in a remote and seldom visited section of Wood Buffalo National Park.[12]

The rarity of a species may even attract visitors thus narrowing further its chances of survival. In California, for example, some groves of trees like the giant sequoia, may be endangered by visitors compacting the ground surface and otherwise influencing the environment.[13]

The unfortunate incidents between grizzlies and recreationists in Glacier Park, U.S.A., in 1967 and in Banff and Jasper Parks in 1968, further illustrate the possibility of conflict between certain wilderness uses.[14] Wilderness areas have a unique and essential role as natural science research areas[15] but again land use conflicts may occur. The research may require certain facilities such as temporary housing, instrumentation or mechanical transport that influence the character of the area. Thus glacier research projects in the Rockies have required construction of temporary huts, and the use of ski-doos and helicopters. Restrictions on human or animal movements may also be required. Failure to note possible conflicts may reduce the quality of several land uses.

Today it is generally accepted that to achieve the many purposes of wilderness conservation a policy of management rather than simple protection of the landscape is required. While some of the

12 N. S. Novakowski, "Whooping Crane Population Dynamics on the Nesting Grounds, Wood Buffalo National Park, Northwest Territories, Canada", *Canadian Wildlife Service Report* Series, No. 1, Ottawa (1966).
13 National Parks Association, "A Preliminary Wilderness Plan for Sequoia-Kings Canyon National Parks and the Surrounding Region," *National Parks Magazine* 41 (232) (1967), pp. 9-13.
14 The problem of bears and humans in Yellowstone National Park is discussed briefly in M. Zook, "Don't Feed the Bears", *National Parks Magazine*, 37 (189) (1963), pp. 7-9.
15 See K. Curry-Lindahl, "Scientific Research in National Parks", *Trends in Parks and Recreation*, 5 (2) (1968), pp. 7-8.

ecological factors involved in wilderness management have been studied, the implications for maintaining quality wilderness recreation have been neglected.

Several decades of quite effective landscape protection in the National Parks have produced certain problems. In the more remote areas of parks, like Glacier, man-made fires were rare and protection has produced high proportions of mature trees and deadfall that are disease and fire hazards.[16] Where protection followed extensive burning, as in the Bow Valley, Banff Park, large areas of even-age lodgepole pine have replaced a forest more varied in age and species.[17] To produce and maintain a healthy forest on a sustained basis, and to prevent the eradication of certain habitats, techniques such as selective burning and logging may have to be employed in park wilderness areas. With careful management, and modern control methods, such practices might be used very effectively to achieve specified ecological goals. However, the impact of these operations on wilderness recreation would require study. Logging and purposeful burning have been absent from most parks for many years and accidental and natural fires have been quenched as fast as possible. A sudden change in policy toward fire and logging could meet considerable resistance, from recreationists and might initially detract from the experience of many wilderness users.[18]

Because of habitat changes, selective protection of animals, and for various other reasons, it will also be necessary to manage the fauna.[19] For example, in Banff, elk must be culled from time to time to prevent overpopulation and the associated problems of overgrazing and disease. Because such practices influence the wilderness environment, and seem somewhat contrary to the preservation philosophy, their impact on the wilderness user and the quality of his experience must be considered.

It may be considered necessary and desirable to eliminate pests or diseases by spraying, as in the Grand Tetons National Park,

16 The need to manage National Park forests is stressed in D. I. Crossley, "Forest Management in National Parks". Brief submitted to the Standing Committee on Northern Affairs, and National Resources, Jasper, (1966).

17 Byrne, op. cit.

18 One study of reaction to logging is R. C. Lucas, "Visitor Reaction to Timber Harvesting in the Boundary Waters Canoe Area", U.S. Forest Service, Research Note, LS-Z, Lake States Forest Experiment Station, St. Paul, Minn., (1963).

19 S. A. Cain, et. al., "Wildlife Management in the National Parks", The Living Wilderness 83, (1963), pp. 11-24.

U.S.A., or by introducing predator species.[20] One can expect the use of such techniques to have an influence on wilderness recreation, as well as ecology, and their introduction must be considered in this light.

Many management techniques will be more directly concerned with wilderness recreation and the impact of these on the ecology will also require close investigation. For example, the impact of trails, campsites and horse grazing on wildlife merits study. The recreational use of wilderness areas has increased markedly in the last two decades and the trend seems very likely to continue.[21]

As increasing numbers of recreationists concentrate on diminishing areas of wilderness the pressure on the environment mounts and the quality of the wilderness and the recreational experience are threatened. In some places and at certain times the situation is already critical, for example around Lake Louise in Banff Park.[22]

The wilderness user has a direct though often subtle impact on the environment that may not be perceived until critical. Plants are picked and trampled, grass grazed, and ground compacted. Some plant communities may quickly be degraded or eradicated by even moderate pressure of this kind. Apart from exerting wear on the environment recreationists cause pollution. In particular, litter accumulates along intensively used trails and water and noise pollution may also occur. More permanent and widespread damage results when fires are started accidentally in back country areas.

In wilderness areas managed for recreation, as in the National Parks, minimal facilities are often provided. Such facilities, as trails, campsites, signs and emergency huts cause changes in the landscape but often they avert the likelihood of more drastic modification. However, as recreational use increases so does the demand for more, and often better, facilities until the area's wilderness character is completely lost.[23] Deciding on what facilities are required to protect the environment and how many can be tolerated in a wilderness area is a difficult matter.

With or without facilities wilderness areas gradually deteriorate under recreational pressure and only careful management can maintain the quality of the environment and the wilderness experience.

---

[20] A. Murie, "Pesticide Program in Grand Teton National Park", *National Parks Magazine* 40 (225) (1966), pp. 17-19.
[21] For trends in the U.S.A. see "Outdoor Recreation Trends", Bureau of Outdoor Recreation, Washington (1967).
[22] Thorsell, *op. cit.*, (1968), pp. 43-44.
[23] Thorsell, *op. cit.*, (1968), p. 21, notes that in Banff and Yoho Parks there is a definite demand for improved facilities in the backcountry.

Even when man's impact on the environment is minimized the quality of the wilderness experience will fall if recreational pressure causes crowding or conflicts between activities.[24] Many people visit wilderness areas, to "get away from it all", to seek peace and solitude. The quality of such an experience will often be inversely related to the intensity of use in the area.

As wilderness use increases conflicts between recreational activities develop and threaten the quality of the experience. Thus trails used by hikers and riders, as in the Lake Louise area of Banff Park, may prove unsatisfactory to both groups when usage is heavy.[25]

Possibilities

The quality of the park wilderness area and the wilderness experience can be maintained only if adequate areas are protected against external land use pressures, on a long term basis. To be adequate, wilderness areas must be of a character and size that allows them to function as ecological units. To satisfy recreation needs they must be accessible and large enough to allow several days continuous wilderness travel.[26] Such units can still be maintained in most National Parks if the basic purpose of parks is re-emphasized, legislation is strengthened and zoning adhered to.

If timber berths and mining claims lie within wilderness areas, as in Yoho and Glacier parks, such areas can only be safeguarded by buying out the owners, even if the cost is high.

The establishment of new National Parks and wilderness areas is a possibility that must be regarded as essential.[27] Such areas might be operated federally or jointly, with provincial and other agencies. An expansion of the wilderness system would reduce internal pressures on park wilderness and provide a better choice and distribution of such areas. Such areas can, however, only fulfill this role if legislation guarantees their survival and quality as wilderness. The term "wilderness area" must mean more than land

---

24 The effects of crowding on wildland recreational quality are discussed in J. A. Wagar, "The Carrying Capacity of Wild Lands for Recreation", *Forest Science Monograph*, 7, Washington (1964).

25 Thorsell, *op. cit.*, (1968), p. 20.

26 The significance of size in defining wilderness is noted in *Wildland Research Centre, op. cit.*, pp. 18-19.

27 Some new National Parks are being considered, for example, on the Pacific Coast and on the prairies. More provincial wilderness areas are being established, for example, in Ontario, Polar Bear Provincial Park, a 7,000 square-mile area fronting on James Bay and Hudson Bay.

not yet required for other purposes, as so often applies today.[28] The possibility also exists of using land outside the National Parks to satisfy those land use pressures that threaten wilderness within the parks. For example, use of the Kananaskis area of Alberta for facility recreation development could reduce the external pressures on wilderness in Banff National Park.[29]

The designation of adequate wilderness areas inside and outside the parks can be done successfully only with a detailed historical-geographic and ecological investigation and inventory as a basis. This would also provide information for deciding on use priorities, management techniques and long term planning. It may be necessary and desirable to zone wilderness, establish priorities for each zone and manage accordingly. Such a system must, however, be flexible to respond to changing ecological conditions and land use needs.

Recreation will probably make the heaviest demands on wilderness in the future. To maintain the quality of the wilderness and wilderness experience many new management techniques will be required. In determining the type and quantity of recreational use permitted in any area, consideration must be given to the other uses of the area, management techniques, the capacity of the area to sustain use, and the availability of alternatives.

In some areas the present minimal facilities and regulations regarding wilderness recreation will be adequate to ensure mainten-ance of the quality of the environment and the recreational experi-ence.[30] Elsewhere and increasingly as recreational pressure mounts, greater protection of the environment and further restriction on use will be required. The development of more and better minimal facilities is a possible short-term development. For example, more trails and wilderness campsites in Glacier National Park would make the park more attractive and help cater for the growing demand for wilderness recreation.[31]

Areal and temporal zoning may also be employed to reduce pressure and conflicts. Certain trails may be allocated to riders and others to hikers or riding may be permitted at one time and hiking

---

[28] Many so-called provincial "wilderness areas" have been influenced by non-compatible uses, such as mining. See "Memorandum on British Colum-bia's Parks Policy", *Park News* 3 (2) (1967), pp. 5-8.

[29] Certain recreation facilities have been provided and a ski area is being developed.

[30] Whether such facilities will be regarded as adequate by recreationists is another matter.

[31] Presently much of the park is inaccessible, even on foot, and there are no official backcountry campsites.

at another. However, eventually it will be necessary to book in advance or pay to gain access to certain wilderness areas. Such methods are already being applied in some countries and can be expected in Canada.[32] In areas that have deteriorated badly, public access may be prohibited completely until the area has recuperated. Where other land uses such as wildlife preservation, have priority access may only be permitted to organized groups with an official guide.[33] It will be possible to maintain the quality of the wilderness and wilderness experience only if such management techniques are used and accepted. Such acceptance and support will require that the National Parks Branch expand its information and education services. More interpretive centres, park naturalists and natural-history publications are required.[34] Hopefully, other agencies, such as schools and outdoor clubs will help the public to understand the role and problems of wilderness conservation.

As the character of the wilderness, its users and problems will change there will be a need for continual research in park areas. Beginning with the basic inventory of parks it is possible that much work may be done on a contract basis using consultants and universities. Only by using current data and flexible management will the quality of the wilderness and wilderness experience be maintained in future.

---

[32] For example in New Zealand and Poland.
[33] This technique is employed in Natal and possibly elsewhere.
[34] Comprehensive guides on most National Parks are still not available and interpretive centres, such as have been developed in the U.S.A., are very rare.

24

Tundra and Taiga

J. R. Mackay

The sparsely inhabited cold regions of northern North America are variously designated as polar and subpolar, arctic and sub-arctic, or tundra and taiga. Perhaps the terms "tundra" and "taiga" are most appropriate for the North American Habitats Study Conference, because of the biotic connotations of the Russian words from which they are derived. "Tundra" is now used in a sense not far different from the original meaning of a level or undulating, treeless plain of northern arctic regions. "Taiga," however, is employed in a more restrictive sense than that of the Siberian swampy, coniferous forests which lie between the tundra and the steppe or boreal forest of the Soviet union.

The topical emphasis in this paper is on the environmental factors in the tundra and taiga, with particular stress on physical processes. The regional emphasis is on the western arctic, because it has a greater potentiality for settlement in Canada, and is best known to the writer. Discussion of plant and animal communities, economic development, and man are covered in other sessions of the Conference and so are only cursorily touched upon here. The specific purposes of this paper are: (1) to examine the combination of physical elements which give character to the tundra and taiga; (2) to discuss the physical processes which are of major im-portance in an understanding of habitats; and (3) to suggest possible future pressures on habitats and changes which might result. Focus will be directed more toward the tundra than toward the taiga, because it offers a sharper contrast to the more familiar middle-latitude environments.

Reprinted from *Future Environments of North America*, eds. F. Darling and J. P. Milton, Natural History Press, New York, pp. 156-71.

Little is gained from the interesting intellectual exercise of debating the precise method of delimiting the tundra-taiga boundary, because the subject has been exhaustively argued in the literature. In many theoretical and practical respects, the problem is akin to defining the arid-semiarid or desert-steppe boundary. Something is to be gained, however, in reviewing the characteristics of the boundary zone, because it helps in understanding the environmental factors involved.

Traditionally, the tundra has been defined as treeless; the taiga as the transitional open woodland (forest-tundra) belt between the tundra and the boreal forest. The definition of tundra therefore hinges on what is a tree, or collectively, a forest. Is the tree line the economic limit of forestry; the last upright tree of a given species in tree form; a combination of the most northerly of all treelike species; or the limit of species, irrespective of being prostrate or treelike (Hustich, 1953)? Should the limit be confined to conifers, or should tree birch and poplar be included? For the purpose of this paper, the tundra-taiga boundary is placed approximately at the present limit of trees which rise roughly ten or more feet in height.

The difficulty in delimiting the tundra-taiga boundary fades by comparison with the problems of specifying the southern boundary of the taiga. In this paper, following Polunin (1959, p. 483), the taiga is described as "sparsely timbered country, especially near the northern limit of arborescent growth." The approximate position of the tundra-taiga boundary is shown in Figure 1. The limit in Canada has been compiled mainly from Halliday (1937) and Rowe (1959) and that in Alaska from Sigafoos (1958). It is obvious that many details, particularly in mountainous Alaska and Yukon Territory, have been generalized on such a small-scale map. No southern limit for the taiga is shown; the southern boundary in Canada is that given by Rowe (1959) for "forest and grassland" and "forest and barren." The complexity of the terrain in relation to map scale makes it impossible to extend the pattern into Alaska and to alpine areas of Canada. Perhaps few would object if the southern boundary, just discussed, was arbitrarily assumed to be that of the southern taiga. For convenience in subsequent discussions: the tundra is inferred to lie "north" of the taiga and boreal forest, although, of course, the tundra may lie to the south, as in southern Alaska; tundra is considered as synonymous areally with arctic, taiga with subarctic; and cordilleran areas of tundra and taiga are generally ignored.

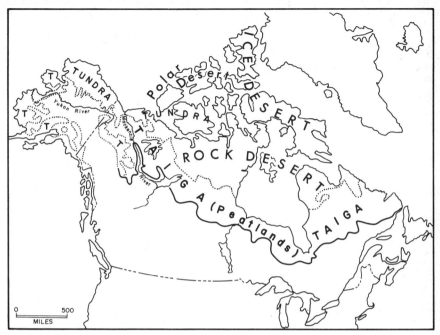

Figure 1. The tundra-taiga boundary.

It might be relevant, at this juncture, to stress the futility of a homologous transference of latitude by latitude or climatic region by climatic region comparisons between the North American and Eurasian subarctics and arctics. The two arctics are quite different (Marsden, 1958-59) and even in North America, there is not just one arctic, but several. To cite but one example, there is the influence of glaciation on soil. The last major glaciation in North America covered by far the greater part of the mainland and the arctic islands of Canada and much of Alaska, but a much smaller area of the northern part of Eurasia.

Climate and Vegetation

Climate, particularly summer temperature, is usually considered to be the major environmental factor responsible for a treeless tundra. This explains the numerous attempts which have been made to relate temperature to the tundra-taiga boundary. Especially well known has been Köppen's boundary line of the 50°F (10°C) isotherm for the warmest month (usually July) of the year. Throughout the north, sizable tundra areas lie south of the 50°F isotherm. Nordenskjöld (1928, p. 73) took into account both summer and winter temperatures by proposing the formula $v = 51.4 - 0.1k$ where v and k represent the mean temperatures of the warmest and coldest months, respectively, in Fahrenheit degrees. In the Nordenskjöld line, the mean monthly temperature of the warmest month required to support tree growth should be at least equal to v or higher. The Nordenskjöld line mostly lies slightly south of Köppen's line and gives a better fit to the tundra limit. In Alaska, a good correspondence has been established among vegetation, the number of degree-days above 50°F, and the mean temperature of the coldest month (Hopkins, 1959). Nearly all weather stations beyond or above the limit of forest had fewer than 130 degree-days above 50°F. Hare (1950) has included temperature and precipitation effects by showing that in Labrador-Ungava the tundra-forest boundary is approximated by Thornthwaite's (1948) potential evapotranspiration index of 12.0 to 12.5 inches. A similar value may apply in northwestern Canada (Mackay, 1958, p. 100). The preceding climatically determined boundaries agree reasonably well with the tundra-taiga limit, but they do not explain it.

During the year as a whole, the tundra is the coldest region with vegetation (vascular plants) in the Northern Hemisphere, simply because most of it receives less solar radiation than areas to the south. Most weather stations experience a large annual mean monthly temperature range of about 50° to 70°F (Thomas, 1960). In areas proximate to the sea, maritime effects may be notable. February, rather than January, is often the coldest month of the year. July is normally the warmest month with mean daily temperatures below 50°F. Coastal temperatures are noticeably affected by ice conditions, the nearby presence of sea ice being conducive to low summer temperatures.

The mean annual precipitation of the tundra is usually less than fifteen inches, the maximum occurring in summer. Parts of the Queen Elizabeth Islands may receive less than five inches per annum; consequently the snowfall is extremely light. The popular image of a deep, snow-covered arctic landscape is false, because the mean annual maximum depth of snow is mostly less than twenty-five inches, except for restricted localities, such as in parts of Ungava.

The presence or absence of snowfall is a most important factor influencing plant cover, ice thickness, and ground temperatures. Once the depth of snow reaches about six inches, a further increase greatly dampens the fluctuations of the ambient air temperature at the ground surface (Krinsley, 1963). For example, when one foot of packed, drifted snow overlies sandy gravel for six months, the shift in mean annual temperature from the air-solid interface to the ground surface would be expected to be about 8° or 9°F, using Barrow, Alaska, as an illustration (Lachenbruch, 1959, p. 29).

Thus, a deep snow cover, such as occurs in parts of the taiga, makes for a sharp vertical environmental gradient (Pruitt, 1957, p. 138). In lakes which are the natural habitat of furbearing animals such as muskrat, mink, and beaver in the Mackenzie delta the role of snow depth and ice conditions is most important. A heavy autumn snowfall helps to reduce the ice thickness. In places where there is an unusually deep and persistent snow cover, as in a gully, ground temperatures tend to be above normal; but if the snow cover persists far into the warming period, subnormal temperatures may result. Snow also has many other effects, both advantageous and deleterious, besides those on temperature. Certain combination of snow load, compaction, and basal snowcreep (Mathews and Mackay, 1963), accentuated by steep slopes, mechanically damage plants. The nature of snow cover is also of importance to wildlife, particularly with grazing animals such as caribou, reindeer, and musk oxen.

The mean wind speed in northern areas differs little from that in more southern latitudes. However, the absence of trees in the tundra reduces the drag force at the earth's surface because the roughness parameter for most tundra vegetation is low, and the velocity profile near to the ground relatively steep. Plants may be subjected to excessive water depletion by exposure to drying winds, especially while the roots are encased in frozen soil and cannot absorb water (Benninghoff, 1952, p. 36). Snow crystals may severely abrade exposed rocks, when driven by high velocities at below-zero temperatures, because the hardness of ice increases markedly with a decrease in temperature (Blackwelder, 1940). Rocks such as granite may be strongly snow-blasted, and it would be surprising, therefore, if unprotected plants escaped injury. Deflation and deposition by wind contribute to changes in the soil. Gravelly pavements (lag gravels) frequently result from the winnowing action of wind. Along bare beaches, lake shores, and stream beds, swirling clouds of fine dust may be lifted up and dropped, as if from a flour sifter, onto vegetated areas. Some of the fines may lodge around the stems and leaves of plants or even smother them. In winter the fines may darken snow and ice and thus contribute to a more rapid melting by absorbing radiation. The "black ice" of the Mackenzie River is an excellent illustration of the preceding.

In the tundra and taiga the interrelated effects of low temperature, snowfall, and wind on vegetation are everywhere apparent, although not fully understood. Despite the long summer days, the annual growth rate is relatively minute, and regrowth of disturbed vegetation may be extremely slow. Climate is also responsible for the widespread occurrence of perennially frozen ground and frost action. An understanding of these climatically induced environmental factors is critical to an appreciation of the distinctive aspects of land utilization in the tundra and taiga.

Perennially Frozen Ground

Continuous permafrost (perennially frozen ground) underlies nearly all of the tundra and discontinuous permafrost is below the taiga (Figures 1 and 3). Because the thickness of permafrost is, in general, a function of the secular mean annual ground-surface temperature, depths decrease southward. At Winter Harbour, Melville Island, the depth probably exceeds 1700 feet; at Barrow, Alaska, and Resolute, Cornwallis Island, the depths are about 1300 feet; at Norman Wells, NWT, about 150 feet; and at Hay River, NWT, permafrost may range from zero to 40 feet thick. Permafrost exerts direct and indirect effects on plant and animal life in numerous ways, such as inhibiting subsurface drainage, contributing to soil instability, and maintaining a steep thermal gradient in the active layer (the layer which freezes and thaws seasonally).

Permafrost tends to form, and persist, where the "long period" mean annual ground-surface temperature is below 32°F. The mean annual ground temperature is usually a few degrees warmer than the mean annual air temperature, because of the insulation provided by snow and a complexity of other factors. Therefore the 32°F mean annual isotherm, recorded for air temperature in a standard weather screen, lies well south of the southern limit of discontinuous permafrost (Figures 2 and 3). Mean annual air temperatures of about 15° to 20°F are required in order to have continuous permafrost.

The active layer varies in thickness from a few inches to several feet, not just on a regional scale, but also on a microscale involving horizontal distances commonly of only several feet (Mackay, 1963, pp. 57-60). Commencing about September-October, freezing of the

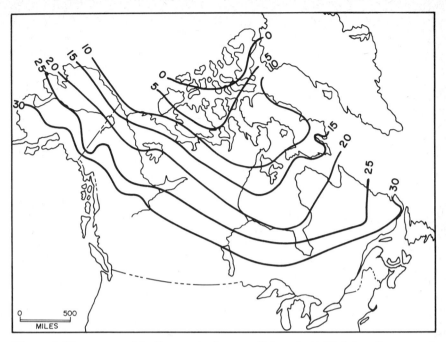

Figure 2. Mean annual isotherms in degrees Fahrenheit. Mainly after Thomas (1953).

active layer progresses downward, at times aided by slight upward freezing from the frost table. Thawing of the active layer starts in May-June, likewise from the surface downward. In most of the tundra, air temperatures may drop below 32°F during any summer month, but the ground itself may not experience a freeze-thaw cycle. For example, at Resolute, NWT, only one annual cycle was recorded at a depth of one inch in 1960 (Cook and Raiche, 1962, p. 68). The annual range at the ground surface was 127°F, at one inch 100°F, at eight inches 82°F; the air (Stevenson screen) range was only 102°F. Thus, roots a few inches below the ground may undergo only one annual freeze-thaw cycle, in contrast to multiple cycles for the exposed parts of plants. As the thickness of the unfrozen ground in the summer months rarely exceeds several feet, the vertical temperature gradient between the frost table at 32°F and the ground surface, possibly at 50°F or above, is steep. Thus, separate parts of a plant may experience a wide temperature range both diurnally and simultaneously.

Frozen ground, whether of bedrock or composed of uncon-solidated material, tends to be quite impermeable. Therefore, ground-water flow—especially in areas of continuous permafrost—

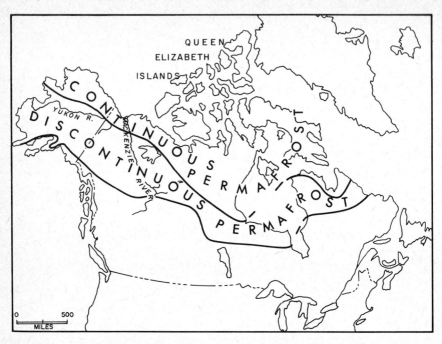

Figure 3. Permafrost boundaries, mainly after Brown (1960).

is lateral rather than vertical and is confined to the active layer, a fact of considerable consequence from the viewpoint of human utilization. Flat terrain is nearly always ill drained. Even on slopes, local undulations of the frost table are often sufficiently pronounced to form closed depressions, like the bottom of an egg carton, so that saturated soils are close to the surface. As a result, ponds, lakes, and soggy ground are common. A concomitant feature, however, is the large amount of moisture available to roots in spite of the low precipitation.

The root systems of plants are normally considered as being restricted to the thickness of the active layer, below which is the thermal hardpan of the permafrost surface. Lateral growth of roots is frequently observed above the thermal hardpan. On floodplains and alluvial fans, where sedimentation adds accretions to the ground surface, the upper permafrost table tends to rise concurrently, thereby maintaining a constant thickness of the active layer. Thus, if the rate of aggradation is rapid in terms of the life span of a plant, the deepest roots become embalmed in the upward-rising permafrost as exposed parts are buried in the active layer. Some plants, such as the white spruce, balsam poplar, and willow, may send out adventitious roots and continue growing even after the permafrost surface has risen above the initial level of the ground when growth commenced. On some Mackenzie River floodplains, the permafrost surface has been elevated more than six feet during the lifetime of spruce trees growing there. On the other hand, degradation of permafrost by a thickening of the active layer—often the result of clearing and removal of shrubs, trees, and organic matter—may cause a depression of the permafrost table, thus giving a thicker active layer, reduced thermal gradient, and permitting a longer growing season.

Although it is generally assumed that the permafrost surface forms an impenetrable thermal hardpan to roots, this may not be the case. Dadykin (1950) has reported roots of cloudberry, sedge, and horsetail penetrating into frozen ground to a depth of three feet while still remaining viable. Root penetration of oats and potatoes into frozen ground was also observed. Inasmuch as fine-grained soils, such as clays, may have a high unfrozen-water content at subfreezing temperatures while still retaining plasticity, the role of permafrost in root development presents intriguing questions.

Soils, Patterned Ground, and Microrelief

Despite the extreme variations between soils of the southern taiga and northern tundra, most localities share one or more of the following features: parent material reflecting late Wisconsin glaciation; soil instability resulting in the formation of patterned ground; and impeded drainage caused by an impermeable frozen substratum.

Most of the tundra-taiga bears the imprint of recent glaciation. In Alaska, glaciation was centred in the montane areas of the Brooks and Alaska ranges, with the lower terrain remaining unglaciated. In Canada, glaciers covered all of the taiga and most of the tundra, with the major exceptions of parts of the Queen Elizabeth Islands and the north-western cordillera. The scouring action of glaciers is still reflected in the large bare expanses of bedrock concentrated primarily in the Canadian shield (Glacial Map of Canada, 1958), the rock deserts of Figure 1. Other areas were veneered with drift of varying thickness. The relative shortness of postglacial time has limited soil development. After all, the Hudson Bay and northern Ontario region had glacier ice only 7000 to 8000 years ago (Lee, 1960). Weathering has been so slow that numerous rocky outcrops still preserve the minutiae of glacial striae. Another facet of glaciation has been the postglacial elevation of coastal strips which range in width from several miles to over a hundred miles. The coastal areas include the shores of

Ungava Bay, Hudson Bay, Foxe Basin, Gulf of Boothia, Queen Maud Gulf, Coronation Gulf, Dolphin and Union Strait, and Amundsen Gulf. On these recently emergent coasts are sited most of the settlements, harbors, and airstrips. Fortunately, the soils tend to be gravelly, well drained, and less susceptible to "damage" than those of more elevated inland regions.

The tundra, and to a lesser extent the taiga, is characterized by soil instability. The soil may be cracked, churned, and over-turned; soil material may be differentially sorted into coarse and fine particles; and all soil moves downslope by slow creep or rapid flow. These processes of soil displacement form patterned ground and distinctive microrelief features (Britton, 1957; Washburn, 1956). The link between specific genetic soils and patterned ground in northern Alaska has been so close, in fact, that two pedologists (Drew and Tedrow, 1962) have suggested a scheme for the classi-fication of soils based upon the association with patterned ground. Many distinct and diverse processes are operative in the develop-ment of patterned ground and microrelief features, but alternate freezing and thawing, with gravity-induced downslope displace-ment, are the most important. In fine-grained soils, ice segregation tends to occur so that the soil in the frozen state contains more water (ice) than it can in the unfrozen (liquid) state; i.e. the frozen soils are supersaturated. The growth of ice layers normal to the thermal gradient tends to produce frost heaving, at times accompanied by stretching or breakage of roots. The growth of ice layers helps to impart a structure to the soil. Lateral expansion from vertical ice veining may exceed 10 per cent and also damage roots. The migration of the freezing plane, whether from the surface downward or laterally from the side of a hummock, may size-sort the soil (Corte, 1963). Alternate freeze-thaw cycles do much, there-fore, to change the microhabitat of plants and animals. These cycles are confined to the active layer; consequently, most features of patterned ground and microrelief are only "skin deep." On slopes, any soil disturbance tends to cause a net downslope movement (solifluction), and where rapid, the pattern resembles frosting flowing down a cake. The overrunning of lower slopes and flats by solifluction debris frequently causes an increase in the organic content of the soil, by burial, and the blockage of drainage leading to soggy flats and elongated lakes.

Patterned ground and microrelief features in the tundra and taiga. Consequently, a disturbance to the surface may set off a active or fossil arctic patterns do occur, however, mainly in the taiga. Consequently, a disturbance to the surface may set off a train of geomorphic and biotic events. A natural or artificial disturbance which tends to accentuate the instability might be locally disastrous. In the tundra and polar desert regions, where frost boils, mudcircles, stone rings, etc., are common, regeneration ranges from slow to rapid, depending upon conditions. Mud circles have been known to begin reforming within a few years of artificial surface grading. If, however, the disturbed patterned ground does not soon reassert itself, then a habitat change may quickly result. To be specific, let us examine some results of common disturbances to terrain with ice wedges and ground ice masses. Such terrain is widely distributed in the arctic.

A characteristic feature of tundra underlain by continuous permafrost is a type of patterned ground usually referred to as an ice wedge or tundra polygon. Ice-wedge growth in these areas is active, in the sense that vertical fissures opened annually by thermal contraction in winter tend to become ice-filled. The ice wedges form a boxlike network, like the unfinished walls of a single-story house. Tens of thousands of square miles of low-lying terrain have very conspicuous ice-wedge polygons; upland areas usually have less distinct patterns. The ice wedges are particularly subject to thermal erosion and upon melting, conical hillocks—the *baidzharakhi* of Yakutia—are left protruding. Streams which follow an ice-wedge network may become beaded; coasts cut into ice-wedge terrain may have long gullies which work headward by thermal erosion along the wedges; and so forth. Thus, ice-wedge terrain is particularly susceptible to change, whether naturally or artificially induced. Disturbances are also critical in thick sections of fine-grained soils with horizontal or irregularly shaped ice masses. The ice content (percentage of ice to dry soil on a weight basis) may average 100 to 300 per cent for the upper few tens of feet of permafrost in fine-grained sediments. A natural or artificial rupture of the surface cover may therefore initiate ground ice slumps which retreat headward, mainly by melting. Coastal recession and gullying are rapid in such areas. A break in the vegetation cover or a blockage in drainage may be sufficient to create a thaw (thermokarst) topography with depressions and cave-in lakes (Hopkins, 1949; Wallace, 1948). There seems little doubt that further study of thermokarst features in North America will show that they are extremely important in causing habitat changes, as has been recognized in Russia.

In the taiga, Raup (1951) has pointed out that forests on actively moving slopes are more or less unstable, root systems may be torn loose from their intimate soil contacts, and mortality is high. Such forests are prone to disturbances, both natural and artificial. The frequent sight of tilted or drunken trees is nearly a sure sign of such a disturbance.

As stressed in the discussion of permafrost, much of the arctic and subarctic terrain is ill drained, and soil development is impeded. Some areas are well drained, however, and there mature soils may develop (Tedrow, Drew, Hill, and Douglas, 1958). Interestingly enough, where well-drained soils occur in the arctic islands, some are dry desertlike in appearance, at times with salts accumulated at the surface, giving the polar desert of Figure 1 (Tedrow and Douglas, 1964).

Man's activities can and do alter the interrelated elements of soil—patterned ground—microrelief. The establishment of a summer campsite for one or more seasons leaves its mark by disturbed vegetation, which in abandoned Eskimo sites is usually recognizable by a more luxuriant growth than in nearby tundra areas (Wiggins and Thomas, 1962, p. 27). Frequent vehicular traffic, if unconfined to a road, may slice up the tundra with remarkable rapidity, especially where track or wheel furrows concentrate drainage into flow channels. A footpath, used for only one season, may persist virtually unchanged for decades. Regrowth of vegetation is so gradual that a disturbance, such as forest cutting, may be perpetuated nearly unchanged for a century. For instance, the Hudson's Bay Company established Fort Anderson (on the Anderson River, 150 miles east of Inuvik, NWT) in 1861 and abandoned it only five years later in 1866. In the intervening century, revegetation has been minimal. Most of the vegetation is still composed of grasses with a few willows. The forest clearing still preserves the original outlines of the stockade. Inevitably such disturbances will increase as man's activities spread; whether they will be harmful in the aggregate is quite another issue.

The Years Ahead

Nearly everyone who has viewed the tundra and taiga from the air or the ground is more likely to ponder on how these arctic and subarctic lands can assure adequate economic support for the existing population, rather than to question why it isn't measurably larger. In our speculating on future habitat changes—the years ahead—for man and other living creatures, numerous questions arise. Some questions are answerable, but most are not. The foremost question is undoubtedly climatic amelioration, because it is the hostile climate which inhibits much development. If the climate cannot be ameliorated, can the pioneer fringe of settlement be moved northward appreciably? If settlement does push farther into the taiga, and small communities (e.g. mining) become established in the tundra, what impacts will there be from land clearing, forest fires, road construction, dam building, hunting, fishing, and tourism?

Should an effort be made to supplant caribou with reindeer and musk oxen? Can the southern part of the treeless tundra be treed (Tikhomirov, 1962)? If it can, would there be an advantage in trying to extend the taiga northward, if even only for a few miles? Can improved long-range weather forecasts, satellite photography, and remote sensors make it possible to predict and follow ice and open-water conditions and thus aid in transportation and the utilization of land, marine, and ocean-floor resources?

Climatic amelioration

Climatic changes of first magnitude have taken place in the past 10,000± 2000 years since the glaciers receded from most of the tundra and taiga. Following the climatic optimum (hypsithermal) of about 5000 years ago, there have been many minor climatic fluctuations, such as the little climatic optimum, 1000-1300 A.D., and little ice age, 1550-1850 A.D. (Bryson and Julian, 1963; Dansereau, 1953). Instrumental records of temperatures in the tundra and taiga are of only short duration, but climatic trends may be inferred by other means, such as freeze-up and breakup records for lakes and rivers. For example, ice records for the Hayes and Churchill rivers, which empty into Hudson Bay, show marked fluctuations since the early 1700s. For the arctic, commencing in about 1920, instrumental records show a noticeable temperature rise until the 1940s, the difference in five-year annual mean temperatures between 1880 and 1940 being roughly 4°F (Callendar, 1961; Mitchell, 1963). However, there is no evidence of trends from historic records (e.g. Wing, 1951) to suggest that the climate in fifty or a hundred years will be warmer or colder than at present, and by how much.

In spite of no positive evidence to favor either a warming or cooling trend, biotic boundaries are not static. Because the tundra-taiga environments are in a youthful stage, there may be a considerable lag in response to past climatic changes. In many places in Alaska at present the forest boundaries are mobile migration fronts rather than static boundaries (Griggs, 1934, p. 92; Raup, 1941, p. 224). On the east coast of Hudson Bay, "Trees are invading tundra areas as soil develops . . . given sufficient time, with climate held constant, forest will occupy the entire area as soils of organic and inorganic nature develop. . . ." (Maar, 1948, pp. 143-44). Tikhomirov (1960) reports a northward and vertical expansion into the Russian tundra. Even some species of birds, whose mobility seems unlimited, are still immigrating northward (Tuck, 1964). Thus, if present climatic conditions remain constant, a low northward encroachment of the taiga into the tundra may continue. If there were a warming trend, the shift should be both accentuated and accelerated. Locally, however, the tundra may replace the taiga along the tree line (personal communication, V. J. Krajina) through the establishment of a sphagnum-moss ground cover, a resulting shallowing of the active layer, and an eventual favoring of a tundra succession.

If there is no evidence suggestive of climatic warming, the question naturally arises as to whether climate can be modified artificially on a macro (regional) or micro (local) scale. Although numerous field experiments have been carried out on weather modification, these have primarily involved rainmaking over a relatively small area, unfortunately with disappointing results (Workman, 1962). The outlook for large-scale weather modification is not, at present, encouraging. The issue can, however, be approached by other means. For example, the unusual appearance of capelin and Atlantic cod in the Ungava Bay area in the 1950s was probably due to a change in the marine climate (Dunbar, 1962). Might it then be possible to alter hydrographic patterns in the arctic to achieve similar desirable ends?

Newspapers have, at times, devoted attention to a "scheme" for a Bering Strait dam to warm the arctic. Is it feasible from an engineering viewpoint? Would it be economical? What effects would such a dam have on arctic circulation either with or without pumping of water? Would there be an amelioration of the Arctic Ocean climate? Dunbar (1962, p. 134) has partially answered these questions: "At all events, the main issue is clear: the damming of Bering Strait, without any pumping of water in either direction, would alter the marine climate of the coastal eastern arctic quite significantly, to an extent which at present can be estimated only within wide limits." Dunbar also points out that to pump the cold arctic layer off the Arctic Ocean, with the purpose of bringing warmer water to the surface, would probably take several tens of *thousands* of years! And if there were an ice-free open Arctic Ocean, would this, in turn, bring about an ice age again (Ewing and Donn, 1961)? Would a smaller hydrographic change, such as the proposed Rampart Dam on the Yukon River, with its 10,850-square-mile lake (Cooke, 1964), affect the local climate? An answer might be suggested by examining the areas adjacent to Great Bear and Great Slave lakes. On balance, the weight of evidence is now against any regional amelioration of climate by artificial means.

The local microclimate can easily be altered, but whether it would be desirable and economical is another matter. Snowmelt may be accelerated by appropriate artificial dusting (Arnold, 1961) or inhibited by artificial insulation. Snow fences, the use of trees as snow breaks, and other means similar to dune control in arid areas can increase or decrease the snow cover. Powdered coal, sprinkled over the ground, may increase soil temperatures by tapping solar energy (Black, 1963). Clearing, cultivation, and drainage may profoundly modify the energy exchange at the ground surface. Methods such as the above may be suitable for changing the local microclimate but are impractical, at present, for any large area.

Any pronounced local climatic warming, if sustained for many decades, would have major consequences on the southern distribution of discontinuous permafrost. As an approximation, under equilibrium conditions the thickness of permafrost is equal to the product of the geothermal gradient and the number of degrees that the mean annual ground-surface temperature is below freezing. Thus, if the geothermal gradient is 1°F per 100 feet, and the mean ground-surface temperature is 31°F, the expected thickness of permafrost is 100 feet. Therefore, if the mean annual ground-surface temperature rises over several decades from slightly below 32°F to slightly above, the discontinuous permafrost, which is already thin, will degrade and may disappear. Even if a zone of relic permafrost still remains at depth, so that winter freezing fails to reach it, drainage conditions should normally improve. In certain marginal areas, there is no reason why complete degradation of permafrost could not be achieved artificially by altering the thermal balance at the ground surface. In areas underlain by continuous permafrost, sustained secular climatic changes of great magnitude would be required to cause appreciable degradation. Thus, the critical areas of permafrost aggradation and degradation are in the southern taiga, not the tundra.

Fires

Forest fires, whether ignited by lightning or by man, have devastated thousands of square miles. Even the treeless tundra has not escaped from fires; some peaty terrain has burnt or smoldered for months. In forested parts of Yukon Territory and Alaska, Hansen (1953) estimates that fire has been more destructive in the past half century than during the rest of postglacial or even Pleistocene times. Sufficiently large areas have been burnt over in the Mackenzie Valley that they are mapped on the hydrographic charts. To cite a specific example, in 1954 an area of 820 square miles of the reindeer winter range area, east of the Mackenzie delta, was 70 to 80 per cent burned and rendered useless for grazing (Cody, 1964, p. 9; Mackay, 1963, p. 168). Ten years later, the lichen flora had not recovered sufficiently to allow reindeer to graze. In Labrador-Ungava, Hare (1959) has mapped burned areas as one of the main cover types. In the "taiga" part of Labrador-Ungava, over 10,000 square miles are shown as burned areas.

The direct consequences of fires are several. There is, of course, the destruction of standing vegetation, and thus the immediate loss of a resource which may not be renewable for generations; in the Mackenzie delta area, 500-year-old spruce grow to the tree line. Frequently, a forest fire consumes organic matter in the upper part of the soil, rendering it sterile for revegetation. A thickening of the active layer is usual as an aftermath to a fire, and if the ice content of the ground is high, thawing tends to produce hummocks, drunken trees, miniature thermokarst features, local ponding, and gullying. It is abundantly clear that control and prevention of fires is necessary in the taiga, and to a much lesser degree, in the tundra. As northern areas become more accessible to hunters, fishermen, tourists, and others, the risk of fire increases.

Soil productivity

Barring an unforeseen breakthrough in agricultural technology, it is most unlikely that outdoor agriculture, beyond the local vegetable garden, will be of consequence in the tundra. Even in the taiga, the future of agriculture is circumscribed both in Alaska and Canada (Underhill, 1959; Bladen, 1962; *Resources for Tomorrow; Science in Alaska*). "When land needs become critical in North America, it is possible that considerably more than a million acres may be farmed in Alaska" (Mick, 1957, p. 107), the number of farms being estimated at about 5000 or 6000 only. In Canada, "it appears that any future agricultural development will be largely limited to the valleys of the Yukon and Mackenzie river systems in the northwest. Here more than a million acres of suitable soil for agriculture may be found." (Nowosad and Leahey, 1960, p. 50) But the occurrence of arable soils does not necessarily mean that the climate is suitable for crops or that they will ripen. Restrictions on agriculture are imposed by the physical environment compounded by a low demand for agricultural produce, excessive costs of production, and continually tightening competition from the southern areas as transportation facilities improve.

The long photoperiod of the subarctic partially explains some of the surprising productivity observed at a few favorable sites, even in areas of continuous permafrost. When land is cleared, the removal of the natural vegetation cover and later cultivation alter the energy exchange at the ground surface, usually toward a net heat gain. For example, in June, 1956, an experimental garden of the Department of Agriculture was started at Inuvik, NWT, at the taiga limit. The active layer, which was about eighteen to twenty-four inches thick in 1956 prior to clearing, has thickened to six feet. Good vegetable crops have been obtained. At nearby Aklavik, vegetables have been raised successfully for several decades. Vegetables have been grown near Fort Chimo, Quebec, in a permafrost area, in both greenhouses and in the open garden.

Problems may arise, however, in the artificial depression of the active layer by cultivation, especially where the ground-ice content is high. Thawing and pitting may result as has been observed in farmlands near Fairbanks, Alaska (Rockie, 1942). In the Yukon Territory and Mackenzie Valley of Canada, much of the potentially arable land has fine-grained soils which probably have a high ice content. Particular caution is required in the utilization of such thermokarst-susceptible soils.

Future developments in agriculture are likely to be in the taiga (subarctic) and will conform to historic patterns. The long hours of summer insolation, advances in agricultural technology, and the demand of local urban communities may stimulate agriculture on a small scale. However, even the most optimistic northern protagonist can hardly envisage the taiga, much less the tundra, as a granary for the future.

Wildlife and man

Although the human population of the tundra and taiga was sparse in prehistory, is still sparse, and is likely to remain so except for special community developments (e.g. mining), man has not played a passive role in affecting the biotic environment. The killing of game to supply whaling ships of the late nineteenth and early twentieth centuries, the introduction of firearms, and the growth of a trapping economy greatly reduced the caribou population and nearly decimated the musk oxen. The caribou population of northern Canada has declined from an estimated 1,750,000 for 1900 to 250,000 at present (Banfield, 1951, 1964). Only stringent protective measures since 1917 have allowed the musk oxen to multiply to the present 10,000 and of these few, most are in the arctic islands.

The exigency for wise use of the wildlife reserve will intensify as arctic and subarctic lands become more accessible. The supply of wildlife, whether migratory fowl, barren-ground caribou, musk oxen, polar bear, grizzly bear, or even fish, is not inexhaustible and easily renewable, as experience has shown. Some uses are competitive. Is it preferable to kill game animals for dog food to support a trapping economy or to support a tourist industry? Some uses might be improvements, such as the domestication of reindeer and musk oxen. These are research problems requiring further investigation.

Conclusions

On the regional scale, low summer temperatures, glaciation, and the short span of postglacial time are three major factors which contribute toward the treelessness of the tundra and the harshness of the taiga. Although significant climatic fluctuations have occurred in the past few centuries, there is no evidence favoring either a warming or a cooling trend in the years ahead. If there is no likelihood of a long-term warming trend, can it be induced economically on a regional scale by artificial means? The present answer is no. However, the local microclimate in which plants live—both above and below the ground—is capable of considerable amelioration through modification of the snow cover, clearing, burning, drainage, use of additives and mulches, etc. Here lies the best possibility for microhabitat amelioration.

The widespread distribution of perenially frozen ground (permafrost) is reflected in soil types, patterned ground, microrelief, and ice segregation. Seasonal freezing and thawing of the active layer above the impermeable permafrost leads to soil instability, gravity-induced down-slope movement, and impeded drainage. Because the ice content tends to be low in coarse-textured soils and high in fine-textured ones, coarse-grained soils are best for construction purposes, whereas fine-grained soils texturally ideal for agriculture are also frost-susceptible and therefore potentially damaging to plants.

There is no present prospect for agriculture in the tundra and a poor outlook for it in the taiga. However, local farms and vegetable gardens may be established adjacent to new mining, transport, and other settlements. With improving accessibility, the total effects of forest fire and local soil disturbance will be magnified, thus leading to large-scale habitat changes in sparsely settled areas. The resource uses of wildlife in the tundra and taiga are posing the problem of alternative choices. Caribou or reindeer? A trapping or tourist economy? In brief, despite the sparseness of human population in the tundra and taiga, and the questionable likelihood of appreciable augmentation, the habitats are still under the influence of man.

References

Arnold, K. C., "An Investigation into Methods of Accelerating the Melting of Ice and Snow by Artificial Dusting", in G. O. Raasch, ed., *Geology of the Arctic*, Vol. II, Univ. Toronto Press, Toronto (1961), pp. 989-1013.

Banfield, A. W. F., "The Barren-Ground Caribou", *Dept. Res. and Develop.*, (1954); "Specially the Caribou" in I. N. Smith, ed., *The Unbelievable Land*, Dept. Northern Affairs and Nat. Res., Ottawa (1964), pp. 25-28.

Benninghoff, W. S., "Interaction of Vegetation and Soil Frost Phenomena", *Arctic 5* (1952), pp. 34-44.

Black, J. F., "Weather Control: Use of Asphalt Coatings to Tap Solar Energy", *Sci.* 139 (1963), pp. 226-27.

Blackwelder, E., "The Hardness of Ice", *Amer. J. Sci.* 238 (1940), pp. 61-62.

Bladen, V. W., ed., *Canadian Population and Northern Colonization*, Univ. Toronto Press, Toronto (1962).

Britton, M. E., "Vegetation of the Arctic Tundra", *Arctic Biol.*, 18th Ann. Biol. Colloquium, Oreg. State Col., Corvallis, Oreg., (1957), pp. 26-61.

Brown, R. J. E., "The Distribution of Permafrost and Its Relation to Air Temperature in Canada and the USSR", *Arctic 13* (1960), pp. 163-77.

Bryson, R. A., and Julian, P. R., eds., Proceedings of the Conference on the Climate of the Eleventh and Sixteenth Centuries, Aspen, Colo. June 16-24, 1962, Notes 63-1., Nat. Ctr. for Atmos. Res., Boulder, Colo., NCAR Tech., (1963).

Callendar, G. S., "Temperature Fluctuations and Trends over the Earth", *Q.J. Royal Meteorol. Soc.* 87 (1961), pp. 1-12.

Cody, W. J., "Reindeer Range Survey, 1957 and 1963", Plant Research Inst., Can. Dept. Agric., Ctr. Exper. Farm, Ottawa, March 23 (1964).

Cook, F. A., and Raiche, V. G., "Freeze-thaw Cycles at Resolute, N.W.T." *Geog. Bul. 18* (1962), pp. 64-78.

Cooke, A., "The Rampart Dam Proposal for Yukon River", *Polar Rec. 12*, (1964), pp. 277-80.

Corte, A. W., "Vertical Migration of Particles in Front of a Moving Freezing Plane", *U.S. Army Cold Regs. Res. and Eng. Lab.*, Res. Rept. 105 (1963).

Dadykin, V. P., "On the Biological Peculiarities of the Plants of Cold Soils", in Russian (1950), *Priroda 5*, pp. 21-29, Abstr. in *Arctic Bibl. 5* (1955), pp. 182-83.

Dansereau, P., "The Postglacial Pine Period", *Trans. Royal Soc. Can.*, 3rd Ser., sec. 5, 47 (1953), pp. 23-38.

Drew, J. W., and J. C. G. Tedrow, "Arctic Soil Classification and Patterned Ground", *Arctic 15* (1962), pp. 109-16.

Dunbar, M. J., "The Living Resources of Northern Canada", in V. W. Bladen, ed., *Canadian Population and Northern Colonization*, Univ. Toronto Press, Toronto (1962), pp. 125-35.

Ewing, M., and W. L. Doon, "Pleistocene Climatic Changes", in G. O. Raasch, ed., *Geology of the Arctic*, Vol. II, Univ. Toronto Press, Toronto (1961), pp. 931-41.

Gates, D. M., *Energy Exchange in the Biosphere*, Harper, New York (1962).

Glacial Map of Canada, Geol. Assn. Can. (1958).

Halliday, W. E. D., "A Forest Classification for Canada", Dept. Mines and Res., Ottawa, *Dom. Forest Serv. Bul. 89* (1937).

Hansen, H. P., "Postglacial Forests in the Yukon Territory and Alaska", *Amer. J. Sci. 251* (1953), pp. 505-42.

Hare, F. K., "Climate and Zonal Divisions of the Boreal Forest Formation in Eastern Canada", *Geog. Rev. 40* (1950), pp. 615-35; "A Photo-reconnaissance Survey of Labrador-Ungava", *Geog. Br., Ottawa, Mem. 6*, (1959).

Hopkins, D. M., "Thaw Lakes and Thaw Sinks in the Imuruk Lakes Area, Seward Peninsula, Alaska", *J. Geol. 57* (1949), pp. 119-31; "Some Characteristics of the Climate in Forest and Tundra Regions in Alaska", *Arctic 12* (1959), pp. 215-20.

Hustich, I., "The Boreal Limits of Conifers", *Arctic 6* (1953), pp. 149-62.

Krinsley, D. B., "Influence of Snow Cover on Frost Penetration", *U.S. Geol. Surv. Prof. Pap. 475-B*, Art. 38 (1963), B144-B147.

Lachenbruch, A. H., "Periodic Heat Flow in a Stratified Medium with Application to Permafrost Problems", *U.S. Geol. Surv. Bul. 1083-A*, (1959).

Lee, H. A., "Late Glacial and Postglacial Hudson Bay Sea Episode", *Sci. 131* (1960), pp. 1609-10.

Mackay, J. R., "The Anderson River Map-area, N.W.T.", *Geog. Br. Ottawa, Mem. 5* (1958); "The Mackenzie Delta Area, N.W.T.", *Geog. Br., Ottawa, Mem. 8*, (1963).

Marr, J. W., "Ecology of the Forest-tundra Ecotone on the East Coast of Hudson Bay", *Ecol. Monogs. 18* (1948), pp. 117-44.

Marsden, M., "Arctic Contrasts: Canada and Russia in the Far North", *Intern. J. 14* (1958), pp. 33-41, Toronto.

Mathews, W. H., and J. R. Mackay, "Snowcreep Studies, Mount Seymour, B.C.: A Preliminary Field Investigation", *Geog. Bul. 20* (1963), pp. 58-75.

Mick, A., "Arctic and Subarctic Alaska", *Arctic Biol.*, Ann. Biol. Colloquium, Oreg. State Col., Corvallis, Oreg., (1957), pp. 100-109.

Mitchell, Fr., J. M., "On the World-wide Pattern of Secular Temperature Change" in *Changes of Climate, Proc. Rome Symp.*, UNESCO and World Meteorol. Org., (1963), pp. 161-81.

Nordenskjöld, O., and L. Mecking, "The Geography of the Polar Regions", *Am. Geog. Soc. Sp. Pub. 8* (1928).

Nowosad, F. S. and A. Leahey, "Soils of the Arctic and Sub-arctic Regions of Canada", *Agric. Inst. Rev. 15* (Mar.-Apr.), (1960), pp. 48-50.

Polunin, N., *Circumpolar Arctic Flora*, Oxford Univ. Press, Oxford (1959).

Pruitt, W. O., Jr., "Observations on the Bioclimate of Some Taiga Mammals", *Arctic 10* (1957), pp. 131-38.

Raup, H. M., "Botanical Problems in Boreal America", *Bot. Rev. 7* (1941), pp. 147-248; "Vegetation and Cryoplanation", *Ohio J. Sci. 51* (1951), pp. 105-16.

Resources for Tomorrow, Vols. I and II, Dept. Northern Affairs and Nat. Res., Ottawa, (1961).

Rockie, W. A., "Pitting on Alaska Farm Lands a New Erosion Problem", *Geog. Rev. 32*, (1942), pp. 128-34.

Rowe, J. S., "Forest Regions of Canada", *Forest Br. Bul. 123*, Dept. Northern Affairs and Nat. Res., Ottawa (1959).

Science in Alaska, Alaska Div., Amer. Assn. Adv. Sci. Annual Proceedings.

Sigafoos, R. S., "Vegetation of Northwestern North America, as an Aid in Interpretation of Geologic Data", *U.S. Geol. Surv. Bull. 1061E*, (1958), pp. 165-85.

Sjors, H., "Amphi-Atlantic Zonation, Nemoral to Arctic", in A. and D. Love, eds., *North Atlantic Biota and Their History*, Pergamon, Oxford, (1963), pp. 109-25.

Tedrow, J. C. F., J. V. Drew, D. E. Hill and L. A. Douglas, "Major Soils of the Arctic Slope of Alaska", *J. Soil Sci. 9* (1958), pp. 33-45.

Thomas, M. K., *Climatological Atlas of Canada*, Nat. Res. Council, Ottawa, (1953); "Canadian Arctic Temperatures", Dept. Transp., Canada, Meteorol. Br., CIR-334, CLI-24, May 9 (1960).

Thornthwaite, C. W., "An Approach Toward a Rational Classification of Climate", *Geog. Rev. 38* (1943), pp. 55-94.

Tikhomirov, B. A., "Phytogeographical Investigations of the Tundra Vegetation in the Soviet Union", *Can. J. Bot. 38* (1960), pp. 815-32; "The Treelessness of the Tundra", *Polar Rec. 11* (1962), pp. 24-30.

Tuck, L. M., "Birds in the Arctic", in I. N. Smith, ed., *The Unbelievable Land*, Dept. Northern Affairs and Nat. Res., Ottawa (1964), pp. 29-33.

Underhill, F. H., ed., *The Canadian Northwest: Its Potentialities*, Univ. Toronto Press, Toronto (1959).

Wallace, R. E., "Cave-in Lakes in the Nebesna, Chisana, and Tanana River Valleys, Eastern Alaska," *J. Geol. 56* (1948), pp. 171-81.

Washburn, A. L., "Classification of Patterned Ground and a Review of Suggested Origins", *Bul. Geol. Soc. Amer. 67* (1956), pp. 823-66.

Wiggins, I. L., and J. H. Thomas, *A Flora of the Alaskan Arctic Slope*, Univ. Toronto Press, Toronto (1962).

Wing, L. W., "Cyclic Trends in Arctic Seasons", *J. Cycle Res. 1* (1951), pp. 20-25.

25

The Quality of the Environment: A Review

I. Burton

The first recommendation of the Environmental Pollution Panel of the President's Science Advisory Committee reads: "The public should come to recognize individual rights to quality of living, as expressed by absence of pollution, as it has come to recognize rights to education, to economic advance, and the public recreation."[1] Most of the Panel's 104 recommendations are more technical, but it seems significant that a group of natural scientists should wish to emphasize so clearly that the problem of environmental quality is political and social as well as technical. Although the Panel gave pride of place to "individual rights to quality of living, as expressed by absence of pollution," it failed to follow with strong recommendations on how these rights are to be secured. For example, on automobiles as a source of air pollution the Panel has five recommendations. These call for (1) recognition of "the special importance of the automobile as a source of pollution problems," (2) "registration before use" of "the addition to motor fuels of substances which are not eliminated by the combustion process," (3) intensification of "surveillance of body burdens of lead and trends of lead in air, water and food," (4) a pilot survey and studies "to assess the significant methods of entry and the accumulation of lead from vehicle exhausts in various soils and

Reprinted from *Geographical Review*, Vol. LVIII (1968), pp. 472-81. Copyrighted by the American Geographical Society of New York.

[1] "Restoring the Quality of Our Environment", *Report of the Environmental Pollution Panel of the President's Science Advisory Committee*, Washington, D.C. (1965), p. 16.

plants," and (5) exertion of "every effort to stimulate industry to develop and demonstrate means of powering automobiles and trucks that will not produce noxious effects." The Panel could have further recommended that the California regulations on automobile exhausts be adopted nationally. Instead they advised: "We must follow carefully the results of California's imposition of special regulations, and be prepared to extend those that prove effective to other smog-ridden localities." Such caution might be thought to reflect deference to the sensibilities of the automobile industry. Another way to put it is to say that "imposition of special regulations" to protect "individual rights to quality of living" is scarcely possible unless the public recognizes such rights and demands that they be protected.

Another reason for the Panel's cautious position is the hiatus between the recognition of a right in principle and the detailed specification of what that right entails. This is well exemplified by the general agreement that pollution should be controlled and curtailed and the almost total lack of agreement on appropriate standards. A comparison with the right to education is instructive. This right has long been recognized, but there is almost constant debate about what it entails, and there is continual redefinition not only for some under-privileged minority groups but also for the majority of white middle-class Americans.

Fundamental Issues

The right to a high-quality environment is only just in course of establishment, and the fundamental issues are now being identified. What are the criteria for a good-quality environment? In what ways will opinion continue to change about the desirable characteristics of environment? Who now has access to a good environment, and who is denied access? Who pays, and who should pay, for preserving or creating good environments? What is an appropriate division of responsibilities between the public and private sectors? How much public money should be spent, and in what ways should it be used? Is there actually danger to public health? Do people really need contact with nature to alleviate the stresses of city life? In what way is environment connected with mental health? How can the benefits of environmental improvements be measured and paid for?

These questions are important, and there is a growing movement to try to provide some answers. One essential point of departure is the need for an agreement on definitions of environments of different kinds. For many specialists working on problems of environmental quality the term "environment" refers to nature or to ecosystems. It covers land, air, water, flora, and fauna and their interactions both "natural" and as managed or modified by man. This is not an adequate definition, however, because the environment may also be taken to include many products of human activity. Automobile exhausts increase the carbon monoxide and sulphur dioxide content of the atmosphere. Human and other wastes change the quality of the water in lakes that are used for recreation. And just as man changes the quality of the environment by his presence in it, so he is in turn penetrated by the environment. Food crops are obviously part of the environment and perhaps remain so after ingestion. The microscopic fauna of the gastrointestinal tract are also presumably part of the environment.

Planners and architects often broaden the definition of environment to include anything physical or tangible and external to man, of whatever origin. Thus buildings and streets constitute a large part of the urban environment, and the size, shape, color, and furnishings of a room are viewed by some as possibly exerting environmental influence on the social activities they surround. If the environment includes (as some would prefer) everything that affects the physical and mental health of the individual, then clearly other persons, their numbers and characteristics, constitute an environment of a social kind. Since social processes are intimately linked with attitudes and states of mind, then environment must extend to include psychic phenomena as well.

The breadth and complexity of the concept of environment are apparent. There is no knowledge or area of specialization that is not intimately concerned with environment. It may be seriously asked, therefore, if the concept is too broad to have any operational value. Like the term "mankind" the term "environment" signifies a concept but does not convey much information. Nevertheless, the concept of environment and the problems it implies have achieved such vogue that universities all over North America are reorganizing to accommodate it. New programs are being established with the word "environmental" being used to describe architecture, archeology, behavior, design, economics, engineering, geology, health, planning, pollution, psychology, and sociology. There seems to be no school of environmental law at present, but it can be only a matter of time before one appears.

Although the academic problems of definition and scope remain unresolved, the current concern with environmental quality has clear justification in that a series of problems exist that are of public interest and are recognized as important political issues, actual or potential. The problems are difficult to resolve and require the cooperation of many experts from different disciplines. The activity in the universities, therefore, is certainly needed from a practical point of view.

The broad social context of the concern about environmental quality has been propounded from a committed viewpoint by social philosophers and moralists such as John Kenneth Galbraith[2] and Paul Goodman.[3] Galbraith was one of the first to draw attention, in 1958, to the contrast between private affluence and public squalor. His statement was quickly followed by reports from Resources for the Future, Inc.,[4] which helped to allay fears about the long-run availability of natural-resource commodities and pointed to environmental quality as a problem of considerable emergency and social importance. These views struck a responsive chord in the new Kennedy administration of 1960, and political action was spurred by the controversy aroused by such books as Rachel Carson's "Silent Spring."[5] Critics agreed that the case was overstated, but overstatement may have been a justified and legitimate way of arousing public concern. New legislation certainly resulted in the first half of the 1960's on air and water pollution, pesticides, landscape pollution and desecration, and highway beautification. In 1965 a White House Conference on Natural Beauty was held.[6] If the pace of innovation has slowed since then it is not because problems have been solved or are less widely recognized, but because of more pressing preoccupations elsewhere. Once these are settled, a renewed attack on environmental-quality problems seems likely.

The political and legislative action was in some respects ahead of available knowledge and understanding, even though it may have lagged behind public opinion. Public concern continues to be

---

[2] John Kenneth Galbraith, *The Affluent Society,* Boston (1958). See also his "The New Industrial State", Boston, (1967).

[3] Paul Goodman, "Like a Conquered Province: The Moral Ambiguity of America", *The Massey Lectures,* 6th Ser., Toronto (1966).

[4] Neal Potter and Francis T. Christy, Jr., Trends in Natural Resource Commodities, Baltimore (1962); Harold J. Barnett and Chandler Morse, Scarcity and Growth: The Economics of Natural Resource Availability, Baltimore, (1963); Hans H. Landsberg, Leonard L. Fischman and Joseph L. Fisher, "Resources in America's Future", Patterns of Requirements and Availabilities 1960-2000, Baltimore (1963).

[5] Rachel Carson, *Silent Spring,* Boston (1962).

[6] "Beauty for America", *Proceedings of the White House Conference on Natural Beauty,* Washington, D.C., (1965).

stimulated by polemical statements about the deteriorating environment. Recent examples include Rienow and Rienow's "Moment in the Sun,"[7] a book that protests the neglect of ecological principles. A brief quotation gives the flavor of the authors' approach: "The redwoods are being slashed into defenseless patches, the mighty Niagara's roar is cut in half, the Grand Canyon has been measured for hydroelectric harness, the Everglades has been drained—then callously flooded—for commercial advantage and its wildlife rots in the receding slime." In the authors' view "already we have passed our zenith," and the moment in the sun will soon pass unless we can control population and accept "a totally new code of values . . . [that will] bring us into equilibrium with our environment." A similar book is Dasmann's "The Destruction of California";[8] doubtless others will continue to appear.

Much of this writing is reminiscent of the conservationist school, which is now reorganizing around the theme of environmental quality. The gloomy forebodings and the shrill cries of protest from authors like Rachel Carson and Raymond Dasmann are countered by the proponents of the technological panacea or the "technological fix" as described by Weinberg.[9] In extreme form the technological optimists are, in their way, no less polemical than the environmental pessimists. A recent example is "The Environment Game," by Nigel Calder.[10] This flight of imagination foresees a world populated by nine billion persons in which agriculture will be a thing of the past. People will be living in cities built on sea or ice, and land will be restored to its natural state. Food requirements will be met entirely by manufacturing processes located in the cities, and the encircling wilderness will be crowded with enlightened mankind hunting animals with crossbows for sport. Such social-science fiction is totally unrealistic or uninformed about social and political processes, but it helps to define the opposite end of the spectrum from the position that all is (almost) lost.

---

[7] Robert Rienow and Leona Train Rienow, "Moment in the Sun", *A Report on the Deteriorating Quality of the American Environment*, New York (1967), references on pp. 123 and 222.

[8] Raymond F. Dasmann, *The Destruction of California*, New York and London (1965). See also Peter Blake, *God's Own Junkyard*, New York, Chicago, San Francisco, (1964), and Henry Still, *The Dirty Animal*, New York (1967).

[9] Alvin Weinberg, "Can Technology Replace Social Engineering?", *Bull. of the Atomic Scientists*, Vol. XXII, December (1966), pp. 6-10.

[10] Nigel Calder, *The Environment Game*, London (1967) (published in the United States under the title *Eden Was No Garden*, New York, (1967).)

Good policies are not likely to emerge from such debates. Morally and ideologically neutral research is needed in which men try to approach the tendentious issues of environmental quality with objectivity and dispassion. Once such a stance has been adopted, broad pronouncements give way to more cautious and reflective opinions; most individuals can speak with authority on only a small segment of the spectrum. The books of a more scientific nature that have appeared in the last few years are therefore commonly multiple-author collections of papers, which, though they frequently lack coherence, provide useful statements.

Ecology and Economics

One of the more outstanding symposium volumes is "Future Environments of North America,"[11] a compilation of the proceedings of a conference held in 1965. The thirty-four papers, together with transcripts of some lively and entertaining discussions, provide fascinating reading, especially on the interrelation between economics and ecology. Two concerns are expressed repeatedly. One is that ecological knowledge is fundamentally weak and is unable to predict satisfactorily the changes in ecosystems that are likely to result from specific human interventions. The same, of course, could be said about much of geography. Could geomorphologists, for example, provide a precise statement of the physiographic consequences of a 15 percent increase in average annual rainfall, which might well be achieved through weather modification? It thus appears that the role of the ecologists often is to give warning about the possibility of serious consequences of human intervention in the environment and to stress the unpredictable and possibly disastrous nature of such consequences without being able to attach any very precise estimate of their probability. The second major concern of the volume is the inadequacy of market-model economic theory to cope with the externalities and intangibles of environmental quality. The latter difficulty continues to attract the attention of economists.

A general statement on the economic approach has been prepared by Herfindahl and Kneese,[12] of Resources for the Future. Their book is subtitled "An Economic Approach to Some Problems in Using Land, Water, and Air," and in it they make strong claims

---

[11] F. Fraser Darling and John P. Milton, ed., *Future Environments of North America,* Garden City, N.Y., (1966).
[12] Orris C. Herfindahl and Allen V. Kneese, Quality of the Environment: An Economic Approach to Some Problems in Using Land, Water, and Air, Washington, D.C., (1965).

for economics. They consider, for example, that "the discipline of economics is central to progress on these problems, for it is economics alone that can formulate these problems in the terms to which they must finally be reduced, namely the balancing of our varied desires in these matters against the costs of satisfying them in various degrees." It is hard to take the authors seriously, and perhaps one should not give them that satisfaction. As they well know, it is not possible to reduce these problems to economic terms satisfactorily at the present time, and it may never be possible. Even if it were, a false underlying assumption is implied, namely that what is best in economic terms is necessarily best in all other ways also. In this view man lives and works to serve the economy and not vice versa. Many students of environmental quality, including ecologists, regard their work as an effort to remove such assumptions and value judgments from a dominant position in the American way of life.

The Herfindahl and Kneese book does contain a good nontechnical statement of the problem of externalities. The crux of the matter is the need "to take proper account of all the costs and benefits" when making decisions. There is also a discussion of the physical, chemical, and biological aspects of pollution, useful for the social scientist unfamiliar with BOD and CO_2. The authors' main interest is to see all problems "in the terms to which they must finally be reduced," and in practice this simply means dollars and cents. The most desirable situation imaginable, in their view, would be that the invisible hand of the market mechanism would resolve all the allocation problems without anybody's needing to worry. The fact that it does not is regretted as "market-failure" and as "less-than-perfect operation of the economy." Faced with this rather deplorable situation, economists should attempt to measure all the benefits and costs. "The question in each case is what a rational consumer or producer would be willing to pay in order to avoid the damage that is done by the pollutant in question." Where this is not feasible, analysis is to be made of the "costs and benefits associated with achieving alternative levels of control."

The authors make few suggestions as to how external benefits and costs are to be measured, and when they do introduce one, it lacks conviction. For example, they propose that the external effects of air pollution might be measured by the "commuting costs people are willing to incur to avoid polluted air." Studies of the spatial variation of urban land values and assessments do not suggest that it is possible to hold all other variables constant while the effect of one of them (air quality) is measured. Even if costs incurred to *avoid* polluted air were measured, this would not necessarily attain the goal of "balancing of our varied desires . . . against the cost of satisfying them in various degrees." The authors do say that "it is apparent that many items of willingness-to-pay and cost information are unavailable and that obtaining them may be a difficult task, if indeed it is possible at all." Nevertheless, they assert, "we believe that sample surveys possibly could yield useful information on the importance individuals attach to values of this type." Another suggestion is that "studies in environmental perception and social psychology would permit us better to gauge the actual values which different configurations of the urban environment can yield." Sample surveys, environmental perception, and social psychology do not sound much like economics. Such approaches are entirely appropriate to the complexity of the problem of environmental quality, but the authors maintain that it is "economics alone that can formulate these problems in the terms to which they must finally be reduced." Their own book seems to show that in practice economics is something less than that.

Legal Solutions

A better case might be made for law as being the discipline "alone that can formulate these problems in the terms to which they must finally be reduced." In a particularly lucid essay in a volume on "Environmental Quality in a Growing Economy" Turvey [13] shows some of the limitations of economic analysis. He argues that prescriptions on how much should be done to preserve or improve the quality of the environment and at what cost "cannot be decided on a purely technical basis by an economic calculation," but he acknowledges that "even though an economic calculation of gains and losses is often not sufficient to reach a well based decision, it is nearly always an essential preliminary."

Where an activity has a deleterious effect on its neighbors, as when the fluorine in the smoke emitted from a brickworks causes damage to crops and animals on nearby farms, it may be possible to resolve the conflict by government regulation, in this case regulation of the quality of the emission from the smokestack. The brickworks may attempt to reduce the toxic effects of the smoke

[13] Ralph Turvey, "Side Effects of Resource Use", in Henry Jarrett, ed., *Environmental Quality in a Growing Economy*, Baltimore (1966), pp. 47-60.

by technical means, with or without a government subsidy. Or the owners may agree in a court of law to pay damages or compensation to the farmers. Often this can be arranged by private contract without resort to legal action.

Where external costs are inflicted on many individuals by one another, as when too many cars crowd an expressway, a possible solution is to use the power of taxation. This is already done on toll roads and turnpikes and might be extended to all other roads.[14] Another legal approach to externalities is to internalize the side effects within the compass of larger decision-making units, as when the sanitation authority of a community that discharges its untreated sewage into a river is merged with the water-supply authority of a nearby community that uses the same river (downstream) as its source of supply. In this way the new larger authority is able to take into account the damaging effects of one of its functions on another.

By such legal and institutional means conflicts about environmental quality can be resolved in the absence of a market mechanism and of well-defined property rights. The application of these devices in a democratic society involves considerations of fairness that require legal or political decisions. Such decisions can be equitable only if they recognize the distribution of gains and costs. The fact that a detrimental side effect exists does not automatically mean that an improvement is possible which is better economically. Only rarely would complete elimination of an existing side effect be economical.

The Role of Technology

The problem of choice in legal and institutional solutions is complex, and answers are sometimes reached only after long delays and high legal costs. A long wrangling process can be extremely frustrating, and it has the added disadvantage that the environment may continue to deteriorate in the meantime. Consequently, the urge to seek for quick solutions is strong, and the solution to which many people turn is some technical innovation that will resolve the difficulty easily and perhaps at low cost. The proceedings of many conferences on polution[15] contain strong and

14 See "Road Pricing: The Economic and Technical Possibilities", H.M.S.O., London, (1964).
15 See, for example, the following: *Proceedings, the National Conference on Water Pollution,* Washington, D.C., (1961); *National Conference on Air Pollution Proceedings,* Washington, D.C., (1963); *Background Papers and Proceedings of the National Conference on Pollution and Our Environment,* 4 vols., Montreal (1966).

eloquent pleas for more scientific research directed in part at the development of technical solutions. In many cases technical solutions can be found, and when the complexities of making economic or legal adjustments confront us, experience seems to have shown that applying new technology to the environment is the path of least resistance. The Achilles heel of the technologists' approach is, of course, that the present problems of environmental quality arise precisely from the application of technological solutions to problems in the past. The new technologies now being developed may in their turn prove to be only palliatives that will pile up greater difficulties to be confronted at a later date.

The advance of science and technology and their application to problems of environmental quality have also been subject to the criticism that the results are not appropriate to the esthetic, psychological, and physiological needs of man even though these results may be technically sound. Planners and architects have been engaged in some serious self-criticism along these lines, as is illustrated in the American Institute of Planners' volume "Environment for Man."[16] The papers in this collection are concerned with the planning and designing of environments that are optimal on a human scale "with man as the measure." The contributions deal with the physiological, psychological, and sociological impacts of the physical environment from a planning standpoint. Taken together, the views expressed amount to a serious criticism of the way in which city planners and architects have failed to produce environments that are as healthy or as psychically satisfying as they presumably should be. An interesting example is Alexander's discussion[17] of the way in which people have moved to cities for human contacts and have found the contacts increased in number but empty and unsatisfying in nature. He then proposes some ingenious designs of urban form specifically constructed to promote intimate contact. A valuable survey of the problems raised by this pattern of thought is provided by Dyckman,[18] who emphasizes the planner's need to draw on environmental and social scientists.

---

16 William R. Ewald, Jr., ed., *Environment for Man: The Next Fifty Years,* Bloomington and London, (1967). See also Robert Arvill, *Man and Environment: Crisis and the Strategy of Choice,* Penguin Books Ltd., Harmondsworth, England (1967).
17 Christopher Alexander, "The City as a Mechanism for Sustaining Human Contact", *Environment for Man* (see footnote 16 above), pp. 60-102, comments, pp. 102-109.
18 John W. Dyckman, "City Planning and the Treasury of Science", *Environment for Man* (see footnote 16 above), pp. 27-52, comments pp. 52-59.

One vital input to the planning process is fundamental knowledge of the process of interaction between man and environment. "Interactions of Man and His Environment"[19] is a book that provides a useful introduction to the already large literature on the technicalities of human physiological response. Topics covered include the thermal environment, hearing and vision, and a field described as "atmospheric ecology." Panel discussions highlight both the need to control and improve the environment, with human physiological responses as the criteria, and the new technical possibilities of doing so.

Human Behavior and Response

Probably the most complex aspect of environmental quality, and certainly one of the most neglected, is that of human behavior and response. There is a growing effort in several disciplines to try to approach the problem in a more scientific manner. The "1967 Directory of Behavior and Environmental Design"[20] lists 270 professionals from thirty disciplines who have engaged in research in the integrative field of environmental design and human behavior. There is even the suggestion that a new science of environment is emerging, which will eventually develop professional loyalties of its own and be accorded departmental status in the universities.[21]

Some of the geographical contributions are reviewed in White's paper on the "Formation and Role of Public Attitudes."[22] Approaches used include analysis of interpretations of environment made by writers and artists in the style of Glacken,[23] Lowenthal,[24]

---

[19] Burgess H. Jennings and John E. Murph, ed., *Interactions of Man and His Environment*, New York, (1966).

[20] *1967 Directory of Behavior and Environmental Design*, Research and Design Institute, Providence, R.I., (1967).

[21] This suggestion is elaborated by Francis T. Ventre in "Toward a Science Environment", *American Behavioral Scientist*, Vol. X, no. 1 (1966), pp. 28-31 (a special issue devoted to environment and behavior).

[22] Gilbert F. White, "Formation and Role of Public Attitudes", *Environmental Quality in a Growing Economy* (see footnote 13 above), pp. 105-127.

[23] Clarence J. Glacken, *Traces on the Rhodian Shore*, Berkeley and Los Angeles (1967). See also his "Changing Ideas of the Habitable World", in Man's Role in *Changing the Face of the Earth* (edited by William L. Thomas, Jr., Chicago, 1956), pp. 70-92.

[24] See David Lowenthal and Hugh C. Prince, "The English Landscape", *Geogr. Rev.*, Vol. LIV, (1964), pp. 309-346, and "English Landscape Tastes," *ibid.*, Vol. LV (1965), pp. 186-222, and David Lowenthal, "The American Scene", *ibid.*, Vol. LVIII, (1968), pp. 61-88.

and Tuan;[25] public-opinion polls; examination of consumer choices as emplified by Wollman[26] and as proposed by Herfindahl and Kneese;[27] study of decision making and choice behavior as exemplified in the work of White, Kates,[28] and others; and experimental research.[29]

"America's Changing Environment," issued by the American Academy of Arts and Sciences,[30] contains fifteen papers. In it Nathaniel Wollman describes the recent work of economists as the "new economics of the environment." Aaron Wildavsky responds that environment economics contains a lot of politics but not much economics. He prefers to cast the net more broadly and advocates a "new political economy." Throughout the book the emphasis is strongly on qualitative changes in the environment.

The dichotomy between quality and quantity is the central focus of a new publication edited by Ciriacy-Wantrup and Parsons[31] and containing fourteen papers presented under the auspices of the Chancellor's Committee on Natural Resources during exploration at Berkeley on how to organize the universities' interest in natural resources and environmental studies.

The potential results of collaboration between psychologists and geographers are well presented in a special number of the *Journal of Social Issues* devoted to "Man's Response to the Physical Environment," edited by Kates and Wohlwill.[32] Collaborative efforts of this kind will clearly encounter some difficulties, one of which is obtaining a mutually acceptable diagnosis of the problems in mutually acceptable terminology. For example, in his paper on

---

25 Yi-Fu Tuan, "Man and Nature: An Eclectic Reading", *Landscape*, Vol. XV, no. 3 (1966), pp. 30-36; *idem.*, the Hydrologic Cycle and the Wisdom of God: A Theme in Geoteleology (forthcoming).

26 Nathaniel Wollman and others, *The Value of Water in Alternative Uses*, Albuquerque (1962).

27 *Op. cit.*, (see footnote 12 above).

28 Gilbert F. White, "Optimal Flood Damage Management: Retrospect and Prospect" in Allen V. Kneese and Stephen C. Smith, ed., *Water Research*, Baltimore (1966), pp. 251-269; Robert William Kates, "Hazard and Choice Perception in Flood Plain Management", *Univ. of Chicago, Dept. of Geogr. Research Paper No. 78* (1962).

29 Little experimental work has been completed, though Joseph Sonnenfeld and Julian Wolpert have studies in progress using slide tests and game theory respectively.

30 "America's Changing Environment," *Daedalus*, Vol. XCVI, no. 4 (1967).

31 S. V. Ciriacy-Wantrup and James J. Parsons, ed., *Natural Resources: Quality and Quantity*, Berkeley and Los Angeles (1967).

32 R. W. Kates and J. F. Wohlwill, ed., "Man's Response to the Physical Environment", *Journ. of Social Issues*, Vol. XXII, no. 4, (1966).

the "Psychological Aspects of Urbanology" Parr[33] emphasizes the lack of stimulus variation in the urban environment that results from the monotony of the cityscape. In contrast, Wolpert's paper on "Migration as an Adjustment to Environmental Stress"[34] describes the urban environment as a source of stress resulting from complexity and overstimulation.

Wohlwill points out that there is not necessarily contradiction in finding both complexity and monotony present simultaneously in the same environment. The extent to which a set of stimuli appear complex or monotonous depends not only on the characteristics of the stimuli themselves but also on attributes of the recipient, including personality. Research by geographers on attitudes and perceptions of the receivers of environmental stimuli is reported in "Environmental Perception and Behavior,"[35] a collection of five papers edited by Lowenthal. In this volume Yi-Fu Tuan[36] discusses the symbolic significance attributed to deserts and tropical islands. Beck[37] uses a symbols test to demonstrate that individuals differ in their "spatial styles," or the way in which they structure the sense of the relatedness of things in their minds. Apparently one way in which geographers differ from nongeographers is in a more marked preference for well-defined boundaries!

In a study of "The Role of Attitude in Response to Environmental Stress" Lee[38] uses the word "attitude" almost synonymously with "response." Thus four attitudes are avoidance, psychological adaptation, physiological adaptation, and constructive behavior. The response of adaptation presents one of the fundamental obstacles to prescriptive findings on environmental quality. Human beings as a species are notoriously adaptive animals. Conditions of environmental quality that initially might be considered intolerable have a habit of becoming quickly accepted and barely noticed.

---

[33] A. E. Parr, "Psychological Aspects of Urbanology", *Man's Response to the Physical Environment* (see footnote 32 above), pp. 39-45.
[34] Julian Wolpert, "Migration as an Adjustment to Environmental Stress", *Man's Response to the Physical Environment* (see footnote 32 above), pp. 92-102.
[35] David Lowenthal, ed., "Environmental Perception and Behavior", *Univ. of Chicago, Dept. of Geogr. Research Paper No. 109* (1967).
[36] Yi-Fu Tuan, "Attitudes toward Environment: Themes and Approaches" in Environmental Perception and Behavior (see footnote 35 above), pp. 4-17.
[37] Robert Beck, "Spatial Meaning, and the Properties of the Environment", in Environmental Perception and Behavior (see footnote 35 above), pp. 18-41.
[38] Douglas H. K. Lee, "The Role of Attitude in Response to Environmental Stress", in Man's Response to the Physical Environment (see footnote 32 above), pp. 83-91.

Sonnenfeld[39] has also been concerned with adaptation to environmental stress; in making a major distinction between natives and nonnatives in a given environment he concludes that natives, with their more limited environmental experience, have greater ability to adapt over time and that "attempts to improve the amount of space and quality of landscape for the native may result in wasted space, expense and effort." People experience different environments as a result of movement or migration and as a result of environmental change at one place. As changes at a place occur more rapidly the difference in adaptability of natives and nonnatives may decline, and as the proportion of nonnatives in the population rises demands for a high-quality environment may also be expected to rise.

Prospects

It seems clear that the current wave of interest in environmental quality will continue for a while longer. Certainly there appears to be no diminution in the magnitude of the problems relating to environmental quality or in the flow of popular and semipopular books urging the public to action.

Public concern is apparently growing, and the research of social scientists adds more than the sum of their findings. Changing our conceptions of the world changes the world itself. There are no simple answers or solutions. "Rights to quality of living, as expressed by absence of pollution" are being recognized by the public, but the price of a high-quality environment is more than eternal vigilance. Quality in environment, as in other things, requires a high degree of self-knowledge. It also requires an ability to observe and measure low degrees of determination in environmental quality and to take action to reverse these before we accept them and cease to notice them.

---

[39] Joseph Sonnenfeld, "Environmental Perception and Adaptation Level in the Arctic," in Environmental Perception and Behavior (see footnote 35 above), pp. 42-59.

Index

NOTE: **Bold** figures indicate pages containing illustrations.

Acid 150; reaction in soils 126; waters 266

Acidic soil parent materials 28

Acidic surface horizons 150

Active soil zone 129

Agriculture 155, 177, 179; influence on wildlife 304; influence on tundra and taiga 340-41

Agricultural areas 155, 186

Aklavik 140, 341

Alaska 10, 19, 69, 127, 128, 131, 135, 136, 139, 151, 152, 196, 198, 201, 216, 250, 286, 288, 291, 292, 294, 326, 327, 337, 341, 349; Highway 211

Alberta 25, 32, 35, 48, 50, 54, 56, 57, 98, 101, 102, 107, 109, 125, 132, 158, 175, 176, 177, 180, 181, 184, 206, 211, 220, 227, 246, 250, 259, 262, 266, 274, 302, 307, 308

Alder 10, 143

Alfalfa 162, 167

Alluvial 332; flats 34; terrace 146

Alpine: communities 36, **37**, 38-39; environment 35; fir 29, 30, 31, 46, 110; plant associations 42-44; plants 36; region 35-36; soils 124; vegetation 36

American Fur Company 221, 236

Amphipods 269

Animal migrations: during Paleocene 197

Animal populations 219-37

Anthropogene Period 195

Antilocapridae 198

Appalachians 123, 189

Arable acreage: British Columbia 182

Arctic 67, 81, 89, 124, 130, 132, 134, 288, 289, 292, 293, 296, 323; brown soils 65, 128, **129**, 130, 132, 151; flora 59, 71, 72; forest 78; Ocean 202, 338-39; Quebec 70, 89; region 127; thicket 64; thicket communities 60-91; tree line 8, 13, 20

Artificial dusting 339; insulation 339

Asbestos Hill 62, 70, 81, 87, 88; mining camp 82

Aspen 10, 11, 36, **52**, 97, 104, 108, 269; grove 93, 95, 96, 97, 98, 104, 106, 175, 177, 181; grove 104-7; parklands 264

Atlantic coastal strip 17, 20, 21; cod 338; shore 13

Atomic energy 164

Avalanche meadow community 39; slopes 35

Awned wheatgrass 101, 104

Baffin Island 61, 128, 288

Balsam fir 8, 10, 11, 14, 22, 107; poplar 10, 107, 108, **332**

Banff **26**, 27-50, 55, 316, 317, 321

Bankhead 48, 315; coal mines **52**

Barren ground caribou 205-17, **208**, 253, 255, 257, 258, 304, 306, 329, 337; decline 342; population 261; range use 209

Barren vegetation type 134

Beaches 64; ridges 108

Beaver 225, 226, 248, 329; landscape 225-30; lodge 158

Bedrock 62, 67, 115

Benthonic foraminifera 197

Beringia 196, 197, 198, 201

Big-game 249, 302; research 261

Biological Survey of the Federal Government (U.S.) 250

Bird species 69, 302; watching 275

Bison 199, 200, 201, 202, 203, 219, 220, 223, 225, 233, 234, 235, 237, 304, 306; effects, on landscape 223-26; elimination 230-36; food source 231-36

Black ash **9**, 11, 15

Black spruce 8, 10, 11, 12, 14, 100, 107, 109, 143, 305; terns 275

Blackbirds 277, 301, 302

Blackearth zone 178, 180

Blackfeet 223, 226, 227, 233, 235

Blowouts: micro-relief depressions 177

Bogs 132, 134, 136; soils **129**, 131, 132, 133, 134, 136

Boreal climax 14, 19; distribution 29

Boreal forest 7, 8, **9**, 10-15, 18, 21, 22, 23, 98, 104, 139, 175, 215, 306, 326; climate 25; conifers 1; covers 15; flora 26; formation 23; mixed forest ecotone 22; plants 72; shrubs 71; type flora 26, 29

Bounty systems 250-55

Bow River 50, 54, 55, 56, 57, 221, 225, 230, 234, 236; Expedition 227; Valley 45-58, 219-37

British Columbia 28, 29, 48, 49, 54, 124, 158, 160, 175, 176, 182, 183, 211, 239, 244, 248, 250, 251, 252, 253, 254, 255, 256, 258, 261, 302; erosion 182-83; Game Conferences 256; Predator Control Division 261

British exploring expedition 222

Brown soil 64, 159

Browsing by wildlife 176

Brunisolic Order 121, 128; soil 124

Brush 96; cleaning 273; wolves 250

Bryophyte layers 3, 4, 39

Buffalo: *see* Bison

Cactus 96

Cadastral grid 95

Calcareous deposits 124; soil-forming materials 28

Calcium 66, 140

Calgary **52**, **53**, 55, 56, 234, 237, 263, 316

Canadian: Arctic Archipelago 71; Board of Geographical Names 62; Department of Agriculture 97, 114; Department of Northern Affairs and Natural Resources 93, 110, 252; Department of Transport 15; Eastern Arctic 61; North-West Mounted Police 222-23; Pacific Railway 46-48, 310; Predator Control Conference 251; Shield 119, 124, 186, 266, 333; Species, Asiatic origin 195; surveys 95; West, grassland formation in 93; Wildlife Service 205, 252, 273, 274

Canopy covers 69, 73, 75

Canvasback duck 263, 268, 270, 306

Carbon monoxide: content 249

Carbonates 144

Caribou: *see* Barren ground caribou

Cascade Mountain **52**; River 48; valley 316

Cash crops 190

Castle Mountain: *see* Mount Eisenhower

Cation-exchange capacity of soil 140

Cattail 268, 275

Cattle-game range, British Columbia 255, 256, 258

Cedar **9**, 11

Cenozoic Era 196, 197

Census, 1951 176, 189

Centrifugation 140

Channels 26, 29, 79

Chars 304, 307

Chernozemic order 119; soil 124

Chironomid larvae 269

Chlordane 279

Chroma 151, 152

Cirques 45

Clay 119, 140, 150, 151

Climate 25-28, 164; amelioration 337; in Canada 15; cold zone 126; distributions (forests) 19; effects on tundra and taiga 227-30; factors 185; floods 50; fluctuations 337-38; optimum 337

Climax association 10, 11; development 97; forest 25, 30; tree line 20

Close-forest 11, 15, 30, 301; growing cover 185

Coal mines in Banff Park area 48, 315

Coast forest region 175; littoral 175; tundra 13

Columbia Basin 227; district 239; forest region 175

Compound '1080' 252, 255

Conifers 8, 10, 14, 19, 46, **51**, 71, 107, 108, 188, 301, 326
Conservation 161, 167, 249, 250, 290; agencies 58; attempts 226-36; funds 254; officers 260
Continental climate 179
Continental Divide 25, 26
Cordilleran Region, British Columbia 124, 158, 326, 333; flora 26, 29
Corn 167, 168, 170, 171, 190
Coulees 264; bottoms 103
Council of the Northern Department 228, 230
Coyotes 250, 251, 252, 253, 303
Cricaceous species 69
Cropping 157, 159, 172, 180
Crops 301; cover 185; damage by ducks 273-74; destroying mice 303; growth 156; production 93; rotation 158
Crown lands 176, 183
Cryopedologic processes 129, 132, 136
Cushion plants 36, 39
Cyanide guns 253
Cypress Hills 103, 109, 233, 236

DDT 277-80
Deception Bay 61, 64, 70, 85
Decomposition 76, 157
Deer 260, 261, 300, 302, 303, 304
Deltas 62, 64, 70, 105, 178
Department: of Agriculture 114, 253, 341; of Natural Resources 93, 110, 252
Depressions 39, 141, 143, 168
DEW line 295
Dieldrin 278, 280
Disease 257, 300, 319
Dispersal of animals 196
Dolomites 28, 45, 144
Drainage 11, 65, 120, 125, 127, 128, 129, 130, 132, 133, 134, 135
Duck 263, 268, 269, 270, 273, 277, 306; breeding 263-65; crop damage 273-74; diseases 272; food 268, 270; potholes 270-71, 304; season 278; territorialism 270
Durum wheat 272

Dutch elm disease 278
Dwarf birch 69; trees 35; shrubs 67, 103; willow-sedge meadow 39
Dystic Brunisol soil group 124

Earth circles 36; slides 182
Eastern Arctic 67; Baffin Island 280; Canada 178, 185, 186, 188, 189, 190, 191, 193; Canadian Arctic 128; Quebec 189
Ecoclimatology 16
Ecological problems 15; pyramid 267; succession 267
Ecology of tree species 29-32, 255, 352
Ecosystem 89
Ecotone 13, 15
Edmonton **51**, 158, 222, 234, 263, 264, 304; House 227, 229, 230
Effective structural aggregates 181
Egg fertility 278, 280; production 278
Elbow River 50, 54
Elk 302, 307, 319
Eluvial soil horizons 150
Environment 348-60; Pollution Panel 347, 348
Equine encephalitis 272, 301
Eskimos 257, 281, 287, 288, 289, 293, 301
Etiolation 73
Exploder 273, 274
Exposure 79, 97

Fallowed land 156, 157, 159, 177, 180, 182
Fauna: cycles 240-50; management 257-62, 271, 319-20; of North America 195-203; Northern American related to Asiatic fauna 199-203
Faunal composition 195
Faunal dispersal 198
Federal Government predator control 250
Federal-Provincial soil surveys 184; Wildlife Conference 255
Fertilization 170
Fertilizer 164; nitrogen 161

Field shelterbelts 161, 180; associations 180

Fire 55, 56, 272, 301, 316, 319; destruction of winter rangelands 205-17; effects on forage 207-9; 212-16; history in Banff Park 31-32, 46-50; on tundra and taiga 340

Fish 280, 301, 304, 305, 306

Floating forms, of plants 267, 268

Floodplains 178, 332

Floods 34, 50, 54, 55, 56, 57, 58, 67; effects of vegetation 56-58

Flora: 28, 29, 32; boreal 71; cordilleran type 26; subarctic 71

Föhn effect 84

Forage crops 159, 163, 190

Forb species 96-104

Forest 11, 48, 60, 97, 158, 301; arctic Quebec 64; associations 41-42; Canadian Shield 119; canopy 59; climate distributions 19; communities 32-35; cover 56; density 57; Eastern Canada 12, 212; fire 29, 30, 31, 40, 48, 49, 108, 183, 206-17, 256, 340; North American Eurasia 12; of Northern Canada 11; reproduction 302; statistics 1953 189; soils 108, 109, 127, 158; tundra 15; tundra ecotone 13; types 11, 12, 107; zonal divisions 19

Forestry 304; influence on wildlife 304

Food and Agriculture Organization: of the United Nations 190

Fossil Faunas 195; soil 87

Fox 69, 268; periodicity 240, 246

Franklin's gulls 275

Freeze-thaw cycle 331, 334

Front Ranges 25, 26

Frost 133; action 36, 128, 134, 330; boils 135, 335; collapse 134; displacement 130; table 331; in tundra 66

Fur Management Division 252

Fur seal industry 286; pelts 257;

Fur trade: development 200; effects on fauna populations 226-36; returns 239-48

Furbearers 243

Furrow method: irrigation 183

Furs 288

Game 255, 278, 300; animals 249; areas 250; birds 275; commission, British Columbia 257; crop 266; depletion 316; fish 300; herds 257; predation 254; species 255

Geomorphic processes 133

Glacial: deposits 67; lake plains 264, lakes 264; moraines 264; movement 62; till 142, 144, 167; till plain 146

Glaciation 11, 62, 327

Glacier National Park 315, 316, 318, 322

Glacier research 318

Glei soils 128, **129**

Gleization 128

Gleying 65, 126; podzolic soils 35

Grain 156, 157, 177, 269, 272, 273, 302; crops 159; elevators 263; growing 156-57, 179, 274, 304; growing effects 157-58; production 163; quota system 159

Grass: competition 95; growth cycle 103; hoppers 279; species 96

Grasses 67, 69, 71, 101, 102; big bluestem 99; blue gramma grass 146; blue joint 99, 102; bunch grass 178; Canadian wild rye 99, 104; common speargrasses 103; deep rooted chokeberry 102; drought resisting 100; grass of parnassis 141; Idaho fescue 104; June grass 99, 102, 103, 104; little bluestem 99; low bush wolferillon 102; marsh grass 104; needle grass 97; niggerwool 103; nodding wild rye 99, 104; northern wheatgrass 99; Parry's outgrass 104; rough fescue 104; sandbergs blue grass 103; western snowberry 102; western wheatgrass 103; wild oatgrass 104

Grasshopper epidemics 183

Grassland 25, 46, 96, 97, 105, 116, 158, 268; pastures 158; plains 264; potholes 268; region 156, 175, 177, 178; sloughs 269; soils 156, 181; soils in Prairie Provinces 123; zones 179

Grass-legume mixtures 182

Gravels 15, 67, 70; pebbles 65; ridges 109

Grazing 104, 269

Great Lakes 8, 123

Great Lakes–St. Lawrence Forest formation 8, **9**, 10, 15, 21

Great Plains 93, **94**, 97, 98, 110, 123, 222; wetland region 263, 264, 266, 275

Great Slave Lake 202, 207, 339

Greenland 202, 285, 286, 288, 292, 295; seal skins 287

Grey-brown podzolic soil 167, 188, 189

Gulf of St. Lawrence 17, 286

Gulf of St. Lawrence – Newfoundland seal hunt 286

Hair-seal pelts 206

Halophytic grasses 102

Hamilton Valley 15, 16, 17; River 22

Hard wheat 272

Hardwoods 10, 11

Harp seal 286, 287, 289

Hawks 301, 305

Hay 100, 156, 159, 163, 167, 168, 170, 275, 302

Heartwood deterioration 76

Heath 12; community 69

Herbicide 268

Herbivores 302

Herbs 11, 71, 72, 75; bunchberry 11; cover corn 69; layer 34, 35, 39; mayflower 107; sarsparilla 107; Solomon's seal 107; strawberry 107; wintergreen 107; wood sorrel 11

Heptachlor 278

Horizon differentiation 115

Horizontal zonation 175

Hudson Bay 8, 13, 20, 72, 201, 220, 333, 334, 337, 338; lowlands 22

Hudson's Bay Company 220, 221, 222, 223, 225, 227, 228, 229, 236, 240, 287, 336

Humic glei 136

Humus 65, 157, 158; rich soils 156

Hunters 257, 275, 286, 292, 294, 300

Hydrocarbon insecticides 280

Hydrogen peroxide 140

Hypsithermal interval 87; period 64

Ice 62; age 117; farm floods 50; jam 67; thickness 328; wedge 335

Illite 150

Illuvial soil horizons 150

Insecticides 277-82; direct effects 278-79; indirect effects 279-80; influences on wildlife 304

Insulation, insulating effects of snow 85

Intensive grazing 93

Interfluves 13

International Commission for Northwest Atlantic Fisheries 286

Internodes 73

Intertilled groups 183

Intrazonal soil: hydromorphic 127, 136

Inuvik 140, 141, 144, 150, 151, 341

Iron 152

Irrigation 160, 161, 177, 183

Isle Royale National Park, Lake Superior 250

Isolated monadnocks 62; plugs 62

Isopleths 22

Isotherm 327

Jackpine 8, **9**, 10, 11, 107, 108

James Bay 14, 16, 18, 22

Jasper 32, 316

Kames 108, 144

Kananaskis, Alberta 322

Kaniapiskau River 13; Valley 15

Kaolinite 150

Kaumajet mountains 89
Kindersley grasslands 271
Knolls 141, 144
Koeleria 177
Koppen's boundary line 327, 328
Kotzebue 292
Krummholz colonies 35, 136

Labrador 15, 21, 89, 211, 340; boreal forest 11; coast 89; current 22, 186; Trough 15
Labrador-Ungava 8, 9, 10, 11, 13, 14, 15, 16, 17, 19, 22, 328; peninsula 7; plateau 12
Lacombe 158, 159; Experimental station 156
Lacustrine basins 124; deposits 188
Lag gravels 329
Lake Agassiz plain 98, 99, 100, 109
Lake Champlain 189
Lake Erie 189
Lake Harbour 60, 61
Lake Huron 189
Lake Louise 27, 316, 320, 321; station 26
Lake Melville 15, 16, 17, 22
Lake Melville-Hamilton River 22
Lake Minnewanka 315
Lake Newen 272
Lake Ontario 189
Lake St. John 14, 17, 21; basin 15; district 188
Lake silt 62
Lake Superior 8, 14, 21, 250
Lake Traverse 190
Lake Winnipeg 99
Land: clearing 274; Classification Surveys 96; use 96, 185, 189, 269, 313
Larch 8, 9
Laurentide Scarp 8, 17
Lavas 62
Leaching 65, 114, 116, 127
Legumes 162, 168, 172
Lesser Slave Lake District 228
Lichens 39, 67, 71, 72, 89, 134, 144; floor 12; layer 34, 35, 39; woodlands 12, 13, 14, 15, 21
Limestone 28, 45, 146

Lindane 280
Livestock 163, 249, 255, 301, 302, 303, 304; damage 255; farming 190; production 254
Loam 65, 79; alluvium 147; glacial till 147
Lodgepole Pine 29, 30, 34, 46, 50, 52, 109, 110, 319
Logging 301, 319; operations 183; roads 14
Lumbering 7, 315
Lure crops 274
Luvisolic Order 119
Lynx: abundance 244; migration 245; periodicity 240

Mackenzie Delta 139, 329; River 139, 141, 146, 147, 201, 202, 210, 215, 333, 341; Valley 19, 139, 340
Macroclimate 97
Magnesium 66
Mammalian fauna 195, 199, 200; species 196
Manitoba 22, 95, 98, 101, 105, 107, 158, 175, 176, 180, 181, 184, 206, 210, 220, 252, 253, 255, 259, 262, 264; escarpment 99, 100, 105; lowlands forest 109
Marine mammals 283; economic importance 285-86
Marine shale 146
Maritimes 186, 188, 189, 250, 310; tropical air 50; type climate 25, 26
Marsh 265; grass 100; hawks 271
Marten 30; migration 245; periodicity 240
Mat plants 36, 39
Mesic vegetation species 134
Mesothermal climates 16
Metamorphic rocks 186
Metamorphosed sediments 62
Microclimate 61, 269; in Arctic 81
Microknolls 143; organisms 114; patterning 132; relief features in soil 134; structure 181; undulating topography 77

Migration: bats 301; birds 264; marten and lynx 245
Mineral parent material 115
Mineral soil 122, 131, 134; horizon 128, 150
Mineralogical analysis 150
Missouri country 227; River 221, 224, 229, 234, 235, 236, 263; Valley 221
Mixed forest 15
Mixed-grass prairie 96, 101-2, 104
Mixed-wood: forest 107-8; vegetation 9, 197
Moisture 156; conservation 164; cycle 18; loss 161
Montane forest 110; plateau 175
Montmorillarite 150
Moose 206, 225, 226, 250, 256, 260, 261, 301, 302; range 209, 256
Moraine 62, 89; areas 265
Morphological lapidity 198
Mosses 11, 12, 39, 56, 67, 71, 72, 141, 143 146; layer 34, 35
Mount Eisenhower 53, 55
Mudcircles 335
Mule deer 303
Musk oxen 199, 329, 337, 342
Muskeg 7, 12, 13, 14, 18, 123, 203, 266
Muskrat 39, 286, 305; periodicity 247

National Parks 47, 57, 58, 176, 300, 313, 314, 315, 317, 318, 320, 321; Warden Service 31
National Soil Survey Committee 118, 140, 191
National Taxonomic System of Soil Classification 118
Natural drainage systems 183; levees 17, 18; vegetation: in high latitudes 8; water reservoirs 183
Nest cover 269; dispersion 271
New Brunswick 14, 123, 189, 190, 301
Newfoundland 14, 16, 17, 22, 116, 123, 186, 188, 189, 190, 305, 307, 310; Royal Commission on Forestry 301

Nitrogen 140, 162, 164; content 157; fertilization 170
Non-irrigated areas 183
Non-stable aggregates 167
Nordenskjold 328
Norman Wells 141, 146, 147, 150
North America 7, 8, 10, 12, 90, 195, 198, 263; fauna 199; Indian 110.
North Pacific 197
North Saskatchewan River 48, 50, 220, 221, 223, 224, 226, 227, 232, 233
North West Company 221, 228
North West Mounted Police 222, 233, 234, 235, 237
North West River 16, 17
North West Territories 139, 206, 210, 252, 253, 255, 257, 261, 286, 331, 341
Northern Council of Hudson's Bay Company 228
Northern Hemisphere 328
Northern reed grass 100; wheat grass 101, 102
Nova Scotia 123, 186, 189, 190, 301
Nuclear power 305; research 164
Nutrients 157

Oats 168, 170, 272
Ontario 17, 123, 186, 188, 190, 211, 251, 259, 260; Agricultural College, Guelph 167; Bounty Act 261; Department of Lands & Forests 255; Manitoba boundary 7
Open boreal woodland 21
Optimum crop growth 162
Organic matter in soils 124, 131, 134, 170, 176; bog 34, 40; horizons 66; matter 115; order 120, 121; preservation 170
Otter: periodicity 248
Otter Lake 85
Overbrowsing 256, 258
Overgrazing 93, 183, 319
Over-harvest 306, 307
Overwash 178, 264

Pack ice 290, 292
Paleartic fauna 199

Paleographic reconstructions 196

Palliser Expedition 233; Triangle 264

Parasites 300, 301; infection 272

Parent material geology 116

Parkland 104, 105, 107, 271, 272; development 315-17; establishment 321-23; potholes 268; recreation facilities 316-17, 320-21; zone 269

Pastoral agriculture: Alberta 177

Peace River 158, 182

Peat 87, 88, 143, 145; deposits 64; moss 34; polygons 141; soil 69

Peneplain 8

Periodicity: badger 247; beaver 248; bear 246; fox 246; mouse 245; muskrat 247; otter 248; racoon 248; squirrel 245; weasel family 246

Permafrost 13, 36, 70, 80, 116, 124-28, **133**, 136-51, 330-41; free area 79; table 84

Permanent drought 274; potholes 266

Permeability 117

Pesticides 277, 280

Pests 319; control 252

P.F.R.A. 181

Phosphate 66, 172

Photoperiod 341

Pinegrass community 34

Pintail duck 269, 270

Plankton 267, 269; algae 267

Plants 114, 267; communities 34, 39, 41; cover 67; development 27; low temperature enduring 28; nutrients 186; population 130; species 73, 74; thermophilus species 28, 318-19

Plant-soils relationship 131

Pleistocene 62, 87, 195, 340; glaciation 29, 86

Podzolization 127, 152; secondary 116

Podzols 116, 124, 128, **129**, 136; order 119; profiles 34; soils 39, 40, 41 188, 189; zone 127

Poisons 252, 255, 272, 277, 302; baits 260; lines 259

Polar: ice cap 290; seas 296

Polar Bear 286, 290 291-97; habitat 291-92; hunting 292-97; movements 296-97; preservation 292-97

Pollution 299, 304, 305, 320, 347, 348, 353-60; legal solutions 354-55; prospects 360

Population dynamics 255

Postglacial xerothemic 72

Potash 172

Potassium 66

Potholes 264, 265, 269, 271, 275; animal inhabitants 269-70; drainage 273, 274; effects of cultivation and land clearing 272-75; floating plants 268-69; food chains 267; use by ducks 270-71

Potential evapotranspiration **17**, 19, 22

Povunguituk group 62

Power-generating rivers 14

Prairie 109, 156, 161, 175; alkaline soils 102; erosion control 180-82; fires 158; grasses 108, 178; grasslands 95; growth 105; heavy clay lowlands 102; in Manitoba 98; in Saskatchewan 98; mixed grass 93, 98 101-2, 105; potholes 264-71; Provinces 93, 123, 160, 177, 265, 271; short grass 93, 98, 101, 105; slough 269; soils 102, 157; soil zones 264; submontane 98; topography 264-71; true grass 98, 101; waterfowl 270, 271; wetlands 265, 266 wildlife value 275-76

Precambrian: area 189; era 305; Shield 186, 188, 305

Precipitation 19, 25, **26**, **27**, 36, 46, 54, 56, 57, 104, 116, 140, 161, 186

Predation 249; of water fowl 227

Predators 259, 260, 271, 302, 303, 308; control 261; management 255; question 255

Preferential browsing of livestock 157

President's Science Advisory Committee 347

Pressure groups: stockmen, trappers, and guides 256

Prince Edward Island 186, 189, 190

Proterzoic granite-gneiss complex 62; sediments 15

Provincial Forest Reserves 176; Parks 176

Pulpwood 22, 176; in Eastern Canada 14

Quarrying 315

Quartz 150

Quartzites 45, 62

Quebec 60, 65, 82, 139, 186, 188, 189, 190, 211, 251, 260, 261, 341; climatic amelioration 89

Rabbits 280, 281; cycles 240-45; girdling trees 106

Rabies 300; control program in Alberta 259; epidemic in N.W.T. 253; in wolves 253-59

Radioactive isotopes 164; wastes 305

Radiocarbon dating 90, 144, 151

Rainfall 134, 167, 185, 352

Red Deer River 219, 223, 224, 230, 235

Red Deer Valley 223

Red pine 10, 11, 15

Red River 99, 219, 232, 233; Colony 231; floods 178

Red River Valley 100, 232

Reforestation 57

Regolith 115

Regosolic order 120; soil 15

Reindeer 199, 329, 337

Reindeer Depot 139-44, 150

Reindeer moss 12, 141

Ridges 128, 168; crests 36; rolling 172

Ring suppression 78; width 76

Ringed seal 286, 287

Rocky Mountain House 221, 227, 229

Rocky Mountains 25, 31, 32, **33**, **37**, 50, 54, 55, 56, 103, 175, 176, 211, 233; East slopes area 31; flora 28; foothills 263; geology 28; soils 28; topography 28

Rodents 250, 281; control 252

Rotation 172, 182; cropping 172; plots 170

Royal Greenland Trade Department 217

Ruisseau Duquet **77**, 78; valley 76

Rundle Massif **51**

Runoff 56, 57, 97, 106 116, 133, 157, 161, 168; control 161; effects of vegetation 56-58

Sage 103, 275; brush 96

St. Lawrence Lowland 16, 123

St. Lawrence River 8, 189

Saline waters: influence on soil 119

Salix alaxensis 61, 67, 71, 75, **77**, 81, 83

Salt: gland 272; in soil 140

Sand 62, 67, 140

Sandbar willow 103

Sandgrass 101

Sandstones 28, 146

Saskatchewan 56, 98, 101, 102, 107, 158, 175, 176, 177, 180, 181, 184, 206, 210, 214, 215, 225, 228, 250, 252, 255, 259, 260, 264, 266, 274, 301; District 228; River Crossing 32

Schist 65; cliffs 61; eroded 62

Scree 35, 62, 57

Seals 292; hunting methods 287-89; pups 287

Sealskins 286; decline in market value 286-88; effects of decline on Eskimos 287-89; income from 286; prices 287; products 287

Sedges 69, 71, 141, 146, 268

Sedimentary strata 28

Sedimentation 140; in potholes 266

Seeds 172, 269; pod 95; germination 85; viable 83, 85

Seepage 39; water 35

Semi-arid brown steppe region 178; brown soil region 177; grasslands region 175, 179
Semi-permanent potholes 266
Sericite schists 62
Sesquioxides in soil 119
Shades 59, 69, 72, 73
Shales 20; knolls 105
Shallow water emergents 268
Sharpsburg: silty clay loan 157
Sheep 250; migrating to America 200
Sheet erosion 186; water 266
Short-grass 102; prairie 96, 97, 102-4
Shrubs 12, 59, 66, 69, 71, 101, 102, 106; cinquefoil 146; communities 60; cover 72, 80, 85; heath layer 34, 35, 39; microclimate 72; species 73
Silt 87, 140; clay 69; sampling wheat 168
Silver City 53
Single-grained soils 181
Sloughs 95, 102, 103, 275; grass 100
Snake River expeditions 239
Snow 54, 56, 57, 69, 81, 168, 260, 329; cover 35, 39, 61, 79, 328-30; depth 35; dispersal 82; distribution 36; drift 82; fall 66, 265, 328, 330; mantle 84; melt 36, 39, 339; patch sedge community 39; storms 83; trap 274
Soil erosion 157, 159, 167, 175, 179, **192**, 267; causes 179-80; classes 191; control 180-82; Eastern Canada 185-93; factors 185; map 191; plots 170; problems 176; program 184; Western Canada 175-93
Soil fertility 155, 160, 163-65; formation in permafrost regions 115-17, 125, 127; genesis 115-17; genetic forces on 113; horizons 65, 113, 114, 127, 140, 151; loss 168, 172; management 151, 155-73; management problems 160-62; mapping 135; micro-relief 133; mineral 113; mineral horizons 126; mineral parent material of 113; mois-

ture 132, 160, 161, 265, 274; morphology 140; mottling 151; movement 36; orders 119, 124; organic 113; parent materials 115; polygons 135, 136, 143; porosity 167, 171; productivity 340; profiles 28, 64, 100, 126, 127, 129, 139, 140, 150, 152, 177; reaction 140; regions 150; sampling 140; solonetzic areas 177; surface 167; survey data 190; texture 95; tilth 159; trenches 135; type 97; under-storey 132; variation 135; zones 121, **122**, 124-26, 264
Soils 113-73, 269; aeration 134; analysis 157; classification 117, 118-24, 152; compaction 167, 171; complex 121; convexities 135; creep 182; density 167; deterioration 176; drifting 178, 184; mountain 28
Solar radiation 79, 328
Solifluction 39, 62, 80, 136, 151, 182, 334
Solum 113, 114, 117, 126, 127, 128
South Saskatchewan River 220, 233, 235, 236
SPCA: New Brunswick 280; Quebec 286
Sphagnum: ground cover 338; moss 12
Spruce **9**, 10, 11, 14, 19, 22, 30, 31, 72, 87, 95; fir association 15; grouse 303
Stone: nets 135; polygons 36; rings 335; stripes 36
Streams 67; flow 57; outwash 178
Strychnine 252, 253
Stubble 168, 272
Subalpine forest 98, 109, 175
Subarctic 124; Gleyed Acid Brown wooded soil 152; minimal podzol 152; Peaty Carbonated Rego-Humic Gleysol 152; shrubs 71; thicket communities 89
Sub-humid grasslands regions 179
Successional trees 30
Sulphur deficient soils 162; dioxide 349; fertilizer 162

Summerfallow 269, 273
Surface drainage 264; horizons 119, 136, 150; soil 118
Swift Current Experimental Farm 102; station 159

Taiga 14, 22, 210, 325-43
Tamarack 8, 10, 11, 12, 14, 108, 109
Technology 355, 356; and pollution 355-57
Temperature 8, **26**, **27**; inversions 27, 28
Terrace 45, **51**, 65, 69, 75, 85; edges 128; terrain 36.
Terrestial forage 213; forms (plants) 267
Thermal conductivity 69; efficiency 16, **17**, 19, 22; gradient 333; hardpan 332
Thermograph 70
Thermokarst 335; activity 134; susceptible soil 341
Thermophile forms 199
Thicket 69, 70; communities 70; forests 75
Tillage 162; operations 181
Timberwolf 250, 257, 262, 306
Topographic depressions 36
Torngat uplift 13; massif 16
Toxaphene 279, 380
Trans-Canada Highway **51**, 316
Transportation 57, 274
Trappers 96, 253, 256, 259, 306
Trapping, competitive 227
Traps 303; lines 259
Tree 56, 186; canopy 84; colonization 30; decadent 30; dog-hair stands 30; dominant 30; final mature stand 30; growth 30, 69, 80, 105; islands 35; offshoots 69; planting 161; root stock 69; seedling growth 30; self-regenerating stands 30; shade-tolerant 30; shade-intolerant 30; shortlived species 30; stands 30; stems 69
Treeline 8, 10, 60, 89, 90
Trembling aspen 105
Troughs 141, 142, 144, 145

Trout 304, 307; streams 305
True prairie 99, 101
Truncated soils 181
Tundra 8, 12, 13, 20, 21, 46, 59-75, 125, 126, **129**, 132, 139, 141, 143, 152, 175, 211, 266, 310, 311, 325-43; associations 13; -boreal forest transition 143; community 310; ground temperature 331-33; profile 126; shrubs 81; slow revegetation 336; soils 64, 126, 127, 131, 134, 136, 333-34; vegetation 116, 135, 139; wolf control program 257; wolves 257-58

Under-harvest 306, 307
Ungava 61, 71, 78, 86, 89, 340; Bay 334, 338; Peninsula 16, 60, 70
United States: Air weather service 15; Bureau of Sport Fisheries & Wildlife 281; Congress: Magnus-Metcalf bill 282; Fish & Wildlife Service 250, 277
Ultrabasic dykes 62

Valley floors 13, 145
Valley-bottom horsetail community 35
Vascular plants 71, 328
Vegetable 302; crops 160; control 162; pre-plough 93; regions of Canada 116; sprouts 85; types 130-33
Vegetation 176; Arctic 59; Great Plains 93-110; soil relationships 130-31
Vegetation areas 97
Vegetation patterns 96, 98
Vermilion Lakes 48, 49
Vertical fissures 335; zonation 175
Veterinary Services Branch: Alberta Department of Agriculture 259

Warm microthermal climate 22; province 16
Water: bath 140; conservation 15; courses 67, 96, 141; erosion **161**, 179, 182, 183; fleas 269; fowl 265, 266, 267, 269, 274, 305; biologist 264

Water fowl: management 306-7
Water-level recorder 168
Waterlogging 69, 116, 126, 130
Waterloss 36, 160, 168
Watershed physiography 57
Watertable 34, 39, 126
Weathering 114, 115, 139, 151
Weeds 156, 159, 272; beds 270; burning 273, 274; control 113
Western Canada 98, 155-61, 175-84, 252; agricultural changes 162-63
Western: grebes 280; hemlock 29; plains 182; red cedar 29; red lily 275; wheatgrass 101, 102; white pine 29
White House Conference on Natural Beauty 350
White spruce 8, 10, 11, 14, 46, 97, 108, 146, 332
Wilderness 50, 313-23
Wildlife 329; and man 309-10, 341, 342; biologists 282; conservation 309-10; damage 274, 302; effects on forests 301-2; management 250, 255, 258; preservation 318; reserves 342; safeguarding 281-82
Wildlife diseases transmissible to man 300-301
Wildlife harvest 306-8
Wildlife problems: categories 299-300, 303-10; solutions 303

Willow 65, 69, 73, 76, 101, 104, 141, 146, 332; forest 60, 67, 70, 80; river 60; thickets 72; valley 60-62, **63, 68, 77,** 78-90
Wind 36, 69, 330; blown drift 177; desiccation 35; erosion 179, 180, 183, 186; exposed slopes 36; in tundra 66; speed 36, 79
Winter cereals 161; mortality of moose 256; ticks 256
Wolf 250-56, 286, 303, 308; control 249-58; poisoning 256; predation 260; research 26
Woodland 269; open boreal 14

Xeric grasses 101; plants 103
Xerophilous vegetation 89
Xerosere 14
Xerothemic 88
X-ray analysis 150; diffractometer diagrams 140; powder diagrams 140

Yukon 252
Yukon River 339, 341
Yukon Territory 127, 240, 248, 252, 326

Zoned divisions 12, 13, 22; forest profile 19, 130; soils 126, 136